FINALIST FOR THE 2020 EDGAR AWARD FOR BEST FACT CRIME

ONE OF NPR'S BEST BOOKS OF THE YEAR

FINALIST FOR THE 2020 DASHIELL HAMMETT AWARD FOR LITERARY EXCELLENCE IN CRIME WRITING

"[An] alarming account of a bank
heist that rocked the country in 1980."
—MARILYN STASIO, *The New York Times Book Review*

"It reads like a crime novel in the best way possible.
But what's truly remarkable about the book is
the depth Houlahan brings to the story . . . An
astonishingly gifted writer, breathing urgent life
into a true story that still resonates today."
—MICHAEL SCHAUB, NPR

"A goddamned thrill ride."
—TOD GOLDBERG, author of *Gangsterland*

"[An] action-packed and thought-provoking read."
—*She Reads,* One of the Best Nonfiction Books of the Year

"An impressively well-rendered true-crime saga."
—*Kirkus Reviews*

D1005064

"This is true crime at its best."
—**DAVID M. OLSEN,** *The Coachella Review*

"[A] deeply researched, thrillingly paced tale."
—**PETER LARSEN,** Southern California News Group

"*Norco '80* blends meticulous details with a strong sense of story arc, character and place . . . The book has a universal message that is needed now."
—**JO KROEKER,** *Greenwich Time*

"*Norco '80* reads like a pre-apocalyptic nightmare, and it's all true. Be warned—you will not get anything done until this book is done with you."
—**JAMES RENNER,** author of *True Crime Addict*

"Want to understand the militarization of modern police forces? Look no further than this nonfiction book, which details how a group of over-armed idiots pulled off a dim-witted bank robbery that became the longest, most dangerous police chase ever."
—*The Oklahoman,* One of Our Favorite Books of the Year

"One of those incredible true crime stories that grab one's attention and does not let go."
—**THOMAS MCCLUNG,** *New York Journal of Books*

PRAISE FOR *NORCO '80*

FINALIST FOR THE 2020 EDGAR AWARD
FOR BEST FACT CRIME

ONE OF NPR'S BEST BOOKS OF THE YEAR

ONE OF *CRIMEREADS*'S BEST TRUE CRIME BOOKS
OF THE YEAR

"[Houlahan] writes with a narrative urgency that perfectly captures the quick and chaotic nature of the robbery. His prose incorporates the vernacular of the officers and criminals; it's hard-boiled, shot through with profanity, but never forced. It reads like a crime novel in the best way possible. But what's truly remarkable about the book is the depth Houlahan brings to the story . . . With his first book, Houlahan proves himself to be an astonishingly gifted writer, breathing urgent life into a true story that still resonates today. *Norco '80* is a fascinating true-crime account that seems likely to be one of the best nonfiction books of the year." —MICHAEL SCHAUB, NPR

"[An] alarming account of a bank heist that rocked the country in 1980 and reflected 'the peculiar zeitgeist of that decade' in all its cockeyed drama . . . [Houlahan's] cinematic treatment of the robbery itself reads like wildfire, the fatal shootout with the police ends in colorful chaos, and the huge manhunt through San Bernardino National Forest conducted by 'Hunt & Kill Teams' is a nail-biter." —MARILYN STASIO, *The New York Times Book Review*

"[An] action-packed and thought-provoking read." —*She Reads*,
One of the Best Nonfiction Books of the Year

"[Houlahan] has compellingly translated a high-octane story to the page without losing traction, leaving the reader satisfied yet craving more."
—LAUREN O'BRIEN, *Shelf Awareness* (starred review)

NORCO '80

The True Story of the Most Spectacular
Bank Robbery in American History

PETER HOULAHAN

COUNTERPOINT
Berkeley, California

The Library of Congress has cataloged the hardcover as follows:
Names: Houlahan, Peter, 1961– author.
Title: Norco '80 : the true story of the most spectacular bank robbery in American history / Peter Houlahan.
Description: Berkeley, California : Counterpoint, [2019]
Identifiers: LCCN 2018052238 | ISBN 9781640092129
Subjects: LCSH: Bank robberies—California—Norco—Case studies. | Violent crimes—California—Norco—Case studies.
Classification: LCC HV6661.C22 N674 2019 | DDC 364.15/520979497—dc23
LC record available at https://lccn.loc.gov/2018052238

Paperback ISBN: 978-1-64009-388-1

Cover design by Jaya Miceli
Book design by Jordan Koluch

COUNTERPOINT
2560 Ninth Street, Suite 318
Berkeley, CA 94710
www.counterpointpress.com

Printed in the United States of America

10 9 8 7 6 5 4 3 2

For my father, who taught me the joy of a great story

Dedicated to Deputy James Bernard Evans

CONTENTS

AUTHOR'S NOTE

THE MOTIVE FOR ROBBING BANKS HAS REMAINED THE SAME SINCE FEBRU-
ary 13, 1866, when members of the James-Younger Gang walked into the
Clay County Savings Bank in Liberty, Missouri, stole $60,000, and shot a
bystander to death in what is widely believed to be the first bank robbery
in United States history. Robbers rob for money and rob banks "because
that's where the money is." The motive for the 1980 robbery of the Security
Pacific National Bank in Norco, California, may have been typical, but the
reason the men who planned it wanted that money was not. They were not
drug addicts desperate for their next fix, a ring of thieves looking to pull
a string of heists, or members of a street gang eager for a roll of hundreds
to flash around. They were none of those things. The two men behind the
Norco bank robbery believed that America was on the verge of a catastrophe
of biblical proportions, one in which only the well armed and well prepared
would survive.

George Wayne Smith and Christopher Harven were certainly not the first
people to conclude that humanity was headed for imminent disaster. They
were part of a long line stretching back at least two thousand years to the time
when an apocalyptic preacher known as Jesus of Nazareth roamed the Sinai

Peninsula warning of the end of the world. The book of Revelation had laid out the general game plan. All George and Chris had to do was untangle the parables, decode the timeline, and match up the current events that would usher in the Rapture, Great Tribulation, and the Second Coming. If one were on the lookout for warning signs of the collapse of civil society and the obliteration of mankind, there were plenty of them to see by May 1980.

To understand why a group of young men with no serious criminal records would attempt a bank robbery that turned into one of the most violent events in law enforcement history, one must first understand the times in which it took place. At the time of the robbery, George Smith and Christopher Harven were twenty-seven and twenty-nine years old, respectively. They had both entered adulthood at the dawn of the 1970s, so whatever beliefs and world views they possessed were formed almost entirely by the peculiar zeitgeist of that decade.

The 1970s were not a hangover from the 1960s, but more like those menacing, early-morning hours of a party that has gone on way too long. It was a decade of national disillusionment and self-destructive indulgence where many of the counterculture philosophies formed in the late 1960s played themselves out in very ugly ways. Drug use became drug abuse as recreational pot smoking evolved into daily pot smoking and then cocaine, crystal meth, and the mind-obliterating angel dust. The idealism of Woodstock became the pure hedonism of Studio 54. Pornography evolved from sexy girls in bunny tails into the explicit raunchiness of Larry Flynt's *Hustler*. Free love became an epidemic of venereal disease and unwelcome pregnancies. Cities descended further into lawlessness, poverty, and bankruptcy while violent crime across the country escalated at a rate that would be almost unimaginable today. Communes turned into cults or business opportunities for predatory self-help gurus. In November 1978, just eighteen months before the Norco robbery, more than nine hundred members of the Peoples Temple died in what cult leader Jim Jones labeled an act of "revolutionary suicide" but was, in fact, mass murder.

The more traditional idea of armed revolution was also particularly active in the 1970s. It was not long before the 1960s idea that you could change society morphed into the belief that you must destroy it first. In the first half of the 1970s, just after their graduation from high school, George Wayne Smith and Christopher Harven witnessed a constant parade of radical groups who not only believed they could overthrow a government, start a civil war, or collapse a society, but actively tried to do just that. Leaders of 1960s sit-ins and protests went underground, made bombs, blew up others and sometimes themselves. There were more than 2,500 bombings by radical groups in the United States over an eighteen-month period between 1971 and 1972 alone. Cops became "pigs," regarded by the radical underground as foot soldiers of a deeply corrupt status quo and targeted for assassination in major cities from coast to coast. It did not matter that groups such as the Symbionese Liberation Army, Weather Underground, and Black Liberation Army had little support and stood no chance of succeeding. What mattered was that for the first time in the country's history, many, including George Smith and Christopher Harven, were looking at American society and seeing a house of cards teetering on collapse. Smith and Harven did not want to change the world, they just wanted to survive it once the whole shithouse went up in flames.

IF CREATIVE INTERPRETATION WAS REQUIRED TO MATCH UP EVENTS AND CULtural trends with End Times biblical prophecy, the means by which that prophecy would be fulfilled was utterly unambiguous. Vast arsenals of nuclear warheads locked and loaded on land, sea, and air assured that the Apocalypse was not only possible but, in the view of millions, inevitable. Never was that threat more acute than in the 1970s. Détente and the SALT I treaty notwithstanding, what made the 1970s so dangerous was the dramatic increase in tactical battlefield nuclear weapons deployed throughout Western Europe by both the United States and the Soviet Union. By 1980, the number of European-based tactical nukes reached well over ten thousand, including missiles and artillery shells tipped with W48, W50, and W70 thermonuclear warheads with kiloton loads reaching well into double digits.

As devastating as a single one of those tactical weapons would have been to the troops in the field, the greater danger they posed was their potential role as a "gateway" nuke to eventual strategic, intercontinental nuclear war-fare. After all, once you've morally justified using the first nuclear weapon, is it really going to be all that hard to justify defending your country with more and bigger ones?

Both George Smith and Christopher Harven were part of the first generation to live their entire lives under the threat of nuclear war. They had spent their early childhood overhearing adults chattering nervously about Sputnik, the Cuban Missile Crisis, and the nuclear arms race. Their school days from kindergarten through twelfth grade had been punctuated by monthly "duck and cover" drills. Both Smith and Harven went straight from high school into the military. Smith was sent to Germany in the shadow of the Iron Curtain for two years as an artilleryman trained in the art of lofting battlefield nukes into enemy forces. Harven, booted out of the army after only two months, still gained an insider's understanding of the implications of the sharp ramping-up of tactical nukes that was underway. The key takeaway for both was simple: We are all going to die.

A less existential yet equally contributing factor to the evolution of the two men from weed-smoking, petty scofflaws to violent bank robbers was rooted as much in the "where" as it was in the "when." When George Smith stepped off the transport plane from Germany, he returned home to Orange County, California, to find himself at ground zero of the biggest religious youth movement since the Children's Crusade.

There is no doubt that the "Jesus movement" had a positive impact on some young lives, especially considering the other counterculture alternatives available in the early 1970s. However, this brand of aggressive theology, intended to frighten the youth of Orange County into the pews and keep them there, was viewed by many as irresponsible, abusive, and dangerous. Born-again ministries such as the Melodyland Christian Center and Calvary Chapel, from which the movement originated, employed Pentecostal-style fire-and-brimstone tactics to keep membership in a perpetual state of terror, afraid that when the Rapture came, Jesus would find them unworthy and leave them behind. Most dedicated themselves unwaveringly to the game plan laid out by the church to assure their entry into the Kingdom of the

Lord. Others saw their destiny as protectors, arming and preparing themselves to ride out the Apocalypse and the collapse of civil society they believed would precede it. George Wayne Smith was one of those.

Christopher Harven was a different breed of cat, but when he looked out at the world, he saw all the same things Smith did. Harven viewed signs of impending social collapse in the alignment of planets, predictions of cataclysmic overpopulation, ecological disaster, and an array of other doomsday scenarios that gained traction during the decade. Harven was not what you would call a follower, but George Smith was a particularly articulate and persuasive young man, adding his own extreme biblical interpretations to Harven's hodgepodge of pseudoscientific beliefs. George and Chris became friends, looked for signs of the approaching Apocalypse together, bought a house together, lost jobs and wives and girlfriends together, and eventually descended into desperation together. So together they made a plan. A very, very bad plan.

While Norco can in many ways be defined by the times in which it took place, it did not occur in an entirely bygone era. Aesthetically speaking, its world looked much the same in 1980 as it does today. The boulevards of Norco are still lined with the same fast-food restaurants, taco joints, gas stations, and convenience stores, many of which have the same names they did back then. The teenagers still wear their hair long and hang out in front of the 7-Eleven and the bowling alley in ripped jeans and ratty rock concert T-shirts. You can still buy a dime bag of weed off a street corner dealer in Rubidoux. Parents still shuttle kids to school and ballet classes or to the Little League field at Detroit and Hamner where the robbers parked their getaway cars forty years before. The Carl's Jr. restaurant where diners dove beneath tables to avoid getting shot is still there, as is the row of small stucco ranch houses that took semiautomatic gunfire through their windows. At the time of this writing, the Security Pacific Bank building is still there. You can even pull your car into the drive-through banking lanes, but no one will help you; it lies empty, scheduled for demolition.

While the men who robbed the bank might be products of their time, the men on the other side of the confrontation were not. The cops involved in the firefight that day were not so different from the cops who came before and after them: working-class guys, many from families with a long history in law enforcement, most of whom knew from an early age that they wanted to be in police work too. Many went into the military first, which in those days often meant a tour in Vietnam. They had rigid definitions of right and wrong. Back then they were more inclined to go outside the official department protocols with a suspect if they felt it was justified, whether that meant giving a car thief an extra whack with the baton after a particularly harrowing pursuit or giving a drunken driver a lift home if they thought he was just a good guy having a bad day. Off duty, they looked like regular blue-collar guys, reflecting the fashion, hairstyles, and trends of the time. In 1980 that meant long sideburns, blow-dried hair, wide lapels, ugly polyester shirts, flared slacks, and, to a man, mustaches.

As always, they boasted that cop swagger and thought themselves immune to any lasting effects from their experiences on the job. But they were not immune, of course, not then and not now. Even today, forty years later, many of the men involved in the Norco shootout break down and cry when recounting it. The helplessness of being completely outgunned or the terror of being shot. The sound of having your cruiser torn apart by military-grade weapons. The thought that maybe you could have done something different that might have saved the life of a fellow cop.

For whatever reason, the passing of years does not seem to help all that much, not for the police officers and civilians terrorized on a spring afternoon by a gang of heavily armed men, and not for the families of the bank robbers who so needlessly threw their lives away. Some of the damage was immediate, tearing friendships apart, ending marriages, destroying careers, and ruining lives. But it just keeps rippling out through the generations, carried forward by heartbroken parents, wives, brothers, and sisters, and handed down to the half dozen children left fatherless on both sides. In this way, the Norco bank robbery is not frozen in time. As William Faulkner wrote, "The past is never dead. It's not even past." In the case of Norco, it seems to go on forever.

NORCO '80

PROLOGUE

1973. Orange County, California.

THE BUS CAME UP OVER THE RISE AND THEN DESCENDED TOWARD THE COVE of white sand, the Pacific Ocean shimmering blue-gray in the afternoon sun. The youngsters inside the bus had been singing one of their favorite songs, but their voices burst into a cheer when they saw the scene below. They were everywhere, hundreds of them, gathered on the cropping of rocks that jutted out into the ocean and on the sandstone bluffs ringing the cove at Corona del Mar. A smattering had waded out into the gentle surf lapping at the sheltered beach, some with their hands lifted to the sky. A young girl gasped. Praise God, praise God, she repeated breathlessly, overcome with joy at the sight of it.

They were for the most part a young crowd in their teens and twenties. The boys wore their hair past the collar with long sideburns, many with beards and mustaches. For the girls, the look was still "natural," light on the makeup, hair swept back on the sides in wings or like Ali MacGraw in *Love Story*, long, ironed straight, and parted down the middle. The dress was relatively conservative for the times, but still plenty of flared bell-bottoms, macramé belts, cutoff jeans, hillbilly hats, and colorfully embroidered peasant tops. They stood in groups or sat on towels facing the ocean, some of the boys with their shirts off taking in the sun. Seen from a distance, they had the appearance of a crowd at a James Taylor concert. Only the banner stretched between two wooden poles like a makeshift volleyball net gave away the true nature of the gathering: GOD'S FOREVER FAMILY.

The young man looked out the window of the bus. He could see his own reflection in the glass, the dark eyes, light brown complexion, round face, and full lips, black hair beginning to grow out from its recent military cut. Just another Mexican kid from the lower-middle-class neighborhoods of Orange County. At least that was what most thought when seeing him for the first time. But if you looked closely, you could see it in his almond-shaped eyes, giving him a gentle, soulful look. Vaguely exotic. Amerasian.

His friends would tell you that he was caring, soft-spoken, a nice guy, someone who would do almost anything for you. Smart, articulate, passionate, but also a bit of a jokester. The army had filled him out a bit, put on some muscle and weight. Just over six feet but still with the lankiness of a teenager. Never a jock, but athletic enough to have lettered all four years on the championship John F. Kennedy High School tennis team, their star varsity player since sophomore year. But he was also brainy, just enough of a geek to have been a member of the chess club and editor of the school newspaper. He still looked so young, but since he had come back from Germany, his mother had seen in him a certain sadness that had not been there before. Being stationed in Germany was a lot better than Vietnam, but something had happened there, and it had changed him.

He felt a tap on his shoulder. George, your fan club is back, his friend Ralph Miranda said in a weary voice.

Huh? the young man answered, snapping out of his trance.

Two young girls, eighth graders, were standing in the aisle looking at him adoringly. Will you go swimming with us, George? one of the girls asked. Everybody keeps saying there are sharks here and now I'm scared to go in the water.

He smiled. Sure, but not right away.

Okay, they giggled and scampered back to their seat.

And don't worry about the sharks, he called back to them. If any show up, we'll baptize them too.

The bus idled as another pulled into the parking lot to disgorge their cargo of the Lord's children onto the beach. Dejected beachgoers trudged up the hill lugging chairs and coolers, looking like a line of refugees fleeing a war zone. They had all seen this sort of shit before. It was 1973, after all, and this was Southern California.

Someone in the bus began to sing and the others followed.

Accept Him with your whole heart
And use your own two hands
With one reach out to Jesus
And with the other bring a friend.

The bus crept forward and came to a stop, the air brakes hissing. Those on the bus grabbed beach towels and moved excitedly through the center aisle toward the doors. The young man remained in his seat, eyes fixed on the beach and its growing number of Believers. George Wayne Smith was just twenty-one years old, looking for some sort of purpose to his life.

If one were looking for purpose in 1973, Orange County, California, was a tough place to find it. It was "fly-over" country, little more than a giant, faceless suburb of Los Angeles. Tying it together was an inadequate freeway network coursing with vehicles moving ant-like through the system at all hours of the day. Here and there, an orange grove could be seen still holding out against the voracious housing development of the past two decades, which had all but eradicated the county of its eponymous fruit. Taken altogether, it was a not unpleasant, yet wholly uninspiring place.

George's father, Walter Smith, had left the oil fields of Wyoming to join the great postwar westward migration in 1956, moving his wife, Judy, daughter Patricia, and four-year-old son to Southern California. Once settled into the little house in Buena Park just a short bike ride to the newly opened Disneyland, Walter and Judy quickly added two more children. Like most young families, they struggled to make ends meet. But the Smiths felt far more at home in postwar Southern California than they had in Casper, Wyoming. Judy was Japanese, Walter Anglo-American. Mixed-race couples in general, and Japanese in particular, had not always been a welcome sight in Wyoming in the early 1950s. But in California, Asians, mixed-race couples, and Amerasian children like George were just another part of the cultural landscape, as common as palm trees, surfboards, and Stage 3 smog alerts.

George and Ralph stepped off the bus, walked over the sandstone bluffs, and went down into Pirate's Cove, a sheltered crescent of beach. They filtered through the crowd of Believers, hundreds strong now and still growing. They kicked off their flip-flops and felt the warm, grainy sand pushing between their toes. The Way, Calvary Chapel's house band, stood on a ledge of the bluffs that ringed the cove, the three woolly faced musicians playing acoustic guitars and singing contemporary songs of praise. Those at the gathering quickly took up the tune until the sound of hundreds of voices drifted up from the beach. The two young men sang as they walked, George's voice clear and in-key. A nice voice.

Two Newport Beach police officers appeared at the top of the bluffs, bemused by the scene. This was one place they did not need to worry about for the next few hours, not with all these Jesus freaks running around. George paused, his dark eyes fixed coldly on them. George had a deep distrust of police even though he had never been in trouble with the law. It was something he got from his father.

There was another reason Walter Smith had wanted to put Wyoming behind him. After three years of blue-collar work, Walter had finally landed a job as an officer with the Casper Police Department. The only thing Walter ever wanted to be was a cop, and he hoped the job with the Casper PD would be the first step in a lifelong career in law enforcement. What he found instead was a culture of corruption and criminal activity on the part of his fellow officers. After being reprimanded for arresting two officers he found burglarizing a shop on Main Street, Walter Smith quit the force after only a year and a half. Feeling disgusted and betrayed, he abandoned any hope for a career as a cop. It was not an experience Walter shared openly with his young children, but somehow George knew.

To Protect and to Serve, George muttered bitterly.

Ralph studied his friend's face. Come on, George, something's going on over there.

A middle-aged man with a receding hairline ascended a low outcropping of rock still wet from the swells washing over it at high tide, its newly replenished tide pools teeming with sea anemones and hermit crabs. It's Pastor Chuck, voices began, hushing the crowd, everyone moving closer and straining to hear what the founder of Calvary Chapel had to tell them.

Pastor Chuck Smith, dressed in casual slacks and white button-down shirt open at the collar, stood with the vast ocean and late afternoon sun as his backdrop and smiled warmly at the flock assembled before him. Today you make that next step of identification, totally and completely with His death, with His burial, with His Resurrection, he called out to the hundreds standing on the sand below him. In baptism, the water is actually a symbol of the grave, the old life, all of the past to be buried here today. They looked up at him dreamily. An ocean breeze ruffled the pastor's comb-over. You are becoming a dead person. All of the past life is being buried. That's all gone, he said, sweeping his hand through the air to emphasize the totality of the statement. That is all dead.

The pastor hopped from his stone pulpit onto the wet sand. A small group of associate pastors and senior church members clustered around him. The gathering of "Jesus People" began to move forward and fan out along the tide line, the water sweeping up the sandy beach and swirling around their ankles. Others scurried up the sandstone bluffs to sit on beach towels along with a smattering of curious passersby to watch. Mexican fishermen stood on the long jetty of boulders with their buckets and poles and stared dumbfounded at the scene unfolding on the beach below. The Way launched into another song, the voices rising again as one.

When they were done conferring, Pastor Smith and his four fully clothed associate pastors spread out and waded waist-deep into the gentle swells of

Pirate's Cove. The atmosphere on the beach became more energized, the air charged with anticipation. A young man with a thin mustache began to sway, eyes closed, head tilted back, face to the heavens. Two young girls clutched beach towels to their chests and bounced giddily on the balls of their feet.

The senior church members acted as shoreline ushers, processing members into the water one at a time, directing them to an available church official or the pastor himself. Quiet words were spoken, a hand placed on their chest and a second on their back as they were gently turned to face the shore. The attending church official encouraged them to hold their nose and close their eyes before lowering them beneath the surface of the water and then lifting them back up, their past now buried with nothing but the Kingdom of God stretched out before them.

George and Ralph moved toward the shoreline to wait their turn. They each had their own reasons for wanting to bury their past. For Ralph, it was the haunting memories from a recently completed tour of duty in Vietnam where he had seen those around him killed while being repeatedly doused in Agent Orange. For George, it was the memory of how Ralph's little sister Rosie had left him within months of their wedding after George had shipped out to Germany for his two-year tour in the army.

George might have felt confused, abandoned, and brokenhearted, but Rosie had had her reasons. George's immaturity and adolescent insecurity had worn her out. She was a playful yet serious young woman even at age seventeen and wanted to have babies. Maybe not right then, but someday. George said no way, that a baby would only come between them. One day, Rosie told George she might be pregnant. It was just a small prank that Rosie figured he would see right through. But George flew into a rage, told her he would cut the baby out of her, and even tried to kick her in the stomach.

Maybe the insecurity, selfishness, and fear of having children were things he would eventually outgrow. But all that talk about wanting to rob an armored car someday and what it would feel like to kill a person? That was different. At first, Rosie figured he was just trying to sound tough, just bullshit teenage boy talk. But he kept at it, even telling her they would be like Romeo and Juliet, joined in double suicide to a life together in eternity. He began to frighten her. There seemed to be an almost pathological detachment between his proposed actions and their inevitable consequences. His disregard for the impact of his actions on others was chilling. You're going to toss a hand grenade into the cab of a Brink's truck? What about the people inside, George? When she asked him questions, it was as if he had never even considered them before. Or maybe he just didn't care.

By the time they were married, Rosie knew she wanted out. George was eighteen, Rosie seventeen. Their reception was held within the cinder block walls of the Miranda backyard. A month after the wedding, George went to Germany and three months after that, Rosie got herself a boyfriend. It was Ralph who finally told George, writing him a letter to say his sister had run off with another man and was not coming back.

The baptism was proceeding with remarkable efficiency. Only thirty minutes in and dozens had already been brought into the water, dunked beneath its surface, and led back onto the sand. Dozens more waited their turn. The profound effect of the experience was on display all along the shoreline. The baptized broke the surface of the ocean trembling, sobbing, arms lifted to the sky in pure joy. Others stood shaking uncontrollably, their eyes rolling back in their heads. They staggered back toward land, their knees giving out, collapsing into the shallow surf and flopping around like grunion washed up at high tide. The eerie babbling of the tongue speakers could be heard rising up from the crowd like the collective mutterings of madmen.

PEOPLE SAY I AM TRYING TO LOOK LIKE JESUS, SAID A MAN STANDING AMONG a group of youngsters seated on the sand, motioning to his beard and stroking the long brown hair falling past his shoulders. Well, there's no one else I'd rather look like. The group crowding around him on the sand laughed, starstruck, hanging on his every word, while George and Ralph stood nearby listening in.

With his flared bell-bottoms, leather sandals, love beads, and multicolored African dashiki shirt, the man could have passed for any acidhead in the swirling crowd at a Grateful Dead show. But that was Lonnie Frisbee's gig: "The Hippie Preacher."

Articulate, charismatic, and handsome in a Jesus–meets–Jim Morrison sort of way, Lonnie Frisbee had burst onto the Orange County born-again scene at eighteen and was now in high demand as a guest on the televangelist circuit. One of the primary founders of the new "Jesus movement," he was also its perfect poster child, a hippie–turned–good guy. The anti-Manson. He was also Pastor Smith's star associate preacher and Calvary's biggest rain-maker. Lonnie Frisbee could round up disillusioned hippies off the board-walk at Newport Beach the way wranglers round up stray cattle on the range.

Wouldn't that be outta sight? Frisbee said, turning to the subject of Adam and Eve. He stared off into the dreamy distance, the Bible tucked under his arm. Walk with God. Eat the fruits of the trees in the garden. Trip around with the animals. An audible sigh came from the circle around him. Lonnie Frisbee and God were blowing everyone's mind.

Frisbee let his arms drop to his side, his whole demeanor darkening in an instant. The crowd held its collective breath. But God is not in every man, he went on, voice rising sharply. That's a lie of Satan. That's the same old trip he was trying to lay on Adam and Eve. You need to receive Him, let Him in, because darkness is coming more and more and more. He looked around him, eyes pausing briefly on one and then the next sheep in turn. These are the last days and Jesus Christ is returning soon to judge the quick and the dead. So repent and save yourself because if you don't . . . He let his voice trail off to allow his audience to finish the thought the same way Mick Jagger let an audience sing the last few words to a popular song. They all knew the consequences if they did not heed the Word of Lonnie Frisbee, the Word of Chuck Smith, the Word of Revelation, the Word of God Himself. Get right with Jesus or when the Rapture comes, you will be left behind.

Revelation might be the last book in the New Testament, but it was first in the hearts of Chuck Smith and the other preachers of the movement. End Times, Rapture, Tribulation, and the Second Coming were the ideas around which their ministries revolved. It was the carrot-and-stick approach to theology intended to keep members immersed in church life. The carrot was salvation; the stick, damnation. In Orange County, they went heavy on the stick.

At Calvary Chapel, the biggest stick of all was the Rapture. When it comes, those who believe in Jesus Christ will be lifted up to the sky to meet the Lord. Those who do not will be left behind to ride out seven years of fireballs, earthquakes, oceans of blood, locusts with human faces, and all the other horrors of the Tribulation. The message was simple and one that Calvary pounded relentlessly into the souls of its young membership.

Once he was back from Germany and trained by Calvary Chapel in the art of interpreting biblical prophecy, it had all become so clear to George. All the signs were there. He had seen the pillars of smoke and fireballs from heaven foretold in the book of Revelation. He had stood on the fields of Armageddon upon which the great battle of East versus West would be fought. He had fired the very weapons that would bring about the annihilation of mankind. George Smith had seen the end of the world and had no doubt it was coming soon.

WHEN THEIR TIME CAME, RALPH PULLED HIS SHIRT OFF, LET IT DROP TO THE sand, and entered the water. George watched as his friend was received by one of the associate pastors. The man spoke to him, said a prayer, and then lowered Ralph into the water. Ralph came back up smiling broadly, wiping the saltwater from his eyes. It was the happiest George had seen him since Ralph's return from Vietnam.

George pulled his own shirt over his head and waded into the ocean. He approached a church leader and stood beside the man, both up to their waists in the gentle swells. George could feel the sun on his skin, the breeze across the ocean's surface, the smell of seawater. The man placed a hand on George's chest and a second on the back of his neck. "I baptize you in the name of the Father, the Son, and the Holy Ghost."

George fell back, the cool waters of the Pacific enveloping his body. He opened his eyes underwater and stared up at the shafts of sunlight streaming beneath the surface and glinting off the specks of fool's gold drifting about him. A calmness and clarity came over him, his purpose in life settled at last. He had been trained as a warrior by the United States Army, shown the light by Calvary Chapel. Soon he would be a foot soldier of God in the battle against the Great Demon.

George got his legs beneath him, pushed off the sandy bottom, and broke the surface, seawater streaming off his body. He swept the salty water from his eyes and fixed his stare across the Pacific, to where the curve of the earth fell away beneath the clear blue sky. When the Apocalypse came, George Wayne Smith would be ready.

1

THE JUPITER EFFECT

April 1980. Mira Loma, California.

CHRIS HARVEN WAS AT THE BOTTOM OF THE PIT. HE SET THE SHOVEL DOWN, leaned against the cool dirt sides of the hole, fished another joint out of the pocket of his denim shirt, and sparked it. He drew in deeply, held the smoke for a long few seconds, and blew it out through his nose. It was his third joint of the day and not yet one o'clock in the afternoon. He might have been out of a job and almost out of money, but he sure as hell was not going to go without weed. Or without guns.

Harven took another drag and looked straight up at the rectangle of blue sky visible above the coffin-shaped mouth of the hole. A figure darkened the opening to the pit, a big man with a full beard and a mound of black curly hair circling his head. Stop bogarting and pass it up, the man said.

Harven reached up with the joint, but the pit was too deep now to hand anything out of it. Throw down that bucket.

The man disappeared for a few seconds. Harven took another hit. A wooden bucket on a rope was lowered into the pit and dangled beside him, a single can of Brew 102 inside. Harven took the beer out and dropped the joint into the bucket. The bucket was hoisted back up by the rope, scraping moist dirt off the walls of the pit and onto Harven.

George Wayne Smith took a toke off the joint and surveyed the hole. It was now twelve feet long, eight feet wide, and ten feet deep, three of the sides crumbling dirt and the fourth partially made of the foundation of the house. Smith crouched down at the edge to inspect Harven's progress in extending the main chamber beneath the foundation of the garage. We better start reinforcing these sides, he said, expelling smoke as he spoke.

Yeah, especially if you're going to stand there on the edge, said Harven. He lifted the ring to the pull top and the beer opened with a hiss. He tilted the can up and drained it, crushing the empty with one hand and tossing it out of the pit.

You just got fuckin' beer all over me, Smith said, dropping the joint back down to Harven and then disappearing from the opening of the hole.

Harven climbed the homemade wooden ladder out of the pit and into the choking smog of another scorching-hot Riverside County afternoon. He raised his hands above his head and stretched out his back, muscles hardened by eight years working as a city parks landscaper. Five days a week of shoveling dirt, wrestling lawn mowers, and stacking pallets of mulch had made him a strong six feet tall, 190 pounds. Not fitness-club strong, but the real kind of strong. Hard-labor strong. Harven had a rugged look that went along with his build. His sandy brown hair was thick and a bit unruly but never worn too long. There was something of a Clint Eastwood squint to his blue eyes, and his mustache curved down at the corners of his mouth.

Christopher Harven and George Smith met on the job, maintaining parks and the grounds of municipal buildings for the city of Cypress in 1973. The two young men hailed from the same sort of working-class Orange County neighborhood, both with very strong personalities, but each in his own way. George was evangelical, engaging, outgoing. Many afternoons mulching out flower beds were filled with his running monologues about the Bible, anarchy, social collapse, and the big plan he had for riding out the great catastrophes soon to befall mankind.

Chris Harven was more stoner than seeker, a burnout rather than a believer. By his own admission, he had always been a real troublemaker, but not maliciously so. While Smith was getting his varsity letters every year and editing the school newspaper, Harven was getting sent to detention, where he often caused so much commotion that they threw him out of there too. George volunteered and served two years with distinction in the U.S. Army, whereas Harven had been drafted and got himself thrown out in two months on an SPN-264—"Unsuitability, Character and Behavioral Disorders"—by simply refusing to do anything he was told. Upon discharge, George received a certificate of gratitude for his service, while Chris, on the other hand, received these parting words from his commander: "I've been serving in the military for over thirty years and the best thing I ever did for the U.S. Army was get rid of you, Harven."

Still, the two young men found common ground in things they both loved: camping, guns, music, and marijuana. Harven had a strong interest in survivalism but was less clear on exactly what he would need to survive. Smith knew what he would need to survive but not exactly how to survive it. So they talked about guns, bomb shelters, Jesus, and the end of the world while shoveling dirt, planting oleander, and mowing lawns, sneaking off every few hours to get stoned.

Chris left Cypress for something a bit closer to home, signing on with the city of Fountain Valley Parks Department in 1976. He was surprised that George had not followed. The supervisor at Cypress, Chuck Morad, did not like George one bit, and thought him an anarchist and troublemaker. He warned other employees, just as he had Harven years before, not to listen to all of George's talk about the Second Coming, overthrowing the government, and "killing pigs" if he had to. "That guy's going to lead you into nothing but trouble one day, Chris," Morad had said.

But by April 1980, Smith and Harven had been fired; both pulling in unemployment checks and doing day labor jobs when they could find them. Harven was bringing in some steady cash from selling pot, but the money was running out for George. He was starting to sound desperate.

Harven wandered into the greenhouse next to the pit to check on the crop of marijuana plants. He pinched off a small green bud from one of the immature plants, crushing it between his thumb and finger and giving it a sniff, and then tossing it aside. The shit wouldn't be ready to sell for months.

He walked out to the backyard. Unlike the carefully groomed plants in the greenhouse, the backyard of the house that the two men owned on 50th Street in Mira Loma was neglected and overgrown with weeds and withering fruit trees. Harven and Smith had scraped together a $5,000 down payment and bought it in the spring of 1979 for $56,000 with a 10 percent VA mortgage in George's name. It was a ratty-looking, stucco, ranch-style affair with three bedrooms.

Shielding the sun from his eyes, Harven looked up at George standing on a ladder, uncoiling concertina razor wire across the top of the greenhouse. It's gonna be at least three months on that bud.

We don't have three months, said George. We'll lose the house by then. Now twenty-seven, George Smith was a little over a year younger than Harven, an inch shorter, and ten pounds lighter. They had the same sort of build: thick around the arms, chest, and shoulders, thin at the waist. Smith made his way down the ladder and removed his gloves. You know what the solution is, he said. You just need to stop being such a chickenshit about it.

The accusation cut at Harven. He cared what Smith thought of him, a fact that Smith was more than happy to manipulate. There's just a lot of shit that could go wrong, Harven said.

Like what?

Harven shrugged. I'm thinking about it, he said, turning away. He wasn't in the mood for getting into that whole bank robbery thing right then. He surveyed the work they had put into the backyard. The entire perimeter of the property was secured now. They had raised the height of the walls separating them from their immediate neighbors by adding three feet of corrugated fiberglass to the top of the cinder block. Razor wire was strung along the fencing, and hundreds of carpet tacks hammered in with the sharp ends sticking up through the wood on top. Harven inspected a cluster of tacks, running his finger over the sharp tips. They rusted up pretty good, he called to Smith.

Sure did, Smith said. Fuck up your hands and give you tetanus too, climbing over that.

The carpet tacks and barbed wire had been Harven's idea, partly to keep the neighbor kids from stealing their weed. The pit was George's brainchild, designed as an escape tunnel leading from the garage to the backyard if the cops ever came busting in. But both had another use, something much bigger than protecting a greenhouse full of pot. The pit would be stocked with food and water to serve as a bunker when the A-bombs started to fall. The perimeter fortifications would help them hold off the bands of marauders who would come after their supplies. For any who managed to breach the perimeter, well, Chris and George had plenty of firepower to take care of them.

The two young men might have had varying visions of how it would all go down, but their beliefs led to the same place: a catastrophic event followed by social collapse, anarchy, and a fight for survival in a nightmarish, post-apocalyptic landscape.

George was still a book of Revelation guy, always on the lookout for current events he could match up with biblical prophecy. For Smith, the sins of man would bring about the wrath of God. Conflict between Arabs and Jews in the Holy Land, the Iranian hostage crisis now in its sixth month, the ritualistic murder-suicide of more than nine hundred people in Jonestown eighteen months before . . . George could see it all coming together, the chaos before the collapse, all of it foretold in the Bible, provided one knew how to read the signs.

In his 1978 book, *End Times*, Pastor Chuck Smith had finally revealed Calvary Chapel's official deadline for the Rapture. Borrowing heavily from Hal Lindsey's 1970 Christian End Times crossover bestseller, *The Late Great Planet Earth*, the pastor used a creative interpretation of Jesus's "Parable of the Budding Fig Tree" to predict the timing of the Second Coming of Jesus.

> If I understand Scripture correctly, Jesus taught us that the generation which sees the "budding of the fig tree," the birth of the nation of Israel, will be the generation that sees the Lord's return. I believe that the generation of 1948 is the last generation. Since a generation of judgment is forty years and the Tribulation period lasts seven years, I believe the Lord could come back for His Church any time before the Tribulation starts, which would mean any time before 1981. (1948 + 40 - 7 = 1981).

With Pastor Chuck Smith's prophecy, George Smith knew he had, at most, eight months to prepare.

Chris Harven could buy into all that End Times stuff, at least enough to add it to his list of doomsday scenarios that included nuclear war, asteroid strikes, population explosions, and any number of ecological disasters bandied about over the last decade. But Chris had recently settled on a specific theory of how the great catastrophe would come about, one he saw as far more pragmatic than the mystical prophecies of some Orange County preacher. There was even a name for it: "the Jupiter Effect."

Published in 1974, *The Jupiter Effect* was a sensational bestseller by British astrophysicists John Gribbin and Stephen Plagemann. The two scientists argued an approaching rare alignment of all nine planets on the same side of the sun would cause an increase in solar activity, altering the Earth's rotation, causing massive tidal shifts, and exerting immense pressure on the world's tectonic plates. The resulting geological instability would produce enormous volcanic eruptions throughout the Pacific Ranges and a massive earthquake that would tear California lengthwise up the San Andreas Fault. The date for all this havoc? March 10, 1982.

CHRIS WENT INSIDE THE HOUSE AND SLIPPED ON A SHOULDER HOLSTER CONtaining the Browning .45 semiautomatic pistol he had bought a few months back. He was hoping his unemployment check had arrived, but he no longer went to the mailbox at the end of the driveway unarmed. The sight of armed men going out to fetch the mail confused the neighbors, a few of whom assumed they were a pair of cops who'd moved in the previous spring. Who else would walk thirty feet to a mailbox packing heat?

Guns were not an unusual sight in Mira Loma. Despite its proximity to Los Angeles, Mira Loma had maintained a rural mentality that extended to gun ownership. Sandwiched between Norco to the south and San Bernardino County to the north, Mira Loma was a scruffy, eight-square-mile island of residential housing surrounded by empty lots, arid farmland, smelly chicken ranches, and pastures of grazing sheep. It was not a city at all, but merely an unincorporated area of Riverside County policed by the Riverside Sheriff's Department and underserved and underfunded by county government.

Originally called Wineville, the area's name was changed in 1930 by local real estate developers following the notoriously grisly Wineville chicken coop murders that gained national attention in the late 1920s. A chicken rancher named Gordon Northcott had a short but prolific run abducting, raping, torturing, and murdering up to twenty young boys, burning some body parts in a backyard fire pit and scattering the rest across Riverside County. Northcott was convicted and hanged at age twenty-three for four of the murders, including that of an unidentified, decapitated Latino boy referred to in the tabloids of the era as "the Headless Mexican."

Still, the area could not entirely shed the memory of the *American Gothic*–style murders, and the neighborhood never rose above the low end of working class. By the 1970s, the community had become a mix of Latino and white homeowners and renters. Housing was cheap and consisted of single-family homes of random design and constructed with a mishmash of building materials. Mira Loma became the land that Building & Zoning forgot with a multitude of non-permitted, do-it-yourself additions haphazardly tacked on without regard to quality, codes, or aesthetics. Maintenance standards of both houses and yards were spotty at best. And in an era of rising crime rates and a lousy economy, it had its fair share of unemployment, poverty, drug dealing, alcoholism, domestic violence, home break-ins, fistfights, and an occasional murder.

Harven opened the mailbox and stood leafing through the collection of junk mail, grocery store discount flyers, and utility bills. In the driveway next door, their neighbor, Denise Sparrow, was lifting a bag of groceries out of her trunk. She paused on the way to her front door. "Boy, you guys must have a whole bunch of gold in there or something," she called over to Harven with a friendly smile, motioning with her head toward the fortified perimeter of the property.

Chris had never met the woman nor any of his other neighbors. He and George avoided them whenever possible, even when they walked over to make conversation. Most had given up trying altogether. Harven flipped the door to the mailbox closed and looked over at the woman. Yeah, he said flatly, turning and walking back to the house.

"How's the little one doing? I haven't seen him around lately," Sparrow tried again in a cheerful voice. Harven ignored her entirely.

The little one was Harven's five-year-old son Timmy. Harven's wife Lani had taken the kid and left Chris two months earlier. The marriage had gone the way of most marriages between a nineteen-year-old boy and a seventeen-year-old girl. Chris had been the crazy high school boyfriend, always in trouble at school, never without money from selling weed. They rode around in Chris's car, got stoned, hung out with friends, went to rock concerts at the San Bernardino Swing Auditorium where Chris always got the best tickets. But when Timmy came along, Chris did not adapt well to the required change in lifestyle. By 1979, he was still smoking a lot of dope, zipping around in a Camaro Z/28, and involved in a secret relationship with a single mother named Nancy Bitetti, a respiratory therapist he met at the Broadway department store.

In February 1980, Lani had finally had enough of Chris's nonsense and was sick of living in a shithole with his weird friend George. So she took off. It was the start of a bad run. In March 1980 he lost his job along with all the benefits of a municipal worker. An argument on Easter Sunday damaged the relationship with Bitetti, but they limped on anyhow. Now he was laying carpet part-time for lousy pay and no benefits and falling behind on house and car payments. Lani seemed to be limiting his access to Timmy. Chris told his mother he felt like his life was going down the tubes.

When Chris returned to the house, George was sitting at the kitchen table, dirty, sweaty, and chugging a glass of tap water. From somewhere in a back bedroom, a radio tuned to KMET blasted a Foghat guitar solo. Chris tossed the junk mail in the trash. He opened a letter from the mortgage company and then slid the envelope across the table.

George read the letter for all of two seconds before sliding it back. We're fucked if we lose this house.

I know it, Chris said, pulling the holster Lani had bought for him for

Christmas over his head. He hung it on the back of a chair and scooped up the keys to his Z/28.

Where are you going? Smith asked.

Drop off some Thai sticks for my brother to sell.

Hope he sells it before he smokes it all, George said doubtfully. Russell Harven was a world-class pothead, even by Harven family standards.

He knows I'll kick his ass if he does, Harven said, walking to the sink to take a long drink of water straight from the tap.

You gonna talk to him? George said.

Harven flipped off the tap and wiped his mouth with the back of his hand. Fuck no. I don't want that little shit involved in something like this.

He already is, George said. Manny asked him yesterday.

HEY, FUCKFACE, HOW DID YOU LET MANNY DELGADO TALK YOU INTO ROBBING a bank?

Thirty miles due west of Norco, Russell Harven was not preparing for the Apocalypse or anything else. He was doing what he usually did: nothing. At twenty-six, a typical day for Russ consisted of lying around in his room smoking dope and jacking off to the *Playboy* centerfolds that papered the walls of the little bedroom in his parents' house in Anaheim.

Russ looked up from the acrylic bong and stared glassy-eyed at his older brother standing in the doorway. He let out an enormous cloud of pot smoke. He said it was your fuckin' idea.

It's George's plan, not mine, Chris said, tossing a baggie of Thai sticks onto the bed.

Russ lifted the baggie and studied the marijuana inside. He looked a lot like his brother, but an inch shorter and thirty pounds lighter. Same blue eyes, same natural squint, same sandy brown hair. But unlike his brother, Russ's hair was long and stringy and, like the rest of him, unwashed. A scraggly billy-goat beard now extended four inches below his chin. His body odor was detectable even through the pot smoke that constantly hung in the air. I didn't tell him I'd do it for sure, Russ said. Just that I'd think about it.

Chris plopped down into the only chair in the room and reached out for the bong. Here, give me that, he said. He loaded the bowl with a bud of Russ's shitty Colombian, flicked a Bic lighter, and the water pipe bubbled ferociously, filling with smoke. Chris took his finger off the carburetor hole and sucked it in deeply.

So, what's the plan, anyhow? Russ said, watching Chris exhale the smoke up toward the ceiling. I don't want to get into anything fucked-up.

Chris bullet-pointed what he knew, leaving out most of the details. Russ was not a detail guy anyhow. They'd rob the bank on a Friday, in and out in two minutes max, pick up cold getaway cars a mile away, and take off to Vegas to change out the hot bills through the casinos.

That sounds pretty good, Russ said absently, opening the baggie of Thai sticks. I guess I'll do it.

It was just like Russell Harven not to ask too many questions, to just go along with something because somebody suggested it. Life seemed to wash over Russ without his direct participation. He wasn't stupid, he was just leading a numbed existence, not even motivated enough to think through a decision like whether or not to rob a bank. He exhibited a profound failure to connect his actions with their logical consequences. At age eleven, he was diagnosed with diabetes, requiring daily insulin injections, usually administered by his protective mother, Mae. Russ's attitude toward the disease ranged anywhere from fatalistic to flippant. He subsisted on a steady diet of candy bars and RC Cola despite maintaining the belief that the disease might kill him before he reached thirty.

Other than an arrest for trespassing on school property, Russ had no criminal record until he was twenty years old and got popped for possession of amphetamines with intent to sell. It wasn't hard drugs, just a bunch of "whites," the same weak cross-tops long-haul truckers eat like candy to stay awake behind the wheel. Although barely stronger than caffeine pills, whites were a Schedule II controlled substance right along with the likes of cocaine, methadone, and PCP. And Russ had thousands on him. He was lucky to get off with a sentence of four months in the Orange County Jail.

Russ was married at the time, but just like Rosie Miranda had done to George Smith when he shipped off to Germany, Russ's young wife took the opportunity of his jailhouse absence to run off with another boy. When Russ got out of the slammer, he was crushed to find his wife and son living with another man. But Russ never fought all that hard to get her back. They never got around to getting a divorce, and Russ continued to wear his wedding band even after Eileen had a second baby with her new man.

Russ picked up a Thai stick and sniffed the length of it. It was strong, real Southeast Asian cannabis sativa tightly wrapped with a thread of hemp around a short bamboo stick. Crystals of pure THC glistened on the surface. He unwrapped the end of one of the sticks and loaded another hit in the bowl.

You smoke that, you pay for it, Chris threatened.

I'll smoke my profits.

As long as I get two hundred bucks when you're done, you can do whatever the fuck you want.

The two brothers were not close. In fact, Russell often wondered if Chris's only purpose in life was to torment him. Chris was better than Russ at everything—sports, school, women, making friends, making money— and frequently reminded Russ of that fact. Where Russ was shy and reserved, Chris was confident and controlling. When he got started, he could be relentless and mean, sometimes taking after Russ's wife, Eileen, until he had demeaned and insulted her to tears. Even then, Russ was afraid to protest for fear his brother would go after him next.

When are we going to do it? Russ asked his brother.

I didn't say you could do it, Chris said. You should stay out of it.

Fuck, Chris, I'm broke. I'm months behind on child support. I could get thrown back in jail for that shit.

Chris let out a long breath and stood up. Fuck, he muttered, fishing the keys to the Z/28 out of the pocket of his jeans. Come over Saturday, we're going up to Lytle Creek to zero out the new guns. I'll show you how.

I know how to shoot a gun, asshole, Russ sneered.

Chris paused at the door and gave his little brother a hard look. Not one like this, you don't.

HARVEN AND SMITH HAD EACH BUILT UP A MODEST GUN COLLECTION throughout the 1970s. For Harven it was simple. He liked the outdoors, going up into the rugged San Gabriel Mountains to hike, camp, hunt, and shoot. From the Harven house on Harriet Lane in Anaheim, Chris could hop in a car, head up to Lytle Creek, and be in some serious wilderness in about an hour. In 1972, at age twenty-one, he bought his first gun, a low-quality Clerke .22 revolver. Two years later he picked up a High Standard 12-gauge pump shotgun. Along with multiple rifles were plenty of handguns, including a Dan Wesson .357, Smith & Wesson Model 59, Browning .45, Walther P48, and the Smith & Wesson .38 he gave to his wife Lani after filing down the hammer so it wouldn't rip up her purse.

Like Harven, George Smith grew up camping on Mount Baldy and shooting in Lytle Creek. Smith also had military training with firearms. In the army, he was one of the best marksmen in his regiment. In 1974, he picked up a Ruger 10/22 rifle, a common starter gun. Less than a month later he went down to Grant Boys in Costa Mesa, not far from Calvary Chapel, and bought an M1 carbine .30-caliber rifle, the same weapon with which he had become so proficient while in the army. Even after picking up three additional guns later in the decade, none of Smith's firearm acquisitions, individually or taken as a whole, were enough to raise any concerns. But it did bother one person, and it bothered her a lot.

In June 1974, George met Hannelore Frolich, a pretty blonde with a round face, originally from Nuremberg, Germany. At thirty-one, Hanne was nine years older than George, fun-loving with a brilliant smile but tending toward serious and reserved. She liked how easy it was to be with George right from the start, how he always seemed to be in a good mood. They went dancing a lot, played tennis, and ran away for the weekends when George didn't have a shift at the Parks Department. On the other side of thirty, unmarried and without children, Hanne was anxious to move forward with life and would normally not have wasted a lot of time on a twenty-two-year-old man. But George had big dreams and Hanne liked people who aimed high. He talked about wanting children and didn't seem at all opposed to settling down. So they did, marrying in the spring of 1975, just nine months after first meeting.

For the first couple of years, Hanne and George talked about their dreams and all the things they might achieve together. They continued to have an active life, but then the baby came along and everything changed.

When Monica was born in 1977, Hanne's focus shifted almost entirely to their baby girl. George seemed to enjoy being a father. He took extra shifts at the Parks Department in Cypress, as well as a part-time gig teaching karate to kids at a local studio. They had enough money, but they stopped going out. George sulked and felt hurt and eventually found other things to do instead of hanging around the house, including running off to the mountains on the weekends with Chris Harven. Their sex life went from infrequent to nonexistent. When George's father, Walter, came over to visit one day, he was alarmed to find George and Hanne sleeping in separate bedrooms.

For George, it was exactly what he once told high school sweetheart Rosie Miranda years before: A baby would only come between them. Had Rosie still been around, she would have told him the same thing she had back then: "George, you're just too selfish to have a baby."

George's evangelical zeal and deep belief in End Times theology had not diminished since his days at Calvary Chapel. He had a talent for navigating almost any conversation to the subject of faith, the Bible, and the need to be prepared, both spiritually and materially, for the approaching Apocalypse. He worked the friends and family circuit particularly hard, converting many around him into born-again zealots. Even Hanne had come to know the Lord through George. Yet no matter how complete their conversion, all politely declined George's invitation to help him trick out some deserted mine shaft with food, gear, and weapons. With Chuck Smith's official Rapture deadline closing in, George was spurred to action. If no one would help him, then he'd do it himself, eventually settling on the goal of buying a remote cabin in the hills of Utah. There he would gather his loved ones, fight the Great Demon, and ride out the horrors God had in store for the creatures he had made in His own image. All George needed was the money to buy it.

The plan was classic George Smith, replete with grandiosity, self-righteousness, and confidence that he knew more than everyone around him. But it could not have come at a worse time for his marriage. Hanne was already stressed, second-guessing all of George's decisions and questioning every cent he spent on anything other than Monica. When George went out over the next few months and added the Colt .45 semiautomatic pistol, Remington hunting rifle, and Sauer .44 single-action revolver along with the ammo, cases, holsters, scopes, and all the other stuff that went with them, Hanne was less than pleased. She was in no mood for blowing the family budget on excessive weaponry while there were buggies, diapers, and baby food to be bought. In April 1979, George and Chris picked up a couple of .38 Specials of the concealable variety usually reserved for liquor store holdups and bar fights. Suddenly George's big plans seemed to Hanne like nothing more than distractions pulling him away from providing for Monica.

Whatever the reason—obsessive mothering, selfishness, Chuck Smith, or guns—by the spring of 1979, George was living in the house in Mira Loma with Chris Harven and without Hanne and Monica. Hanne was introspective enough to recognize her role in the disintegration of the marriage, but she had also seen something in George she knew would only become a bigger problem as time went on. "I think his dreams are just too big for what he can really do."

By Christmas 1979, George Smith was without a job, without a car, and without a family. It was a demoralizing condition for a young man who had always thought of himself as destined for great things. George struggled with a painful cognitive dissonance between who he thought he was and what he had really become. He had a solid support system of family and friends, but to fall back on it was utterly unimaginable to him. George was the one who always saved other people, whether it be with a few extra bucks, a solution to a problem, or the salvation of their very souls. What other people might have seen as merely a rough patch, George Smith saw as a desperate situation and one that he needed to escape at any cost.

George told Chris that he and a twenty-one-year-old co-worker from the Cypress Parks Department named Manny Delgado were going to rob the Denny's restaurant in Corona. Chris told him it was a ridiculous idea. "If you're gonna rob anything, why don't you just rob a fuckin' bank?"

With his situation growing ever more dire, and the Revelation time clock running out as fast as his bank account, George's behavior became increasingly erratic. He stopped cutting his hair so he would be able to weave it into seven braids like Samson. He convinced Chris that it was time to start turning the Mira Loma house into a fortress, complete with escape tunnel, fallout bunker, and fortified perimeter. After all, if they were not going to have enough money to buy the cabin in Utah, they better make damn sure they were prepared to ride out the Apocalypse right where they were.

But the Mira Loma house was only a contingency plan. George had not entirely given up on Utah. We got to get the fuck out of California, dude, or we're gonna die here. He'd been thinking about what Chris said about robbing a bank. As usual, George was thinking big. None of this passing a note and cleaning out the teller line for ten thousand bucks. Why not take over the whole bank and go for the vault? On a Friday payday, who knows, there could be $50,000; $100,000; $300,000 in cash in there. All we need are enough guys to pull the whole thing off, fast.

Chris remained noncommittal even as George got more and more detailed in his planning. Whenever Chris questioned the plan or pointed out a flaw, George would get defensive and question Chris's manhood, calling him a "yellow-belly" and a "coward." Chris would just brush him off. Throughout the New Year, Smith continued to poke and prod to get Chris on board, alternatingly bullying and begging his roommate. They'd lose the house soon. He didn't have enough money to pay child support to Hanne. You gotta fuckin' help me out, Chris.

One day, George came home and announced he had just finished casing the perfect bank for the job: the Security Pacific Bank in Norco. Chris was amazed. You're going to rob your own fucking bank?

When Chris's life began to fall apart too, he started to cave, retaining his doubts about the wisdom of the enterprise while committing himself to its execution. Okay, he'd do it under one condition. I'm not going into any bank unless we're armed up. You know the cops will be shooting at us, so we might as well be prepared to fight back if we have to.

WITH THE DECISION MADE, THE TWO EMPTIED MOST OF THEIR REMAINING savings accounts on more guns. Why not? George said. They'd either end up with a shitload of money from the job or die trying. In January 1980, Chris Harven visited two gun stores and bought a High Standard 12-gauge shotgun and a Browning semiautomatic pistol. On February 3, Harven and Smith went to Dave's Guns in Costa Mesa and picked up a second Browning .45 along with a far more serious weapon, a Heckler & Koch HK93. The HK93 was a top-of-the line German-made .223-caliber assault rifle, the civilian semiautomatic version of the M16 used by American forces in Vietnam. But it still wasn't enough. On February 13, Harven came back to Dave's and bought a sawed-off, antipersonnel version of the Remington 870 Wingmaster shotgun known as a riot gun. A week later, Smith stopped in and picked up hundreds of rounds of .223 ammunition, a high-powered rifle scope, and forty rounds of German Rottweil Brenneke shotgun slugs powerful enough to crack the engine block of an automobile.

In March, Chris brought Russ with him to Dave's Guns to look around and left after buying a .45 Long Colt single-action revolver with a six-inch-long barrel. Russ did not know at the time that his older brother was arming up for a bank robbery. On April 28, Chris went to the Gun Ranch in Garden Grove and purchased his second .223-caliber assault rifle, this time a Colt "Shorty" AR-15. The "Shorty" was as powerful as the M16 Colt manufactured for the military but with a collapsible stock and shorter barrel for use in confined spaces. Along with it he bought a handful of forty-round, high-capacity magazines. By the end of April, Christopher Harven had completed his arsenal.

George Smith, on the other hand, had not. Concluding that everyone involved in the robbery should be armed to the teeth, he made his biggest purchase yet—and the one that finally raised eyebrows at Dave's Guns. Smith picked up a standard Colt AR-15 and a Heckler & Koch HK91 semi-automatic assault rifle. The HK91 was essentially the same gun as the AR-15 but chambered for a .308-caliber round three times the size of the .223. A .223 might kill you, but a .308 would literally blow your head off. There was not an animal in the world that could not be brought down with a single round from a .308.

Guns like these might have been legal, but they were not big sellers in 1980. "What are you doing," clerk Dave McNulty joked, "getting ready to start World War III or rob a bank?"

Smith just laughed.

The date was May 2, 1980.

2

ZEROED OUT

May 3, 1980. Lytle Creek Canyon, California.

CHRISTOPHER HARVEN TOOK A LENGTH OF ONE-AND-ONE-QUARTER-INCH schedule 40 PVC plumber's pipe and screwed it snugly into the vise. With the hacksaw, he cut it down to three inches and used an electric drill to bore a small hole through one side in the middle of the white plastic tube. After sealing off one end with a PVC endcap, he tore a strip of newspaper off the front page of the *Riverside Press-Enterprise*, wadded it up, and pushed it down the pipe into the endcap. Picking up a six-inch length of green waterproof safety fuse, he threaded one end through the hole he had made in the side of the pipe. He stood the piece of pipe up on its capped end and gently tightened it down in the vise and left it there to dry.

When's Russ getting here? George asked, standing at the workbench emptying buckshot out of a shotgun cartridge into a metal Band-Aid box.

Harven took a rag off the table and dried the sweat off his forehead and neck. You know Russ, he could show up whenever.

Okay. Just as long as he's not thinking about backing out on us.

Chris tossed the rag onto the workbench. I'm sure every one of those guys are thinking about it.

George tilted the shotgun cartridge, rolling it between his thumb and fingers until the gunpowder charge began to pour out into a can of Copenhagen dip already half filled with the stuff. I can talk to him.

Don't talk to him, Chris said, pulling on a pair of powder-blue rubber gloves. We should have left him alone to begin with. He reached out and slid three canisters of black powder in front of him. He had worked with gunpowder before, making his own fireworks and M-80s strong enough to blow a home mailbox to shreds and then setting them off down at Huntington Beach on the Fourth of July. But the shit still made him nervous, especially with all the oily rags, solvents, and cans of gasoline sitting on shelving they had haphazardly thrown up with cinder blocks and boards. The whole place already smelled like a fucking bomb.

Harven took the canister of FFFG-grade smokeless powder from the shotgun shells and poured it into one containing black flake powder. To that he added DuPont-type powder, tiny black cylinders that looked like bits of pencil lead. Screwing the lid onto the metal canister, he gently shook it to combine the three into a Red Dot–type gunpowder mix. Using a small funnel, he poured an ounce and a half of the mixture into the PVC pipe, enough high-grade, smokeless gunpowder to fill thirty shotgun shells. He capped the other end and laid the four-and-a-half-inch detonating device in a row along with the others, over a dozen in all.

You need to catch up, he said to George, peeling off the kitchen gloves and tossing them onto the floor.

George set the last emptied shotgun cartridge to the side and stepped over to the odd collection of materials laid out in various containers: unfired lead bullets extracted from .358 rounds, concrete and duplex nails, barbed wire staples, shards of broken glass, and the lead pellets of #4 buckshot he had emptied out of shotgun cartridges. He took a final look at his copy of *The Anarchist Cookbook*, an instruction manual for an array of illegal activities such as making drugs, setting booby traps, tapping phone lines, and, of particular use to Harven and Smith, a section on "How to make an antipersonnel grenade."

Taking a twelve-ounce Budweiser can into the lid of which he had cut a star shape and peeled back the metal, Smith poured in a combination of the materials, inserted one of Harven's detonation devices in the center, and filled in the area around and on top of it with more of the lethal shrapnel mix, two and a half pounds in all. He bent the cut metal strips of the lid back down, took a second lid cut from another beer can, pulled the fuse from the detonator up through the opening, and pop-riveted the second lid to the top of the main can. When he was done with that, George wrapped the whole business in masking tape and set it beside the others.

It's not like these guys have anything to lose, George said, walking over to the card table with the launching devices he and Chris had made earlier (page 98: "Converting a shotgun into a grenade launcher").

Everybody's got something to lose, Chris said.

George slid one of the beer can grenades into a launcher and gave it a small shake until it held snugly in place. The launching device was simple: a twelve-ounce Coke can with the lid cut off and the bottom screwed down onto a half-inch circular plywood plate, which in turn was attached to a five-eighths-inch dowel, nineteen inches long. By setting the explosive device into the Coke can "grenade holder," sliding the dowel down the barrel of a shotgun, lighting the fuse on the bomb, and firing the shotgun loaded with a shell emptied of its buckshot, Harven and Smith had a devastating anti-personnel grenade with a launch range of one hundred yards. The shotgun could also be used to launch the incendiary bombs that Smith would add to the collection later: sixteen-ounce Blue Nun wine bottles filled with leaded gasoline, one of Harven's PVC detonators placed inside the neck.

When they were done, George and Chris surveyed the arsenal. Chris shook his head. I don't know, George, he said. This is some pretty heavy shit.

Well, we don't have much choice, George said, wiping the gunpowder and cellulose off his hands with a beach towel. We already spent all our money on guns. He picked up *The Anarchist Cookbook* and flipped through the pages. Think you could make one of these? he said, holding it out for Chris to see.

Harven studied the page. What's this for?

Diversion bomb. We'll set it off on the other side of town just before we go into the bank.

Harven let out a long breath. Sure, I can make that.

GEORGE TOOK THE NYLON RIFLE BAG OUT OF THE TRUNK OF THE CAMARO, UN-zipped it, and removed the Colt AR-15 he had bought the day before from Dave's Guns. He lifted the rifle and sighted down the barrel into the wash at Lytle Creek Canyon. Between two cottonwoods was the rusted hulk of an abandoned Ford Pinto. A Maytag washing machine pockmarked with gun-fire sat at the base of the hill along with an assortment of tires, furniture, and hundreds of beer cans and soda bottles. Half a dozen watermelons lay torn apart among it all, their red guts splattered over anything within twenty feet.

A hawk glided by and George sighted in on it with the AR-15 and fol-lowed its flight but did not fire. He lowered the gun, laid it down on the case, and took out a Zippo lighter. Trick I learned in the army, he told the boy who was standing by watching. He flicked a flame and held it just below the iron sight at the end of the barrel and slowly moved it back and forth. Blackens the sight to give it some contrast, he said.

Why are you doing that? Billy Delgado asked, moving a bit closer. He didn't know shit about guns, had never owned one himself. Coming from one of the worst barrios in Orange County, a seventeen-year-old kid like Billy didn't have much money for anything, let alone a rifle. Only the drug dealers and gang members in Crow Village had guns, and Billy wasn't either of those.

Zeroing out the sights, George said. Adjusting them for accuracy. He lifted the gun up to his shoulder and looked down the barrel, then lay the gun down again. You okay, Billy? he said without looking at the teenager. How are those vitamins I gave you working out?

Billy stretched out his arms. I'm all right, he said, even though it wasn't really true. Billy was always in pain, diagnosed with rheumatoid arthritis one doctor told him would rob him of his ability to walk by age twenty-five.

George had gone to the library, done some research, and put Billy on a vitamin regimen that was supposed to help.

Billy had known George since his older brother Manny got his landscaping job at Cypress Parks Department, when Billy was twelve. Even though George was ten years older, he always took the time to talk to Billy, asking how he was feeling, what the latest doctor had said, what medications he was on. In addition to the vitamin program, George also put together an herbal regimen for the psoriasis that caused dry, blotchy rashes all over Billy's face, arms, and hands. Billy hated the skin disease more than the arthritis. Together they kept him from sports, girls, and anything requiring physical exertion.

That's good, said George, taking a forty-round magazine of .223-caliber ammunition from the trunk of Chris's Z/28.

There was the sound of gunfire from somewhere down the canyon, a single, uninterrupted burst of at least twenty rounds, the reports echoing back and forth off the canyon walls. Billy looked across the wash, as wide as a football field and strewn with boulders, to the granite outcroppings soaring hundreds of feet off the canyon floor.

Sounds like somebody up here's got an automatic, Chris called from a few dozen feet away. Harven lifted a rifle and cracked off five quick rounds down into the wash, the rounds pinging off metal. The Heckler's good, he said.

Billy watched as George snapped the magazine into the bottom of the AR with a solid clicking noise, took a small backpack, and walked to the edge of the turnout where the hill sloped down into the wash. You nervous?

Not really, Billy lied. George turned and gave the kid a doubtful look. Well, maybe a little, Billy conceded.

George nodded. Yeah, me too. He tossed the backpack on the ground and then lay down prone with the rifle barrel resting on the pack. He steadied the gun, sighted through the back and front sights, let out a long breath of air, and slowly pulled the trigger. There was a sharp crack and Billy could feel the concussion deep in his chest. George repeated the process, firing another round. He took a set of binoculars and looked down into the wash. Come here, he said. I'll show you what I'm doing. Billy walked over and knelt beside George. I was aiming right at the middle of the door on that washing machine, he said, holding the binoculars up to Billy. Look at where they hit.

High, Billy said.

Yeah, George said. He took an unspent round and used the lead tip to click an adjustment on the iron sight at the end of the barrel. This direction to bring the sight down, he said. He lay back down in the prone position, steadied the gun again, and slowly squeezed off a shot. He adjusted the sights again until the bullets were hitting in tight groupings directly in the middle of the washer door. There, he said, getting back to his feet and dusting the dirt off his shirt and pants. He handed the gun to Billy. This is the one you're going to have.

Billy hesitated, staring at the black steel and composite weapon.

Just keep it on the seat beside you in case you need it.

Billy nodded, positioned himself, and lifted the gun exactly the way he had seen George do it. He swallowed, aimed down at the washing machine, and fired off three quick shots.

Not bad, George said. He left Billy and walked up the hill to where the others were shooting.

There was a booming sound. Is this fucking thing even legal? Manny grinned, holding the shotgun with the short barrel and pistol grip.

Riot gun, George said flatly. If anyone fucks with us, fire it into the ceiling.

Manny held the gun low at the hip and blasted off another three shells.

You better go talk to your brother, George said.

Manny looked over at Billy firing the AR and then handed the riot gun to George.

Manny Delgado was twenty-one years old but not all that much bigger than his little brother. Both were bantamweights, barely over five feet tall and weighing in at about 120 pounds. But whereas Billy looked boyish and easy to pick on, Manny carried himself like a tough little motherfucker. But when you came from the barrio, a kid had better be tough. Manny was all that, but he never gave anyone a bad time unless they gave it first. He looked after his wife and small child, held down a job, and stayed out of trouble. Well, mostly stayed out of trouble. Manny had gotten himself into a minor scrape with the law and was doing some weekends in the county jail. Nothing he couldn't get past, except now he had missed two weekends in a row planning for the bank job with George.

Manny had already gotten the hell out of the Crow Village neighborhood of Stanton and was living in Garden Grove with his wife, Juanita. If a kid in Crow Village had any job at all, it probably involved street drugs, stealing cars, or gang shakedowns. But Manny got a job through a work program when he was just sixteen years old, digging up irrigation pipes and planting trees at the Parks Department for the city of Cypress. He had worked there together with George for almost a half dozen years. Manny worked his ass off and the supervisor there called him an "ideal young man," but frequently asked Manny what the hell he was doing hanging around after hours with that troublemaker George Smith.

All George had to do was suggest the bank job and Manny was in. He already had one child under age two and was expecting another with Juanita in a few months. Succeed or die, George told him. Manny was down for that, too. He quit his job at Cypress and told them he was moving to Arizona. His only hesitation was getting Billy involved, but a little bit of money could get Billy a long way out of Crow Village.

Billy lowered the gun when he saw Manny approaching. I thought I was just driving, he said. What do I need this for?

What are you so fucking worried about? Manny said in his heavy Chicano accent with its unique mix of staccato and elongated syllables. You don't have to do it if you don't want to.

It's okay, Billy said, staring down at the gun in his hands. He knew it was too late now to back out without letting down his brother and George.

Manny took the gun from him. It's going to be okay, Belisario, he said softly, using his brother's given name. Nothing's gonna happen.

CHRIS POPPED THE EMPTY MAGAZINE OUT OF THE COLT "SHORTY" AR-15, tossed it into a cardboard box, and snapped in a new forty-round clip. This one's all set, he said, handing the gun over to Russ. Give it a try.

Russ lifted the gun and squeezed the trigger. The rifle gave a sharp crack and kicked back against his shoulder. Russ smiled and reeled off three quick shots in the direction of the abandoned Pinto. Crack, crack, crack. The first shot hit metal, but the gun jerked and pulled up and to the left, sending the next two way high of the mark.

Try to keep it in the canyon, shithead. Chris walked over to the Z/28, reached into the open trunk, and dug around in a duffel bag. Who wants to throw a bomb? he said, walking back with one of the fragmentation grenades they had made.

I'll fuckin' toss a grenade, Manny said with a smile.

The others gathered around as George showed them how it worked. Light the fuse, throw it, and then get the fuck down before you get your guts torn out by shrapnel. He pulled out the Zippo. Ready?

None of that shit better hit my car, Chris warned.

George flicked the lighter. Throw it way over there, he said to Manny, nodding in the direction of the Pinto down in the wash.

Manny extended his arm back, clutching the grenade. When George lit the fuse, Manny stepped forward and hurled the canister like an outfielder throwing a runner out at home plate. They all hit the dirt and lay on their bellies waiting. Three seconds later there was a sharp explosion and the sound of shrapnel striking metal, trees, granite boulders, and everything else down in the wash.

Slowly, they all pushed themselves up from the dirt and walked to the edge of the wash. For a few seconds, they stood staring down at the smoke rising up from the canyon floor. Chris Harven shook his head. Holy shit, he said.

3

THE RSO

May 9, 1980. Riverside, California.

THERE WAS NO WAY ANDY SHOULD HAVE ENDED UP A COP. THE ILLEGITIMATE child of a poor, fifteen-year-old Latina with drug and alcohol problems. Abandoned by his birth mother, raised by a grandmother who died a violent death, passed around among relatives who either could not afford or did not want him, placed under the jurisdiction of Child Protective Services, in and out of facilities run by the California Youth Authority. On paper, his childhood history was the familiar trajectory that led far too many young Mexican Americans into street gangs and the California correctional system.

The difference was Andy had never done anything wrong, never broken a single law in his life. Andy's childhood had been one of abandonment, rejection, and tragedy, but it had also been one of salvation.

Andy's birth mother was first-generation Mexican American, part of a large family of migrant workers who followed the picking seasons or any other employment opportunity throughout the Southwest. His father was Italian, a successful restaurateur in Tempe, Arizona. It might have been a great love story except that Esperanza Espinoza was the fifteen-year-old babysitter and Leonard Monti was a much older married man with three kids of his own.

Leonard Monti was not cruel or heartless, but there were all kinds of reasons why a pillar of society, a member of the Chamber of Commerce, a Goldwater guy might want to cover up the fact that he had knocked up his underage Mexican babysitter. Whatever the arrangement, Esperanza quietly went on her way and had her baby in Modesto, California. Some guy named Delgado stepped in for Leonard Monti on the birth certificate, so Andy became the only Delgado in a family of Espinozas, an uncomfortable detail no one ever bothered to change.

Three days into his life, Andy was handed over to his grandmother. It was obvious that his birth mother could not care for a newborn. Alcoholism and addiction made sure she would never play that role in Andy's life. Andy was raised by his grandmother Marcelina, a woman he would forever refer to as his mother. They were poor, a single woman with six kids to support. They rattled around the Southland, living in the migrant camps or trailer parks. But it was okay. Andy had a family, siblings to play with, a place to belong. But like most things in Andy's young life, it did not last.

In 1963, when Andy was ten, they were living in the Warehouse District of Los Angeles. One day, his grandmother rented a trailer, loaded it up with used appliances and furniture, and, along with Andy and her three youngest children, drove to the border town of Mexicali. They spent the day delivering the goods and visiting with relatives. At the end of a long day, they headed back, swinging by the L.A. suburb of El Monte to drop a few items off at their Aunt Olga's house.

A man named John R. Barkus was driving through El Monte that night too. He was drunk. When Marcelina Espinoza stepped between the trailer and the car to get something out of the trunk, John R. Barkus slammed into the back of the trailer at high speed. Marcelina was crushed, pulled to the pavement and plowed over by the trailer. What Andy saw that night was his grandmother, his mother really, crumpled, broken, and dead, the clothes ripped off her body by the force of being dragged across asphalt by the undercarriage of the trailer.

Of the six orphaned children, five were absorbed into the families of relatives. The three younger ones, the kids with whom Andy was closest, went together to the home of an aunt in Hacienda Heights. Andy, the youngest, was the odd kid out. He was different than the others, not one of Marcelina's kids at all, more like an adopted child, the only one with a different last name. He was passed around among the aunts and uncles, many of whom already had large families and problems of their own and were either in no position to take on an extra kid or simply did not want to. Andy could tell. Many treated him as an outsider, or worse. With his family jerked out from under him, Andy was quickly becoming anchorless, bouncing around from school to school, neighborhood to neighborhood, house to house. That's when an El Monte cop named Darrell Creed showed up in his life.

Creed was in his early twenties, a gangly six-foot-four transplant straight out of rural Kansas. He looked the hayseed part with ears that stuck out, arms that dangled almost to his knees, and a wide, crooked smile. But he was a smart and decent young man who could see all the warning signs in Andy, the sort of rootless and unstable existence that turned good kids into juvenile delinquents. Creed began to stop by the house on his off hours to check in on Andy, maybe take him over to the park, buy him a burger, or even drag him along for dinner at a friend's house. The El Monte PD thought this was a very bad idea and told Creed so. He ignored them. Creed became a big-brother figure Andy could look up to.

But then Andy moved on to another relative in another town, away from Darrell Creed. That situation did not work out either. Now there were no more relatives willing to take him in. One of them handed him over to Los Angeles County's child protective services system. Whatever paperwork or hearings or judicial machinery that might have been grinding away in the background to determine his fate was invisible to Andy. All he knew was that he was getting stuffed into an overcrowded youth facility called MacLaren Hall while his brothers and sisters were tucked away with family members.

Even at age ten, Andy Delgado knew a shitty situation when he saw one. The place was creepy, sad, and mean, and he wanted out. So he left. Just walked the fuck right out of the place. At MacLaren Hall, they called that "escaping" and brought him back and put him in the lockdown area with the juvenile offenders. He left again, this time climbing onto the roof and over a perimeter fence. In all, he climbed in and out of youth facilities for the better part of a year until all the "escapes" officially made Andy a juvenile offender.

Meanwhile, the system was making some decisions about Andy Delgado's future. They placed him in the Los Padrinos facility in Downey. Same thing, different place. A parole officer named Betty McCold took over Andy's case and was dismayed at what she found when reviewing his records. Andy was about to be become a long-term inductee into the juvenile corrections system even though he had committed no crime beyond wanting to get the hell out of some lousy, county-run, lockdown orphanage. She asked Andy if there wasn't someone, *anyone,* who would take him in? No, he said. Nobody. And then he remembered that cop in El Monte who had shown him some kindness a few years before. Darrell . . . Something. Andy did not even know the man's last name.

It was an absurd idea. Betty McCold could have done what most overworked caseworkers would have done: shrug her shoulders and stuff the Andrew Delgado case into a filing cabinet until his upcoming date before a judge to determine his fate. But instead, Betty McCold called the El Monte PD. Did they have a cop named Darrell who used to hang out with a ten-year-old kid named Andy? They used to, but he was not on the force any longer. McCold followed the trail, but when she finally tracked down the big lanky cop from Kansas, it looked as though it might be too late.

Andy sat before the judge in the Child Protective Services disposition hearing to determine what they were going to do with him next. There was nowhere for him to go but a lockdown facility within the system; otherwise he would just run away again. Well, the judge said, is there anyone present who is willing to take responsibility for this kid? There was. Andy looked over and saw Darrell Creed for the first time in months. He was there with his new bride. Yes, they would take responsibility for Andy. Yes, they would be his foster family until he was old enough to go out on his own.

From then on, Andy had a home. However, the experience of being abandoned, locked up, bullied, and treated so unfairly was one that Andy never forgot. For the rest of his life, the injustices inflicted upon him as a child would play a huge role in how he viewed the world and interacted with the people around him.

As a father, Darrell Creed instilled in Andy the values of loyalty, honesty, and integrity. It was the loyalty part that was particularly attractive to Andy because he had seen so little of it in his life. He listened in on the conversations Creed and other cops had while drinking coffee around the kitchen table. Stories about always having each other's back, trusting your partner with your life, and, above all, never leaving a fellow officer alone in a fight. Andy revered these values, these men, and, by extension, all policemen and the institution of law enforcement. From then on, Andy Delgado knew exactly what he wanted to do with his life.

ANDY WAS JUST COMING OFF PATROL THE EVENING OF MAY 8, 1980, WHEN HE found deputy chief Ron Bickmore waiting for him, smoking a cigarette in an area just off the dispatch center called "the pit." The normally gruff Bickmore seemed even more annoyed than usual. "I want to see you in Sheriff Clark's office tomorrow, oh-seven-hundred sharp." When Andy asked what the meeting was about, Bickmore took a last drag off the cigarette and crushed it out on the floor. "It's personal." Shit, Andy thought. I knew it would catch up with me.

The whole thing had been fucking stupid, a dustup during a party at deputy Fred Chisholm's house two weeks before. Chisholm was a tall, good-natured, and deceptively tough transplant from a blue-collar town just outside Boston who still retained his thick regional accent. Andy had been his training officer, and the two had become friends. Chisholm had managed to get hold of a video of the movie *Animal House* and invited a bunch of the boys over to his new house one afternoon to throw back some beers and watch the movie. When Andy got to the party around three o'clock, it was mostly a bunch of bleary-eyed deputies from the graveyard shift who had come straight off the overnight and had been pounding beers since. Andy did not know these guys well and what little interaction he had had with them was not always good.

There was one deputy Andy especially did not like, one of those on the force for whom every black man was a "jungle bunny," every Mexican a "beaner," and every Asian a "gook." There were too many guys in the department like that. "Do you not see me standing right here?" he had snapped after a fellow deputy dropped a few too many "spics" and "wetbacks" into a story about an encounter with a group of Mexican migrant workers. If Delgado had any triggers—and he certainly did—one was his Mexican heritage and the other was his size, a generous five foot four, 145 pounds.

Andy had not been at the party long before the slurring deputy from the night shift was working both of Andy's triggers. Delgado tried to deflect the confrontation but eventually the man—a solid six-footer who outweighed Delgado by sixty pounds—extended an invitation for Andy to step outside. Andy did not want to cause Chisholm and his young wife any trouble in their new home. "If this wasn't Fred's house," Andy told the guy, "I'd give you that opportunity." By then, Fred had enough of the asshole too. "Don't let that bother you, Andy. Kick his ass, or I will."

The smart money was on the bigger man when the two Riverside deputies took their disagreement to Chisholm's backyard to settle it once and for all. What most did not know was that Andy had been a star wrestler on the high school team and in the Marine Corps and a judo black belt by age sixteen. Andy tackled the man, tossed him, twisted his limbs, pinned him in wrestling holds, and even punched him clean off Fred's porch before another deputy stopped it.

There had been an ominous silence from the department brass for the two weeks following the incident as news of the fight spread among deputies. The higher-ups had to know all about it, but so far none of them had said a word. Maybe they never would. Then again, maybe they were preparing Andy's termination papers.

Delgado knew he must be getting close to a promotion to detective. Seven years of service, with a reputation for dedication, honesty, dependability, and effective policing. If Andy was told to go into an area and suppress crime, Andy did it. Along the way he had a number of big arrests and had even saved a woman trapped inside her car in a torrent of rising floodwaters.

He was also taking a full course load at Cal State San Bernardino and closing in on a degree in public administration and criminal justice. The promotion was important to Andy, not just for the additional pay and status, but also for the recognition that he was a damn good cop.

Andy was starting to think the whole thing was just going to blow over until Bickmore intercepted him in the pit. That night he went home and told his wife, Lucretia. "I'm in trouble," he said, preparing her for the worst. "I'm never going to make detective."

THE SUN HAD CRESTED OVER THE SOARING SAN GABRIEL MOUNTAINS ON THE morning of Friday, May 9, when the rest of the deputies on the 6:00 a.m. to 4:00 p.m. "two-shift" began arriving at the Riverside Sheriff's Office. The RSO, as the men who worked there called it, inhabited offices within a larger municipal complex in the center of the city of Riverside that included the county jail and courthouses. The Riverside Police Department occupied another municipal building directly across the street from the RSO. Other than geographical proximity, the two law enforcement agencies could not have been further apart.

The officers of the Riverside PD were city cops, their jurisdiction confined within the borders of a modern and mostly suburban city. Most of the larger cities in Riverside County had their own self-contained police departments. The California Highway Patrol ruled the freeways. The Riverside County Sheriff's Department got what sheriff's departments always got: everything else.

For the RSO, "everything else" meant responsibility for most of a county larger than the state of Delaware. Covering more than 7,200 square miles, Riverside County is a crude rectangle of arid land running west to east from the edge of the Los Angeles metro area to the Arizona border. Within this area, the Riverside County Sheriff's Department was responsible for operating county jails, guarding county courthouses and municipal buildings, and patrolling all wilderness areas, unincorporated population centers, and "contract" cities too small or too poor to take on the cost of maintaining a police force themselves.

Other than the resort town of Palm Springs, the area east of the San Gabriel and San Jacinto Mountains consists of vast and forbidding wildlands, Indian reservations, and a few small desert towns sprinkled over thousands of square miles of the barren Colorado Desert. While this area contained three-quarters of the land mass of Riverside County, three-quarters of its population was centered in an area west of the mountains known as the Inland Empire.

The Inland Empire was the brand name given by early real estate developers and civic leaders to promote the collection of cities occupying the far western end of Riverside and San Bernardino Counties. "Inland" because it is, "Empire" because it just sounded good. The I.E., as locals call it, was a rather ill-defined contiguous sprawl of residential housing, agricultural land, dry washes, factories, fast-food restaurants, taco stands, and distribution centers. Without road signs announcing you had passed into one city from another, you wouldn't even know it. Air pollution generated by the entire Los Angeles metro area was pushed by westerly winds into the I.E. where it backed up against the San Gabriels, obscuring the mountains in a brown haze. First- and second-degree smog alerts were the norm, the toxic air burning the lungs upon each deep inhale.

The I.E. of May 1980 was a dusty, hot, and smoggy land populated by a blue-collar, redneck, ragweed-smoking, hard-rocking population as tough as that of any Pennsylvania steel or Texas cow town, of which it was a little of both. While trends, fashions, and fads were being created by designers and movie stars just a few dozen miles down the road in Los Angeles, they were going mostly unnoticed in the Inland Empire. Disco was hated, punk rock unknown. AC/DC, Led Zeppelin, Ted Nugent, and Lynyrd Skynyrd ruled the airwaves.

The area had always been a rough place, and with unemployment rising along with the proliferation of gangs and street drugs throughout the 1970s, it only got rougher. Cops were increasingly coming up against weapons they had never seen before. Methamphetamine addiction was savaging the local population, its manufacture and distribution controlled by murderous rival motorcycle gangs.

There were already rumblings among the RSO deputies about their need for more powerful, high-capacity weapons to combat the firepower emerging on the streets. But arming the average patrol cop with anything more than a sidearm and shotgun was a step very few law enforcement agencies in the country had been willing to take. Most viewed it as an unnecessary, expensive, and dangerous escalation in weaponry. Those who did make the jump to high-powered rifles kept them tightly under the control of SWAT teams.

Riverside sheriff Ben Clark deflected the issue, seeing no reason to increase the firepower within a force that still relied on SWAT teams from neighboring departments. Clark had come out of the administrative side of the house and had a more sociological approach to the modernization of the force. Few of the deputies had the balls to put their concerns in writing to the sheriff, but one did. He was a veteran deputy named James Bernard Evans.

DEPUTY JIM EVANS CAME INTO THE BRIEFING ROOM WEARING HIS BROWN-and-olive patrol uniform and a Stetson cowboy hat, as usual. Evans was a Texan, a Special Forces Green Beret who had seen combat on some of the riskiest deep-jungle missions in the Vietnam War. At thirty-nine, Evans was one of the older deputies on the force, easygoing and highly respected by the other deputies. If you got into trouble on the streets, Jim Evans was the guy you wanted backing you up.

Evans was handsome, six feet tall, and trim, with sandy-blond hair and mustache and hazel eyes that looked out at the world through the thick lenses of sixties-era tortoiseshell eyeglasses. He had a soft West Texas drawl and countrified vocabulary. He was never without his John B. Stetson and cowboy boots while off duty and even sometimes behind the wheel of a sheriff's department cruiser. Fred Chisholm had been surprised to come upon Evans on the side of the road one afternoon writing a motorist a ticket, the cowboy hat still perched proudly on his head.

Deputy Dave Madden entered the room. Evans looked him over. "Are those new boots you got on, Brother Madden?" he said.

"Indeed, they are," Madden replied with a smile, taking a seat next to Evans.

Dave Madden was a curiosity to his fellow deputies. He always wanted to be a cop and had the temperament for it, but he was also a seeker. He was a big fan of science fiction, not for the rocket ships or aliens, but for the philosophical exploration and social commentary contained within. Raised a Roman Catholic, he could nevertheless quote the Jewish philosopher Maimonides, reference Kabbalah, and speak intelligently on the teachings of Buddhism and Hindu polytheism. From the ancient Greeks to the Beatles to the book *Zen and the Art of Motorcycle Maintenance*, Madden had quotes up his sleeve for almost any situation. He spoke fluent Klingon, responded to calls with the theme to *Star Wars* blasting from a handheld tape player, shaved his head on a whim, and consistently confounded his colleagues. They shook their heads in dismay, called him a hippie, and nicknamed him "Mad Dog" Madden.

Madden's best friend on the force was Andy Delgado, a pairing that on the surface made no sense at all. But the two men found common ground in their views of the world around them. It did not hurt that the intense Delgado found Mad Dog's eccentricities and antics massively entertaining.

Hey, man, how's J.B. Jr. doing? Madden asked Evans. Born on Christmas day, the four-month-old James Bernard Evans Jr. was just getting over the measles and still running a fever.

I guess he's all right, Evans said. Gonna stop by the house on my way out to Moreno Valley and check in on him.

Giving Evans a ride home the night before, Madden was surprised to see the impressive collection of military decorations mounted in a case in the living room, including two Bronze Stars and a Medal of Valor. Although they had been on the force together for four years, Evans had never mentioned anything about his military career. "I should stop calling you Jimmy," the much-younger Madden said, "and start calling you sir." Evans laughed it off with his usual modesty. He was more interested in introducing Madden to his new son. Evans held the baby and told Madden his plans for teaching the boy to ride horses by the time he was three.

Jim Evans had been a city cop but felt penned in by its urban landscape and made the move to the more far-ranging sheriff's department. In every way, being a sheriff's deputy fit the personality of a Texan like Evans. The mystique of the Old West sheriff lingered deep in the consciousness of every American boy, especially the men of the RSO. Sheriffs were cowboys, lawmen, savers of damsels in distress, gunslingers in white hats. They roamed the range fearlessly handing out American-style justice to rustlers, bandits, murderers, and train robbers with a sock on the jaw or from the barrel of a gun. Sheriffs and deputies had patrolled the mean streets of Deadwood, Tombstone, Dodge City, and the brawling boomtowns of Nevada. They guarded the pony express, Oklahoma Territory, and the Alamo. Wild Bill Hickok was a sheriff. So were Doc Holliday, Bat Masterson, and Wyatt Earp. Gary Cooper was the sheriff in *High Noon*. Clint Eastwood played one, too. And, of course, John Wayne. Especially John Wayne.

Shift sergeant Ed Giles set a folder down and took a seat at the head of the table. "All right, men," he said. "Listen up." The men wrapped up their conversations and turned their attention to the briefing. It was routine: watch the numbered streets in Mira Loma, lots of car break-ins lately, keep up the traffic patrol in Norco, the town is grumbling about ticket revenues again, same old shit in Moreno Valley. The only notable issue on the briefing list was the trouble brewing at Rubidoux High School. Rubidoux was one of the roughest areas in the county, one of its few African American communities. It was poor, plagued by drugs and gang activity, and made up mostly of run-down single-family homes and subsidized housing projects. Giles told the men to expect trouble there. He used the word *riot*. The men groaned. Patrolling Rubidoux was bad enough and none of them wanted anything to do with a riot. Giles assigned Rubidoux to the youngest deputy in the department, A. J. Reynard, along with one of his veterans, Ken McDaniels, and told them to keep a high visibility around the school.

With the assignments made, Giles shifted to one of his periodic briefings on a crime that had been skyrocketing to epidemic proportions over the last four years: bank robbery.

If you had robbed a bank in the greater Los Angeles metro area on May 9, 1980, you would not have been alone. Los Angeles had long been labeled "Bank Robbery Capital of the World" among FBI agents responsible for investigating the crime. It was a title well earned. For decades, one-quarter of all bank heists in the United States fell under the geographical jurisdiction of the Los Angeles field office of the FBI, which included Riverside and San Bernardino Counties. By 1980, an average of six banks were being robbed each business day. More than fifteen hundred a year. The reason was simple: freeways.

The Southern California car culture had resulted in a physical landscape ideal for bank robbery. A relative latecomer to the ranks of the big cities, the Los Angeles area's population exploded 117 percent between 1940 and 1960 to more than six million inhabitants. With the automobile age in full swing, the second great American western migration flooding the region with newcomers, and a vast coastal basin within which to put them, Los Angeles did not grow up; it grew out. By 1980, the total population of the Los Angeles metro area was more than ten million people spread out over five thousand square miles.

The great enabler of this mass suburbanization was the automobile and a vast network of freeways that, rush hour aside, allowed the population to move long distances in a short period of time. And nobody wants to move farther and faster than a bank robber. By hitting a bank near a freeway on-ramp, a holdup man could jump on and off and be anonymously cruising side streets five miles away in a completely different police jurisdiction before the cops even arrived at the crime scene. Have the foresight to park a second "cold" getaway car a few miles away and you are gone-baby-gone. Try putting that kind of distance between yourself and the bank you just hit in New York City, Philadelphia, or San Francisco and you would likely find yourself bogged down in crosstown traffic or standing on the nearest subway platform waiting for the No. 6 train to show up before the cops did.

It did not take long for the word to get out. Follow a few simple rules and you could rob a bank in Los Angeles with little chance of getting caught:

Don't rob locally where people might know you, never stay inside a bank too long even if it means a shitty take, and always hit a bank close to a freeway on-ramp.

With a consumer market in love with convenience and the newly de-regulated savings and loan industry eating their lunch in the lucrative home mortgage market, the traditional retail banks began locating branches closer and closer to freeway on-ramps throughout the 1970s, making the L.A. sprawl a target-rich environment for bank thieves. In Riverside County, the cities straddling the 60 and 91 freeways such as Corona, Moreno Valley, and Riverside were particularly hard hit. Less so, the areas located farther away from the major freeway corridors.

While not immune to bank heists, the small town of Norco had no major freeways running through it. (The existing segment of Interstate 15 bisecting Norco had not yet been built in 1980.) Geographically speaking, one of the safest locations for a bank in the entire Inland Empire was the in-tersection of Fourth Street and Hamner Avenue, right in the center of town. From there, it was four miles south to the 91 and nine miles north to the Pomona Freeway, much of it through heavy traffic areas. Not surprisingly, a bank was located at that exact intersection: the Norco branch of the Security Pacific National Bank.

AT THE CONCLUSION OF THE BRIEFING, THE DEPUTIES OF THE TWO-SHIFT went to the board, grabbed a radio and keys to one of the available cruisers, checked out a shotgun for the day, and then headed out to the vehicle yard to pick up a patrol unit. Unlike many local police forces, the RSO was strictly one officer per vehicle.

Ken McDaniels was a veteran with all the confidence that goes with hav-ing a half dozen years on the street. He had been diagnosed with Hodgkin's disease a year before and had worked half shifts every Friday for the past year to make his weekly radiation treatments. Ready for a riot? McDaniels said to deputy A. J. Reynard as they walked together to the vehicle lot.

Fuckin' Rubidoux, Reynard said, shaking his head. At least you're off early today.

Nope, McDaniels said, smiling. Today was supposed to be my last treatment, but they called me up yesterday and canceled it. Said they had counted wrong and my final one was actually last week. For the first time in months, Ken McDaniels would work a Friday shift until four o'clock in the afternoon, just like every other deputy on the two-shift.

Man, that's great, Ken, Reynard said, slapping his fellow deputy on the back.

At twenty-three, A. J. Reynard was still a "probie" with three months left on his eighteen-month initial evaluation period and desperate to do everything right, make a good impression, and, most importantly, keep his job. Reynard was part Cajun by heritage but a true born-and-raised Southern Californian with a unique mix of hyperkinetic energy and laid-back attitude to go along with a vocabulary somewhere between surfer and stoner, of which he was neither. He was quick-witted, a bit of a prankster, and a full-on adrenaline junkie. He was smart enough to have been accepted into the pre-med program at UCLA, but in his heart, he wanted to be a cop. He dropped out of school after a year, did a stint in the Marine Corps, and then began putting in for jobs with the different police agencies in the area. He was quickly snatched up by the RSO.

His fellow deputies liked A.J., even if they might have initially resented the fact that he was one of the few recruits ever fast-tracked straight into Patrol & Investigation without working the traditional twelve- to fourteen-month initiation period inside the county jail. But right off, they could tell A.J. had the instincts for the job: streetwise, able to defuse tense situations, while at the same time unafraid to mix it up with a suspect when all else failed.

The experienced McDaniels was giving Reynard a few tips on how to handle a gang riot as they reached Reynard's patrol unit for the day. Slightly distracted and perhaps a bit more hyped up than usual after all the talk about a riot, A.J. slid the key into the door lock of the Plymouth Fury and heard a snap. McDaniels stopped midsentence. A.J. looked down at half a car key in his hand, the other half broken off in the door lock. Fuck, Reynard said. How much shit am I going to be in for this little maneuver?

You still on probation? McDaniels asked.

Yeah.

That's too bad, McDaniels said, suppressing a smile. You could definitely get terminated for destroying county property. Probably extend your probation period another six months at the very least.

Reynard looked nervously around the vehicle yard. Help me out, Ken, he said, nodding in the direction of the kiosk in the center of the yard where the notoriously ill-tempered garage attendant guarded the extra keys to the fleet of sheriff's vehicles. Distract him while I grab the keys to a different cruiser.

McDaniels looked over at the little man, who eyed the two deputies with suspicion. He flashed A.J. a smile and headed in the direction of the kiosk.

While McDaniels chatted with the man, Reynard leaned inside the kiosk and quickly slipped a set of keys off the board. It was a close call.

Whadya get? McDaniels asked as they walked away from the cage.

Reynard looked at the keys for the first time. One of the Chevys, he said with equal parts excitement and concern. Everyone preferred the Impalas over a Plymouth Fury or, worse, the Dodge Aspens. The Chevys were newer, had way more pickup and top end, far superior handling, bigger inside cab, and great A/C. It didn't hurt that a higher dashboard meant a few more inches of cover should a semitruck or fleeing suspect send some sort of projectile through the front windshield. The problem was, the veterans on the shift sure as shit did not want probies like A. J. Reynard snagging the best cruisers out from under them. Uh-oh, Reynard said.

Uh-oh is right, McDaniels agreed, pointing at the Impala. That's Franklin's 511 unit you just took.

Everyone at the RSO knew about deputy Kurt Franklin and the 511 unit. He loved that goddamn thing.

Shit, Reynard said under his breath. He glanced at the attendant in the kiosk. Too risky to try another swap.

Not good, McDaniels said, walking to his own unit. But you might as well enjoy it while you got it.

A few minutes later, Kurt Franklin arrived at the vehicle lot to begin his shift. He stopped and looked around. Who took my 511 car?

ANDY DELGADO SAT OUTSIDE SHERIFF BEN CLARK'S OFFICE WAITING AS THE clock ticked past the 7:00 a.m. meeting time. Bickmore came out smoking a cigarette and looking aggravated. Get in here, Delgado, he barked. Clark, who had been sheriff for the last seventeen years, glanced up at Andy and then went back to reading some paperwork on his desk.

Andy swallowed hard and took a seat beside Bickmore and waited while Clark leafed through a few last pages and then set the papers aside in a neat stack. He took a sip of his coffee, studying Delgado over the rim of the cup. Well, Andy, he said, finally. Here it comes, Andy thought. I've been reading nothing but superior reviews about your performance for years now, the sheriff went on. Our deputy chief here says you'd make a good detective. Is that something you would be interested in?

Andy Delgado reflected on his life as he drove the sixteen miles east to his beat in Norco. The mother who gave him away, the grandmother who loved him and died, the relatives who abandoned him, and the cop who saved him. After all he had been through, things were finally falling into place. A family of his own, on the verge of a college degree, and now a promotion and pay raise to detective. The child Andy Delgado had been could never have imagined any of this.

Andy arrived in Norco twenty minutes later. He had grown quite fond of Norco and all its quirkiness and stubbornly Old West feel. Where else in the greater L.A. metro area did residents ride their horses down to the supermarket to pick up a loaf of bread? The Inland Empire might have been called "Cow County," but Norco liked to call itself "HorseTown USA." The almost constant presence of horses walking down the main drag and residential side streets and tied up in front of the feed stores, country diners, and family-owned establishments of downtown supported the claim.

Norco was no Kentucky bluegrass Thoroughbred country. Like most of the Inland Empire, Norco was scrappy, working-class all the way. These were real horse people who were willing to put every last cent of extra income into their animals. You would not find any lush grazing meadows, whitewashed four-rail fences, or fancy jumping rings in Norco. Every inch of the town was zoned for horses, and most kept theirs in backyard corrals and rode them among the cottonwoods and rattlesnakes down in the Santa Ana River basin bordering Mira Loma. Although far from a life of equine luxury, owners were expected to keep up standards of care and living space for their animals. Neglect or mistreatment might result in a call to animal control or a pistol-whipping from members of the Norco horse-owning community. Live and let live might have been the attitude toward one's neighbors in Norco, but don't ever fuck with a horse.

Still, Norco was not immune to the encroachments of the far less charming aesthetics of modern twentieth-century Southern California. Bisecting the town on a straight north-south line was Hamner Avenue, the real main drag of modern Norco. Hamner was more boulevard than avenue in feel and function, with two lanes running in each direction, a "suicide lane" down the middle for left turns, and an additional lane flaring out at major intersections to accommodate right turns. The forty-mile-per-hour speed limit was widely interpreted to mean somewhere between fifty and sixty miles per hour on the one-mile stretches between traffic lights. To jaywalk or cross against a light on Hamner was to put one's life in serious jeopardy, a fact deputy Andy Delgado acknowledged by ticketing anyone he saw stupid enough to try it.

The south end of Hamner itself was lined with 7-Elevens, IHOPs, dry cleaners, supermarkets, gas stations, banks, hardware stores, and a dizzying array of fast-food chains. This was the area of Norco where most of the day-to-day consumer business took place and which made it utterly indistinguishable from dozens of other main commercial thoroughfares throughout Southern California. However, head north beyond Fourth Street, and commercial properties rapidly grew fewer among the empty lots of dirt and dead grass. Just past Seventh Street, Hamner passed over the usually dry Santa Ana River bottom and the area transformed into the Riverside County of old—mostly rural farmland, wide-open fields with grazing cattle, horse corrals, and rows of lettuce, tomatoes, and beans. There Hamner marked the western border of the Mira Loma neighborhood that Chris Harven and George Smith called home.

As usual, Delgado began his patrol by driving the length of Hamner Avenue. If you wanted to get the current pulse of Norco, Hamner was the place to do it. It was a usual busy Friday but otherwise calm. Andy decided to allow himself to do something he rarely did: relax a little bit and enjoy his accomplishment instead of aggressively seeking out the bad guys.

Andy Delgado was not always easy to get along with and he knew there were some on the force who would not be so happy to hear of his promotion. He had a fiery personality and could be confrontational when he felt he had been slighted or let down by another officer in the field. He drew his conclusions quickly, forming strong, often immovable opinions of his fellow deputies or supervisors, divvying up the men around him into categories often based on a single incident. Lion or coward. Good cop or shitty cop. Stand-up guy or goddamn liar. Friend or enemy. Andy was the type of cop he thought everyone else should be, a composite of all the brave, honorable, and loyal peace officers like Darrell Creed and the others who had sat around the kitchen table when he was a child. In Andy's view, most of the deputies at the RSO were, but he had been let down by more than a few along the way. Those experiences had eroded many of Andy's cherished ideals about the nature of police and police work.

By midafternoon, deputy Chuck Hille noticed Andy was not generating his usual amount of radio traffic running plates, reporting suspicious activity, or bringing in arrests. Hille was an experienced cop who had lateralled over from the city of Orange PD. He was a stout, tough ex–high school football star whose mere presence was often enough to deter a confrontation with a suspect. Some of the other deputies found Hille, a smart guy with an intellectual manner of speaking sprinkled with long words, a bit off-putting. He and Delgado had first met while working out of the Blythe substation years before, and their history together had not always been positive.

About three in the afternoon, an hour before the end of their shift, Hille radioed Delgado for a 1087 meet-up at the Stater Bros. supermarket parking lot at the intersection of Fourth Street and Hamner Avenue, the busiest intersection in town. In addition to the always-bustling market, the intersection was anchored by other popular businesses: a Carl's Jr. fast-food restaurant, which occupied the corner of the Stater Bros. lot, Redlands Federal Savings Bank, and Murphy's Hay & Grain store. Directly across Hamner Avenue from the Stater Bros. was the Norco branch of the Security Pacific National Bank.

Arriving at the parking lot a few minutes later, the two deputies pulled their patrol cars side by side pointing in opposite directions, so they could talk out the driver's-side windows to each other.

"You're pretty quiet today, Andy. You okay?" Hille asked.

"Just taking it easy," Andy answered, having been told by Bickmore to keep word of the promotion quiet until the official announcement. But Andy was dying to tell someone the news, even if he was not especially close to Hille. "Actually, Chuck," he said. "I just got promoted to detective this morning."

Hille nodded his head approvingly and smiled in his understated way. "That's great, Andy," he said. "You're a good cop and I'm really happy for you."

Andy was surprised and a bit touched to hear Hille say it.

Over the radio they heard deputy Glyn Bolasky sign on to start the "cover watch" that bridged the transition between the two-shift and night shift. Between the hours of 3:00 and 4:00 p.m., the RSO would have three deputies patrolling Norco rather than just two.

"Come on, I'll buy you a cup of coffee," Hille offered Delgado. "I'll meet you at the Donut Corral," he said, referring to a shop a mile north on Sixth Street between Hamner and Sierra Avenue.

The two deputies might not have taken any special notice of the green van parked just fifty feet away in the supermarket lot. But the five heavily armed men sitting inside the van had certainly noticed them. The unexpected arrival of the sheriff's patrol units had even caused them to consider calling the whole thing off. But when the two RSO units suddenly peeled off and headed out of sight up Hamner Avenue, the leader of the men inside the van made his decision.

The time was 3:25 p.m.

4

TAKEOVER

May 9, 1980. Norco, California.

GARY HAKALA KNEW ALL ABOUT HOW A PERSON'S LIFE COULD CHANGE IN AN instant long before he drove his van into the parking lot of the Brea Mall, twenty-five miles west of Norco. Orphaned at age six when both of his parents died unexpectedly within months of each other, Gary had found himself on a train headed from his home in sunny Southern California to the cold and barren coal-mining country of Central Wyoming to live with relatives he had never met. There he learned early that when you're an outsider and smaller than the other kids in a place like Rawlins, Wyoming, your choices were to run or to fight. Gary chose to fight, eventually getting good enough at it that the other kids left him alone. At thirteen, Hakala began working summers as a ranch hand, spending brutal fourteen-hour days stacking hay, mucking stalls, breaking wild horses, mending barbed wire fences, and riding the range. His fellow ranch hands were tough, unforgiving, hard-drinking men who had no affection for some teenager living among them. It was there that Gary learned how to exist among dangerous men.

Now thirty-five, with seven children and in the middle of a rough divorce, Gary owned a small, single-machine dehydrated food–canning operation in nearby Fontana. Hakala was in the process of making payments on a dark green 1975 Dodge Tradesman van still bearing the name of the previous owner's company, D'MANNO CAPPUCCINO, written across the logo of a large coffee mug with a frothy wave cresting above the rim. The Tradesman was big and powerful enough to pull the rented flatbed trailer Hakala used to carry his usual pickups of dehydrated foods for his canning operation.

Although Hakala chose the van purely for work purposes, it came with the custom interior of a vintage seventies SoCal shaggin' wagon. Behind the two upholstered captain chairs in front was a cargo area tricked out with gold shag carpeting and simulated wood-grain paneling throughout. At the far back, cushioned faux-leather seating blocked access to the rear doors and extended in an L shape several feet along the passenger side. Two passenger-side cargo doors swung out for easy loading. Running along the driver's side of the cargo area were sixteen-inch-deep floor-to-roof wooden cabinets. The only windows in the cargo area were the two large tinted ones on the rear doors. When not in the service of the canning business, the Tradesman was roomy enough for hauling around all seven of Gary's children and comfortable enough for him to camp in on hunting and kayaking excursions.

The men who kidnapped Gary Hakala on the morning of May 9 did not give a shit about his life, his divorce, or his big order to fill; they just wanted his van. The problem was, none of the three men assigned to the task had any experience carjacking, let alone kidnapping. They had already screwed up once that morning.

Steve Cantelli was only a few hours into his shift as a field service representative for General Telephone when he pulled his company van into the Westminster Mall parking lot at 9:30 a.m. to look up the location of his next customer. Glancing up from his Thomas Guide map book, he was surprised to see three men standing beside his window, one of them aiming a .38 Special straight at his head. When ordered to "get out of the fucking van, now!" Cantelli stepped out and then just kept going, running as far away from the thieves as possible.

Sitting in his car several feet away, Anthony Savala was just as surprised as Cantelli. As Savala watched, one of the men entered the van through the side cargo doors, only to jump back out seconds later shaking his head. Not surprisingly, the cargo area of a telephone company service van was filled top to bottom with telephone equipment. The three men abandoned their catch and fled the scene in a blue Matador headed for the Brea Mall twenty-three miles away.

That morning, Hakala was pulling the rented flatbed trailer behind the Tradesman on his way to pick up a big order of powdered food in Los Angeles. He exited the 57 Freeway and pulled into the parking lot of the Brea Mall to fix a loose side mirror and, on a more practical level, to take a piss at the Sears department store. Upon entering the lot, Gary took note of the three suspicious-looking characters staring at him through the windshield of what he would remember as an early 1960s metallic-blue customized Chevy lowrider.

Parking sixty feet away from the blue car, Hakala decided he would take the extra step of padlocking the trailer to the van hitch should the men have any designs on stealing it. He had just climbed into the cargo area to grab the lock when the side cargo door and both front doors of the van flew open at once. In an instant, Hakala was looking down the barrels of three handguns pointed at him.

"Get down, get down, get down!" Manny Delgado barked at him, jumping inside through the driver's door, climbing past the front seat and into the cargo area. "I told you to get the fuck down now!" growled Delgado, pushing Hakala facedown onto the carpeted floor, planting a knee in the small of his back, and striking him on the back of the head with the butt of the gun. Hakala caught a brief glimpse of a second man standing outside the cargo door before the man slammed it shut, ending any chance that someone in the parking lot might see what was going on inside.

"Get back here and tape this motherfucker up," Manny yelled at Billy, standing by the passenger door.

Billy Delgado clambered over the seat holding a roll of nylon-reinforced, heavy-duty packing tape and began taping Hakala's legs together, wrapping him from the ankles nearly up to his knees.

Manny took the tape from his little brother and, still pinning Hakala down with a knee, wrapped the length of his forearms together behind him.

"I swear to God we will fucking kill you if you try anything, you fucking understand?" Delgado threatened when he was done.

"Yeah," Hakala managed to say under the weight of Delgado's knee in his back. "But could you put my glasses somewhere, they cost me a lot of money."

Manny Delgado did not answer, but the face of a younger Hispanic man with a wispy mustache entered Hakala's field of vision. Jesus, he's just a boy, thought Gary. The kid looked almost apologetic for what they were doing as he gently removed Gary's glasses. "I'll put them in the glove compartment for you," the boy said. It would be the only act of kindness shown to Gary Hakala that entire day.

Gary complained the tape was cutting off circulation to his hands. Manny told him to shut the fuck up and waved a hunting knife menacingly in front of his hostage's throat. The van began to roll. Hakala tried to keep track of the location of each of his tormentors. The mean little Mexican still had a knee in his back and someone was driving the van. Gary could not see Russell Harven trailing them in the Matador. To him, the man he had briefly seen standing outside the cargo door seemed to have disappeared entirely.

After a few minutes, the van stopped and Gary could feel the trailer being unchained and lifted off the hitch. They entered the on-ramp to the 57 Freeway minutes later. With his head turned sideways Gary could look out the back window and see the drivers of big semitrucks following just behind the Tradesman. One came up so close that Gary thought he had made eye contact with the driver, but the truck changed lanes and was gone.

Manny Delgado had noticed it too. He jumped off Hakala and began smashing the shelving out of the rear side cabinet of the van with the handle end of the hunting knife. When he was done, he jerked Gary to his knees and ordered him inside the cabinet. The guy had to be joking, thought Hakala; there was no way he could fit in that. With a little extra encouragement from the hunting knife, Gary did his best to comply. Once inside, Delgado shoved a paper grocery bag over Hakala's head and began wrapping a nylon cord around his neck. A chill went through Gary. So that's it, Hakala figured. This punk is going to strangle me to death.

With the cord secure, Delgado jerked it hard several times but left it loose. He pressed the knife to Gary's stomach, screamed more threats, and then slammed the door of the cabinet closed, throwing his full weight against it to get it to latch. Gary's hands and legs soon went numb from being so tightly bound. Exposed nails in the cabinet dug into his flesh. He was facing the back of the van, trapped in a partial standing position with his knees bent, not unlike a stress position used in torture interrogations.

INSIDE THE MIRA LOMA HOUSE, GEORGE SMITH AND CHRIS HARVEN HAD BEEN smoking weed and working their way through a six-pack of Budweiser to keep their nerves down and their courage up. Laid out on the carpet of a back bedroom, an arsenal of weapons and survival supplies were grouped by purpose and ready to be loaded into a half dozen military duffel bags. The two yellow MacDonald walkie-talkie radios to be used between Billy in the getaway van and George inside the bank sat off to the side.

Chris, Russ, and George would each enter the bank armed with semiautomatic assault rifles, Chris with his HK93, Russ with the Colt "Shorty" AR-15, and George with the Heckler .308. Manny would have the riot gun. The serial numbers on all the guns had been covered up with electrical tape to avoid being readable on bank surveillance tapes. Each of the men would carry at least one sidearm, George with a Browning .45 semiautomatic pistol shoulder-holstered and another at his hip. Both George and Chris had hundreds of additional rounds of ammunition in fully loaded magazines strapped across their chests. In the front seat of the getaway van, driver Billy Delgado would also have a Colt AR-15 to go along with the .45 Colt semiautomatic handgun tucked into a holster strapped around his right ankle.

For the rifles, George and Chris had made dozens of "jungle clips" allowing them to eject an empty magazine, flip it over, and load a full one in its place in a matter of seconds. Piggybacking three forty-round magazines together up-down-up as George and Chris had done gave the weapon a devastating 120-round capacity, which they were capable of emptying on a target in a little over a minute. Chris Harven alone had seventeen forty-round magazines: 680 extra rounds in total. In addition to this, boxes of extra ammunition, more than 3,000 rounds of varying calibers, had already been packed into duffel bags.

Zipped up in two of the bags destined for the trunk of each cold getaway car was survival gear that included map books, compass, water purification tablets, field glasses, mess kits, gas masks, emergency blankets, extra clothing, and insulin vials and three syringes for Russell Harven. Half a dozen hunting knives, a nine-inch Bowie knife, and two machetes were split among survival kits. A Remington hunting rifle with scope and hundreds of rounds of H&H .375 cartridges would go into each trunk. The H&H .375 cartridge was designed primarily for taking down large and dangerous game. In other words, an "elephant gun."

And then there were the bombs, a dozen twelve-ounce homemade fragmentation grenades, a half dozen sixteen-ounce shotgun-launch versions, three Blue Nun Molotov cocktails, and a curious item that consisted of a cardboard box containing six beer bottles filled with leaded gasoline surrounding a small detonation device. George would bring two of the antipersonnel grenades into the bank, shoved deep in a pocket of his military-green duster.

When they were done loading all the weapons, bombs, ammunition, and survival gear, they moved the duffel bags to the back seat of Chris's Z/28. George just kept adding more supplies, the last being a samurai sword with a twenty-three-inch blade sheathed in an ornate scabbard and protected by a gym sock pulled over the handle. George placed the sword in the back seat with the other weapons. Try as he might, Chris could not come up with a single reason why anyone would need a goddamn sword to rob a bank.

"WHERE'S THE DUDE?"

Gary Hakala did not know he was in a Kmart parking lot in Riverside County when he heard the side door of the van slide open, but he knew "the dude" they were talking about was him. He was more angry than afraid, but was nevertheless relieved when he was not immediately jerked out of the cabinet, shot in the back of the head, and dumped in an empty field.

Hakala still had no idea what the end game was, but he knew it might include killing him somewhere along the way. So far, he had been riding on freeways and side streets for almost two hours with Manny Delgado occasionally jerking the cord around his neck and threatening to kill him while his hands and feet turned a waxy white from lack of circulation.

Chris Harven stuck his head inside the cargo area and looked at the bulging door of the cabinet. You put him in there? he said, amazed that any human being could fit in such a small space.

Where the fuck else was I going to put him? Manny spat, looking nervous, sweaty and jumpy, an unsheathed hunting knife beside him on the carpet. Considering Manny's condition, Chris figured the dude was lucky to still be alive. Let's just get this shit in here, said Chris, hoisting the first duffel bag into the back of the van.

Russ and Billy took the Z/28 and the Matador and headed north on Hamner to drop the two cars off at the Little League field parking lot a mile and a half north of the bank at Detroit Street, the van following close behind. The Friday-afternoon traffic at Hamner and Fourth Street was heavy, the Security Pacific Bank parking lot on the southeast corner mostly full of customers coming and going. A steady line of cars streamed into the intersection from the west side of Fourth Street where the Naval Sea Systems Command base was disgorging a day shift eager to cash their weekly paychecks.

When they got to the Little League field, Billy and Russ parked the two cars side by side in the empty lot, noses facing Hamner just a few dozen feet off the busy avenue. Manny and Billy had stolen two sets of license plates from cars parked at the Westminster Mall the night before, which had been put onto the "cold cars" that morning. If things went according to plan, George and Chris would jump in the Z/28 and head off to Vegas and the others would either go home or head up into the mountains to lay low depending on how hot the situation was after the robbery.

For the first time that day, all five of the Norco bank robbers piled into the van to make final preparations. From inside the cabinet, Gary Hakala could hear hushed voices but could only make out some of the words. Someone was using military jargon: "the mission," "the objective," "the diversion." He could hear a walkie-talkie crackling, maybe even a police scanner. There was movement, unpacking of bags, the sound of people dressing, pulling on jackets, the unmistakable sounds of weapons being loaded and readied. And then the van began to move again.

George Smith worried that it was getting dangerously late in the day. There would be much more cash walking out of the bank on a payday than there would be walking in. It was almost 2:00 p.m. and they still had one more important piece of the plan to execute before hitting the bank.

Chris got behind the wheel and they rolled south on Corona Avenue parallel to Hamner back in the direction of the Kmart. Edging the van down an alley just off Hamner and a mile south of the bank, Chris brought it to a stop behind a strip mall under construction at 1780 Commerce Street. A few minutes after two o'clock in the afternoon, George opened the side door of the van and jumped out carrying the cardboard box containing six beer bottles filled with leaded gasoline. Hurrying to the back of the building near a wooden shed, George set the box beneath the meter regulating the main source of natural gas to the structure. Using the Zippo, he lit the delay fuse of the detonator and ran back to the van. Let's get the fuck out of here, he said.

Chris drove off as a spiral of black smoke began to curl up into the air. In a few minutes, the detonator would go off, starting a gasoline fire that would heat the gas main until it exploded. Every emergency vehicle, including the cops, would be at the scene of a gas main explosion at least a mile south of the bank.

What occurred behind the building at 1780 Commerce Street just about the time the van was pulling into the Stater Bros. parking lot at Fourth and Hamner was something different than planned. At 2:11 p.m., William Clark looked out the window of his cabinet shop to see black smoke rising from the construction site just across the alley. Clark observed a small flame coming from a box containing what looked like a six-pack of beer placed next to the back wall of the building. And then he saw the gas main. While Clark might not have fully comprehended what he was looking at, he certainly understood the severity of a fire burning directly below a gas main. And then one of the bottles exploded with a loud pop, throwing flames ten feet into the air, igniting the wall above it.

While Clark ran to warn everyone at the construction site, a passing motorist saw the flames too, grabbed a fire extinguisher from his truck, and quickly put the whole thing out. By 2:15, a critical part of George Smith's master plan had ended in a fizzle. It was the first sign that things were about to go very wrong.

THE MEN IN THE VAN PARKED ACROSS THE STREET FROM THE SECURITY PA-cific Bank pulled on their matching drab-green military ponchos, readied black ski masks on their heads, checked their weapons one more time, and waited for the blaring of sirens and the procession of emergency vehicles heading south on Hamner to begin. By 2:45, Chris and George began to bicker over who was responsible for the failure of the bomb to blow up the gas main. They waited some more. About 3:00, they sent Billy over to the Carl's Jr. to grab a few drinks. They argued among themselves about whether they should call the whole thing off. But what about the fucking dude in the cabinet? They were already guilty of a crime that could send them to prison for life.

By 3:15 p.m., George Smith had decided he was no longer running a democracy. He wanted to make one last surveillance of "the objective." They drove to the far edge of the Stater Bros. lot, the nose of the van just a dozen feet from Hamner Avenue, facing the bank. As customers left the bank, George knew that each was leaving with cash that could have, should have, already been his. George gave the order to make final preparations. And then somebody spotted deputy Andy Delgado pulling into the Stater Bros. parking lot for his 1087 meetup with deputy Chuck Hille.

Fucking cop, right there.

They waited breathlessly, their eyes shifting from one to another. In the passenger seat, George leaned forward and took a sip of soda, trying to look as casual as possible. Just a couple of drive-through customers pausing to eat their burgers and fries. The sheriff's car drove within twenty feet of them, swung around, and stopped fifty feet away, angled across several empty parking spots facing the van. The guy looked like he was waiting for backup. They could have been spotted at the site of the diversion bomb, after all. They would not be all that hard to find with that giant cup of cappuccino painted on both sides of the van.

Keep your guns ready.

When a second sheriff's car entered the parking lot, the situation grew even tenser. The second cruiser pulled up next to the other and the two deputies sat talking to each other through the driver's-side windows. George let out a long breath while eyeing the two cruisers in the side mirror. I don't know about this shit, someone whispered in the back. Nobody answered. They waited. The cop cars headed for the exit, one after the other, turned left onto Hamner, and sped north until they were out of sight. At least now we know where all the cops in Norco are, George said.

But George Smith was wrong. He did not know about the RSO "cover shift" that placed an additional deputy in Norco during the transition between day and evening shifts. An hour earlier, deputy Glyn Bolasky had changed into his uniform at Riverside HQ, checked out a shotgun and radio, and picked up a Chevy Impala cruiser. On his way to Norco he stopped at the 7-Eleven to buy a ginger ale and pack of sour apple bubble gum, and was at that very moment headed south on Hamner Avenue in the direction of Fourth Street.

George was done waiting. From inside his cabinet prison, Gary Hakala heard a shouted command. "It's on. Go, go, go!" When the van began to move, Hakala knew that whatever was going to happen to him was about to happen right then. The van came to a sharp stop less than a minute later. The voice called out "Go, go, go!" one more time and the side door swung open hard. The van bounced and rocked from the weight of the men piling out. A child screamed. And then that voice again, this time from outside the van: "Everyone hit the fucking floor or I'm going to blow your fucking heads off!"

OUTSIDE THE ENTRANCE TO THE SECURITY PACIFIC BANK, TWO MOTHERS AND their Cub Scouts were selling magazine subscriptions when four men in military ponchos and black ski masks carrying assault rifles exploded out the side doors of the green van directly in front them. As George Smith leapt from the van, he shoved one of the young Scouts out of the way. The boy screamed as Smith and the others charged into the bank.

Eighteen-year-old James Kirkland had just come from work and was filling out a deposit slip in the middle of the bank when he heard someone threaten to blow his fucking head off. When he turned to look, Chris Harven stepped in front of him, pulled an assault rifle out from under a green military poncho, and aimed it straight at his head. Kirkland hit the fucking floor.

"Everyone down," George Smith commanded, swinging his HK91 from one terrified customer to the next until all dozen or so had complied. "This is a robbery, everyone down!"

Customer Beverly Beam was seated in a chair against the wall next to the entrance waiting for the new accounts manager when the masked men burst through the door. With all four men only steps away with their backs turned to her, she was afraid any movement would surprise the gunmen and get her killed. She froze. George Smith caught sight of her out of the corner of his eye, whirled and aimed the Heckler at her. "Do you want your fucking head blown off?" he shouted. She shook her head, no. "Then get on the floor." Beam went down onto her stomach.

Seated at her desk, assistant branch manager Sharon Higman saw an opportunity to trigger the silent alarm mounted just below the edge of the desktop. But the moment she began to move her hand, Chris Harven had the assault rifle trained on her from twenty feet away. "If you hit that fucking alarm, I will shoot your fucking head off," he growled. Seeing the eyes through the hole in the ski mask, Higman had no doubt that the man meant it. She put her hands back where he could see them and sat down on the floor beside her desk.

"If there are any alarms or anything," Smith barked, roaming between customers flattened out on the marble floor, "there are going to be a lot of dead people here. We have explosives. We won't be afraid to use them."

Manny Delgado crossed the bank lobby holding the riot gun at his hip and then vaulted the teller line. Standing atop the counter, he swept the barrel of his shotgun along the row of four cashiers manning their windows below. "You heard him, hit the fucking floor!" he bellowed.

Standing behind the teller line sorting checks, proof operator Denise DeMarco was so frightened at the sight of the shotgun that she began to back away rather than sit down as ordered. "Get down on the floor!" Delgado exploded, lifting the shotgun in her direction. The petrified DeMarco continued to back away as Delgado screamed at her over and over to get down. "Please get down, Denise," one of the tellers begged. DeMarco reached the rear wall of the bank. Terrified, but unable to retreat any further, she slid down the wall and took a seat on the floor.

"Cashiers, stand up!" Delgado ordered the four line tellers. The women glanced at each other before getting back to their feet. Delgado threw a blue drawstring bag onto the counter in front of the closest teller, Janet Harper. "Put the fucking money in it!"

With her face just feet from the end of a shotgun in the hands of a very jittery man, Harper froze, too frightened to reach for the bag. Standing beside Harper at window 2 was lead teller Sharon Marzolf, a fearless and commanding former security guard whose previous job had been apprehending shoplifters at a local department store. Marzolf calmly took the bag and held it open for Harper. "Go ahead Janet, empty your bus," Marzolf said, referring to the teller's cash drawer. Harper did. Next Marzolf emptied her own drawer and handed the bag to the third teller, Teresa DeRuyter. DeRuyter was careful to add her traceable bait money to the contents of the bag before passing it on to the last teller in the line.

"You down there, hurry up," Delgado ordered Marlene Faust. Faust had been the last of the tellers to obey Delgado's command to sit down, taking time to make sure a stunned customer at her window complied before taking a seat herself. While Delgado had been busy threatening Denise DeMarco, Faust had remained calm enough to trigger the silent alarm button mounted beside her drawer.

Once pressed, the alarm system installed at the Security Pacific Bank in Norco relayed the alert over a dedicated phone line directly to the police department dispatch center. Officers in the field were immediately dispatched to the local Security Pacific Bank for a 211—bank robbery in progress. But Marlene Faust's silent alarm would do the customers and employees in Norco no good. Due to an installation error, the alarm had been transmitted to the police department of the neighboring city of Corona. Within minutes, police units were descending on the Corona branch of the Security Pacific National Bank, five miles away from the scene of the robbery in Norco.

Sitting in her pickup truck in lane 2 of the drive-up banking window, Elaine Jones had just put her checkbook into the capsule and dropped it inside the pneumatic delivery tube when she noticed all the tellers on the other side of the plexiglass window had suddenly vanished. In their place, Jones saw a man in a ski mask standing atop the teller counter swinging the barrel of a shotgun back and forth. "Is that what I think it is?" she called over to the man in a car in the lane closest to the bank. The man nodded. "Yeah, I think so," he said. Jones leaned as far back in her seat as she could, not sure what to do. Turning to her right, she got the attention of a woman in lane 3. "There's a bank robbery in progress. See if you can get out of here and get some help."

Behind the teller counter, Sharon Marzolf walked the bag of money back to Manny Delgado, who was growing more jittery and threatening as the seconds ticked by. "Do you want the coins too?" Marzolf asked him.

"Every fucking bit of it," Delgado answered.

This guy has no idea what he's doing, Marzolf thought. What bank robber wants a bunch of heavy coins? She dutifully went down the teller line again, emptying the coin changers into the bag and then handing it up to Delgado. He took the bag, ordering the tellers down to the floor again. The four sat down. "Is this good?" Marzolf asked.

"I want you belly down, kissing the fucking floor," Delgado said, waving the riot gun at them. The women did as they were told.

While Manny Delgado terrorized the teller line, Christopher Harven worked on getting at the big money. "Get up," Harven shouted at assistant manager Sharon Higman, now seated on the floor beside her desk after her attempt to trigger the silent alarm. He crossed the bank toward Higman, his rifle trained on the woman. Higman stood, keeping her hands visible. "I want your keys," Harven ordered.

"I don't have any keys," Higman replied.

Chris lifted the rifle to his shoulder. "Give me the fucking keys."

Higman followed the simple rule of bank robbery: Give them whatever they want and get them out of the bank as soon as possible. "He's the manager," she said calmly, pointing to branch manager Ron Richter seated on the floor a few feet away. "I'll get the keys from him."

Harven turned his rifle on Richter. "Come on, Manager, we're going across the lobby." He motioned back to Higman with the AR. "You come too."

Higman knew that she and Richter were about to have a serious problem on their hands: There was no more money in the vault. Just an hour before, Richter had called for an armored car delivery of additional bills to meet the end-of-day paycheck rush from the nearby Naval Sea Systems Command base. But the delivery was late. Anticipating a volatile situation that might develop once the gunman realized there was no more cash in the main vault, Higman called over to the second assistant branch manager, Cynthia Schlax. "Cindy, give me the keys to the nests," she said, referring to the individual teller back-up currency in the vault, usually about $2,000 to $5,000 each.

Chris Harven was in no mood for the transferring of keys from one employee to the other. "Stop stalling!" he exploded at Higman. Pressing the barrel of the gun into her ribs, he ordered the woman to sit down again. "You come instead," he said to Schlax. As soon as she was on her feet, Harven herded Schlax and Richter across the lobby.

"One minute left!" George Smith called out, checking his watch as he continued to pace the floor back and forth, menacing the prone customers with the Heckler. On all sides of him, George could see the faces of bank employees he knew, people who had greeted him with a smile while he conducted his business there. "Hurry the fuck up!"

Smith looked over at Russell Harven, who upon entering the bank had dutifully headed to the west entrance facing Hamner to guard against anyone going in or out during the heist. Standing behind an artificial ficus tree, Harven was transfixed on the activity within the bank, neglecting the only task he had been assigned. "Watch the fucking door!" Smith barked at him.

When Russ turned back, it was too late. A woman opened the side entrance and walked inside the bank clutching her purse. Already a nervous young lady, Sheila Deno now seemed utterly paralyzed trying to comprehend the scene before her. Almost as surprised as Deno, Russell Harven stepped out from behind the tree, lifted the "Shorty" AR to his shoulder, aimed it at Deno from five feet away, and ordered her to the ground. Deno stood stone still, her eyes darting from the bodies strewn facedown across the lobby floor to the man standing on the teller counter waving a shotgun and back to the one in the ski mask aiming the gun in her face.

"Get the fuck down!" Russ yelled again.

Sharon Higman, seated on the floor at Deno's feet, reached up and took ahold of Deno's wrist, yanking her to the floor.

The moment vault teller Janet Dessormeau realized there was a robbery in progress, she had pulled closed the steel side entrance door to the vault, locking herself and employee Gail Altenburger inside. However, she had no time to swing shut the heavy main vault door. Now the only thing between the two women and the heavily armed man coming toward them was the grill gate.

"You better get this vault open," Harven threatened, sticking the barrel of the Heckler through the bars of the gate, "or there will be a lot of dead fucking people in here."

"Janet," manager Ron Richter said in as calm a voice as he could muster. "Open it up for us."

Dessormeau nodded, went to the side door, and opened it. Chris pushed

Richter and Cindy Schlax inside and then shoved Dessormeau up against the wall of the vault with his rifle. "Don't look at me," he said. Dessormeau shifted her eyes to the floor as Schlax opened the teller nests, hoping Harven might not notice that the larger reserve area of the vault was completely bare. Ron Richter scooped bills from the teller nests into a drawstring bag held by Schlax. "We have no reserve currency," she whispered to him. "I know," he said.

"Stop wasting time," Chris growled, poking Richter in the ribs with the gun.

George called out from the lobby area. "Thirty seconds left!"

At the west entrance to the bank, Russell Harven had another problem on his hands. Hiding behind the plastic tree again, Russell did not notice Miriam Tufts approaching the door to the bank until the woman had pulled it wide open. Tufts caught sight of the customers on the floor and froze in the doorway. Russ stepped out from behind the plant to face her. Tufts looked back at the two eyes staring out from the ski mask and then glanced down at the jet-black assault rifle in the man's hands. Without a word, Tufts turned and left, the door swinging shut behind her. "Don't go in there, the place is being robbed," she warned two customers crossing the parking lot.

At the same time, seventeen-year-old getaway driver Billy Delgado was running into trouble of his own outside the main entrance. Heart pounding, gulping in shallow breaths, Billy had been so busy checking mirrors and leaning across the passenger seat to see what was going on in the bank that he never saw Debi Paggen approaching. Paggen was running late and just wanted to pop into the bank quickly to get some cash for the weekend. Hurrying to the entrance, she walked directly in front of the green van. Something about that nervous-looking kid on the other side of the windshield caused her to pause and look back just as she reached for the entrance door. When she did, Paggen found Billy Delgado leaning across the passenger seat pointing a handgun out the window at her.

Paggen let go of the door handle. "Go ahead and rob the bank," she said, "I'm not going in there."

The boy with the gun said nothing, his hand shaking as he aimed it at her. Paggen backed away slowly and then turned toward the rear of the van and out of his line of fire.

At the two-minute mark, George Smith called out again. "Time. Now!"

Clutching his bag of coins and bills, Manny Delgado leapt down from the teller counter and made his way to the middle of the bank. Russell Harven abandoned his post at the west entrance and joined the other two. When Chris Harven did not immediately appear, Smith ran to the vault. "Quit stalling," he screamed at bank manager Ron Richter. "It's taking too much time!"

But they had already run out of time. Two minutes earlier, a customer getting out of her car at the Redlands Federal Savings Bank on the other side of the intersection happened to look in the direction of the Security Pacific Bank. Racing inside Redlands Federal, the woman approached teller Maria Casa Grande. "I just saw four men with guns go inside the bank across the street!"

At 3:32 p.m., veteran dispatcher Gladys Wiza took an incoming call at the headquarters of the Riverside County Sheriff. Wiza scrawled the info on a note card and handed it to deputy Gary Keeter, who was working the dispatch mic at the time. At about the same moment George Smith yelled "Time. Now!" Keeter dropped a priority alert tone over the Riverside County Sheriff's radio system: *Riverside to all Norco units. 211 in progress, Security Pacific Bank, Fourth and Hamner.*

Billy Delgado had just slid the .45 Colt automatic back into the ankle holster after scaring off Debi Paggen when his side mirror lit up with flashing blue and red lights. Jerking his head around, he settled on a police car making a left turn from Hamner onto Fourth Street, its light bar whirling. Billy fumbled for the walkie-talkie in his lap and pressed the talk button.

Inside the vault, George Smith's radio crackled to life. "The cops are here," came the trembling voice of Billy Delgado.

George and Chris looked at each other. "There's no fucking way," Chris said.

"Let's go, let's go!" called Smith, bolting from the vault area to the north entrance of the bank.

Still lying on the floor of the bank lobby, eighteen-year-old James Kirkland kept his cheek to the carpet as the boots of the four men stomped by inches from his head. "We've been seen," one of the men called out as they passed. "Let's go, we've been seen." The door flew open and the men ran out. Before the door swung itself closed again, Kirkland heard a final voice yell, "There's one!"

That's when the shooting started.

It was 3:35 p.m.

5

THE END OF THE WORLD

May 9, 1980. Norco, California.

THE ONLY WAY RIVERSIDE COUNTY SHERIFF'S DISPATCHER GARY KEETER could explain what went down in Norco that day was that it had all happened so goddamn fast.

Riverside to Norco units, have a 211 in progress at the Security Pacific Bank at Fourth and Hamner.

3-Edward-50, 1097, deputy Glyn Bolasky responded two seconds later, indicating his radio ID and 1097, the code for "officer on scene."

Bolasky was already 1097? thought Keeter. He was never en route. *Riverside to all, clear the air,* Keeter added, instructing all nonessential radio traffic to cease. Keeter's flat, rural accent made the request sound more like *Riverside t'all* . . .

Keeter was a veteran patrol deputy on desk duty at the time because of a blown-out knee. When it came to dispatch, the woman seated next to him, Gladys Wiza, was the real pro. But at that moment, Keeter's patrolman instincts were telling him that Glyn Bolasky might be in more danger than he knew. With everything going down so fast, did Bolasky understand he was on scene of a confirmed 211 in progress, rather than a 211 silent, most of which turned out to be false alarms? Bolasky ought to be holding off for backup, but so far he had not reported his exact position to Keeter. Was Bolasky headed straight into a 211 in progress all alone?

Still on the phone with the Redlands Federal Bank teller who had reported the robbery, Gladys Wiza was furiously writing information on an index card. She slid the card in front of Keeter. Keeter looked down. Shit, he thought, now we got a real problem.

CHRIS EVANS AND HER FRIEND JENNIE LEWIS WERE ON FOURTH STREET IN Evans's black 1979 Chevy Camaro waiting for the light while checking out the cute deputy about to make a left turn in front of them. Is that "Sexually Frustrated"? Evans asked, laughing.

Lewis worked at Winchell's Donut House, where the girls had nicknames for all the cops who frequently stopped in to chat them up. She leaned forward to get a closer look. Nah, that's not "Sexually Frustrated," she said. I don't know who that guy is.

The light bar on the roof of the deputy's car abruptly lit up. Well, whoever he is, there he goes, Evans said as the Chevy Impala patrol car made the turn onto Fourth, crossing in front of them. Just then the two young women heard what they thought was a pack of firecrackers going off and a hard thud! as something hit the Camaro. An object came through the driver's-side window and struck Evans above the eye and bounced into the lap of Jennie Lewis in the passenger seat. Evans put a hand to her head. What the hell was that?

Lewis lifted a pancaked and melted-looking piece of gray lead out of her lap and studied it. The furthest thing from her mind was that she might be looking at a bullet.

The light changed, and the two girls continued across Hamner.

Deputy Glyn Bolasky left his siren off as he made the left onto Fourth Street headed toward the east entrance of the parking lot, scanning the lot and bank building as he went. The only thing between him and the bank were a pair of split rail fences marking a horse path bordering the parking area. The place was busy with customers parked in the lot or waiting in the drive-through lanes, but nothing looked all that unusual.

Bolasky heard a muffled popping noise and saw red and blue plastic falling around his unit. What the hell is going on with my light bar? he thought. A bulb had been replaced on the Visibar that morning and Bolasky figured it must have blown when he turned it on. If Bolasky had not had his windows up and air conditioner running, he would have recognized the popping noise was really the crack of an assault rifle. Had he heard that, Bolasky probably would have realized that what sounded like bottles breaking in the street was a bullet shattering his light bar. And if he had not been distracted by colored plastic raining down around him, he would have spotted the man in the ski mask and military poncho standing next to a green van aiming the assault rifle at him. And if Glyn Bolasky had seen that, he certainly would not have done what he did next.

At that very moment, Gary Keeter was radioing Bolasky the information written on the card Gladys Wiza had slid in front of him moments before.

3-Edward-50, the suspect vehicle is a green van with weapons.

If Bolasky heard the transmission at all, it was too late to do anything about it. As he swung his patrol car into the bank parking lot, four men in black ski masks and olive-drab field jackets came into view standing no more than two car lengths in front of Bolasky's unit. An instant later, Bolasky's windshield glazed into an intricate spider web as three rounds crashed through it. He felt his face and arms go hot as flying glass and metal peppered him like birdshot. The young deputy's mind began to play tricks on him. This isn't real. It must be a training exercise. What the hell is this?

The side mirror of the Impala exploded, snapping Bolasky back to reality. He threw his body across the bench seat to take cover below the dashboard. Bolasky reached up and grabbed his radio mic. Seconds after reporting a green van with weapons, Gary Keeter heard a desperate, nearly unintelligible transmission come across the radio, the rapid popping of gunfire clearly audible in the background.

3-Edward-50 taking fire!

Keeter, Gladys Wiza, and a third dispatcher, Sharon Markum, whipped their heads around to look at each other. Only twenty-eight seconds after initial dispatch, was it possible Bolasky was already taking fire? How could things have gone so badly so fast? Keeter keyed up the mic. *It's a green van. It's Fourth and Hamner. They are shooting.*

They were all shooting now, the gunshots cracking with the irregular cadence of popping corn. Manny Delgado walked in front of the van, lowered the riot gun, and unloaded several booming shotgun blasts. "We've got a hostage in here!" George Smith screamed in Bolasky's direction, but the only thing Glyn Bolasky could hear were bullets ripping into the metal surrounding him, blowing out windows, the muzzle blasts echoing back from a cinder block wall bordering the lot behind him. There was sharp pain in his left shoulder as a round came through the dashboard, sending fragments of lead and copper jacketing into his flesh.

Whoever these people were, Glyn Bolasky had no doubt they were going to kill him if he did not get the hell out of there. Still lying across the bench seat with his head below the line of the dashboard, he grabbed the steering wheel with one hand, jerked the gearshift on the steering column into reverse with the other, and slammed on the accelerator. Bolasky could still hear the bullets pinging off the Impala as it shot backward out of the parking lot, traveling thirty feet east on Fourth Street before skidding to a stop sideways in the middle of the road.

As he rose up and threw the release on the shotgun mount positioned at the center of the dashboard, Bolasky felt blood running down his face and arm. He clutched at the mic again. *I've been hit!*

Two seconds later, Keeter sent out the transmission that changed everything: *Officer hit. Clear the air. 1199.*

Across Riverside County, every patrol car in the field, every detective at a desk, every undercover narc on stakeout, every helicopter in the sky, every law enforcement officer from California Highway Patrol, Riverside PD, or RSO with a gun stopped what he or she was doing to converge on the intersection of Fourth and Hamner.

In Rubidoux, deputy Rolf Parkes stopped writing a traffic ticket, shoved the driver's license back into the hands of the stunned motorist, and ran to his unit. Fred Chisolm was already responding from Mira Loma on the original 211 dispatch, but now he jammed the accelerator to the floor as he went south on Pedley Avenue. A. J. Reynard pushed Kurt Franklin's 511 car over one hundred miles per hour on the Pomona Freeway wondering, as were others, how the hell a 211 could go from dispatch to "Officer down" in less than one minute. Sergeant Ed Alvis and three other undercover narcotics detectives bailed out of a surveillance stakeout behind the nearby Lions Club and headed south on Hamner.

At RSO headquarters, detective Mike Jordan leapt up from his desk, grabbed his holstered .38 from the hook on the door, and raced headlong down the hallway toward the department vehicle yard. Others poured out of their offices along with him. California Highway Patrol officer Doug Earnest heard the transmission on scanner, notified fellow patrolman Bill Crowe, and the two left the freeway, self-dispatching to Norco. Riverside City cop Mike Watts did the same, along with others from the neighboring Corona Police Department. In Moreno Valley, deputy Jim Evans aimed his unit in the direction of Norco. Even lit up like a Christmas tree with sirens screaming, it would take him at least twenty minutes to get there, maybe more. But it did not matter. It was an 1199. It was Mayday. It was the end of the world.

IN THE PASSENGER SEAT OF THE CAMARO, JENNIE LEWIS HEARD THE GUN-fire. She turned and looked out the back window just in time to see Bolasky's unit come flying out of the parking lot in reverse, shedding glass and debris in the roadway. She saw the deputy jump out of the vehicle and then disappear behind it. "Shit," she said. "That guy is down."

As Evans and Lewis pulled across Hamner away from the gunfire, they passed a 1964 Ford Thunderbird headed straight into it. Fifteen-year-old Jody Ann Tygart was behind the wheel taking a driving lesson from her father. Darryel Tygart had instructed his daughter to cross Hamner and continue on Fourth Street past the bank and into the quiet neighborhood behind it. Once through the light, however, the Tygarts found the neighborhood anything but quiet. The moment Tygart caught sight of Bolasky's unit in the bank parking lot, he saw the right rear tire of the sheriff's vehicle explode, followed by the sound of heavy gunfire. Tygart immediately recognized what was going on.

"Jody, step on the gas. That bank is being robbed," he shouted to his daughter. The teenager hesitated, trying to comprehend her father's instruction.

The Thunderbird was about to pass the entrance to the parking lot when Darryel Tygart saw the sheriff's vehicle reversing into their path. "Get down!" he yelled, lunging across the center console. He threw his body over his daughter, grabbed the steering wheel, and jerked it to the left to avoid Bolasky's unit and the gunfire being directed at it. Tygart waited for the impact, but somehow, Bolasky's unit barely clipped them. Tygart lifted his head above the dashboard and found he was now traveling in the oncoming lane with another automobile headed directly at them. He jerked the wheel back to the right, but the Thunderbird sideswiped the oncoming car, hard. The impact nearly tore the side off Marvin and Ernestine Holtz's Buick Regal, sending it into the dirt shoulder where the elderly couple cowered, both injured, as bullets began to strike the pavement around them. Tygart's Thunderbird continued to career eastbound on Fourth Street until it struck a curb and came to a stop seventy-five feet beyond Bolasky.

When Darryel Tygart raised his head to check if they were still in the line of fire, there was a sharp crack as a bullet came through the back window, grazed Tygart on the side of the head, and slammed into the center of the dashboard. He threw his body over his daughter again to protect her, putting a hand on her back to keep her as low as possible. But when Darryel Tygart looked down at his hand, it was covered in the girl's blood.

THERE HAD BEEN NO BREAK IN THE GUNFIRE RIPPING GLYN BOLASKY'S UNIT apart. Now crouching behind the Impala holding his shotgun, Bolasky waited for a pause in the firing before daring to put his head up for a look. When he did, he saw the green van rolling slowly in his direction, headed toward the bank exit onto Fourth Street. In addition to the driver, another man sat in the passenger seat with the barrel of a gun sticking out the side window. The van accelerated toward Bolasky. Afraid of taking gunfire at close range, Bolasky dove forward and curled up with his shotgun behind the front tire, where he would be protected by the wheel and the engine block.

The possibility also existed that the van would ram the Impala in an attempt to flee in the direction of Sierra Avenue. If it did, Bolasky would be crushed.

THE MINUTE HE SAW THE FLASHING RED AND BLUE LIGHTS APPEAR IN HIS SIDE mirror, Billy Delgado knew he had made a terrible mistake. Why had his brother gotten him into this? *It's going to be okay, Belisario. Nothing's gonna happen.* That's what Manny had told him all along. But what about now? What about those blue and red lights in the mirror?

Billy had watched the cop turn onto Fourth Street, the light bar whirling blue and red, praying that it might just keep going past on its way to somewhere else, maybe the gas main fire a mile south. Fumbling with the walkie talkie, he radioed George that the cops were there. Seconds later, they all came crashing out the bank door.

"There's one!"

Crack! Crack! Crack!

Billy saw red and blue plastic flying off the roof of the sheriff's unit and half the light bar go dark. Seconds later, the black-and-white was right in front of the van, almost nose-to-nose, half a light bar still whirling away. There was a moment when Billy could see the face of the man behind the wheel. A young guy in a tan uniform. And then the whole car seemed to explode. First the windshield, and then glass, metal, and plastic flying off in all directions. Billy glanced out the open cargo doors and saw all four of them shooting at once. His own brother stepped in front of the van and fired the shotgun straight at the deputy from no more the six feet away. That cop was dead. He just had to be. No one could live through all those bullets. *Don't worry about it, Billy. We're never gonna have to use no fucking guns.*

Then Billy saw something he could hardly believe. Somehow that dead cop in the shot-up car in front of him was not so dead after all. The car suddenly came to life, accelerating in reverse, tires screeching, sliding to a stop sideways in the middle of the road and blocking their escape route to Sierra Avenue. They would have to go up Hamner instead. George had said it would be crazy to go that way. Too much traffic, too many witnesses, too many cops. But now Hamner Avenue was the only hope Billy Delgado had left.

As soon as the police car backed away, the guys all dove into the van through the open cargo doors at once, their guns still smoking with a metallic smell. Manny climbed into the passenger seat beside him and pointed the shotgun out the window. Fuck, let's go! Billy gunned the van toward the exit and the cop car parked sideways in the road. When he got close, he saw the cop again, out of the car now and hiding behind the wheel. Just as the van reached the exit, the cop poked his head up and Billy could see he was holding a shotgun. The sight of the gun startled Billy and he whipped the hard left onto Fourth Street toward Hamner but took the corner too damn fast. He could hear the guys in the back being thrown around along with the duffel bags of bombs, guns, ammunition, and Molotov cocktails. One of the cargo doors swung wide open. Someone managed to dive for the door and jerk it back shut before anyone tumbled out onto the road.

Tires screeched on pavement as he completed the turn. Everyone was pissed off and screaming at him as they scrambled to their knees.

Crack! Crack!

A gun went off right behind Billy's head. Glass shattered. Russell Harven was so close behind Billy's seat when he opened fire straight through the back window that the shell casings from the "Shorty" AR ejected onto the dashboard of the van. The others began firing too, so many rounds going off all at once, like a wall of sound, deafening in the confined space of the cargo compartment.

In front of him, Billy saw nothing but road all the way to Hamner Avenue only a hundred feet ahead. The intersection was clear, with all the traffic stopped at the light. Some people were out of their cars gawking in disbelief at the scene unfolding before them. All that empty road suddenly looked a lot like hope to Billy. If he could make the turn onto Hamner, it would come down to a sprint to the cold getaway cars parked at the Little League field. If he could just make that one last stretch of road, they really might get out of this after all. Then never again. Never ever again would he let himself get talked into any shit like this, not even by Manny.

But then something happened that made no sense to Billy. His body seemed to disappear on him. He could not feel it at all. His hands slid off the steering wheel and fell uselessly to his sides like dead meat. He could not even hold his head up; it just sagged, chin resting on his chest, eyes staring down. He could see his body below him but had no ability to control it at all. The only thing he could feel was a sharp stinging at the back of his neck. But even that did not last long because right then Billy Delgado began the process of slowly drowning in his own blood.

CROUCHED BEHIND THE FRONT WHEEL OF HIS SHERIFF'S VEHICLE, DEPUTY Glyn Bolasky heard the screeching of tires, the sound of the van turning away from him toward Hamner. Bolasky moved to the rear of his vehicle and leveled the shotgun from the hip, but before he could get a shot off, the back windows of the van exploded out and he began taking fire from the men inside. With bullets striking the body of the Impala in front of him, Bolasky gripped the fore-end of the shotgun and pumped all four rounds in the direction of the van from a distance of twenty-five feet. He saw even more glass fall from the back window and knew at least one of his shots had hit the mark, maybe more.

It is unclear precisely how many shots of buck from Glyn Bolasky's shotgun had gone through that van. There are twenty-seven pellets of #4 buck, more or less, in every cartridge, each pellet about the size of a standard BB traveling 1,300 feet per second. Bolasky had pumped off four blasts from the Wingmaster. So . . . twenty-seven? Fifty-four? Eighty-one? There had been at least one full cartridge for sure, the one that entered squarely through the rear window, flew straight through the cargo area, and then out the front windshield in a tight twelve-inch spread pattern. Well, most of it had anyhow.

There had been that one pellet in that one load of buck that did something other than waste everybody's time. A single quarter-ounce ball of lead flew through the rear window, past all the Molotov cocktails, beer-can bombs, bags of cash, and thousands of rounds of ammunition. It went past Russell and Christopher Harven, past George Wayne Smith and Manny Delgado. It even went past Gary Hakala. It went right the fuck past everyone. Everyone except Billy Delgado.

When it got to Billy, that solitary lead orb weighing no more than a fat raisin went through the captain's chair and into the back of his neck, midline at the base of his skull, punching a hole through bone like it was rice paper and entering the cranial cavity just north of the medulla oblongata. At that instant, Billy's somatic nervous system ceased to relay voluntary commands below that point, and Billy's body was no longer his own. But the medulla itself dutifully carried on its job of running the autonomic nervous system that kept Billy's vital organs functioning. When it had finished its business in Billy's brain stem, that shot of buck continued its journey, puncturing the cartilage wall of his trachea, allowing his heart to pump blood into his lungs, gradually filling them from the bottom up.

Without Billy, the van decelerated and drifted harmlessly into a chain-link fence on the north side of Fourth Street, coming to a stop just a few feet short of what had been the teenager's last great hope: Hamner Avenue.

THE SECOND GEORGE SMITH WHIPPED HIS HEAD AROUND TO SEE WHY THE van was not moving, he knew what had happened to his driver. Billy was pitched forward, slumping limply to the right side. In the passenger seat, Manny was already shaking him, calling his name, trying to push him back up straight, but Billy's body was dead weight. Manny tore off his own ski mask, lifted his little brother's head, and saw the eyes filled with terror, darting crazily around in their sockets. Get him the fuck out of there, somebody yelled. Manny, drive!

It was hopeless. Manny could not move his brother's body out of the way. I'm getting out of here, Chris yelled. I'm not getting toasted in this van.

Go out the back, George said, grabbing duffel bags and tossing them in the direction of the side cargo door. We need another vehicle.

Chris put a foot up on the upholstered back seat and went straight out the shattered back window still holding his Heckler. He fell onto the street and then popped up, aiming the assault rifle toward the police car still sideways in the road. A moment later, Russ followed his brother out the same way with the "Shorty" AR.

While Chris and Russ were diving out the back window, George grabbed Manny and pulled him away from Billy, whose body had begun involuntarily convulsing. Help me get these bags out of here, he yelled. Instead, Manny grabbed the riot gun, climbed over his dying brother, and went out the driver's door onto the street.

Alone in the van, George tossed one more duffel bag toward the cargo doors, grabbed his Heckler .308, and prepared to offload the bags. Before squeezing out the tight space between the van and the chain-link fence, Smith took a final look around the van for anything else they might need. His eyes settled on the cabinet holding their hostage and saw it punctured and gouged with buckshot. That dude was fucking dead, for sure.

GLYN BOLASKY NEVER SAW THE VAN DRIFT OFF THE ROAD. THE YOUNG DEP-uty was busy tossing his empty shotgun onto the pavement, drawing his .357 Python service revolver, and scrambling to the shelter of the front wheel. When the gunfire abruptly stopped, Bolasky peeked up over the hood of his car, expecting the van to have disappeared around the corner onto Hamner. What he saw instead surprised him. The van had come to a stop just before the traffic light. It was mostly off the road with its front end up against a chain-link fence bordering a strip of dirt used as a horse trail.

Standing at the rear of the van was a man holding a rifle at his hip with the barrel leveled directly at Bolasky. With the mask pulled over his head, staring through a single hole for his eyes, he did not look so much like a man as he did some sort of gothic nightmare, a hooded executioner about to drop the guillotine.

The two men fired at each other almost simultaneously, Bolasky getting off a single round, which he saw hit low, throwing up a puff of dirt and asphalt. He dove back down behind the front tire as rounds struck his patrol unit. The deputy made himself as small as he could behind the wheel and engine block. The bullets kept coming, hammering into one side of the Impala and out the other, zinging off the pavement to his left and right. They flew so close he could feel the concussion from the air they displaced and hear the sharp crack as they broke the sound barrier while whizzing homicidally overhead.

There was another short break in the gunfire and Bolasky popped up again. There was a second man alongside the first now, each firing from the hip. Bolasky raised his .357 and got off two more rounds before the gunmen commenced firing on him, so many rounds striking the Impala that he thought the entire car would be torn to pieces. Bolasky went down again and immediately saw his rear tire blow out. Then something jerked his left arm backward. When he looked down, there was a hole on the inside of his left elbow. Blood began squirting onto his face.

A MILE DIRECTLY NORTH ON HAMNER AVENUE AT THE DONUT CORRAL ON Sixth Street, deputies Chuck Hille and Andy Delgado threw down their coffee cups and jumped into their vehicles at the first 211 dispatch. The two men split up, Delgado heading down Hamner and Hille paralleling him on Sierra. Hille and Delgado were coming into the situation blind with no information on the location of the van, the number of suspects, or the firepower they would be up against. For all they knew it could be a strung-out junkie popping off a Saturday night special; it usually was. Splitting up and approaching from two sides was a basic tactic intended to locate a suspect fleeing in an unknown direction. But the two deputies did not know at the time that they were about to execute a classic pincer movement on four heavily armed men.

Turning westbound onto Fourth Street from Sierra, Chuck Hille immediately began scanning the scene. One hundred fifty yards in front of him and dead center in the road, Hille saw Glyn Bolasky crouched behind the front wheel of his unit and taking heavy fire. Even from that distance, Hille could see that something was very wrong. A moment later Hille heard the first rounds striking the radiator and hood of his own patrol unit with a guttural thump. The bullets hit so hard that Hille felt the impacts resonating through the frame of the Plymouth Fury. *2-Edward-59, we're taking fire now,*

Hille radioed. *Unit's been hit.* Why the hell are these guys still here? Hille thought. Every bank robber he had ever encountered just wanted to get away from the bank and the cops as fast as possible. So why were these guys still hanging around?

Hille could not pick out the source of the gunfire from the landscape in front of him, but he knew he was headed straight into it. He began zigzagging his car left and right, employing the serpentine evasive driving tactic he had learned in a training course just a week before. Two more rounds hit his vehicle. Just before he reached Bolasky's location, he jerked the wheel right, sending the Plymouth into a dirt lot, fishtailing to an outbuilding 150 feet off Fourth Street. As he skidded his cruiser to a stop, Hille heard a chilling transmission coming from Bolasky.

3-Edward-50, I'm bleeding badly. I have an artery hit. I need help!

Leaving his sheriff's unit behind the outbuilding, Hille threw open the driver's door, turned on the portable radio on his hip, and headed toward Bolasky's position. He still had no visual on the suspects, but he could hear the crackling of gunfire, the bullets zinging off pavement and striking Bolasky's vehicle. Holy shit, thought Hille, they're firing automatics. There was the deep booming of a shotgun. How many of these sons of bitches were there? Hille eyed Bolasky's position and scanned the scene again for the source of the shooting. There was a large bush on Fourth Street near the corner of Hamner. Other than that, Hille was looking at a wide-open field of fire between himself and Bolasky. Another transmission from Bolasky came over the radio.

3-Edward-50, the suspects are stranded, their vehicle is disabled at Hamner and Fourth. Roll help. I need an ambulance. I'm bleeding badly.

The transmission was enough to focus Hille on the urgency of reaching the wounded deputy and getting him out of there. He took off running toward Bolasky's unit and immediately began taking fire, bullets thudding into the dirt around him. The gunfire intensified as Hille dashed the last fifty feet to Bolasky's unit and crouched behind it. When Hille turned his attention to Bolasky, what he saw alarmed him. There were fragments of glass embedded in his fellow deputy's face, and blood was dripping from his chin and cheeks onto his uniform shirt. Bolasky was pale white and appeared to be slipping into shock. There was considerably more blood around Bolasky, streams and droplets in all directions, as though someone had been shooting a squirt gun full of it in random directions. Hille searched for the source and saw Bolasky gripping his left elbow.

Let me see it, Hille said. Bolasky lifted his hand off the wound and a jet of blood spurted onto Hille's uniform. Hille gripped his hand over Bolasky's elbow to stop the bleeding. Another tire on the Impala took a round and blew out. Bullets hit the pavement, bounced under the vehicle, and came through the frame in lethal fragments. We've got to find another place, Hille told Bolasky, who seemed to be growing even more disoriented. It's not safe here.

Hille crouched low behind the Impala and eyed a row of thick-trunked eucalyptus trees lining the south side of the street just behind them. Hille reached for Bolasky's .357. He emptied the spent rounds from the cylinder, reloaded, and pushed the gun back into Bolasky's hand. Bolasky held the gun in his left hand while gripping his hemorrhaging elbow with his right. Let's get to those trees, Hille said, helping Bolasky to his feet. There was the sound of more shotgun blasts and then the cracking of rifle rounds, but none of it was hitting near them. The two men took off running.

Chuck Hille did not realize the reason he and Bolasky were no longer taking fire was that the gunmen had shifted their focus to the man standing behind the open door of a Riverside County Sheriff's patrol car pumping shotgun blasts into their midst.

ANDY DELGADO CUT HIS SIREN AND CRESTED THE RISE BETWEEN FIFTH Street and Fourth Street going seventy-five miles per hour. *Where the suspects at?* Delgado radioed. Bolasky had not yet reported the van disabled at Fourth and Hamner. The only thing Andy knew was that he was looking for a green van. Seconds later he saw it pulled off the road on Fourth Street just short of Hamner. There was activity about the vehicle. Andy tried to take it all in. Figures darted out from behind the vehicle and disappeared again. Two came to the front. There appeared to be someone still behind the wheel and another standing directly outside the driver's door. Yet another stood between the open side cargo doors and a chain-link fence unloading what looked like duffel bags. Andy began to hear gunfire, so much that he assumed it must be automatic weapons fire.

When he got close enough, Andy saw they were all wearing military jackets and black ski masks and holding military-type rifles. Delgado's initial thought was that he might be facing a band of Middle Eastern terrorists. After all, more than sixty Americans were still being held hostage in Iran, and others had died just two weeks before trying to free them in a military raid. Video footage of mobs chanting "Death to America!" had become a staple of nightly news coverage.

Andy sized up the situation but it was impossible to get a definitive count because they were constantly moving. Four to six of them, he estimated. He swung his patrol unit into the empty northbound lanes and angled it toward the side of the road, bringing it to a stop at a forty-five-degree angle at the curb fifty yards short of the intersection. Now he could see more clearly what the men at the front of the van were doing. Three of them were taking turns stepping out from behind the van to fire down Fourth Street, where Bolasky must be. Delgado immediately recognized it as a variation on a military tactic called an Australian peel. Now these guys really did look the part of a terrorist gang: well armed and well trained.

Delgado exited his vehicle with his shotgun and stood behind the V of his open driver's door. He knew right away that he was at the effective range limit for a shotgun. Andy was a pretty good shot with a long gun and figured even with a wide spray pattern from that distance he could land a pellet or two on at least one of them.

There was another factor Delgado needed to take into account: There were people everywhere now. Vehicles were backed up fifty yards deep on Hamner in both directions. Motorists were out of their cars trying to figure out just what the hell was going on. Gawkers streamed from the Carl's Jr. or wandered across the Stater Bros. parking lot to see what all the commotion was about. Andy estimated close to fifty civilians in the immediate area. With buckshot spreading out wider and wider, he could easily cause collat-

eral damage if he was not careful. But for the moment, Andy's field of fire
was free of civilians.

Andy lifted the Wingmaster shotgun over the top of the open door of his
patrol car and unloaded three rounds of buckshot. The result was . . . nothing.
Or at least nothing that he could see.

In reality, Andy had hit three of the four bank robbers in his initial volley. One pellet grazed the back of Chris Harven's neck. One inch over and
he might have suffered a fate similar to that of Billy Delgado. When Russell
Harven turned toward the source of the shotgun blasts, he felt a burning sensation in his scalp, like a cat clawing at his head. A shot of buck had burrowed
under his scalp at the hairline and tunneled its way beneath the tissue all the
way to the back of his head without penetrating the skull or resurfacing. Still,
the force of the tiny pellet felt like a blow from the small end of a ball-peen
hammer, staggering and dizzying him.

It was the shot Andy fired in the direction of the man offloading duffel
bags from the side cargo door of the van that did the most damage. With
a spread pattern almost six feet in diameter from a distance of fifty yards,
the blast from Andy's modified-choke Wingmaster haloed George Smith in
buckshot, rattling pellets off the thick exterior of the van. Two shots of the
#4 buck found their target. Turned in profile while dropping a bag onto the
horse trail, George felt something dig into the meat of the inside of his left
leg, up high in the groin area. Simultaneously, a second struck the outside of
his right thigh, coming to rest deep inside the tissue of his buttocks. In the
midst of an adrenaline surge, George did not realize he had been shot until
he felt the warm wetness spreading down his inner thigh. He saw the dark
stain of blood and immediately recognized that his situation had just gone
from dire to hopeless.

Andy was surprised to hear the scene grow momentarily silent. Maybe
he had hit one or two of them, but why was there no gunfire coming from
Bolasky and Hille? He took advantage of the break and fired the last round
he had left in the Wingmaster.

The moment he was down again behind the door, the gunfire returned. This time it was aimed at him. The first two bullets ripped into

Andy Delgado's vehicle, one in the hood on the driver's side and another in the molding at the roof line. A third hit the pavement, sending fragments through the open door he was using for cover as though it were nothing more than a shower curtain. That's when the fear began to grip him. For all his military and police training and six years on the streets, he had never been shot at. He never dreamed it would be anything like this.

CHRIS AND RUSSELL HARVEN WERE THROUGH BEING SITTING DUCKS. RUSS moved to a position on the driver's side of the van for protection, peeking around to fire shots in the direction of the cop who had just put a shotgun pellet under his scalp. Chris lay prone on the pavement, sighting over the barrel of the gun, reeling a dozen rounds at Andy Delgado's radio car. He rolled to his right, ejected the banana clip, flipped it over, and locked a fresh one into the magazine port.

Andy had six more shotgun shells in a stock sling strapped to the butt end of the gun. He slipped out two loads of buckshot and a rifled slug—a one-ounce monster chunk of lead the size of a Civil War Minié ball. He pushed them into the magazine port on the belly of the gun. Over the gun-fire, he heard the radio transmissions from Bolasky that he had an artery hit and was bleeding badly. That explained why Bolasky was no longer laying down fire on the suspects. He had heard Hille report being fired on while driving into the scene but nothing from him over the radio since. Hopefully he was still in the fight, pinning these bastards down in a cross fire.

Andy racked the first shell into the chamber, stood, and fired off both rounds of buckshot. In the process, he caught sight of the two men who had been at the front of the van. One stepped out from behind the van and lev-eled a rifle at Andy. The other was lying prone in the road in a sharpshooter position. Andy saw the muzzle smoke and there was an explosion of gunfire. He threw himself to the ground. Rounds struck the pavement and the side mirror on the driver's door shattered, the frame around it exploding. Frag-ments erupted from out of the dashboard inside the vehicle just to his right.

There were a few more seconds of silence and a terrible feeling came over

Andy. He could sense he was alone, that Hille was no longer firing either. There was no way out for him now. He fought back the urge to turn and run, the emotions rising up in him. An image of his seven-year-old daughter flashed through his mind and then one of Darrell Creed telling him to keep fighting.

Andy stood and fired his seventh round, the rifled slug, missing the suspects and punching a hole in the side of the bank building. He ducked down again, no longer taking the time to assess the effects of his fire. He pushed his last three shells into the magazine port. He would have preferred them all to be buckshot, but all he had left was one buck and two slugs. He heard the desperate voice of Glyn Bolasky come over the radio for the last time.

Roll anyone, CPD, we got to get people out of here. We need the highway blocked at—

Another officer stepped on Bolasky's transmission and Andy could not make out the rest of it. The radio crackled with transmission from sheriff's units responding to the scene. A chorus of sirens swelled in the distance. Andy stood and fired two more rounds and went back down. All he had now was one slug and his .38 revolver. He set the shotgun to the side, drew the six-shooter, and waited.

GEORGE SMITH WAS DIZZY WITH PAIN AND WANTED TO VOMIT. HE KNELT down and gripped his leg to stop the bleeding, but the blood just oozed between his fingers. There were two more shotgun blasts from the north on Hamner and pellets struck the van again, this time high, near the roof. He let go of his leg and threw three of the duffel bags to the rear of the van, took his Heckler, and limped after them. He eyed the sheriff's unit in the middle of the road on Fourth Street but there was no sign of anyone. That guy's probably dead too, just like the one in the cabinet in back. The whole plan had fallen apart. They had stayed in the bank too long.

George looked toward Hamner and saw Manny Delgado standing by the driver's door holding the riot gun. He had thrown off his mask and poncho. I'm hit, George yelled at him. Help me with these bags. Manny came back and lifted one by the strap and slung it over his shoulder. He took the other two and carried them to the other side of the van. George followed. Take a bag, he yelled to Chris and Russell Harven. The two fired a few more rounds in the direction of Andy Delgado and then each took up a duffel bag. Fan out, George ordered, pointing toward the two lines of cars backed up at the light south on Hamner. We need another vehicle.

The three men spread out and moved toward the lines of cars, the Harvens with assault rifles tucked under their arms, Manny with the riot gun at his hip. The scene at Fourth and Hamner became one of total madness as masked and heavily armed men descended on the trapped motorists, menacingly swinging high-powered rifles, approaching windows and looking in, sending drivers and passengers, including children, running for their lives. Terrified onlookers fled back into the Carl's Jr., Murphy's Hay & Grain, and Redlands Federal Savings Bank, where some crawled beneath desks or dove for shelter behind the teller line. A large woman ran screaming south down Hamner and into the parking lot of the Century 21 Real Estate office that shared the building with the bank. An agent named Jim Lyon ran out and grabbed her and dragged her into the office. Other bystanders followed as they ran from the men with the guns.

At that moment, George Smith and Andy Delgado shared the common belief that they were going to die. Smith was no longer afraid as he flipped the jungle clip at the bottom of the Heckler .308, locked in a fresh forty-round magazine, and limped out into the middle of the intersection. Once there, he calmly surveyed the area, people fleeing in all directions. He looked down Fourth Street, but there was still no movement there. He turned and looked up Hamner and saw the deputy who had shot him couched behind the door of his sheriff's unit. Smith raised the .308 to his hip and began to fire.

ONE HUNDRED FEET DOWN FOURTH STREET, CHUCK HILLE COULD SEE THAT the short sprint to the eucalyptus trees had taken a toll on Glyn Bolasky, but they were still not out of danger. If the gunmen chose to leave the scene by way of Sierra Avenue, they would pass right by their position. We're going to have to move again, he told Bolasky. Over there, behind that house.

When they stood up to make their move, a man was running at them from the direction of the intersection. Get down, get down! Bolasky screamed at the man. Hille reached for his gun but then saw that the man was just a bystander running for his life, shirt unbuttoned and flapping behind him. Hit the ground! Bolasky screamed. This time the guy did, diving facedown onto the dirt and making himself as flat as possible.

Shaken, the two deputies darted the ten yards behind a small stucco house. Hille could see he would need to retrieve his patrol car from the other side of Fourth Street and come back to pick up the wounded deputy. After checking with Bolasky, he ran back to the eucalyptus tree, checked the street, and spotted one of the gunmen for the first time. A lone figure stood directly in the center of the wide intersection of Fourth and Hamner. The man was wearing a ski mask and a long military-green duster, pants tucked into his boots. In his hand was a rifle, the stock resting on his hip, the barrel straight out at a ninety-degree angle aimed at something north on Hamner Avenue.

For a second time, Hille crossed the field of fire to his unit at the far end of the dirt lot. He could hear sporadic gunfire but had no idea if any of it was aimed at him. Reaching his patrol unit, Hille swung a big looping U-turn, crossed the dirt lot and Fourth Street, jumped the curb, threaded between two eucalyptus trees, and pulled up to Bolasky's location behind the house. He jumped out and swung open the rear door. Get in, Hille yelled.

I'm not getting into the cage, Bolasky protested, referring to the fenced-in back seat area usually reserved for suspects.

Is he fucking kidding me? Hille thought. You've got to get in now!

There was the sound of another burst of gunfire. Bolasky dove into the back seat, and Hille took off east on Fourth, away from the intersection. He drove as far as he could over the front lawns until a drainage canal blocked his way and forced him back onto the asphalt road. Hille made the final stretch and turned right onto Sierra, out of the line of fire. Only then did Hille glance back and notice that the back door of the patrol unit was still wide open and Bolasky's legs were hanging out. Hille brought the unit to a stop and helped Bolasky climb the rest of the way inside. Hille aimed his vehicle south on Sierra focused on a single task: get Glyn Bolasky to Corona Community Hospital before he bled out in the back seat of an RSO patrol unit.

HOLDING HIS REVOLVER, ANDY DELGADO PEEKED OVER THE DOOR TO HIS PAtrol unit. The intersection had erupted into chaos with people running everywhere. The cars on his side of Hamner were now backed up evenly with his position on the opposite side of the road. He scanned the scene for suspects and saw two walking between the rows of cars. Where were the rest? There were just too many goddamn people, too many independent situations developing at once to figure it all out. He saw the driver of a tan Cadillac jerked out of the car and thrown to the pavement before running away. Or had the man simply fallen trying to get away and the other guy was helping him up? Out of the corner of his eye someone ran toward the feed store to his left and disappeared inside. Who the hell was that? More were fleeing into the Carl's Jr. and toward the bank parking lot. Were any of those suspects?

Andy could hardly believe what he saw next. A tall man in a ski mask and military-green duster, pants tucked into black boots, came out from behind the van and walked, no, *strolled* out to the very center of the busiest intersection in Norco. The man positioned himself right where a traffic cop might stand and coolly surveyed the area. Andy could tell by the way the man stood there in the wide open, flat-footed and unafraid, that he was the leader of the group. No question. The man did not look at all concerned that it had come down to a firefight.

The man turned toward Andy, lifted the assault rifle to his hip, and began firing. The first two rounds struck Andy's patrol unit with such force that the entire vehicle seemed to shudder from the impact. One round entered through the grill, passed through the radiator, slammed into the engine block, and fragmented. Shards of lead and copper cut the hood cable in half and passed though the dashboard and into the interior of the vehicle.

Delgado lay on the ground as more rounds cracked the sky above him and struck the road in front of him, spraying the area with a lethal mix of asphalt, lead, and copper. This is it, Andy thought. This is where it all ends.

A TWENTY-FOUR-YEAR-OLD HEAVY-MACHINERY MECHANIC NAMED MIKEL Linville was driving a service vehicle northbound on Hamner coming back from a job at the Corona Airport when he stopped at the light at Fourth Street. The company vehicle was a 1969 Ford F-250 pickup mounted with steel utility cabinets on the sides of the bed, an air compressor in back, and tall cylinders of compressed oxygen and acetylene secured upright just behind the cab. Sundry welding equipment, a five-gallon can of gear oil, and tools of the heavy mechanic trade lay scattered about the bed of the truck. The truck was painted a yellow-orange similar to that of local road maintenance departments. The company name, Pascal & Ludwig, was painted on the doors of the cab.

Linville slowed to a stop in the far-left lane with only one car in front of him. His mind was on dumping the truck at the yard in Upland, cashing his paycheck, and starting his weekend when he heard the popping of gunfire and saw men standing next to a green van firing their rifles down Fourth Street. Linville lay across the bench seat of the truck as the shooting intensified. When he peeked his head up again, he saw a man in a ski mask and drab-green poncho holding a military rifle walking into the center of the intersection as though there were not a damn thing anyone there could do to stop him. Then he spotted three other men—two wearing ski masks and the other, Hispanic, with his face exposed. All three were carrying duffel bags and rifles. They fanned out and began moving through the lanes of stopped traffic, leveling their guns at passengers. One was headed directly for Linville.

To Mikel Linville, the man headed in his direction seemed huge, at least six foot three, 250 pounds. It might have been the ski mask or the poncho that made Chris Harven look that big, or it could have been the semiautomatic rifle he lowered and aimed directly through the windshield. Either way, Linville knew it was time to leave. He threw open the door to the truck and jumped out, in the process popping the clutch, which made the truck jump forward, strike the car in front of it, and stall out. The athletic Linville darted between cars, making sure to stay clear of anyone else wearing a fucking ski mask. He sprinted for the parking lot of the Security Pacific Bank, scrambled up a cinder block wall, and vaulted onto the roof of the Century 21 Real Estate offices.

From there, Linville could see the big man who had aimed the rifle at him climb into the driver's seat of the truck. Another man in a ski mask ran for the truck, hurled a duffel bag over the side cabinets, and scrambled into the bed after it. The one without the mask climbed into the passenger side of the cab. But the one in the intersection, he just stood right where he was, firing from the hip in small bursts, one after the other, over and over, in the direction of a lone cop hiding behind the door of his sheriff's vehicle.

THERE WAS A SUDDEN BREAK IN THE SHOOTING. ANDY DELGADO PUSHED HIMself up and looked over the door to his unit. The man in the intersection no longer had the rifle on his hip and had turned to face the other direction. There was some commotion around some sort of service vehicle. One of his suspects was standing beside the driver's door waving a gun around. It appeared to Andy as though he was aiming the gun in the direction of the passenger seat, forcing someone to get back inside. Andy figured it must be a hostage because the person who jumped back inside wore no mask, no green field jacket. He saw another gunman in a ski mask run through traffic toward the yellow truck and jump into the bed. But had there been a second guy with him? A second hostage? The man in the intersection turned and fired another burst of gunfire in his direction and Andy ducked down again.

Andy tried to tally it up. Two shooters in the back. The one who was waving his gun around must be the driver, so that's at least three. The guy in the passenger seat makes one hostage and very possibly another in the bed of the truck. Shit, so where were all the other suspects? He had guessed anywhere from four to six. They must still be in the area, maybe inside that tan Cadillac he had seen before or in Murphy's Hay & Grain.

Out of the chaos, Andy saw the yellow truck lurch forward, swing out of its lane, and pull into the intersection. The truck slowed while the man standing in the center of the intersection walked to the rear and handed his rifle up to the man in the back. He seemed to be in no hurry at all. He stepped up onto the bumper and swung himself over the tailgate and disappeared into the bed. The truck accelerated, angling back into the northbound lanes heading toward Andy's location. God almighty, Andy thought, these guys are coming to kill me. Andy lay down on the pavement between his cruiser and the curb, using as much of the front wheel as he could for cover. He could hear the engine of the big truck as it drew closer. He put his head to the pavement, holding the .38 and peering under the patrol car, looking for any boots that might hit the ground. If they did, he would shoot at them.

The truck never slowed down, but there was a rapid Bam! Bam! Bam! of gunfire as George Smith fired the Heckler over the tailgate of the truck, one .308-caliber bullet gouging a deep, five-inch trench in the metal roof of Andy's unit. Andy could hear the truck accelerating away, the big 360-cubic-inch V8 engine straining up the low grade between Fourth and Fifth Streets. Andy grabbed his shotgun off the pavement, aimed at a figure in the bed of the truck, and fired the last shotgun slug as the truck crested the hill and disappeared.

Andy grabbed his radio mic and breathlessly communicated the best information he had been able to gather under the circumstances. *3-Edward-51, three suspects fled, a yellow pickup north on Hamner. They have two hostages.*

Gary Keeter parroted the transmission for all units to hear. *Riverside t'all, yellow pickup has fled with two hostages northbound on Hamner.*

THE INTERSECTION AT HAMNER AND FOURTH WAS EERILY QUIET EXCEPT FOR the crackling bursts of radio traffic coming from Andy Delgado's shot-up cruiser and the wail of sirens closing in fast. The whole event had taken just four minutes and two seconds from the time of Gary Keeter's 211 dispatch to Andy Delgado's broadcast that the robbers had fled the scene. But to the officers flooding the scene minutes later, that seemed almost impossible to believe.

Hundreds of empty shell casings littered the bank parking lot, Fourth Street, and the intersection at Hamner. To Riverside City PD officer Fred Grutzmacher, it seemed as though he could not take a step without crunching at least one underfoot. In the end, only fourteen shotgun cartridges and three spent .38 shell casings were Riverside county-issue rounds. The others, more than five hundred spent shells in all, had come from the private collection of George Wayne Smith and Christopher Harven.

There were bullet holes everywhere—forty-six having hit Bolasky's car alone, several in each of Hille's and Andy Delgado's units, one in Darryel Tygart's Thunderbird, another in Chris Evans's El Camino, and more in civilian vehicles abandoned or parked in nearby lots. Six rounds had whistled through the walls of Murphy's Hay & Grain and another through the radiator of an employee's truck parked out front. Others went into houses, cars, sheds, and storefronts. In the row of apartments just behind the bank, John Leighton herded his family to a back room after a bullet smashed through a bedroom window, cutting a metal lamp in half.

On Fourth Street, a Thunderbird was crashed against the curb with Darryel and Jody Ann Tygart still lying across the front seat, the daughter telling her father she was okay, but pleading with him not to stick his head up again. A little farther up, a two-tone Buick Regal was facing Hamner, its driver's side smashed in by the Thunderbird, Marvin and Ernestine Holtz trembling inside. Bolasky's Chevy Impala was sideways in the road, riddled with gunshot holes, every window and three of its tires blown out, with blood on the front seat, on the side of the door, splattered on the asphalt beside it, and trailing away in droplets to a row of trees.

Inside the Security Pacific Bank, customers and employees were only now daring to get off the floor. The teller drawers and bank vault were still open and empty. Denise DeMarco picked up a ringing telephone. It was the Corona branch. "Did you guys just get robbed?" Elaine Jones, the woman who had been in the drive-through lane when she spotted Manny Delgado waving a shotgun around, had jumped from her truck to stop a group of small children from running straight into the gunfight and was now shielding them behind a cinder block wall.

Adjacent to the bank, Jim Lyon had almost forty bystanders lying on the carpet and behind desks in his Century 21 office, while Mikel Linville was crawling down from its roof. Dozens of others, including Chris Evans and Jennie Lewis, were wandering out of the Carl's Jr. while restaurant manager Chuck Anderson tried to calm those still too frightened to come out from under the tables. Cowering in the bathroom at Murphy's Hay & Grain were two mothers and their Cub Scouts who had been at the entrance to the bank when it all began. Others were coaxed out of closets and phone booths, from under cars or behind houses, trees, and walls.

With responding units from Riverside Sheriff's Department, Riverside PD, Corona PD, and California Highway Patrol now flooding the intersection of Fourth and Hamner from all directions, there was a radio transmission from Chuck Hille as he raced to the hospital with Glyn Bolasky. *2-Edward-59, Bolasky is shot in the shoulder, leg, and arm. He needs AB blood.*

On Fourth Street, the green van, still stuck in drive, was rhythmically rocking back and forth against the chain-link fence, rolling a few feet forward until the tension of the fence rolled it back. Slowly forward, slowly back. Over and over. A teenage boy sat slumped in the driver's seat convulsing, a .45 Colt semiautomatic strapped to his ankle, an AR-15 on the floor beside him. In the cargo area in back, a cabinet door still bulged from the weight of the man taped up inside. Scattered across the floor of the van was the cause of it all, a sad little mix of wrapped and loose bills and coins. What was already one of the most violent bank robberies in history had yielded one of its shittiest takes: $20,112.36.

Through the glass doors of the Security Pacific Bank, eighteen-year-old James Kirkland watched the green van rocking back and forth against the chain link fence. And then something very peculiar happened. A head emerged out the back window of the van and seemed to be shouting something. Moments later, a man with his arms and legs bound in packing tape, a rope tied around his neck, squirmed his way out of the window and flopped onto the pavement below.

Andy Delgado was the first to catch sight of Gary Hakala on the ground and advanced toward him, gun drawn. Having no reason to expect anyone other than a bank robber to come out of the van, Andy leveled his .357. Then he saw the arms and legs bound with packing tape. This was no bank robber. This was a hostage.

"Come toward me! Come toward me!" Andy yelled at the man, his gun still drawn as a precaution against God knew what else might come out of that van. Several of the cops who had just arrived on scene turned toward the van and leveled their sidearms and shotguns at the screaming man emerging from behind the suspect vehicle.

"I'm a hostage! Help me!" Hakala continued to call out, relieved to see so many cops. Hakala bunny-hopped his way toward Hamner Avenue before his feet, asleep after five hours bound in tape, went out from under him and he flopped onto the asphalt. He felt the rope slip from his neck and began rolling across Hamner Avenue while dozens of bystanders and cops looked on dumbfounded at the spectacle of a bound man crossing a major boulevard like a rolling pin.

After rolling almost the entire width of the wide avenue, Gary Hakala's ordeal finally ended when a Corona PD cruiser advanced into the intersection, two officers running alongside, weapons drawn. When they reached Hakala, they scooped him up like a giant sausage, chucked him onto the back seat, and drove him a few hundred yards north on Hamner.

INSIDE THE VAN, BILLY DELGADO'S BODY WAS COMING TO THE END OF ITS struggle. With a dozen jittery lawmen now inching forward with their guns drawn, Billy drew his final bubbly breath. It had taken fifteen horrifying minutes for his heart to pump enough blood through the hole in his trachea to fill his lungs and suffocate him to death. A moment later, the van's engine also gave up its futile struggle against the chain link-fence, and it died too.

6

WINEVILLE

May 9, 1980. Wineville, California.

SIX THOUSAND MILES AWAY FROM CALIFORNIA, A MEETING WAS TAKING place in a vacation home on a lake in Velden, Austria. The owner of a modest manufacturing facility specializing in curtain rods and army knives had gathered together a collection of Europe's leading military, law enforcement, and sporting firearms experts. The Austrian military had just opened contract bidding to choose the supplier of a new sidearm to replace the outdated Walther P38. The man hosting the meeting had a single question to ask the assembled group: What would be the ideal characteristics of a new handgun?

Gaston Glock had no experience whatsoever designing or manufacturing firearms, but he had recently retooled his shop and begun working with advanced synthetic polymers whose strength and lightweight characteristics he was sure could be applied to create a superior weapon. Within months, he had. The semiautomatic Glock 17 pistol was lighter, more durable, and more reliable than anything before it. Glock won the contract.

But it was another feature of the Glock 17 that would cause it to sweep through American law enforcement in the years that followed, eventually reaching an industry-leading 65 percent rate of use by police agencies. Feeding from a double-stock magazine housing NATO-standard 9 mm rounds in the grip, the Glock 17 allowed the user to peel off seventeen rounds of semiautomatic fire before pausing to reload, an action that took only seconds to execute.

Glock was certainly not the first firearms company to manufacture a semiautomatic pistol, but when a string of lethal shootouts in the 1980s proved the need for law enforcement to increase round capacity, it was the Glock 17 that had the right performance, specs, and price point. The first in that string of shootouts to usher in the militarization of America's police forces occurred the same day as the meeting from which the Glock 17 was born: the Norco Bank Robbery.

Of course, the Glock 17 would arrive too late for the deputies shooting it out with four heavily armed bank robbers on the streets of Norco. To say the Riverside County Sheriff's Department was outgunned on May 9, 1980, is to vastly understate the situation. Like most local law enforcement agencies at the time, the RSO was still arming its deputies with two weapons: a six-shooter and a shotgun. The standard county-issue Smith & Wesson .38 Special revolver and Remington 870 Wingmaster shotgun both experience ever-diminishing accuracy and penetrating capability, making them nearly ineffectual at distances beyond forty-five yards. Neither will accommodate high-capacity magazines, requiring frequent and time-consuming reloading.

In contrast, a bullet fired from the HK91, HK93, or Colt AR-15 assault rifles used by the Norco bank robbers travels at almost three thousand feet per second, close to three times the speed of sound, and can kill a man from five hundred yards away. A .308-caliber round from George Smith's Heckler HK91 strikes a target with a staggering 2,200 pounds of energy, eight times that of a Smith & Wesson .38 Special, punching through car doors like aluminum foil.

Both the .223 and .308 are "full metal jacket" bullets with hard copper sheathing and a soft lead interior that tumble and fragment upon impact, sending shards of metal on random, homicidal journeys throughout the human body. Armed with forty-round magazines taped together up-down-up "jungle style," any of the Norco bank robbers were capable of firing 120 rounds in just over a minute.

GEORGE SMITH SAT IN A POOL OF HIS OWN BLOOD IN THE BACK OF THE STOLEN pickup and watched the Security Pacific Bank recede into the distance. The Ford F-250, now being driven by Chris Harven, was a three-quarter-ton pickup with a powerful 215-horsepower V8 engine and a body clad in fabricated steel. Metal utility cabinets mounted on the sides were filled with heavy tools providing three-feet-high impenetrable cover for the full length of the bed on both sides, the perfect height and width for steadying a weapon upon while firing. The thick cast iron of the four tall cylinders of highly pressurized oxygen and acetylene gas mounted upright against the back of the cab could never be penetrated by what law enforcement was firing. Instead, they provided excellent cover for anyone shooting over the top of the truck and protected the driver from gunfire from the rear. For all intents and purposes, the yellow truck that rolled northbound on Hamner with four heavily armed men on board that day was the equivalent of a military vehicle in both armor and firepower.

George released an empty magazine out of the bottom of the Heckler and snapped in a fresh jungle clip. They crested the hill and continued north. There was no sign of any police cars, no sound except for the wail of distant sirens closing in and the V8 engine straining to keep the heavy truck moving. All they needed to do was make it one mile more up Hamner, switch to the cold cars parked at the Little League field, and get the fuck out of Norco.

George looked up and saw Russell Harven standing behind the cab of the truck holding the "Shorty" AR. We stayed too fucking long in the bank, George yelled.

Russ just stared at him through the hole in the ski mask, studying the man who had talked all of them into this bullshit to begin with.

I can't stop the bleeding, George said, motioning to his blood-stained pants.

Russ knelt beside George and checked the wound on his inner thigh.

Warm blood stained George's pants from his crotch all the way down to his left knee and smeared the bed of the truck beneath his leg. George pulled a red bandana from his pocket and Russ helped him tie it tightly high up on his left thigh to put pressure on the wound, but it did little to stop the bleeding.

Did you get hit? George asked him over the wind whipping through the open bed of the truck.

I got shot in the head, Russ said flatly.

You got fucking what?

Russ went back to his post, setting the barrel of the "Shorty" AR-15 on the roof of the cab between two acetylene tanks and scanning the road in front of them.

Behind the wheel, Chris shifted into fourth as the truck finally reached a higher speed. His eyes darted between the side mirrors and the road ahead of them, scanning for cops. Just one mile, he thought, a minute and a half, max, and they'd be at the cars.

As they approached Fifth Street, Chris saw a problem. Firefighters at a department at Hamner and Fifth Street had heard the RSO radio traffic on scanner and took it upon themselves to position an engine across the southbound lanes of Hamner to block traffic headed in the direction of the shootout. With the northbound traffic stopped at a red light, there was only one thing he could do.

Ivan Hopkins was stopped at a red light when something struck his Datsun compact pickup from behind. When he whipped his head around to see what it was, a large yellow utility truck pushed up against his back bumper. Hopkins saw something else too. Manny Delgado now sat on the window frame of the passenger door, his entire torso out of the vehicle. He had ditched the riot gun and was using Chris's HK93, aiming the rifle at Hopkins and screaming for him to move. Before he could react, the yellow pickup began pushing Hopkins's smaller vehicle forward. Hopkins instinctively kept his foot hammered down on the brake, but the yellow truck was too powerful and continued to push him, tires screaming on pavement, into heavy traffic crossing on Fifth Street.

With the truck still blocking their way, Russell Harven vaulted over the side cabinets and ran out into the intersection holding the "Shorty" AR. "Move it or I will blow your motherfucking head off!" he screamed, aiming the rifle at Hopkins from no more than five feet away. Hopkins released the brake on his pickup and accelerated through the intersection.

Instead of running back to the yellow truck, Russ whipped around and leveled the gun at a man named George DeVol standing in the intersection a dozen feet away. DeVol had also heard about the gun battle raging at Fourth and Hamner and, with another man, was attempting to direct southbound traffic down Fifth Street instead. For a moment, Harven and a stunned DeVol stared at each other before DeVol threw himself prone onto the pavement and began to pray. Instead of gunshots, he heard something metal hit the pavement near him. Then the yellow truck pulled up and the gunman scrambled over the tailgate into the back. When they were gone, DeVol found a twenty-round magazine lying in the intersection where the man in the ski mask had been. When he checked, he found it still contained live rounds. Jesus Christ, DeVol wondered, with all the commotion maybe the son of a bitch accidentally hit the release on the magazine port instead of the trigger.

RUSSELL HARVEN HAD BARELY SCRAMBLED BACK TO HIS POSITION BEHIND the cab before the yellow truck had traveled another half mile to Sixth Street, where more cars were backed up at a red light. This time, there was no fire engine, so Chris swung the yellow truck into oncoming lanes and barreled through the intersection, slamming into the side of a car making a left turn off Sixth Street. The big pickup sent Levester Dietsch's Plymouth Champ spinning out of its path. Chris Harven shifted the truck into third gear and stomped on the accelerator, roaring out of the intersection.

Chris Harven had only another quarter mile to reach the Little League field and the cold getaway cars. So far, they had not seen a single cop car on Hamner. Chris pulled into the right lane to pass a slower car. As the truck went by, the driver, Janice Cannon, saw two men in ski masks in the bed. The one standing up began shooting over her car at something on the other side of the road. Cannon looked over and saw a Riverside Sheriff's unit racing down Hamner in the opposite direction, its light bar flashing. When she looked back, the man standing behind the cab swung his gun around, aimed it at her, and fired. Cannon slammed on her brakes and jerked the car onto the right shoulder. She ducked down, cowering in the front seat until someone from the local VFW post ran to check on her.

Riverside deputy Darrell Reed had just crossed over the Santa Ana River bottom southbound on Hamner and crested a rise in the road when he caught sight of the yellow truck. He saw at least two men with rifles aimed at him. Both fired. Reed ducked down in his seat and heard four shots in all before the two vehicles passed each other. It was the second of those shots that went right through the sheriff's star emblazoned on the driver's door of his unit and straight into Reed's left leg just below the knee. *I've been shot*, Reed called over the radio, but it was mostly lost among the flurry of other transmissions.

Reed pulled into the next side street to quickly check the wound. The bleeding was controllable, so he decided not to wait for an ambulance. *They're shooting from the back of the vehicle*, he radioed. *I'm headed to the hospital.*

He resumed southbound on Hamner until he reached deputy Andy Delgado, gun drawn and crouched behind the door of his patrol unit just north of the bank at Fourth Street. He heard Delgado yell something to him about taking up a position or something. "Andy," Reed called back matter-of-factly. "I can't. I've been shot."

Andy stared at Reed for a second and then darted across Hamner to Reed's unit after asking a plainclothes narcotics detective to cover him. He opened the door and helped the wounded deputy out onto the pavement. "I'm going to have to cut those pants to get at it."

"I just bought these pants, Andy," Reed protested.

"Fuck the pants," Delgado said, searching through his first aid kit. "You got a knife on you?" he asked Reed, unable to find his own.

"I thought all you Mexicans carried knives," Reed said, managing to flash Delgado a smile while grimacing in pain from the gunshot.

Andy shook his head, deciding this was one comment he would let slide.

AFTER THE CONFRONTATION WITH IVAN HOPKINS'S BLUE PICKUP AT FIFTH Street, Manny Delgado continued to ride sitting on the window frame, aiming Chris Harven's Heckler over the roof of the cab. When he began firing at Darrell Reed's patrol unit, Chris leaned across the seat, grabbed Manny by the back of his shirt, and yanked him back inside the cab. What the fuck are you doing? Chris screamed. We're just about at the cars. Now we can't stop because you just drew attention to us! Manny wrestled out of his grip and climbed back out to his perch on the window frame just in time to take a last look at his Matador as they passed the Little League fields.

He passed the cars! George Smith screamed to Russ, watching the Matador and Z/28 parked in the Little League lot fade into the distance behind the speeding truck. Why did he pass the fucking cars?

Russ leaned out over the side of the truck and hollered something into the window at his brother. He turned back to Smith. Too many people, too many cops.

Where are we going to go now? George yelled.

Chris pushed the truck past sixty miles per hour north on Hamner, over the Santa Ana River Bridge and into flat farmland and grazing pasture beyond. When Harven downshifted and swung a right turn onto Schleisman Road, George had his answer. They were headed back into Mira Loma. They were going home.

DEPUTY DOUG BORDEN WAS THE FIRST TO COME UPON THE YELLOW TRUCK AT a bend in the road on Schleisman. Borden never saw the truck until it was right on him, guns already blasting away. Borden took evasive action by driving his car into the front yard of a dairy farm. The men fired on him as they passed, punching a hole through a water tank twenty feet above him and spraying gunfire into a pen of milk cows. *The vehicle is on Schleisman headed toward Etiwanda*, a stunned Borden shouted into his mic. *I've been hit by fire.*

Dispatcher Gary Keeter relayed the information. *Riverside t'all, units on Schleisman are being fired on.*

Driving on 68th Street, California Highway Patrol officer Doug Earnest could hardly believe what he was looking at when he saw the yellow truck appear from Schleisman and head toward him. Earnest had been monitoring RSO radio traffic on his scanner and self-dispatched the instant the call turned into an 1199. Only seconds before, he had heard Borden's report of taking fire and now found himself staring down the barrels of three rifles. With more than a dozen years in the field, Earnest thought he had seen everything. But, Jesus, this was like going up against a tank. And what the hell was that guy doing sitting out the passenger window aiming over the roof?

There was a muzzle flash and the telephone pole just outside Earnest's driver's-side window exploded in a hail of wood splinters. Earnest ducked across his seat and heard more than a dozen gunshots go off in the seconds it took for the truck to go by. One tore into the roof and a second into the center post separating the front and rear doors of his patrol car. Even after they were past, Earnest could still hear firing and bullets zinging off the pavement and corral fencing around him. When it stopped, he sat back up, U-turned, and fell in with Borden in pursuit. By then the truck had disappeared, passing the site of the Wineville chicken coop murders and veering off 68th Street onto Holmes Avenue, where Riverside deputy Rolf Parkes was waiting for them.

WITH A NAME THAT BELIED HIS TRUE HERITAGE, ROLF PARKES WAS OF MOSTLY Hawaiian descent, born on the island of Oahu and adopted at birth by a Caucasian, nonnative "haole" couple who lived there. When his parents divorced, Rolf and his mother left the beaches of Waikiki for the beaches of Southern California, where Rolf grew up the only child of a single mother just blocks off the water in the Belmont Shore area of Long Beach. He was a good-looking kid with black hair and dark eyes who, by virtue of local demographics, was assumed to be Hispanic. But once teachers and friends learned he was Hawaiian by blood, it all made perfect sense: the Islander's smile, the smoky complexion, his love of sun and water. It also explained his middle name: Napunako.

Rolf developed a passion for flight at an early age and was soloing a Cessna in the skies above Long Beach by age seventeen. He wanted to be a professional pilot, but with all the veterans returning home from Vietnam in the mid-1970s, the labor market was glutted with experienced fliers. Parkes earned a four-year degree from Long Beach State, worked for a while as an EMT, and then decided to enter police work at the encouragement of some cop friends.

At twenty-seven and with less than two years on the Riverside force, Parkes was highly regarded by his fellow officers. Andy Delgado considered Parkes one of the "lions" on the force: a quiet, brave cop who would be there when you needed him. Reserved by nature, Rolf kept a few close friends on the force but did not fraternize much after work because of the ninety-minute commute back to Long Beach. Rolf liked the ocean, the beach, and his childhood friends too much to move to the landlocked smog belt of Riverside County.

It was Rolf's desire to be closer to Long Beach that led him to accept a lateral move to the Irvine Police Department. He was headed into his final week at the RSO when he arrived for the cover shift the afternoon of May 9, 1980. At the shift briefing, Parkes had tried to grab the Norco beat ahead of Glyn Bolasky to avoid working in Rubidoux, but Bolasky was having none of it, pulling rank on Parkes with a sly smile. Bolasky kept his Norco shift while Rolf hit the streets that day with the call sign 3-Edward-13—*3* for the three-shift, *Edward* for Riverside station, *13* for Rubidoux.

When the 1199 went out, Parkes responded in the direction of Fourth and Hamner by way of Mira Loma. Trying to follow reports of the suspects' location over the increasingly cluttered radio traffic, Rolf listened as every one of his fellow deputies who encountered the bank robbers took fire or was wounded, maybe even killed. He heard Doug Borden report being fired on at Schleisman. The next transmission put the suspects on 68th

Street headed in the direction of Holmes Avenue. Turning off Etiwanda onto Holmes, a two-lane road lined with ramshackle houses, double-wides, and animal pens, it suddenly occurred to Rolf that he might be seconds away from a battle in which he would be outgunned, outmanned, and utterly alone.

Rolf abruptly slowed and pulled his cruiser onto the dirt beside the metal fencing of a horse corral to give him time to consider his options. Before he could make any decisions, the yellow truck appeared, traveling at an ominously slow speed. To Parkes, it did not look like a vehicle fleeing police as much as it did one daring anyone to get close to it. And now it was 150 feet away, headed directly toward him.

At once, three men with rifles simultaneously turned their weapons on Rolf. Bullets ricocheted off the pavement in front of him with a singing sound as they fragmented. Others cracked like bullwhips overhead as they shattered the sound barrier on their way to God knows where. There was the tearing sound of rounds striking his vehicle, ripping through multiple layers of metal, plastic, and glass with a guttural, three-dimensional quality. Fragments lacerated the interior and seats while heavier rounds from George Smith's .308 passed through one side of the vehicle and out the other. Rolf had been around plenty of guns, but this was like nothing he had ever heard before.

Closing in on him, the truck methodically crossed the dotted line, veering into his lane like a trapper walking up to a snared animal to blow its brains out. The fucking thing seemed to amble, in no hurry at all. These sons of bitches are not trying to get away from me, he thought, they are trying to kill me. He was out of options. In the move of a desperate man willing to put anything between himself and death, Rolf Parkes did the only thing he could think of: he rolled up his side window.

A calm resignation came over him. He wondered if he would die slowly or quickly and how much it would hurt. He lay across the bench seat on his right side, all the shit mounted on his dashboard preventing him from getting down on the floorboard. Rounds were already tearing through the interior of the Monaco. He reflexively lifted his left arm up to shield his head, peering out from underneath his elbow.

The truck slowly rolled into his field of view no more than a yard away from his window, drifting by like a pirate ship pulling broadsides on some helpless, wallowing frigate. Time seemed to slow down as they appeared one by one, looking like pirates themselves. The wild eyes of Christopher Harven stared out at him from behind a black ski mask. With one hand on the steering wheel, Harven reached out with the other and fired the .45 Long Colt revolver at point-blank range, the bullets striking the quarter panel and door. Manny Delgado managed to get off a few shots over the top of the cab, gouging ruts in the roof of Parkes's unit. There was an explosion of gunfire coming from multiple weapons and then the face of Russell Harven appeared above Parkes, looming like some sort of insane hillbilly while aiming his rifle down at a violent angle, shooting fish in a barrel. Broken glass sprayed Rolf in the face. He shut his eyes against it. Something whizzed by, cleaving his scalp right down the middle, just above the hairline. Finally, it was George Smith's turn, firing over the edge of the tailgate into the body of the Monaco as they pulled away, the last round from the .308 exploding the back window of the patrol unit.

Rolf could hear the truck accelerate away. He opened his eyes and felt his head. There was only a spotting of blood from a flesh wound on his scalp. A few inches lower and it would have been the proverbial bullet right between the eyes. There was glass all through his hair and a stinging in his right eye, but Rolf Parkes knew the impossible had just happened: He had survived.

PARKES SETTLED HIMSELF BEHIND THE WHEEL OF THE MONACO. I HAVE ONE week left in this place, he thought to himself. Do I need this shit? With just about every window blown out except the windshield, bullet holes through the doors, fenders, hood, and roof, and his hair parted down the middle by a round from a .223, who would blame him for shutting it down and calling it a career at the RSO? But the thought did not last. Parkes just didn't have it in him to bail out on his partners in the middle of a fight.

Fred Chisholm passed Rolf's position, having just had his own harrowing head-on confrontation with the yellow truck a hundred feet beyond Parkes.

Chisholm drifted by, staring in disbelief that Rolf was not dead amid the destruction of the Monaco. *You okay, Rolf?* he asked over the radio. Parkes nodded yes, pulling a U-turn and taking the lead in the pursuit. Chisholm fell in behind Parkes as the CHP unit with Doug Earnest at the wheel suddenly came flying off 68th Street and onto Holmes, itself riddled with gunfire but most decidedly back in the hunt.

At the far end of Holmes, Parkes could see the yellow truck, George Smith sitting in military sharpshooter pose with one leg tucked under him, rifle stock resting on the other knee, still peeling off round after round in their direction. Under heavy fire again, Parkes grabbed his mic and radioed that the truck was coming up to the T-intersection at Etiwanda Avenue. *3-Edward-13, behind the vehicle. They have fired on us. They have high-powered rifles.* It was the first time anyone had mentioned that important fact.

Approaching the pursuit head on, Deputy Herman Brown radioed back to Parkes. *I'm at Etiwanda and Limonite at this time.*

Parkes responded with an urgent warning to Brown and anyone else who might be in the path of the yellow truck. *Get your shotgun out immediately! They are firing numerous rounds.*

Just around the corner at the intersection of Etiwanda and Limonite, Brown along with Riverside deputies Dave "Mad Dog" Madden and Ken McDaniels were only moments away from finding themselves directly in the path of the yellow truck.

SIRENS WAILED FROM ALL SIDES AS CHRIS TOOK A HARD LEFT AT A T-intersection off Holmes, northbound onto Etiwanda. Russ flipped the magazine on the AR, locked in a full one, and then steadied the gun between the two acetylene tanks and waited. Coming up on a busy four-way intersection at which Chris had no intention of slowing down, Riverside deputies were suddenly everywhere.

The first took a right turn off the cross street, Limonite, and was no more than twenty-five feet away when both Manny and Russ opened up on him. Deputy Herman Brown knew the truck might pop out somewhere on Etiwanda, but never expected it to be right on top of him. The moment he saw the truck and the two gun barrels aimed at him, Brown ducked his head and heard his windshield shatter. There was a cascade of gunfire and more bullets tore into his unit. Brown never saw it, but as the truck passed him going the other way, Chris Harven stuck the Long Colt out the driver's window and fired into his unit.

Brown attempted to make an evasive maneuver onto a side street, but a pickup truck suddenly pulled up to the stop sign. Brown jerked the wheel hard and threw his car into a sideways slide to avoid the truck, tearing his rear tire off the rim and coming to a stop on 63rd Street facing Etiwanda.

Brown sat staring at his shattered windshield in disbelief. It did not feel as though he had been shot, but his body seemed to sting everywhere. He felt blood on his neck and coming from his left knee. His left arm burned. A bullet from a .223 had struck his hood just below the windshield and fragmented, penetrating his left arm with more than one hundred tiny shards of copper jacketing from his shoulder down to his wrist. Another had come through the door, also fragmenting enough to puncture his leg with fifteen shards while leaving half of the slug buried so deep into his knee it would never be taken out. But it was the first bullet that should have killed him. That one had punched a hole through his windshield and grazed the back of his neck. Had Herman Brown not ducked the instant he saw rifle barrels pointed at him, he would have been shot through the face.

Turning onto Etiwanda directly behind Brown had been a green pickup truck driven by Gilbert Peña. Peña was on his way home from work when he decided to stop at a grocery store at Limonite and Etiwanda. Making a left turn onto Etiwanda behind Brown, Peña's windshield suddenly shattered and he felt something graze the side of his face. More bullets struck Peña's truck, shattering his rear window. Then his side mirror blew up. He saw a yellow truck pass him and the face of a man who seemed to be sitting out of the passenger window. The man was still shooting at him. Peña dove to the floorboard of his pickup. Two more bullets came through his door, and another missed the cab and went through his tailgate. And then it suddenly stopped. He could still hear gunfire, but it was getting farther away. He opened the door and stepped out of his truck, dazed.

A woman rushed up to him. "Are you hurt?" Patricia Sanchez asked breathlessly, seeing blood on Peña's face and shirt.

"Well, I don't know," Peña answered, feeling his body. "What happened?"

"Didn't you see that son of a bitch with a machine gun?" said Sanchez.

THE NEXT TO TAKE FIRE AT LIMONITE AND ETIWANDA WAS DAVE MADDEN. MIN-utes earlier, Mad Dog had been listening to the radio traffic and predicted the truck would come out on Etiwanda near Limonite. Reaching the inter-section, Madden threw the release on his shotgun, grabbed the weapon, and positioned himself in a field a few dozen feet off Etiwanda. Madden's plan was to empty his shotgun through the front windshield of the truck the in-stant it turned off Holmes. A moment later, he heard another radio report on the suspect vehicle that made him change his prediction and race off in the direction of Hamner.

When he heard the truck had changed its direction again, Madden sped back toward Etiwanda, receiving the warning from Parkes *to get your shotgun out immediately* seconds before making the right turn, falling in just behind Gilbert Peña. By the time he saw the yellow truck, all Mad Dog could do was jam on the brakes and duck beneath the dashboard. The two vehicles passed each other so quickly that the men shooting from the back barely had time to fire off a couple of rounds at Madden before they were through the intersection at Limonite.

Had Madden held his original position, it was possible he could have killed both Chris Harven and Manny Delgado with four shotgun blasts through the windshield at close range, ending the pursuit right there. For years, Dave Madden would roll the sequence of events over and over in his mind, wondering . . . What if?

Madden turned around and fell into the pursuit line behind Parkes, Chisolm, and Doug Earnest. Seeing deputy Herman Brown's unit shot up on 63rd Street, Madden slowed. "You okay?" he mouthed. Brown looked dazed, but waved Madden off. Mad Dog took off after the truck while radioing dispatch. *Officer hit, Etiwanda and 63rd.*

DEPUTY KEN MCDANIELS WAS THE THIRD MAN TO BE SHOT AT THE INTERSEC-tion of Limonite and Etiwanda. McDaniels had been approaching on Limonite when he saw the yellow truck blow through the intersection in front of him, one gunman standing in the bed and another out the passenger window aiming a rifle over the top of the cab. Although the yellow truck raced across the intersection at high speed, McDaniels was sure he had seen something on the face of the man leaning out of the cab window. He would testify later that the man had been smiling.

McDaniels, who had planned to be at his last radiation session that afternoon until the doctor realized they had miscalculated the number of treatments, turned left on Etiwanda less than a hundred feet behind the truck. As he straightened his unit out of the turn, he took a round from George Smith's .308 through his windshield that fragmented on impact, penetrated the heavy metal screen between the front and back seats, and blew out his entire rear window. McDaniels felt a sharp pain in his right shoulder. *I've been hit*, he radioed. Hearing even more gunfire whizzing by his window, McDaniels pulled his unit to the side of the road and ducked down. A car skidded to a stop beside him.

"You okay?" Doug Earnest asked him from his CHP unit.

"Yeah, but we are taking fire right now," McDaniels called out to him.

"I know," Earnest replied. "I already got too close to these guys once." The next moment, the big patrolman was gone, taking off directly into the firing line of George Smith.

McDaniels pushed himself up in the seat, pulled back onto the road, and headed north on Etiwanda until he reached the Pedley firehouse. He stopped in front of the engine bay doors to check how badly he had been injured. He was bleeding through his uniform.

The fire chief at Pedley had been monitoring the pursuit on scanner and ran out when he saw McDaniels. "What the hell is going on out there?" the chief asked.

"I think I just got shot," McDaniels said, unbuttoning his shirt to see where he had been hit. "It's not bad," he said, ready to rejoin the pursuit.

"No way," the firefighter said, opening the passenger door and jumping in beside McDaniels so he could not drive away. "You're going to the hospital."

McDaniels shook his head and grabbed the mic. *I'm on my way to the hospital*, he radioed. *I took a round in the shoulder.*

When the transmission came in from Ken McDaniels to RSO dispatch, Gary Keeter, Gladys Wiza, and Sharon Markum looked up from what they were doing. Only twelve minutes and twenty-seven seconds since Keeter's initial 211 dispatch and they already had five deputies wounded. The shooting of McDaniels, Herman Brown, and civilian Gilbert Peña—the last of which dispatch still knew nothing about—had occurred on a one-hundred-yard stretch of Etiwanda in a matter of ten seconds. Now reports had the yellow truck leaving Wineville and headed into the neighborhood of Mira Loma. As unimaginable as the first twelve and half minutes had been, something told Gary Keeter things were about to get worse.

7

THE GRAVEYARD
OF CARS

May 9, 1980. Mira Loma, California.

ROLF PARKES HAD JUST CROSSED THROUGH THE INTERSECTION OF LIMONITE and Etiwanda when a round from George Smith's .308 whistled through his windshield, hissing maliciously as it passed within inches of his head before blowing out what remained of his back window. Parkes lay on the brakes and pulled his Dodge Monaco patrol unit onto the dirt shoulder.

The moment Parkes pulled over, Smith put a round into Fred Chisholm's radiator. The rookie slid his cruiser onto the shoulder behind Parkes, dove out of the vehicle, and lay down behind it for cover. Seeing the RSO units on the side of the road, Dave Madden pulled behind them while taking fire himself. "This guy's got us dialed in," Parkes told him. "We gotta give him some space." Madden agreed. *We're gonna have to lay back because of the amount of rounds they're firing at us,* he radioed dispatch.

Doug Earnest thought differently. Notoriously aggressive in vehicle pursuits, CHP officers took it very personally when a motorist tried to outrun them, and as a personal defeat whenever one succeeded. Earnest was already feeling very insulted by these clowns for shooting up his patrol unit at 68th and Schleisman. It was no surprise then that after pausing momentarily to check on the wounded McDaniels, Earnest was right back in the fray, this time at lead position in the pursuit line. After pulling over to give George Smith's .308 a few hundred yards of space, Dave Madden pulled into the number-two spot behind Earnest with Parkes and Chisholm right behind.

A good quarter mile ahead of him, Earnest saw the yellow truck take a hard right off Etiwanda onto 54th Street, the road marking the southern border of the suburban neighborhood of Mira Loma. As aggressive as they might be, the CHP were anything but reckless, easily the most highly skilled and well trained in the business of chasing down a fleeing suspect. Earnest knew better than to come barreling around a blind corner in a pursuit. When he got to 54th Street, he slowed to a crawl and began to edge the nose of his Dodge patrol unit into the intersection. Immediately two rounds tore into the metal hood of his vehicle. Through a break in the shrubbery that had been blocking his view, he saw the truck at a dead stop in the roadway just a half block down 54th, three men aiming rifles back at him. Doug Earnest had just been ambushed. Only his instincts and training had saved him.

With rounds striking the nose of Earnest's patrol unit, above him the newest entry into the pursuit arrived on scene. Riverside Police helicopter Baker-1 with spotter Paul Benoit on board had finally located the pursuit and swooped in to hover five hundred feet above the yellow truck. The loud chopping of the rotor blades drew the gun barrels of George, Russ, and Manny away from Doug Earnest.

Shoot the fucking thing down, George said, lifting the barrel of the .308 skyward. But before he could get off a shot, Chris hit the accelerator again. As George and Russ tumbled across the bed, the truck raced a hundred yards up 54th and then left onto Troth Street, plunging into the heart of Mira Loma.

IT WAS A BUSY TIME OF DAY FOR MIRA LOMA, ESPECIALLY ON A FRIDAY. KIDS were still returning from school, dozens of them walking along the dirt shoulders or in school buses working their way through the four-square-mile grid of suburban homes. Many of the adults had ended their workweek early and were already home watering their lawns, checking their mailboxes, or chatting with neighbors in the driveway. But now the residents of Mira Loma stopped and turned their eyes to watch Baker-1 overhead. The wail of sirens began to fill the air, coming closer as the sound of gunfire reached their ears for the first time. In an area familiar with trouble, it was obvious to the people of Mira Loma that something very big was on its way.

The moment the yellow truck with masked men standing in the back shooting in all directions entered Troth Avenue, children and adults scattered, diving behind parked cars or fleeing back into their houses. Chris zigzagged his way through the neighborhood to confound any attempt by Baker-1 to establish an intercept point for the units on the ground. One block up Troth, right one block on Jurupa, left onto Marlatt ... With Baker-1 outside its usual Riverside City patrol area, Paul Benoit was less familiar with the street names and could not always keep up. The narrow streets lined with houses, rows of oleander, and cinder block walls built right up to the road prevented pursuing units from getting a visual on anything coming at them from a side street. With only a general idea of the location of their suspects, most never saw the yellow truck until it was right on them.

Rolf Parkes had anticipated the truck's direction and was limping his shot-up unit along Marlatt when the truck suddenly appeared from his left coming off Jurupa, making a left turn directly in front of him. All three gunmen opened up on him, hitting his vehicle again. Parkes felt the Monaco pull sharply to the side. He slowed down and rolled toward the intersection ahead.

Doug Earnest's CHP unit came out of Jurupa directly in front of Parkes and turned up Marlatt in close pursuit of the truck. Way too close, in Parkes's opinion. Earnest was trailing the truck as closely as fifty feet at times, despite taking constant gunfire.

Dave Madden came up Marlatt and slowed beside Parkes to see if he was okay.

They're northbound, go, go. Go, go, go! Parkes radioed, motioning Madden on. *Northbound! GO!*

Madden took off, but not before he radioed Parkes. *You got a flat tire, Rolf.*

Fred Chisholm appeared from Jurupa Road and skidded to a stop. *Pull over, get your shotgun, and come on*, he radioed Parkes.

Rolf grabbed the gun and jumped in the passenger seat beside Chisholm, leaving the Monaco dead on the side of the road. Chisholm took off again, driving with his head below the dashboard, telescoping up only long enough to keep the car on the road. "Where are they, Rolf?" the jittery rookie asked repeatedly. "Can you see them?" For the moment, Rolf could not.

Like Chisholm, Doug Earnest was now driving mostly with his head ducked down below the dashboard. He did not see the truck make a sudden right turn onto 50th Street, and drove straight through the intersection without turning. A young boy ran out onto Marlatt, pointing wildly down 50th. Earnest slammed on the brakes, threw his patrol car into reverse, tires screeching, and headed east on 50th over a low rise in the road. When he crested the hill midblock, the yellow truck was stopped in the middle of the road less than fifty feet in front of him. They're ambushing me again, Earnest thought, laying on the brakes. But this time the men in the truck did not fire on him, never even pointed their guns in his direction. They all seemed to be looking at a house near the corner of Dodd and 50th. Earnest did not know that the men were looking at their own house, assessing their chances of bailing out of the truck and into their barbed wire compound and the safety of the pit.

Chris knew it was impossible with Baker-1 overhead and cops traversing the neighborhood. George had far too much faith in their little fortress with its half-built tunnel anyhow. It was one thing to hold off starving marauders staggering around a postapocalyptic wasteland, but quite another to take a stand against a SWAT team with a helicopter circling overhead. Chris hit the gas and turned left up Dodd toward Bellegrave Avenue, a major road to the north just a few blocks away.

When Doug Earnest tried to follow, a school bus full of kids obliviously turned in front of him, getting between him and the truck. He jockeyed for position until he was finally able to swing his patrol unit around the bus and race past it. Behind him, Dave Madden did the same. By then, however, Earnest had lost sight of the truck. He put out a transmission to warn patrolman

Bill Crowe, the other CHP officer in the vicinity, which direction the truck had been headed. It was a transmission Earnest would regret making for the rest of his life.

BILL CROWE WAS A RELATIVE LATECOMER TO LAW ENFORCEMENT, JOINING the California Highway Patrol in his late twenties. Originally from Detroit, Crowe moved around a lot as a child, joined the army in 1965, and, like George Smith, was trained in artillery, including tactical nuclear battlefield weapons. After the service, he moved to California, tried his hand at a few different jobs, and began taking college classes at night. When he finally decided to take a shot at police work, he was one of three applicants out of thousands to be offered a position with the elite California Highway Patrol.

Crowe was sent to the Santa Ana station in the heart of Orange County for training and assigned to work alongside a six-year veteran named Doug Earnest. Earnest took to Crowe immediately. Seven years older, six foot six inches tall, and 250 pounds to Crowe's five foot nine, 150 pounds, Earnest looked after Crowe as he would a little brother. The two men grew close. Although Crowe was more than capable on his own in the field, Earnest remained protective of him even after Crowe completed his training. Earnest seemed to appear whenever Crowe called for backup, no matter what beat he was covering that day.

But on May 9, 1980, they were covering the same beat: Interstate 15 and the Pomona Freeway in the area of Norco, Rubidoux, and Mira Loma. Unlike Earnest, Crowe did not have a scanner and could not hear Riverside Sheriff's radio traffic. He learned of the 1199 in Norco only when Earnest radioed to CHP that he was self-dispatching to the scene of an officer down. Crowe finished issuing a ticket to a motorist on the Pomona Freeway, jumped in his patrol car, and headed for Hamner Avenue, sometimes reaching speeds of up to one hundred miles per hour on the wide surface streets. His only information about the location and direction of the suspect vehicle came from Earnest's updates over the CHP frequency.

Doug Earnest was doing his best to feed Crowe as much current information as possible, even while under heavy fire. Crowe had once lived in the area and knew the streets relatively well, but Earnest did not want him stumbling into heavy gunfire at a blind intersection. Following Earnest's reports, Crowe was eastbound on Bellegrave when he saw Riverside deputy A. J. Reynard standing beside his vehicle at Troth Street stopping traffic. Crowe hit the brakes and used the external PA speaker on his roof to relay the latest information from Earnest. "They're northbound on Dodd, headed for Bellegrave right up there," he called. Riverside deputy Rudy Romo pulled beside Crowe and together they sped off, hoping to get a roadblock set up at Dodd before the suspects arrived there first. Reynard scrambled to his unit and raced to catch up.

Bellegrave Avenue was a long, straight, two-lane stretch of road marking the northern boundary of Mira Loma. On the north side was nothing but pasture and vineyards. To the south, the side streets of Mira Loma terminated at T-intersections every quarter mile. Martin, Troth, Marlatt, Dodd, Bain. After that, Bellegrave intersected busy Van Buren Boulevard. After hearing Earnest's latest transmission, Bill Crowe covered the half mile from Troth to Dodd in less than a minute with Romo following behind and Reynard trailing a hundred feet back.

Above in Baker-1, Paul Benoit could see what was unfolding beneath him. The yellow truck coming up Dodd and the three police units eastbound on Bellegrave were going to reach the intersection at the same time. *Better advise those units on Bellegrave they are approaching that vehicle at this time*, he radioed urgently.

Had there not been an open dirt lot on the corner of Dodd, Bill Crowe probably would have crashed his CHP unit into the yellow truck without ever seeing it as it blew the stop sign onto Bellegrave. As it was, Crowe was fifty feet short of the intersection when he looked across the field and caught sight of the yellow truck speeding up Dodd with Russell Harven standing in the bed firing. Crowe slammed on the brakes and went into a skid.

The first volley strafed the entire right side of Crowe's patrol car, rounds going through the front fender and both side doors, shattering the rear passenger-side window, and blowing out the two tires on that side. Crowe stood on the brake as his skidding unit continued to close in on the yellow truck now making the right off Dodd onto Bellegrave directly in front of him. By the time his vehicle came to a stop in the middle of the intersection, he was only twenty feet behind the tailgate of the truck. He was so close, in fact, that Russell Harven had to point the "Shorty" AR at a downward angle in order to shoot Bill Crowe through the windshield of his patrol car.

The first bullet from Harven went through the right side and out the rear window, shattering it. The second hit dead center, tore the rearview mirror in half, and fragmented, sending shards of copper into Crowe's arm and leg, lodging others under his scalp and in his sternum. Another pierced a hole through the soft pinna tissue of his ear. Crowe was ducking for cover when the last bullet came through the driver's side of the windshield, entered his body through his left bicep, tunneled through the flesh of his upper arm, and exited his back just above the shoulder blade. The truck sped away, leaving Bill Crowe stunned and bleeding in the front seat of his CHP unit.

Rudy Romo had also jammed on the brakes in a hail of gunfire at the same time Crowe did. He ducked below the line of his dashboard the instant before a bullet came through the windshield and blew the headrest clean off the driver's seat above him. Like Parkes and Brown before him, Rudy Romo had come within inches of taking a direct head shot from an assault rifle.

While Russ and George were keeping their weapons firmly trained on the police cars converging on them from Bellegrave, Manny Delgado was firing wildly at anything that caught his eye. Immediately after making the turn onto Bellegrave, he sprayed gunfire into two civilian vehicles headed the opposite direction, hitting both. Passing a third car pulled over on the far side of the road, Delgado pivoted and sent two rounds through the back window, nearly hitting the two passengers taking cover inside. When Russ spotted three young boys riding their bikes on the dirt shoulder of the road, he screamed at them to get back. But as the truck roared by, Manny turned his AR on the group and fired at close range. One of the children fell off his bike with a scream, a bullet from the .223 having clipped the end of a finger as he gripped the handlebars of his Stingray.

With the first two police cars now shot up and sideways in the road,

George and Russ watched as a third steadily closed in on them from be-hind. While George reloaded, Russ leveled the "Shorty" AR and fired three rounds directly through the windshield. The car just kept coming. When it got within twenty feet of them, Russ noticed something very strange: There was no one driving the car.

But there was. Inside the ghost ship RSO unit, the youngest deputy on the force, A. J. Reynard, was lying across the front seat of Kurt Franklin's 511 car, pinning the accelerator to the floor, with blood running down his arm and absolutely no idea that he was headed straight into the back end of a truck with two men firing assault rifles at him.

Reynard never saw the yellow truck that day. Approaching Dodd, he came up fast on Crowe and Romo, planning to join the two men in forming a road-block at the intersection. As he slowed and pulled alongside Romo, he glanced over in time to see Romo duck out of sight. An instant later, a bullet came through the bottom right corner of Reynard's windshield followed by a sec-ond round that blew out his rear passenger-side window. Thinking the gunfire must be coming from the field directly to the right of him, A. J. ducked down across his seat and stomped on the accelerator to get clear of the line of fire. He did not know that the men shooting at him were actually in the back of a truck coming up Dodd. With his head ducked down below the dashboard, he never saw the suspect vehicle turn onto Bellegrave directly in front of him.

When Russ Harven opened up on him, Reynard heard three rounds smash through his windshield and then it felt as though someone grabbed ahold of his arm and jerked it off the steering wheel. When he looked, there was a large hole on the inside of his left elbow and blood was rushing out onto the radio, dashboard, and paperwork beside him on the seat. Assuming he was still headed away from the source of the gunfire, Reynard punched the accelerator to the floor. He reached up with his bloody arm and grabbed the steering wheel again, not realizing he was now hanging off the rear bumper of the yellow truck just feet away from the business end of a "Shorty" AR.

Five hundred feet overhead in Baker-1, a dumbfounded Paul Benoit radi-oed an urgent message over the RSO frequency. *Riverside, you better tell that unit to back off.*

In all, Reynard traveled over a quarter mile down Bellegrave at full acceleration without looking up once. With Russ Harven just about to unload on Reynard at arm's length, Chris Harven spotted a two-car police roadblock just ahead and turned sharply right onto Bain Street. Reynard kept going.

Baker-1, the [suspect] has just turned southbound off of Bellegrave, the SO unit just passed him, Benoit radioed.

When A. J. Reynard finally did peek up over the dashboard, he was headed straight at two RSO units blocking the road in front of him. He moved his foot over to the brake and slammed it down, pitching the front end of the 511 car forward into a hard slide. The Impala, with its windows blown out, its body riddled with bullet holes, and front seat soaked in blood, came skidding to a stop in front of one of the deputies manning the roadblock. It was Kurt Franklin.

The other deputy, Bill Eldrich, helped Reynard out of the Impala and looked at his elbow. "Let's just take him to Riverside General in one of our units," Eldrich said.

The amped-up Reynard was having none of it. "Fuck that," he said, pulling away from Eldrich. He drew his .38 and gripped it in his left hand. "Look, I can still hold a gun," he said to Franklin, raising the weapon in the air to demonstrate.

"Uh-huh," Franklin said, looking past Reynard at the demolished vehicle sideways in the road. "That's not my 511 car, is it?" he asked.

DOUG EARNEST HAD BEEN MAKING UP GROUND ON THE YELLOW TRUCK ON Dodd when he approached the intersection at Bellegrave. When he saw the CHP unit racing toward the intersection, he knew it was Crowe, but it was too late to warn him off. With the first crack of gunfire, Crowe's unit went into a full skid. *I'm hit!* Earnest heard Crowe cry out over the CHP radio frequency. There was more gunfire and Crowe's unit seemed to disintegrate before Earnest's eyes, exploding from the inside out, glass and metal flying in all directions.

Earnest was out of his own vehicle almost before Crowe's had come to a sliding stop just short of Dodd. He sprinted to his fellow patrolman's unit and jerked open the passenger-side door, using it for cover as rounds continued to hit the asphalt around them and snap overhead. Crowe was sitting up, but leaning to the passenger side of the vehicle, his arms limp at his sides, eyes glassy and fixed, staring straight ahead. There was blood coming down his face, in his hair, on his uniform and still-holstered gun. Earnest called his name. Crowe did not respond. He's dead, Earnest thought, and it's my fault. I'm the one who guided him straight into the truck and they killed him.

Rudy Romo reached Crowe's patrol car and pulled open the driver's door. "Shit," he said when he saw the CHP officer sitting unresponsive in the seat. But at least the guy was breathing. "He's going into shock," Romo told Earnest. Earnest ran back to his own unit, retrieved a first aid kit, and came around to the driver's door. He called out sharply to Crowe. This time Crowe responded and began to sit up in the seat, still pale and waxy but at least somewhat coherent.

Dave Madden emerged out of Dodd Street and pulled beside Crowe's disabled unit. Madden could hear rounds passing overhead with a high-pitched crack! "Do you need help?" Madden called out to Earnest.

Earnest knew Mad Dog and was relieved to see him there, but no one was going to take care of Bill Crowe but Doug Earnest. "No. Go get those bastards," Earnest called back to him. "I'll take care of my own man."

Of all the wounds, the arm concerned Earnest the most. As he began wrapping the wound, a young photo journalist for the *Riverside Press-Enterprise* named Jim Edwards appeared at the passenger door and quickly snapped the photo of Earnest bandaging Crowe that would appear on the front pages of newspapers across the country the next day. Edwards and writer James Richardson had been alerted to events while monitoring the police scanner in the newsroom. Jumping in separate cars, they each raced toward the action. Edwards intercepted it perfectly, but Earnest was not happy to see him, barking at Edwards to get the fuck out of there. Edwards got his photo and leapt back into his car, speeding off to catch up with the pursuit.

Rolf Parkes and Fred Chisholm came out onto Bellegrave from Marlatt and raced eastbound to Dodd. What they found there shocked them. A CHP unit was cockeyed in the road, utterly destroyed, a seriously wounded patrolman being worked on inside. Beside it, Rudy Romo's unit had a hole through the windshield and the back window was completely blown out. Parked a dozen feet away was Doug Earnest's patrol car, its hood and sides punched through with bullet holes. Facing the opposite direction were three civilian cars shot up and disabled, their occupants standing in the road, either stunned or hysterical.

Riverside, 3-Edward-13, Parkes called into the mic, his voice straining above the sirens and chaos around him. *Roll an ambulance to Bellegrave and Dodd. Officer shot!*

Copy. Bellegrave and Dodd. Officer shot, Keeter acknowledged flatly. *Ambulance en route. We'll also roll rescue.* That was six men down.

Moments later, Kurt Franklin was on the radio. *2-Edward-73. I am transporting Officer Reynard, he's taken a round in the arm, to the hospital.*

Now Keeter was confused. *10-4. Is this the officer from Bellegrave and Dodd?*

No, he's a CHP officer, Dave Madden corrected.

At RSO dispatch, Keeter, Wiza, and Markum were too overwhelmed trying to keep up with all the phone calls and transmissions to say anything to each other, but they were all thinking the same thing: Reynard was number seven.

There remained confusion in the field over the status of hostages. *Do we have hostages on this vehicle that's shootin' everybody?* a lieutenant inquired. *That's unknown*, Keeter answered.

People were everywhere on Bellegrave now, jumping out of their cars or streaming from houses onto front lawns, all feverishly pointing Parkes and Chisholm in the direction that the truck had fled. Trying to decipher the reports coming from Baker-1, the two deputies headed toward the major intersection of Bellegrave and Van Buren Boulevard, passing the shot-up 511 car on the way. Passing the ruins of seven vehicles within a single block, Rolf Parkes decided on a name for the place. He called it "The Graveyard of Cars."

ON BAIN STREET, A HALF BLOCK SOUTH OF BELLEGRAVE, DOROTHY CRAIG WAS in her kitchen when she heard the deafening sound of the helicopter flying low over her house. Running out to her front yard, she saw a yellow utility truck cruising by at an almost leisurely pace. There was one man sitting out of the passenger window and two more seated in the bed of the truck. All three were aiming what appeared to be assault rifles straight up into the air. Then she realized they were firing up at the helicopter.

When they reached the end of the block, Chris Harven made the right turn onto 50th and accelerated. Passing their own house again, Harven did not even bother to slow down. There was no point. They had not been able to drive off Baker-1, the sound of the blades still chopping the air right above them. They would never see the Mira Loma house again.

Unharmed and only vaguely aware they might have been fired upon, Baker-1 continued tracking at low altitude, radioing out the location. Chris Harven pushed the truck to forty-five miles an hour on 50th Street back toward Etiwanda. As far as Chris was concerned, Mira Loma was a lost cause. They just needed to get the fuck out of there as fast as possible. There was another thing they needed to do: get a different vehicle. Every cop in the Inland Empire must be looking for a bright yellow pickup at this point and it wasn't exactly hard to spot. Taking the right turn northbound onto Etiwanda at high speed, Harven saw an opportunity to swap out their ride.

At the southeast corner of Etiwanda and Bellegrave was a small mom-and-pop convenience store called the Can Do Market. As usual, it was busy on a Friday with at least a dozen cars parked in the small lot outside. A railroad crew of about fifteen men stood around a picnic table, finishing off their workweek with a few beers in the shade of a cottonwood. A white panel van waited its turn at one of the two gas pumps in front. Chris cut sharply into the market parking area, scattering the terrified customers.

From Baker-1, Paul Benoit could see the chaotic scene unfolding below him and tried to relay the information as best he could. *Baker-1, suspects are bailing out of the vehicle, it appears it's going to be at Etiwanda and Bellegrave. There are a couple of people still in the vehicle. Vehicle is still moving. There is a small red brick building. A couple of the suspects apparently rushed inside. I don't know if they are suspects or people running from this vehicle.*

Harven brought the yellow truck to a stop beside the white van waiting to get gas, grabbed the Long Colt, and jumped out of the truck while Manny Delgado leapt from the passenger side waving the Heckler. Behind the wheel of his 1974 GMC van, a Vietnam veteran named Robert LeMay was about to pull forward to an open pump when Chris Harven appeared at the driver's window aiming the Long Colt at his head. "You better get the fuck out of there," Harven yelled at him. LeMay looked down the barrel of the gun and then looked at Harven. He then did what he thought would be wise considering the circumstances: He drove away.

With their intended target now gone and more than a dozen burly railroad workers staring at them, there was nothing left to do but pile back into the yellow truck and get the hell out of the Can Do Market. Manny Delgado moved back to the passenger side while leveling the Heckler at the railroad workers, sending them diving to the dirt.

Vehicle at this time is resuming its northbound traffic on Etiwanda, Baker-1 updated. *Northbound again.*

The moment the yellow truck crossed Bellegrave, every cop in the Inland Empire knew exactly where it was headed. These bank robbers were doing what every bank robber in Southern California does: They were headed for the freeway. Only these bank robbers had headed there way too late.

Vehicle is still northbound, approaching Highway 60, Paul Benoit announced from Baker-1.

For the first time that day, dispatcher Gary Keeter sounded almost defeated as he relayed the information. *Northbound, coming to Highway 60*, he said wearily. The men who had just robbed a bank and shot seven cops and five civilians in his county were not only leaving Mira Loma, they were escaping Riverside County entirely. For the last twenty-one minutes, Keeter had been dealing with a complete disaster. Now he would have to inform the San Bernardino Sheriff's Office that the disaster was most likely headed straight into their county.

8

INTERSTATE

May 9, 1980. San Bernardino County, California.

RACING EASTBOUND ON BELLEGRAVE IN AN UNMARKED BROWN FORD CROWN Victoria with its dash-mounted emergency light whirling away was Riverside sheriff's detective Joe Szeles. *Don't forget to put on your raid jackets*, he heard someone radio the responding units, referring to the bulletproof vests every RSO officer in the field carried in their vehicle. Szeles pulled over and quickly threw on the vest before speeding off again, hoping to intercept the suspect vehicle at Etiwanda.

As Szeles approached the intersection at high speed, the yellow truck suddenly bolted out of the Can Do Market and crossed Bellegrave directly in front of him. The detective slowed sharply and jerked the wheel to the left, falling in just thirty feet behind the tailgate of the truck. Within seconds, a man in a ski mask standing in the back peeled off three rounds at Szeles. The gunman then coolly ejected the spent magazine, replaced it with a fresh one, and resumed firing.

Edward-214, the veteran detective radioed in his calm, clear voice. *I am behind the vehicle northbound. They are hooded subjects. Just put another clip in the weapon and fired at this officer.*

The ease with which the gunman handled the rifle left an impression on

Szeles. "The suspect was not fumbling with the clip," he wrote afterward in his incident report, "but precisely placed it in the weapon as if he knew how to handle the weapon."

Dropping back one hundred feet and zigzagging back and forth in an evasive maneuver, Szeles was acutely aware that he was alone in the pursuit. "There were no other black and white units or other plain units in the area at that time," his incident report would read. Of the dozens of police units that had engaged the suspects so far, those who had not been wounded or had their vehicles shot out from under them were now being diverted to the Can Do Market to address the possibility of a hostage situation inside.

Szeles knew his suspects were headed for the Pomona Freeway, the local name for Highway 60, but from there . . . where? If they went east on the Pomona, they would be headed back into Riverside and nothing but cops all the way to Palm Springs. Westbound and they would quickly find themselves in Los Angeles County. L.A. had shitloads of cops and heavily armed SWAT teams strategically placed throughout the county. In L.A., they shot suspects from helicopters. If those guys want to go into L.A. County, be my fucking guest, thought Szeles.

Szeles had a suspicion where they might be headed: Interstate 15 North. Three lanes in each direction, the newly extended I-15 went straight through San Bernardino County on a stretch known as the Devore Freeway before bisecting the San Gabriel Mountains through the Cajon Pass. After that, it was a whole lot of nothing until Las Vegas. But nobody was stupid enough to try to outrun the cops across two hundred miles of the wide-open Mojave Desert. If these guys went north on I-15, they were headed for San Bernardino National Forest, 1,200 square miles of winding mountain roads, deep canyons, and rugged wilderness. The nearest access to the San Gabriels was sixteen miles away at the Sierra Avenue off-ramp and then straight up Lytle Creek Canyon Road. In Southern California, bank robbers headed for the freeway. But there was another place bank robbers went, especially with the sheriff on their tail: They headed for the hills.

Just as Szeles expected, once on the Pomona Freeway, the truck stayed in the right lane heading for the transition ramp to I-15 North, just a quarter mile ahead. With traffic unusually light for a Friday afternoon, Szeles followed the truck on the Pomona Freeway. Driving at over fifty-five miles per hour, Szeles looked on in amazement as one of the gunmen in the back of the truck suddenly climbed on top of the metal cabinets, leaned far over the side, pulled open the passenger door, and swung inside. The truck took the sweeping on-ramp onto Interstate 15 and accelerated to sixty-five miles per hour. Moments later, the passenger door flew open again and the man climbed back over the cabinets and into the bed of the truck. Szeles was so stunned he never even radioed it in.

Szeles would have been even more amazed to know that Manny Delgado had actually made the trip three times, once while holding a rifle. After climbing from the cab to the back of the truck, George had yelled at Delgado to go back and ask Chris where he was headed. That's when Manny began the round-trip journey witnessed by Szeles. *He knows where the fuck I'm going!* Chris barked at him after Manny reappeared in the cab beside him. Manny opened the door and returned to the rear.

George handed the Heckler back up to Manny. Without a word, Delgado began firing on the only cop car still chasing them, a brown Crown Victoria with its dashboard light flashing. George set his .308 to the side, dug deep into the pockets of his duster, and pulled out the two beer-can grenades he had carried into the bank. Ducking low behind the cabinets to shelter the wind, Smith used his Zippo to light the fuse and then tossed the hissing grenade over the tailgate before it went off in his hands. The bomb skipped over the asphalt, trailing the truck for a few seconds before losing speed. The Crown Victoria gained on the grenade and then drove directly over it.

To Joe Szeles, it sounded like a shotgun blast going off just behind his car. *Suspect throwing something out of the back of the pickup truck,* he radioed. *Northbound on Interstate 15 toward Interstate 10.*

Just after tossing the grenade, George Smith discovered he had a bigger problem on his hands than the brown narc car following them. This particular problem had just come in from the east to replace Baker-1 and was now eight hundred feet directly above them.

LIEUTENANT JON GIBSON AND FLIGHT SERGEANT RON HITTLE RAN OUT TO THE Hughes 500 helicopter parked on the tarmac at the Rialto Airport and began preparing for launch. RSO dispatcher Sharon Markum had contacted San Bernardino minutes before to request a chopper to replace Baker-1, which was running low on fuel. When the order to launch San Bernardino County Sheriff's helicopter 40-King-2 finally came, pilot Gibson and observer Hittle had their craft in the air within seconds.

The yellow truck was just entering the northbound lanes of Interstate 15 as 40-King-2 took to the air. Hittle contacted Paul Benoit on Baker-1 over the Ontario Airport frequency and got the rundown. A bunch of bank robbers in the back of a yellow pickup truck with automatic weapons were shooting the hell out of everything in their way. Was it true they might have a CHP officer hostage? Hittle wanted to know. No, but there had been radio chatter from the units on the ground about possible hostages. Benoit had one other thing to tell 40-King: We're not sure, but it's possible we took fire from these guys over Mira Loma.

Lieutenant Jon Gibson knew all about taking fire in a helicopter. Gibson had done twenty months of heavy combat flying Hueys in Vietnam. Like most experienced combat chopper pilots, his senses were supernaturally tuned to the subtle aeronautics of a bullet in flight, especially one aimed in his direction. Even with the noise of the spinning blades, Gibson could detect a bullet passing by his Huey Cobra and determine the caliber of the round from the concussion the projectile made as it flew by. If he did come under fire, he knew when he could fly through it and when it was time to get the hell out of there. Most importantly, on those occasions when he did catch a round, Jon Gibson usually knew whether he was about to go down and how much time he had before he did.

As Gibson swept the Hughes 500 over the sprawling grounds of the Kaiser Steel plant, spotter Ron Hittle got his first visual on Baker-1. The Riverside PD chopper acknowledged its San Bernardino counterpart and did a low run over the yellow truck to identify it before peeling off to return to base for fuel. Gibson moved in at an altitude of eight hundred feet and engaged the suspect vehicle by shadowing it directly overhead. Hittle confirmed three men in the bed of the truck armed with long guns, possibly AR-15s. That was when Lieutenant Gibson heard that familiar noise.

The first four were in rapid succession. A thick whooshing sound as they flew by close to the cockpit. He felt the concussions deep in his chest. This was not .223 fire. It felt bigger, more guttural. Like a .308, maybe.

We're taking fire, Gibson said calmly, pulling sharply to the right in an evasive move. There was a fifth whoosh and then a loud crack, as if someone had hit the bottom of the chopper with a baseball bat. The cockpit began to fill with blue smoke. Gibson recognized it by the smell. Electrical. Check the radios and panel, he said.

Hittle began to comb over the controls while Gibson pulled the craft away from the freeway and back over the empty Kaiser plant, testing its airworthiness and responsiveness. It seemed to be holding up okay for now, but Gibson knew things in a wounded airship could change in an instant. As the smoke began to clear, he checked his fuel and oil gauges for signs of leaks.

We lost our Riverside radio, Hittle reported. Also, a hole through the bubble, he said, pointing to the plexiglass encasing the front of the craft. Hittle looked around some more and spotted another hole through the belly of the airframe directly between his knees. A .308 round from George Smith's Heckler had passed through the titanium alloy landing skid below the cockpit and fragmented into three parts that penetrated the airframe, ripping apart electrical panels and wiring. We got one down here, he said, relieved he had not just had his dick shot off.

I knew we should have put a chicken plate on this thing, Gibson said, referring to the protective metal plating that can be fitted onto the underbelly of the Hughes 500. He angled the helicopter back toward the freeway but kept his altitude up. Get King-1 in the air. We should be able to stay engaged until they get here.

Hittle got on the working radio and reported in to the Ontario com center. Ontario copied Hittle's request for King-1. There was a long pause. 40-King-2, 10-9 your transmission. Did you say your craft has been hit by gunfire?

That's an affirmative.

John Plasencia, the spotter on 40-King-1, came on the radio. They were already in the air, coming up on King-2 from the south. Be careful, Hittle warned their replacement. These people will shoot at you.

Two minutes later, San Bernardino County Sheriff's helicopter 40-King-1, with Ed Mabry piloting, descended and fell in behind 40-King-2. Jon Gibson pointed his wounded craft northeast toward Rialto Airport. It would have been closer to land at Ontario Airport, but Gibson and Hittle had just heard another transmission from the Ontario com center. The largest passenger airport in the Inland Empire was shutting down their airspace and diverting all air traffic to Orange County. They did not want any commercial jetliners getting shot out of the sky by a bunch of crazy bank robbers from Norco.

SAN BERNARDINO COUNTY SHERIFF'S DEPUTY D. J. McCARTY STOOD IN FRONT of his locker in the Fontana substation dressing room, slowly unbuttoning his uniform shirt, one ear on the scanner feed coming over the squawk box mounted on the wall. It was just after 4:00 p.m. and McCarty was coming off the two-shift, changing back into street clothes before heading out. From the radio traffic, it sounded like there was some serious shit going down just over the county line in Riverside.

McCarty took his cowboy boots out of his locker and thought about what he might do that night. Maybe he'd go down to the local bar for a few pops with his old high school buddies, maybe land in bed with a new girl or one of his regulars. Maybe he'd just go home and watch some TV. Any was just as easy as the other for a handsome twenty-six-year-old with a quick wit and magnetic personality.

One of the other men coming off shift came into the room. Riverside's getting their ass kicked. McCarty hadn't heard a thing about it while in the field; he did not have a scanner in his unit. It had never made any sense to him that San Bernardino and Riverside could not communicate with each other, considering how often cases, criminals, and pursuits crossed county lines.

D.J. took off his uniform shirt to reveal an undershirt bearing the Zig-Zag Man, a bearded seagoing chap smoking what appeared to be a marijuana cigarette. Zig-Zag was an old brand of cigarette rolling papers but had become a favorite among joint-twisting stoners everywhere.

Nice shirt, the sergeant said sarcastically.

D.J. shrugged. It had been gently suggested that he stick to regulation clothing, but, you know . . . whatever. He really couldn't give a fuck. Even though he had only been on the force a little over a year, D.J. remained an irreverent Inland Empire shitkicker. He was instantly popular on the force, a local boy with a sweeping Glen Campbell hairstyle who knew the flatlands and mountainsides of San Bernardino County well. He was also an adrenaline junkie, young and inexperienced enough to be excited that the pursuit going on in Riverside might be coming their way.

San Bernardino dispatch came over the radio with reference to a Riverside pursuit with armed and dangerous suspects northbound on Interstate 15. Holy shit, McCarty thought. He threw a bright red windbreaker over the Zig-Zag shirt. A few seconds later, D.J. heard the radio transmission from deputy Jim McPheron that sent him running out of the locker room in search of the only assault rifle in the entire department.

SAN BERNARDINO COUNTY SHERIFF'S DEPUTY JAMES MCPHERON WAS JUST starting his 4:00 p.m. shift as D. J. McCarty was getting off his. The two men were very different. At thirty-seven, McPheron, "Mac" to the guys on the force, was a dozen years older than McCarty with seven years' experience working the streets of San Bernardino County. Named for two military generals—James Doolittle and Douglas MacArthur—James Douglas McPheron was the son of a preacher. Tall and soft-spoken, McPheron always knew he wanted to be a cop, but he sure took a long time getting there. He was almost thirty

years old when he quit his job as a grocery clerk and signed on with the San
Bernardino County Sheriff's Department. McPheron had married his wife,
Patricia, two years before and they were on their way to building a family that
would include two children. While tough, McPheron's nature tended toward
the quiet and gentle as compared to the brash and colorful McCarty.

Mac was an old-school cop who always referred to himself as a "peace
officer," but the half dozen years of law enforcement were beginning to take a
toll. He was starting to feel as though maybe he had seen too much. In 1975,
McPheron had watched one of his closest friends on the force, a huge, likable
deputy named Frank Pribble, die on the emergency room table after a shooting. And there was the time a four-year-old girl died in McPheron's arms
after her drunken father tried to race a train through a crossing at eighty
miles per hour. Or the man Mac had shot in the head after a pursuit when
the suspect tried to back over him in a stolen car. It was all starting to get to
him, but he was a cop and he didn't want to do anything else.

McCarty and McPheron were not especially close, but they bullshitted
together in the locker room and chatted when they ran into each other in the
field. They patrolled the same terrain, frequently backing each other up on
tough calls. Both liked working out of the Fontana substation for the same
reason: action. Even by Inland Empire standards, Fontana, including Lytle
Creek, was extremely rough turf.

McPheron thought the pursuit going on in Riverside might be headed
into San Bernardino County via Interstate 15. He was halfway to the freeway
when he heard the report from 40-King-2 that they had been grounded by
gunfire and heavier weapons would be needed.

McPheron wheeled the Ford Fairlane patrol unit into a sweeping U-turn
across the four lanes of Foothill Boulevard and grabbed the mic of his radio.
I'm headed back to Fontana station. Somebody get the AR.

The San Bernardino Sheriff's Office, or SBSO as it was referred to,
had not approved automatic weapons for use in the field and had no such
high-powered rifles, at least not officially. But Fontana did not always play by
the rules. Several months before, deputies had seized a fully automatic Colt
M16 rifle stolen from the U.S. military and ditched out a car window by a

drug dealer during a high-speed chase. Other than some unsightly road rash, the thing worked just fine. After the military said they didn't want the damn thing back, the .223-caliber rifle hung around in the evidence locker along with the four twenty-round magazines.

Pulling his duty boots back on, McCarty heard McPheron's request for the AR, a generic reference to the class of weapon that included the M16. McCarty knew the weapon was currently residing in the trunk of a shift sergeant's vehicle parked outside in the vehicle lot. As a nonregulation weapon, no one in the department had been trained on the M16, but there were plenty of Vietnam vets on the force who knew how to fire one. D. J. McCarty was not one of them. He had only a passing familiarity with other rifles in the AR class. How different could this one be?

D.J. found Sergeant Mendoza in a hallway and they ran out to the vehicle yard. Mendoza popped the trunk and handed McCarty the weapon. D.J. dug around in the trunk until he found the four magazines taped together in pairs, jungle-style. He grabbed the magazines just as McPheron came racing into the vehicle lot, the passenger door of the Fairlane flying open like something out of a TV cop show. D.J. jumped in the passenger seat.

Let dispatch know we have the AR, said McPheron, tires screaming as they tore out of the lot. They need to tell everyone to get the hell out of our way.

McCarty steadied the unloaded M16 between his knees and relayed the request over the mic while McPheron sent the Fairlane racing down Alder Avenue. At Foothill Boulevard, they blew through the only traffic light between the station and the Sierra off-ramp of I-15, where they thought they might be able to intercept the pursuit. McPheron quickly had the Ford Fairlane reaching an exceedingly high rate of speed as they headed toward the mountains, Taco Bells, 7-Elevens, and IHOPs blurring past. McCarty sat pinned in his seat, wondering which he should be more worried about: a band of heavily armed bank robbers or Jim McPheron's driving.

OF ALL THE DEPUTIES WHO ENGAGED THE NORCO BANK ROBBERS IN RIVERside County, the only two to continue into San Bernardino County were

Rolf Parkes and Fred Chisholm, both now in Chisholm's unit. The reason they had not ended up at the Can Do Market like the others was because Fred Chisholm inadvertently missed a turn and ended up at the major intersection of Bellegrave and Van Buren Boulevard. As they entered the intersection, Baker-1 radioed another change in direction, but spotter Paul Benoit was not familiar with the neighborhood and called out an incorrect street name. Confused, Chisholm began circling the intersection while Parkes tried to figure out what direction the pursuit had really gone. Go north on Van Buren. Wait, back on Bellegrave. Shit, I think he means southbound. Hold on. Goddamn it! They circled the wide intersection three, four times with lights and sirens, to the stunned amazement of their fellow motorists. After the fifth time around, Parkes yelled, Stop! Chisholm hammered on the brakes and they came to a dead stop in the middle of the intersection. Fuck the radio transmissions. Parkes stuck his head out the window and got a visual on Baker-1's location in the sky and instructed Chisholm to go northbound on Van Buren.

Van Buren took the two deputies directly to the Pomona Freeway on-ramp at Mission and onto Interstate 15 a half mile behind Joe Szeles and the yellow truck, but gaining fast. Without any visual on the suspects, Fred Chisholm was growing jumpy behind the wheel. Parkes understood. Chisholm, only a few months on the force, had never been fired on. The guy had every right to be frightened; Parkes sure as hell was.

"Is that them?" Chisholm kept repeating. "What about right there, is that them?"

"No, it's not them!" Parkes snapped after already answering the question at least five times. A semitruck in front of them changed lanes, revealing the yellow truck a quarter mile ahead. Immediately, rounds began striking the pavement around them, bullet fragments and asphalt hitting their vehicle. "*That's* them!" Parkes said.

"Get me my helmet, Rolf. I need my helmet."

"It won't help you," Rolf told him, trying to keep his eye on the truck.

"I need my helmet," Chisholm insisted.

"Your helmet's not going to help you, Fred," Parkes told him again. More rounds struck the pavement around them. "All right!" Parkes said, fishing around on the floorboard among all the equipment that had been tossed around during the pursuit. He handed him the helmet, but Chisholm never put it on.

Gunfire was not the only thing Chisholm and Parkes were contending with on the Devore Freeway stretch of Interstate 15. All around them, civilian cars were jamming on their brakes, swerving wildly, and bailing off the freeway. Harold Phibbs was driving with his girlfriend in his wine-red 1977 Dodge van when a yellow utility truck began to pass them in the number 2 lane. As it slowly edged past, Phibbs caught sight of two men in black ski masks standing in the bed of the truck, each holding what looked like military rifles. Phibbs's girlfriend, Elizabeth Campbell, gasped at the sight of them. As the truck continued to overtake them, one of the men looked down at Phibbs, making eye contact. The man lowered the rifle, firing a round into the front of the van just below the windshield. Steam immediately hissed from the radiator. Phibbs jammed on the brakes and pulled into the breakdown lane.

A few hundred yards behind Phibbs, Parkes and Chisholm began taking fire again. "Fall back behind that semi so they can't see us," Parkes instructed. Chisholm took his foot off the accelerator and then drifted behind the cover of a big tractor trailer. It didn't work. The men in the truck simply turned their fire on the semi. The truck took two rounds into its engine compartment, slowed sharply, and then veered onto the median, exposing Parkes and Chisholm yet again. Another bullet struck their unit. Parkes was stunned; the yellow truck was at least a half mile ahead of them. He leaned over and turned off the switch to their light bar, realizing that's what was drawing the fire.

They passed Joe Szeles to take the lead in the pursuit, but had plenty of company now. Riverside deputy Jim Evans had taken the Pomona Freeway all the way from Moreno Valley and was third in the pursuit line after entering Interstate 15. He soon began to overtake Parkes and Chisholm. Other fresh horses began to enter the pursuit, most notably the California Highway Patrol. The freeway was CHP turf. Units flooded onto I-15 from all directions. Riding together in an auto-theft unit, patrolmen Steve Batchelor and Peter Vander Kamp merged off Interstate 10 northbound onto I-15. To Vander Kamp, the bullets flying by their vehicle sounded like the buzz of giant bees. Patrolman Ronald Kauffman was out of his vehicle manning a roadblock to keep civilians from entering the freeway when the truck went by. Bullets kicked up dirt around his feet. After taking cover, Kauffman jumped in his unit and joined the pursuit.

Along with the CHP, units from five additional police agencies entered the chase, most taking fire the instant they came within sight of the truck. Ontario and Riverside city PD units joined at the Jurupa Road on-ramp. North of Highway 10, San Bernardino County Sheriff's deputies out of the Fontana substation began to appear along with Fontana city PD. A police unit from the town of Perris far to the south had somehow caught up with the pursuit.

RSO detective Mike Jordan entered Interstate 15 in an unmarked vehicle with red and blue dashboard lights whirling. Although the suspects were nowhere in sight, Jordan heard rounds striking the asphalt around his vehicle. At the same time, a radio transmission put the location of the truck at the Interstate 10 interchange. Jordan was astonished. The men shooting at him were almost a mile away. Others had noticed the range and accuracy the suspects' weapons were capable of. *Keep your lights off, they've been firing from a half mile hitting units*, an RSO unit radioed. Jordan killed his emergency lights.

Operating over separate radio frequencies, officers from different agencies resorted to hand signals or mouthing words to get urgent messages across to the each other. With all these amped-up cowboys joining the chase, the message Rolf Parkes frequently found himself trying to get across was "slow down before you get your ass shot off."

When the CHP unit driven by Joe Haughey came charging up the fast lane with a Riverside deputy just behind, other Riverside units tried to warn them off.

Be advised, they are firing. I wouldn't get too close, Joe Szeles cautioned.

Haughey and the overly aggressive RSO deputy advanced past Parkes and Chisholm's 2-Edward-13 unit. *Whoever's ahead of 13, you're getting too close,* they were warned. *That's the vehicle right in front of you, man, look out.*

Is that the bright yellow one just in front of the next car? the Riverside deputy asked.

Yeah, that's it. Watch out, they'll shoot at you.

Chris Harven saw the two units racing up behind him and was having none of it. He slowed the truck sharply, drawing the two cop cars in precariously close to the gunmen in the back. All three opened fire, spraying the police units with gunfire. Haughey and the RSO deputy dropped back.

After pulling the wounded A. J. Reynard out of the shot-up 511 car at Van Buren and Bellegrave, Riverside deputy Bill Eldrich had managed to catch up to the pursuit and was only one hundred yards behind the suspects when he entered I-15 from the Baseline Avenue on-ramp. Within seconds, Eldrich heard bullets whizzing over his unit and then rounds smashed into the front of the vehicle. *They're still firing, I just took two,* he radioed. A mile later, steam hissed out from under his hood and the car lost power. Eldrich managed to roll his dying vehicle onto the center median. *2-Edward-71, this unit is hit and down. Officer is 10-4,* he transmitted, indicating he was okay.

I'll pick you up, Joe Szeles radioed, pulling in behind him. Eldrich grabbed his shotgun and jumped into the passenger seat of the brown Ford. Together they rejoined the chase.

A Highway Patrol unit driven by Patrolman Dennis Johnson accelerated onto the freeway. Parkes motioned him back, mouthing, "They have high-powered rifles." As the patrolmen pushed forward anyhow, Parkes saw something fly out from the back of truck and explode in the air beside Johnson's vehicle. Shrapnel peppered the body of Chisholm's unit, sounding as if someone had thrown a handful of gravel against it.

They're throwing explosives out of the vehicle, a deputy who saw it reported.

Have they got explosives? another asked, surprised.

That's affirmative, Parkes responded. *They've thrown one explosive device out the rear.*

Okay, that was a similator, Jim Evans radioed in his West Texas accent, mistaking the explosive for a harmless training device.

Similator, my ass, thought Parkes.

An RSO lieutenant monitoring the traffic from back in Norco decided he had heard enough and ordered all pursuing units to fall back and give the fleeing suspects plenty of room. The unmarked units were told to back off even farther. Dispatcher Gary Keeter asked for a roll call of Riverside units still in the pursuit. Eight acknowledged.

A sergeant suggested they *figure out what we're gonna do here.*

Wait until they run out of gas or ammo, Szeles responded.

A mile short of Sierra, Fred Chisholm's unit began to cough and lose speed. After taking multiple rounds and shrapnel from a fragmentation grenade, the Plymouth Fury had finally had it. Other black-and-white units began to overtake them. Rolf was despondent. This was his chase, goddamn it. He and Chisholm had been in it the longest. Parkes told Chisholm he might as well keep riding the accelerator hard until the fucking thing died. Parkes had already had one car shot out from under him that day.

Over the radio, RSO units tried to figure out where the yellow truck might be headed.

Where are they, Joe, I can't see them, one radioed Szeles.

Get off on Sierra? another unit wanted to know.

That's affirmative, Jim Evans answered, his unit speeding up to fall in behind two CHP units leading the pursuit.

As Chisholm limped off the freeway and down the ramp at Sierra Avenue, Rolf eyed the San Gabriel Mountains towering above the valley floor just two miles to the east. Like Szeles, Parkes had a strong suspicion that was where the truck might be headed. He hoped to God he was wrong. The next transmission put the yellow truck heading under the Interstate east on Sierra Avenue. Now there was no doubt: These guys were headed straight up Lytle Creek Canyon. Instantly, the pursuit took on a more ominous feel. When it came to law enforcement, nothing good ever happened in Lytle Creek.

9

AMBUSH

May 9, 1980. Lytle Creek Canyon, California.

LYTLE CREEK CANYON IS A PLACE THAT MAKES NO ATTEMPT TO HIDE THE madness of its origins. Geologically speaking, the San Gabriel Mountains through which Lytle Creek has carved itself are "new" mountains, part of the Southern California Transverse Ranges created when the North American and Pacific tectonic plates shifted direction along the San Andreas Fault, crashing and grinding their way into each other. The result was a transtensional force so awesome it rotated an entire section of the Pacific Ranges anywhere from 80 to 110 degrees in a northwesterly direction from its original north-south orientation.

The Transverse is a freak of nature, a miracle of geologic deformation that is still actively moving, forming, heaving up, and tumbling down. The mountains rise abruptly from the valley floor, reaching elevations over four thousand feet so quickly that a 7.5-minute topographical map of the range looks more like a solid blotch of ink than it does the usual concentric figures separated by white space. The wide creek bed is strewn with boulders of white and gray granite, for which millions of years of water and wind is not nearly enough time to settle or make smooth. It all makes for extremely uninviting terrain, unstable and unpredictable enough to give experienced climbers pause before taking it on and outwardly forbidding enough to let inexperienced hikers know that they might very well die trying. Only the bighorn sheep want anything to do with it.

Not much farther up Lytle Creek, the elevation of the nearby mountains soars to over eight thousand feet at Ontario Peak and almost nine thousand feet at Cucamonga Peak. Above it all, at just over ten thousand feet, is Mount San Antonio, more popularly known as Mount Baldy. On a clear day, Baldy is visible for miles in all directions, the highest peak in the San Gabriel Mountains. It is bisected by the San Bernardino County–Los Angeles County line, with the summit and northern side lying within L.A. County. Rain and snow fall on the southern side of the mountain lands in San Bernardino County, much of it flowing into Lytle Creek Canyon. The hillsides above the creek bed are covered with California chaparral made up of scrub oak, manzanita, buckbrush, sumac, and sage. In some places it is taller than a man's head and impenetrably thick. At higher elevations, the ecosystem changes to scattered pine groves of Douglas fir, ponderosa, and sugar pine.

Lytle Creek has never been an easy place to inhabit for man or beast. It still experiences frequent earthquakes, rockslides, wildfires, and flash floods. Freezing temperatures and snowfalls measured in feet can come in quickly and late in the season at higher elevations. Hard rains and quick snow melts sweep sediment, shrubbery, and dead trees down feeder streams, transforming the main channel of the creek bed from a trickle to a torrent that tears the hell out of roads, trails, and bridges before sweeping out into the flatlands. The city of Fontana owes its southward-sloping elevations to the fact that it is built atop the alluvial fan of rock and debris swept out of the mouth of the canyon since the Cretaceous period. Serrano Indians, Spaniards, Mexicans, and Mormons have all tried to call Lytle Creek Canyon their home, all with eventual failure.

Many of the streams, ridges, campsites, and trails in the area are named for early settlers, pioneers, gold miners, trappers, moonshiners, scoundrels, and horse thieves who hid their stolen animals up the canyon. Meyers Canyon, Nealeys Corner, and the tiny Happy Jack settlement, named after miner Joseph "Happy Jack" Pollard, all reference early inhabitants. The Applewhite

Campground was named after a family related by marriage to the Glens of Glen Ranch. The relationship did not stop James and Ollie Applewhite from shooting John and Silas Glen to death in 1893. Twenty years earlier, a dispute over a productive gold claim ended when a driverless team of horses pulling a wagon arrived at the Texas Point mine with one of the contestants to the claim lying dead in the back. These were not the first murders in Lytle Creek and far from the last. In fact, it got worse. Much worse.

As dangerous as it is beautiful, Lytle Creek is notorious for both its geological and manmade violence. The place has always attracted loners, outsiders, and outlaws. The wanted and the unwanted. Like any wilderness area in the west, guns have always been part of life in the canyon due to the practical need to hunt and to protect oneself from wild animals and bandits intent upon taking one's property, livestock, or life. But as the population grew in the Inland Empire below and the Kaiser Steel mill began filling up with blue-collar workers, more and more people came up Lytle Creek just to blast away at shit. Many were responsible recreational gun enthusiasts, but a lot of them were reckless, untrained, and unsafe. Many ignored the formal shooting ranges in favor of pulling their cars off the road at any old place to fire illegal automatic weapons or toss an occasional pipe bomb into the canyon without regard for who or what might be down there. In addition to pumping rounds into the appliances, automobiles, propane tanks, and watermelons they dumped down the hillside, they often sent rounds into the houses of residents or tents of campers. People and pets died. By the 1970s, any trip into Lytle Creek Canyon was accompanied by the crack of gunfire and the frequent sight of impromptu firing lines of gun nuts alternately shooting and wandering into the wash to set up a new target while their fellow yahoos continued firing over their heads. And if you did not have a semiautomatic weapon of your own, you could always upgrade by shooting someone who did and taking theirs. That happened more than a few times.

The explosion of illegal street drugs starting in the late 1960s represented an even darker turn for Lytle Creek. Drug traffickers moved into the canyon alongside the population of six hundred or so permanent residents and began growing marijuana plants up the side canyons and brewing up batches of crystal meth in their bathtubs. Their friends joined them—addicts, dealers, parolees, and bail jumpers hiding out from the law. The busiest day at the Lytle Creek Post Office became the day the welfare checks arrived. Sirens of San Bernardino County Sheriff's units became more common as they raced up Lytle Creek Road responding to one unpleasantness or another. Other times they snuck up the canyon to serve a warrant on some wayward felon or to raid another meth lab, often resulting in standoffs and shootouts.

Visits from the county coroner's van also became more common. If they were not rolling their cars down hillsides or shooting themselves, their friends, or strangers, the really bad guys were dumping bodies in Lytle Creek Canyon. It was a plague common to any mountain wilderness area that ran up against big population centers, the preferred dumping ground for drug gangs, child murderers, psychos, and serial killers. Kill a hitchhiker or a hooker down in the flatlands and dump the body off the side of a mountain road up in one of the canyons and it might not be found for months, if ever. When San Bernardino sheriff's deputies patrolling the canyon came upon unaccompanied young women in Lytle Creek, they usually ordered them to leave and shadowed them all the way down to Fontana to make damn sure they did. It might have seemed unfair, but the chances of a young woman being raped or killed up there were simply too great.

SAN BERNARDINO COUNTY SHERIFF'S DEPUTIES D. J. McCARTY AND JIM McPheron both had their taste of death in the canyon. At the end of a long shift that same year, McCarty had been dispatched to Lytle Creek on the report of a missing person. A long-time Lytle Creek resident said her husband had gone up the canyon to shoot for a bit but never came back. D.J. found the man's car by the side of the road, empty gun cases resting on the trunk. He did not have to go far to find the body, shot and dragged into the chaparral, his guns gone. McPheron located the bloated body of a drug dealer dumped into the creek bed only a few hundred yards into the canyon. Another time, McPheron responded when a teenager's handgun went off while the youngster was carrying ammunition boxes down a canyon trail, blowing the top of his head off. Neither man wanted much to do with the place, so they were not happy when they heard the pursuit of the Norco bank robbers was headed into the canyon.

Despite holding the commandeered M16 rifle between his knees with the muzzle pointed up at the roof and four fully loaded ammo magazines on the seat beside him, D. J. McCarty's main concern was not the gun. He and McPheron's immediate task was to get to the front of the pursuit. Until they did that, it made no difference whether D.J. was holding a machine gun or a slingshot; it would be of no use to anyone. In the meantime, the last thing McCarty wanted was a loaded rifle bouncing around in the front seat of a Ford Fairlane blowing stop signs at seventy miles per hour.

For the man blowing the stop signs, Jim McPheron's strategy was simple: drive as fast as possible in the oncoming traffic lane. By the time he caught up with the pursuit on Sierra Avenue just beyond Interstate 15, there were close to forty law enforcement vehicles strung out through Lytle Canyon, all of them also moving as fast as they could in the same direction.

One of the first they came upon was Fred Chisholm's shrapnel- and bullet-ridden patrol car, smoking and dead on the side of the road. Chisholm and Rolf Parkes were standing dejectedly beside it, shotguns in hand. Moments after McPheron blew past, the two were picked up by Riverside detective Mike Jordan in his unmarked vehicle. By that time, the whole pursuit pack had already passed their location, leaving them far back in the chase.

In addition to having the living shit scared out of him by McPheron's driving, D. J. McCarty had another problem. Among the pack of vehicles in front of them now were units from no less than half a dozen law enforcement agencies, only one of which McCarty had any ability to communicate with. He was having no problem getting his fellow San Bernardino units to pull over, but word that a marked SO unit with an automatic weapon was trying to make its way to the front was slow to spread through the phalanx of other agency vehicles moving up the mountain. McCarty's only option was to shout at each of them through the PA speaker until they finally got out of the way. "Let us pass! We have an automatic rifle! Let us pass!"

It was the same old problem: Each agency was operating on a different radio frequency. The few with scanners could hear select frequencies but not communicate back. Riverside deputies had been fussing and griping about the limitation for years, but none had been more concerned about the situation than Jim Evans.

We are a quarter mile from the ranger station on Sierra Road in the National Forest and they are firing like crazy.

With Evans's cool West Texas country drawl and calm delivery, there was no question in the minds of the Riverside deputies which one of their men was now the lead RSO unit in the pursuit. It was only the content of Evans's reports that betrayed just how perilous his situation had become since plunging into the mouth of Lytle Creek Canyon.

> Jordan: *Do you have visual contact with the suspect?*
> Evans: *That's affirmative, we're right behind 'em.*
> Evans: *2-Edward-74, they're firing.*
> Jordan: *Watch out they don't bail out when you come around the corner.*
> Evans: *I think my unit just got hit with three rounds.*
> Jordan: *Evans, you okay?*
> Evans: *Yeah, I'm okay. They're shooting automatics for sure.*
> Spain: *Edward-20 to Evans. Give these guys plenty of room.*
> Evans: *Fall back, they are really firing now.*

Evans might have been the lead RSO unit, but he was only the number-three car in the pursuit. Coming off Interstate 15, two CHP units had had grabbed the one and two spots with Steve Batchelor and Peter Vander Kamp riding together in the lead vehicle and patrolman Joe Haughey just behind. It was not surprising that CHP would have come off a freeway pursuit in front. There was no way they were going to let some deputy sheriff or beat cop come off that freeway ahead of them.

After a straight two-mile run up Sierra Avenue, the two-lane road entered the mouth of the canyon near Convict Spring, crossed the wide creek bed, and ran along the base of Penstock Ridge. *Somebody tell the Forest Ser-*

vice, Evans requested. *We're going right into their station and they don't know we're coming.*

Attempts by the CHP units to keep their distance in the canyon were countered by ambush tactics on the part of Chris Harven. On straightaways, Harven accelerated the truck up to speeds of fifty miles per hour only to lay back on curves so Russ, Manny, and George could open up at close range when pursuing units appeared around the bend. In the lead vehicle, Steven Batchelor had taken to hanging back on sharp curves until he could get a visual on the truck farther up, but all the units near the front of the pursuit, including Evans and San Bernardino deputy Mike Lenihan, were still taking considerable fire. *Okay, we got him up here*, Evans radioed. *We had to slow down, he laid a barrage on us at that last curve.*

It was a deadly game of cat and mouse that continued for five miles up the canyon until the pursuit reached the first of the only two settlements of any size in Lytle Creek Canyon.

The tiny community of Scotland, California, owes its origins to an 1860 gold strike and its location to the confluence of the north and middle forks of Lytle Creek, which join to form the main Lytle Creek channel. The Scotland Store was a convenience market with a small café that served as the de facto meeting hall for the entire Lytle Creek community. Late in the afternoon of May 9, 1980, San Bernardino sheriff's lieutenant Robert "Bunny" Lorimer had been sent to the Scotland Store to hear residents' complaints of rising crime rates and inadequate police protection in the canyon. Lorimer was attempting to pacify the locals when his efforts were interrupted by a cacophony of gunfire. Lorimer and the concerned citizens of Lytle Creek rushed outside just in time to see a yellow truck race past with three heavily armed men in the back spraying gunfire, followed by forty police units in close pursuit.

After initially scattering for cover at the sound of sirens and gunshots, a pause in the firing sent four young siblings of the Hoeppner family running back toward the road to check out the action. As the truck rolled by within feet of the four children, one of the men in the back turned his head and looked straight at them through the hole in his black ski mask. Brenda Hoeppner gasped at the sight of what looked to her like a monster holding a very scary gun. But instead of trying to kill them, the monster clearly motioned with one hand for them to stay back from the road. It was the second time in the pursuit that Russell Harven had warned children to get out of the line of fire.

A mile past Scotland was Lytle Creek Village, the last settlement in the canyon. With the cops hanging back to prevent an active gun battle in the community, the pursuit drifted through the village in an eerie silence. George Smith used the break in the action to catch his breath. Since exiting the bank, it had been forty-five minutes of nonstop fight and flight. Only now did he realize how weak he had become, a quarter of his blood supply already drained from his body. As Chris floored the truck out of the village, George stared up at the sky, shivering, breathing heavily, and watching the mountains blur by on both sides. Above him, Russell Harven stood leaning back against one of the tall acetylene tanks with the "Shorty" AR pointing up. At his feet, Manny Delgado was crouched, resting the barrel of Chris's Heckler .223 on the tailgate, waiting.

Beyond Lytle Creek Village lay only campgrounds, firing lines, and raw wilderness virtually unchanged since the days of the Wild West. Since entering the canyon, they had climbed to an elevation of 3,000 feet. What had been a clear, warm spring day in Norco now had a bite of cold and a cloud cover moving in. Above them another 3,500 feet, patches of snow still held out on the hillsides of Baldy. Soon the paved road would give way to a rain-rutted dirt track suitable only for four-wheel-drive vehicles.

As he sped up the canyon, Jim Evans knew there had to be a police helicopter somewhere in the skies above him but figured it would not do him any good. Anything up there was bound to be a San Bernardino sheriff's chopper with which he had no ability to communicate. There was only one outside chance that Evans would ever be able to get reports from any SBSO helicopter.

The California Law Enforcement Mutual Aid Radio System, or CLEMARS, was a rather simple solution to the vexing problem of interagency radio communications: a dozen radio channels set aside for communication among multiple agencies during emergencies and special operations. While the solution might have been simple, implementation was decidedly more complicated and costly, requiring additional radios be added to vehicles. The RSO had been slow to deploy the system throughout the department, their current capability limited to several handheld CLEMARS radios. But at that moment, one of those radios just happened to be in the hands of an RSO sergeant on narcotics detail named Don Bender.

Bender: *Edward-320. We got communications with the chopper.*
Evans: *Okay. Is the chopper on Sierra? Can you see him?*
Bender: *Affirmative, he's almost to the end of the paved road.*

It was far from a perfect solution. Bender would need to receive information on the CLEMARS from spotter John Plasencia on board 40-King-1 and then relay the info to Evans over the Riverside frequency. The result was a ten- to fifteen-second communication lag each way between 40-King-1 and Evans. But at least Evans now had a pair of eyes to tell him the one thing he wanted to know most: Was he about to get ambushed?

Evans: *320, can you tell us how far behind we are?*
Bender: *Just a minute, we'll check with the chopper.*
Evans: *We got blind curves. We want to know how far back we are.*

In the Hughes 500C helicopter above, 40-King-1 pilot Ed Mabry was battling bursts of severe turbulence as warm air from the basin funneled into the canyon and collided with the cooler air at higher elevations. As Mabry steadied and positioned King-1, he and Plasencia watched the extremely dangerous situation continuing to unfold in the canyon below. Plasencia did his best to communicate developments, especially changes in the truck's speed, to Bender as quickly as possible.

Bender: *Starting to slow down. Okay, now he's moving out again, continuing northbound on the paved road.*

Evans: *We're still behind him.*

Bender: *Okay, just going around the first large curve at the end of the pavement.*

Neither of the two CHP units ahead of Evans had CLEMARS in their units, but patrolman Ron Kauffman, holding the number-five position in the pursuit, did have a scanner with which he could monitor 40-King-1 and relay the information to the CHP units ahead of him. It amounted to a giant rolling game of telephone with multiple agencies monitoring, relaying, and communicating by means of scanners, CLEMARS, PA speakers on the roofs of their vehicles, or via their dispatch centers when all other means failed them.

Reaching the dirt portion of Lytle Creek Road, the pursuit abruptly slowed to speeds ranging from thirty miles per hour to below ten miles per hour in the bad spots. The farther up they went, the worse it got. Even with its annual grooming, the road was a washboard track punctuated with basketball-size rocks and deep ruts, barely wide enough for two vehicles to pass, usually not even that. Pursuing units also had to contend with clouds of thick dust kicked up by the vehicles in front of them. It was not long before law enforcement sedans began dropping out.

Adding to the rapidly growing number of disabled or destroyed police units, a San Bernardino sheriff's deputy twenty miles away in the Cajon Pass was positioning his patrol unit to block one of the feeder roads to Lytle Creek when the vehicle became stuck on the tracks at a railroad crossing. As the deputy furiously attempted to free his unit using a tire jack, a Union Pacific freight train pulling almost one hundred cars slammed into the vehicle, dragging it hundreds of yards while the deputy looked on sheepishly.

It had been Chris Harven's expectation that the rough road conditions in Lytle Creek would favor the F-250's higher clearance over the low-slung police sedans. Disabling a lead unit could stop the entire pursuit line in its tracks until the offending vehicle was dragged out of the way. If the roadbed was not going to do it, Harven was determined to have his shooters in the back do the job. Approaching a tight horseshoe bend carved into the hillside, Chris spotted an opportunity. Jim Evans could sense something was up.

Evans: *They're pulling up on us up here. Looks like they're gonna lay back on the*
curve, next one coming up on us. Have that chopper keep watching.
Bender: *Okay, he's still moving northbound according to the chopper.*
Evans: *Tell him if they stop, that's what we want to know.*

Coming out of the bend in the horseshoe, Harven abruptly brought the truck to a halt. In the back, Manny and Russ stood up and fired across the ravine at Evans and the two lead CHP units on the other side. A line of bullets kicked up dirt on the hillside just above the hood of Batchelor and Vander Kamp's patrol car. But Harven accelerated out of the horseshoe before his shooters could adjust their aim and take out the lead CHP unit.

Riding with Fred Chisholm in detective Mike Jordan's unmarked unit two dozen vehicles back in the pursuit line, Rolf Parkes spotted a civilian walking along the shoulder carrying a rifle. Parkes told Jordan to pull over. "That might be a .30-.30," he said, leaping from the vehicle. Getting their hands on a large-caliber weapon with the long-range capability of a rifle would represent a significant upgrade to their current firepower. It was no Heckler, but many a hunter had dropped a deer in Lytle Creek from two hundred yards with a .30-30 Winchester. Parkes rushed up to the bewildered gun owner. "We need to borrow your gun," he told the man. Having already been passed by the yellow truck and dozens of police vehicles with sirens screaming, the man did not need much convincing. Parkes took the gun and handed the man his department business card. "Do you have ammunition?" The man fished in his pocket and dumped a dozen loose rounds in Parkes's hand. When Rolf saw the dinky little shells rolling around in his palm, his heart sank. He jumped into the back seat and told Jordan what he had. Jordan raised his eyebrows doubtfully and reached for the mic nonetheless. *We commandeered a lever-action .22,* he radioed unenthusiastically.

STILL BACK IN THE PACK BUT GAINING IN POSITION, DEPUTY JAMES McPheron's task of getting D. J. McCarty and the M16 to the front of the pursuit had become much harder now that the paved road had given way to a narrow dirt track. At least word of their approach was getting out to most of the agencies. CHP and the city cops had begun pulling over to let them pass without McCarty having to do too much screaming through the PA. It was not until a Riverside lieutenant named Wayne Daniels caught wind of the situation over a scanner that the RSO deputies heard anything about it. If Jim Evans heard Daniels's instruction to yield to the San Bernardino unit with the automatic weapon, he did not immediately acknowledge it.

After almost five miles of dirt track, Lytle Creek Road passed the mouth of Coldwater Canyon and abruptly turned west to cross the wide creek bed. At the center of the wash, the yellow truck splashed through the shallow waters of the North Fork and began a straight run up an eight-hundred-foot grade to a campground known as Stockton Flats. The CHP units in the lead vehicles heard rounds striking rocks in the streambed around them as the gunmen in the truck fired down the grade.

As the pursuit continued into Stockton Flats, the elevation rose to six thousand feet. The road began to cut through thick stands of Douglas fir and ponderosa pine. Above in 40-King-1, pilot Ed Mabry and spotter John Plasencia began to lose sight of the yellow truck for as long as twenty seconds at a stretch. With makeshift dirt roads forking off the main roadway into the campground and nearby smaller canyons, the radio communication among Plasencia, Bender, and Evans became even more urgent.

Slowing the truck on another blind curve, Chris Harven paused just long enough for Russ and Manny to toss two highly explosive acetylene gas cylinders out of the back of the truck along with a five-gallon can of diesel fuel. As Steve Batchelor and Joe Haughey weaved their CHP units past the obstacles, George Smith attempted to detonate the tanks with rounds from his .308. The tanks failed to explode. Soon after, Haughey's unit died on him due to road damage. He had to abandon the vehicle. He watched as Jim Evans and San Bernardino deputy Mike Lenihan raced past him into the second and third spots in the pursuit before fellow CHP officer Ron Kauff-man pulled over and picked him up.

JIM MCPHERON AND D. J. McCARTY STILL HAD NO IDEA WHERE THEY WERE IN the pursuit line because of all the dust being kicked up in front of them. They knew they must be getting close. McPheron estimated they had already passed thirty to forty vehicles at that point. As the road leveled out in a grove of pines and entered Stockton Flats campground, they came up fast on a CHP unit. Equipped with a scanner, patrolman Ron Kauffman had a good idea who was on his tail and pulled over to let it pass.

McPheron shot past Kauffman's unit and right up on the rear bumper of another San Bernardino black-and-white. D. J. McCarty did not know it, but the driver was his roommate, Mike Lenihan. Along with Lenihan was a civilian reserve deputy named Margaret Martin in her first-ever ride-along, now wondering what the fuck she had gotten herself into. Like Kauffman, Lenihan recognized the unit behind him and pulled over to let McPheron and McCarty fly past.

That left only the RSO unit with Evans and the CHP unit with Batch-elor and Vander Kamp between McPheron and the yellow truck. After pull-ing his own CHP unit over, Ron Kauffman radioed up to Batchelor and Vander Kamp that the SO unit with the automatic was coming up behind them. Batchelor began to angle his CHP car toward the side of the road. For a moment, Evans seemed to follow. But just as McPheron accelerated to pass both vehicles, the Riverside unit swung back out into the road in front of him and maintained its position.

Okay, I got the lead unit now, Jim Evans radioed.

McCarty and McPheron could not hear Evans's transmission and did not know there was now only one patrol car between them and the sus-pects. Within seconds of the Riverside unit cutting in front of them, the road suddenly changed, pitching upward and narrowing to the width of a single vehicle. In all the dust, there was no way Jim Evans, D. J. McCarty, or James McPheron could have seen the sign the Forest Service had posted there: DANGEROUS ROAD. NO UNAUTHORIZED VEHICLES BEYOND THIS POINT.

ETCHED ALONG THE WESTERN FACE OF THE TALLEST MOUNTAIN IN THE SAN Gabriel range, Mt. Baldy Road rises from a 6,012-foot elevation at Stockton Flats to a summit of almost 8,000 feet in 3.9 miles. Labeled Baldy Road on Forest Service topo maps, it is referred to by rangers and serious hikers as Baldy Notch Road after its destination point. Originally constructed in 1894 by the Hocumac Mining Company to reach fourteen gold mines on the mountain-side, the road replaced a wagon trail built earlier to access the Banks Mine at Baldy Notch summit. The previous trail was so inadequate it required that the wagons be raised and lowered by winch at points. With the mines tapped out, the road was taken over and improved by the Forest Service to provide access to remote regions for emergency personnel and equipment to fight the raging brush fires that frequented the mountainsides there.

While the engineering was sound, any trip up Baldy Notch Road was a harrowing journey of steep inclines, declines, and sharp 180-degree switch-backs on a single-track dirt road clinging to the mountainside with drops of up to five hundred feet on one side and an incredibly unstable upslope on the other. "Dirt" was a kind description for a road surface that was mostly gravel and sizable rocks. Maintenance by bulldozer was an ongoing battle against erosion, landslides, and falling pines.

Dangerous in the best of conditions, a run up Baldy Notch under heavy gunfire was unthinkable, the stuff of nightmares. Now in the lead position, Jim Evans was being followed closely by McCarty and McPheron. Mac was still trying to push past Evans at every widening of the road with nothing but a two-foot berm of dirt standing between the Ford Fairlane and a tumble down hundreds of feet of rocky hillsides to Stockton Flats below. The San Bernardino unit with Mike Lenihan remained in third position. Just behind Lenihan were the two CHP vehicles, with Batchelor and Vander Kamp in the first and Kauffman and Haughey on their tail.

With the road beginning its sharp ascent up the mountainside, and the men in the truck firing down on him, the strain of the situation could be heard in Jim Evans's increasingly frequent requests for information. *What are they doing? I'm coming into the curve*, Evans asked, his voice a vibrato as he bounced over the washboard surface of the loose roadbed. *They're moving slow. They're moving slow*, Bender relayed. *I'm hittin' a blind curve, what does he say?* Evans asked again seconds later.

For the moment, the truck was obscured from 40-King-1 by a stand of pines, so Bender had no report to relay to Evans. Fifteen seconds later, the truck came into Evans's view again. *Okay, I got him. It's still movin'.*

A few hundred yards into the climb, the road horseshoed back on itself. The three gunmen in the back of the truck opened up on the units still moving through Stockton Flats. In the narrow canyon, the gunshots echoed sharply back and forth off rock-face cliffs on three sides, making a dozen rounds sound more like thirty-six coming at them from all directions. *Left side, they're shootin' down the ridge*, one of the deputies on the Flats radioed urgently. The pursuit line was strafed with gunfire.

Chris Harven hit the accelerator and the truck disappeared around a tight curve. *302, I got a bad curve coming up here, what are they doing?* Evans asked, nervous enough now to have begun addressing Bender by the incorrect call number 302 instead of 320. *302, can you get him? I can't see him*, he asked seconds later when he did not receive a reply the first time.

He's still movin', he's still movin', Bender relayed, but the delay in getting the information to Evans had been almost fifteen seconds.

Above them, 40-King-1 was fighting worsening conditions. In addition to more and more pine stands blocking his view, pilot Ed Mabry had the narrow canyon and descending cloud cover to contend with while trying to reposition the chopper to maintain a visual on the truck.

The road flattened out and cut in where water runoff had eroded a wide cleavage in the hillside. Sweeping back on the other side of the gully, Chris Harven slowed the truck as Manny and Russ stood up in the bed and fired across the mouth of the ravine at their pursuers. Again, the sound of the gunshots echoed back and forth off the canyon walls. The truck headed up a steep incline directly across from Evans. Evans spotted an opportunity and tried to have a message relayed to the SBSO unit with the automatic weapon. *That San Bernardino unit, if you can come up, you can catch them going up that ridgeline over there with the mountain backdrop.* Evans had no idea that the San Bernardino unit he was trying to reach was the one directly behind him.

Still down on Stockton Flats with the CLEMARS, Don Bender heard a barrage of gunshots echoing down off the mountainside. *Are they up that hill to the left?*

Yeah, take the left turn, the left turn, Evans answered, accelerating across the slide area and continuing up the grade a hundred yards behind the truck. Evans increased his speed to twenty-five miles an hour and watched as the truck disappeared around a bend to the right leading into a straight, sharp ascent. *302, are they movin?* he asked Bender. There was no reply. Fifteen seconds later, Evans came around the bend and had his answer.

Okay, we're hit! Evans screamed into the mic so sharply it distorted the transmission, making it almost unintelligible. But everyone who heard it knew that something very bad had just happened.

Jim, talk.

Evans, you there?

Edward-20, unit with Evans?

Evans, are they in the truck?

Evans, who is in the truck?

There was no answer. There was no one left in the truck.

SEATED IN THE BED OF A STOLEN PICKUP TRUCK COMING AROUND THAT FINAL bend, George Wayne Smith was finally able to see the magnitude of what he had created. A quarter mile away on the far side of the wide ravine, Baldy Notch Road descended like a ribbon draped across the mountainside. All the way down to Stockton Flats, law enforcement vehicles were snaking up the road, light bars whirling red and blue like a trail of electric ants. It might not have been how he wanted it, but for the first time in his life George was part of something huge, just like he always knew he would be.

Behind the wheel, Chris Harven leaned forward and checked the sky to get a visual on the helicopter that had been tracking them all the way up the canyon. He found it 1,500 feet overhead, hovering out over the canyon above Stockton Flats. The road beneath his wheels was as steep as it could possibly be now, the tires alternately slipping and gripping the coarse rock, spinning, kicking stones and dirt behind it. Chris pushed the F-250 into third gear as he gained traction up the grade, deciding he would use the straight stretch of road ahead to make a run for the cloud cover. He stole another glance out the side window to find the chopper, but a line of enormous pines on the downslope blocked his view. The next time he looked through the windshield, the road in front of him was completely gone. In its place was a fifty-foot-wide stretch of the mountainside that had given way, taking Baldy Notch Road with it.

Harven hammered on the brakes and leapt from the truck holding the Long Colt revolver. Debark! he yelled. Everybody out! We have to hoof it from here.

Manny Delgado vaulted the tailgate and stood behind the truck, leveling the barrel of Chris's Heckler down the road. Manny wasn't going anywhere. Russ scrambled over the side cabinets and positioned himself at the driver's-side rear of the truck with the "Shorty" AR. George crawled over the tailgate and fell to the ground, got up, and lifted the Heckler .308 to his hip. The three stood at the rear of the truck aiming their assault rifles at the empty road behind them, waiting. A few seconds later, the first cop car appeared.

The explosion of gunfire from all three rifles was instantaneous and overwhelming, the reports echoing off the canyon walls, multiplying the muzzle blasts into a solid cacophony of sound. With nothing but the Long Colt, Chris turned and began to head up the road, but something slammed into his back with such force that it knocked the wind out of him and threw him forward onto the dirt. He lay there gulping air, trying to figure out what the fuck had just happened. There was a burning sensation in his back, just below the shoulder blade. Chris Harven realized he had just been shot.

THE INSTANT JIM EVANS TURNED THE BEND, HE SAW THE MUZZLE FLASHES coming from three men standing seventy-five feet in front of him. A round crashed through the passenger side of his windshield and exploded out the rear window. *Okay, we're hit!* he called into his radio mic as he threw open his door. As Evans dove from the vehicle, three more rounds came through his windshield on the driver's side. Any one of them would have been a direct head shot had Evans still been behind the wheel. In an instant, Evans was on his feet behind the protection of the V of the open car door with his .38 revolver drawn. Evans turned and assumed a defensive combat firing stance, peeling off rounds—Pop! Pop! Pop!—as he shuffle-stepped to the rear of his patrol unit. Once there, he dropped to one knee, ejected the spent shell casings from the .38, and used a speed loader to quickly reload six live rounds into the cylinder of the revolver.

Evans did not know it, but he had just done something remarkable. Using a .38 revolver while under heavy fire, Jim Evans had hit his target from a range of seventy-five feet, striking Chris Harven several inches below the left shoulder blade and knocking him to the dirt.

D. J. McCarty saw it all happening in front of him as though watching a movie through the windshield of the Fairlane. One second they were following the RSO unit around a bend in the road and the next he was being thrown forward as McPheron slammed on the brakes. "He's bailing out," McPheron yelled as he flung the driver's door open and leapt out himself. Alone in the passenger seat, D.J. saw the Riverside deputy dive out of his vehicle just as the rear windows of the RSO unit exploded. McCarty tried to process the activity unfolding before him as he gripped the unloaded M16, his eyes riveted on the deputy discharging his revolver as he retreated to the rear of the unit.

As Evans ducked behind his vehicle to reload, McCarty saw a gunman with wild, bushy hair rise up off to the right, one foot on the hillside, aiming his rifle down over Evans's unit. He could make out two figures farther up the hill near the rear of the truck, both with rifles. *Don't come back up in the same place you went down*, McCarty thought, watching Evans reload.

An instant later, Evans came up again to fire. D.J. saw his head suddenly jerk back. Evans spun to his right, discharging a round from his .38 into the dirt as he fell, a spray of liquid ejecting out from the area of his head. As he went down, D.J. could see a massive hole in his face. And then Jim Evans disappeared, falling dead just feet in front of the hood of McCarty's unit.

The rounds that came crashing through the windshield of McCarty's patrol unit a moment later were a continuation of the volley that had just killed Jim Evans. The first punched a hole through the safety glass high on the right side and dug into the roof of the Fairlane. McCarty let go of the M16 and rolled to his left, lifting his right arm to shield his face. When the second round came through, D.J. saw the sleeve of his red windbreaker puff out as the bullet tore a chunk of soft tissue off the inside of his right elbow.

McCarty knew he needed to get out of the car or he would die there. Sitting up quickly, he grabbed the handle to the passenger door and kicked it open. Rounds immediately struck the front quarter panel of the Fairlane and the side of the open door. Forgetting about the M16 now lying on the seat beside him, D.J. tried to unlatch the shotgun from its mount at the center of the dashboard, but the maneuver required two hands to perform, so he gave up. With a cascade of gunfire echoing off the canyon walls and rounds hissing overhead, D.J. made a desperate crawl across the front seat and spilled out the driver's side onto the dirt roadway, unarmed. There was another burst of gunfire, even closer this time as rounds struck off the roadbed. Out of options and certain he would be killed at any moment, D.J. did the only thing he could think of: He began to dig.

Even with the low clearance of the Ford Fairlane, McCarty somehow managed to clear away enough of the loose roadbed to get most of his body underneath the patrol unit. Lying on his stomach, he heard McPheron calling to him from the rear of the vehicle. "D.J., are you all right? Are you all right?"

"I'm okay, but I don't have a weapon," McCarty called back. There was another volley of gunfire, this time the muzzle blasts sounding much closer than they had before. They're coming to execute me, he thought. "Mac, give me a gun," he yelled back to his partner. There was no reply from McPheron. D.J. turned his head to see if he could spot the legs of the suspects from underneath the vehicle. What he saw instead was the body of Jim Evans lying in the road, his glasses shattered beside him and a gaping wound where his right eye socket had been. Please, God, don't let me end up like that, D.J. thought. That's when he remembered the M16.

Clawing his way out from under the Fairlane, McCarty reached up and blindly swept his hand over the front seat searching for the weapon. He grabbed ahold of the barrel of the gun, and the M16 and two magazines fell out onto the dirt beside him. McCarty shoved one of the magazines into the bottom of the weapon. He grabbed the bolt and pulled it back to chamber a round, but the magazine just fell out onto the dirt. Bullets struck the road around him. He tried it again. The magazine fell out again. He looked into the breech and saw that the rod had failed to forward the round. If this thing is broken, he thought, I'm fucking dead. There was another burst of gunfire. In a panic, McCarty beat the M16 against a large rock on the roadbed and then tried the loading procedure again. This time the magazine locked in place and the rod forwarded the round into the chamber.

D.J. leapt to his feet and caught a glimpse of movement at the rear of the pickup truck. He lifted the M16 above his head and emptied half of the twenty-round magazine in the direction of the yellow truck, sweeping the weapon back and forth to cover the width of the road with gunfire. It was only when he ducked back down that D.J. realized he had been so afraid of being shot that he had closed his eyes the entire time he was firing.

It was suddenly silent. McCarty looked over the door, scanning the roadway in front of him. The figures were gone. He took a deep breath and advanced to the rear driver's side of Evans's unit. He lifted the gun, sighted in on the back of the yellow truck, and fired, sending rounds into the tailgate, trailer hitch, and through the back window. He saw something lying in the road that he thought might be a body and emptied the remainder of the clip at the object, but it turned out to be nothing more than a rag.

Jim McPheron moved up from behind the Fairlane to D.J.'s previous position behind the open door and took the shotgun out from the unit, crouching behind the open door.

McCarty flipped the jungle clip over and this time it locked easily into the magazine port. He knelt beside Evans. Suddenly there was the booming of four shotgun blasts just behind him. McCarty jumped, accidentally discharging a round from the M16. McPheron had decided to lay down some cover for D.J. without telling him.

Deputy Mike Lenihan advanced to the rear of the Fairlane from his own unit one car back. Along with him was Highway Patrol officer Steve Batchelor. Lenihan motioned to Batchelor and together they darted forward in a crouch to Evans. The two men dragged him back to the driver's side of the Fairlane, McPheron emptying all six rounds from his .38 as cover. When they were back, McPheron retrieved a first aid box from the trunk of the Fairlane and dressed a bandage over Evans's grotesquely enlarged eye socket. It was the only thing he could think to do. The men huddled behind the two patrol units with their weapons drawn. "If they still want to kill us," Lenihan said, motioning with his revolver toward the thick brush on the top of the hill above them, "that's where they'll go." McCarty stood and fired a dozen rounds from the M16 up the hill.

WATCHING THE ACTIVITY AT THE WASHOUT SITE FROM A BEND IN THE ROAD far below, detective Mike Jordan put out an urgent plea for all RSO personnel to clear the air of all the goddamn radio chatter. *E-229, can you copy. We request that you maintain minimum traffic. We have a very hazardous situation on Sierra. We got several officers shot and we don't know what the status is with all this traffic.*

10-4. All units minimum traffic, even on emergency, Keeter relayed. *Reference Sierra Avenue.* Keeter's transmission was calm and measured, but the meaning was not lost on those who heard it: Something had gone terribly wrong in Lytle Creek.

Hovering above in 40-King-1, John Plasencia and Ed Mabry had watched helplessly as the firefight unfolded on the roadway below. Mabry had momentarily lost sight of the truck behind a row of trees and when he finally reestablished a visual on the suspects, they were already standing in the road. Thirty-six seconds after Jim Evans had asked if the truck was moving, Bender finally came over the radio with the answer from 40-King-1: *The vehicle is stopped. They're on foot.* Now Plasencia and Mabry could see something else happening below: The suspects were getting away.

Chris Harven pushed himself up to his hands and knees and began to crawl up the road. It felt as though someone had stuck a knife in his back. After five yards, he got to his feet and walked to the tumble of gravel, boulders, and tree trunks that had rushed down the mountain and buried Baldy Notch Road. He picked a route and began to climb his way across. Ahead of him, Manny scrambled across, still holding Chris's Heckler. When he got to the other side of the washout, Delgado just kept walking and never looked back.

Chris saw his brother crossing the washout just above him, carrying the "Shorty" AR-15. Where's George? Chris called. Russ paused, looked around, and then motioned downhill. George was below the level of the roadbed, still carrying the .308 and moving slowly, his feet slipping out from under him on the loose shale. I'm done, George called up to them, breathing heavily, his face pale and waxy, pants blood-soaked down to the knee. I'm bleeding out.

Chris took the Heckler from George and squinted up at the chopper cruising just below the cloud cover, the blades cutting the air with a guttural sound. He looked at the road ahead of them. A hundred yards farther up, it curved around the back of the mountain, the dirt and gravel seeming to disappear into the gray sky. Just get up around that bend and you can go over the side, he said to George. They began to slowly walk up the hill. Russ hoisted the "Shorty" over his shoulder and followed behind them. Ahead, Manny reached the top and disappeared around the bend.

After another few minutes, Russ, Chris, and George came to the sharp bend that would take them to the other side of the ridge. Russ Harven took one last look at the scene below them, the long line of cars, the blue and red lights flashing against the canyon walls in the falling dusk. I knew this was a fucked-up idea, he said to himself before disappearing around the bend with the others.

On the other side of the mountain, the road was just as steep as before. George went to the edge and stood looking down the hillside of chaparral. I'm gonna slough off here, he said. He stepped over the edge and slid down a few feet on the loose dirt. Chris handed the Heckler down to him. George took the gun and went down the hillside a few dozen more feet before abruptly tossing the rifle aside and then continuing down.

Chris and Russ moved on. A few hundred yards up, Chris suddenly veered off and went over the edge. When Russ looked back, he was just gone. Russ kept going, all alone now. After another bend in the road, he went over the side himself. The loose dirt kicked out from under his boots and he fell back and began to slide and tumble down the hill. He got his feet under him again and kept going. Reaching a group of fallen trees, he found an opening beneath one and shoved the "Shorty" AR underneath it. It was one thing to be holding the cops off from the back of a speeding pickup truck, but there was no way they were going to shoot their way out of a canyon on foot. The only thing a rifle would do now was slow him down.

A little farther down he came to a stand of fir trees and leaned against a boulder among them to rest. He ran his hand along his head until he came to the bump where the pellet of buckshot was nestled beneath his scalp. An inch lower and I'd be right there with Billy, he thought. He sat and looked out over the canyon, his breath visible in the cold air. Below him, Coldwater Canyon opened up to the North Fork of Lytle Creek. He could see the stretch of Lytle Creek Road they had traveled a short time before. Law enforcement vehicles were still streaming up the road toward Stockton Flats. The San Bernardino sheriff's helicopter that had been following them made one last pass and then swooped down into the canyon just below the cloud cover and headed back toward the Inland Empire. He watched it go.

CROUCHED BEHIND THE REAR FENDER OF JIM EVANS'S PATROL CAR, D. J. McCarty heard the last transmission from 40-King-1. Give me a cigarette, he asked Lenihan, even though he rarely smoked. Lenihan shook a pair of Marlboros out of his pack and the two men sat smoking behind the cover of Evans's unit.

Lenihan checked McCarty's wounded elbow. A chunk of flesh the diameter of a golf ball had been torn off. We should get you out of here, he said. McCarty shook his head. There was another radio transmission. An eight-man SWAT team from San Bernardino PD was at Stockton Flats and making its way up the mountain. I'll leave when they get here, he said, lighting a second cigarette off the first.

RIVERSIDE DETECTIVE JIM HOPKINS WALKED UP THE HILL TO WHERE ROLF Parkes, Fred Chisholm, and Mike Jordan were standing beside Jordan's unit far back in the pursuit line. Hopkins had been behind the wheel while Don Bender was working the CLEMARS. I hear you're wounded, he said to Parkes.

Parkes pulled back his hair to display the shallow rut etched into his scalp. "It's nothing."

Look, Rolf, Hopkins said patiently. Nothing else is going to happen up here tonight. Do me a favor and take the chopper out of here and get that thing looked at.

Rolf had been trying to rally the other deputies to form a posse and go after the escaping bank robbers on foot, but he knew Hopkins was right. He handed over the lever-action .22 and headed dejectedly up the hill toward the landing site.

Coming down the hill at the same time to be evacuated by the Huey 500 was another wounded deputy. D. J. McCarty had finally relinquished the M16 to San Bernardino sergeant Dennis O'Rourke and was headed in the direction of the landing site a few hundred yards below. In the fading daylight, McCarty passed the SWAT team headed up to the ambush area. "If you see 'em, shoot 'em," McCarty told them as he passed. "Don't try to capture 'em; just fucking shoot 'em."

The heavily armed SWAT members were expressionless. D.J. saw it in their eyes, the look of soldiers marching into a battle they knew they might not survive. SWAT was accustomed to surrounding houses and bringing superior firepower to bear on a suspect, not walking into a remote wilderness in the dark to go up against equally well-armed men. There was none of the usual SWAT team swagger and bravado. These guys are scared, D.J. thought.

D. J. McCarty and Rolf Parkes had never met before and had no idea what the other had just gone through. Once they had jammed themselves into the cramped compartment of the police Huey, Rolf asked McCarty what had happened up there. McCarty told him how Jim Evans had died. Parkes nodded silently. "What happened with you?" McCarty asked. Rolf told him. The blades of the Huey cranked up to a deafening roar and the chopper lifted off, McCarty and Parkes staring down as the mountainside faded into the distance.

Below them on Baldy Notch Road, the painstaking process of backing dozens of law enforcement vehicles down to Stockton Flats was underway. It grew dark and a freezing rain began to fall. Back at RSO dispatch, Gary Keeter began a roll call to account for all the Riverside personnel in the field.

"2-Edward-21?"

"2-Edward-21, copy."

"Edward-320?"

"Edward-320, copy."

On the mountainside, the blue and red lights still swirled, flashlights swept the ridgeline, and deputies huddled against the cold. Over the Riverside frequency, Keeter could be heard calling out the identification codes, amplified throughout the canyon by the vehicle radios and portables hanging off the hips of the deputies.

"2-Edward-71?"

"2-Edward-71, copy."

"Edward-20?"

"Edward-20, copy."

"2-Edward-74?"

On Baldy Notch Road, the men leaned against their patrol units and listened, studying the outline of the mountain against the dark sky.

"2-Edward-74?"

"Deputy Evans?"

All was silent on the mountain.

10

SOME MEN NEVER GET TO SEE THEIR SONS GROW UP

May 9, 1980. Norco, California.

AT THE INTERSECTION OF FOURTH AND HAMNER, RIVERSIDE SHERIFF'S LIEU-
tenant Floyd Oden found himself with overall responsibility for a crime scene that extended unbroken for more than forty miles, the largest in U.S. law enforcement history. After a very public screaming match between Oden and lieutenant Jack Reid over who should have command of the scene, deputy chief Ron Bickmore stepped in and assigned the job to Oden.

The first thing Oden did was split Fourth and Hamner into two primary responsibilities to which he assigned two of his best investigators. Detective Joe Curfman was put in charge of the bank itself, interviewing employees and witnesses and gathering evidence.

Oden designated everything immediately outside the bank "Crime Scene #1" and assigned it to his top evidence investigator, John Burden. Burden was a big walrus of a man with a bushy mustache and a meticulous eye for detail. His first challenge was to secure the crime scene and stop all the sergeants and lieutenants from waltzing their way through to gawk at Billy Delgado, now handcuffed per protocol and slumped over dead between the two front seats. What should I do with all this brass wandering around here?

Burden asked Oden after receiving his assignment. Tell them to get the fuck out of there, Oden said. So that's exactly what Burden did.

Burden and his team had just started the painstaking task of finding, marking, gathering, and logging every last piece of evidence when a sergeant approached. "Oden needs your help," the man said, motioning to an unmarked car just north of the intersection. "Delgado won't give up his gun."

Burden let out a sigh and lumbered over to the car. Floyd Oden and Andy Delgado were sitting in the back seat arguing. Burden opened the door and slid onto the seat, using his ample girth to push Delgado into the center. Andy was now sandwiched between the two much larger men. "Give him the goddamn gun, Andy," Burden said.

Delgado dug in. "You're not going to leave me unarmed," he said.

"Goddamn it, Andy, you know the rules," Burden barked. "It's evidence. We have to take it."

"But I never even fired it!" Andy protested.

"Just give him the gun," Burden said, softening his tone. Andy let out a sigh, took the .357 out of the holster, and handed it to Burden. Burden flipped open the cylinder and shook out the six unspent rounds. "Thank you," he said, opening the car door and heading back in the direction of the green van.

Shortly thereafter, an ID tech named Sue Dobson came over to Burden, gingerly holding a .45-caliber pistol she had just found lying in the dirt outside the van door. Loaded and cocked, the woman told him.

At 5:58 p.m., Burden got on the radio with Larry Brown of the Norco Fire Department. There had been some sort of incendiary device detonated under a gas main just south of Second Street. A witness reported seeing a green van speeding away from the scene. "I think these might be your guys," Brown said.

Carefully sorting through the contents of the van, Burden spotted what looked like a dozen wooden dowels projecting out of a duffel bag. When he looked and saw what was inside, he immediately ordered everyone away and put in a request for the Riverside Police Department bomb squad.

At 6:34 p.m., head of the RPD bomb squad, Bill Miller, began clearing the van of explosives—ten stick bombs, three Blue Nun Molotov cocktails, and a half dozen fragmentation grenades—and laid them out on Fourth Street. After that, Burden's team went in and began pulling out gas masks, field glasses, a compass, forty-round banana clips, a machete, an AR-15, handguns, and unopened ammunition boxes, more than one thousand rounds in all. The MacDonald walkie-talkie on the passenger seat next to Billy Delgado was still turned on and crackling with static. The last item taken from the van was a samurai sword with a gym sock pulled over the handle.

At 7:38 p.m., deputy coroner Doug McCoy arrived and removed Billy from the van. While searching the area around the body, he found a wallet and handed it to Burden. Burden opened the wallet, anxious to find out the identity of his dead suspect. He looked at the photo of a very white, middle-aged man with owlish eyeglasses. Who is this guy? One of the other investigators checked out the photo. That's our hostage.

John Burden's job was far from over. In fact, Burden would not get to sleep for another sixty hours. At 2:00 a.m., he and Joe Curfman were at Grimes Funeral Home on Hamner watching pathologist Rene Modglin dissect Billy Delgado. Billy was X-rayed and sliced open, long needles sunk into his heart and bladder to drain out fluid samples contained therein, his stomach cut open and contents removed. His cranial cap was sawed and detached, his brain set on the table next to him while the doctor fished out the quarter-ounce ball of buckshot from the base of Billy's cranial cavity.

He dropped the tiny pellet into an evidence baggie and handed it to Burden. The detective stared at it, no bigger than the scrawniest kernel in a can of corn. This is all your fault, isn't it? he thought. Just a few inches to the left and this thing is harmlessly rolling around a gutter on Hamner Avenue, Jim Evans is home rocking his infant son, and Billy Delgado is lying in a motel room in Vegas with his first hooker instead of on a stainless steel table with his brain beside him. And all because of you, you little motherfucker.

AFTER A WHILE, SOMEONE TOLD ANDY DELGADO HE WAS NO LONGER NEEDED on scene. He was driven home and dropped off at the curb in front of his house. Andy stood on the front lawn for a long time trying to figure out what he should do now. He went inside and told his wife, Lucretia. He ate dinner with his seven-year-old daughter, Tanya. He fidgeted while watching news reports of the incident, grew restless and wandered around the house. His car was still back at the RSO, so he could not even go for a drive to clear his head. He called the station. Sure, they'd send someone over to pick him up; they needed to interview him anyhow.

Around eight thirty that night, three deputies pulled up in an unmarked vehicle. They had a case of beer with them. We'll take you to HQ, but we're going to stop by the hospital first, they told him, tossing Andy a beer.

The other deputies had been only peripherally involved in the incident but were still amped-up like athletes after the biggest game of their lives. Andy grew quiet and began running the whole gun battle over and over in his head, slowing it down so he could examine every decision he made in excruciating detail. Did I do everything right? Yeah, he was sure he had. He went back through it again, right from the 211 to when the yellow truck had disappeared over the rise. But the question would not go away: *Did I do everything right?*

Glyn Bolasky and Darrell Reed had been moved out of the ER and were sharing a room, doped up on painkillers and flicking through local channels until they could find another report of the Norco bank robbery. Reed's leg was elevated and bandaged, half the .223 bullet still lodged just below the knee. Bolasky's elbow was wrapped in gauze, and his face, chest, and shoulder were patched up where bullet fragments and broken glass had been plucked from his flesh. Still, the young deputy was in good spirits.

Delgado stood at the back of the room studying Bolasky's bandaged elbow. He had expected it to be worse. Much worse. How bad is that arm? Andy asked. How many stitches? Just two or three, but it hit an artery. Well, I'm glad it's not that bad, Andy said. Andy continued to watch Bolasky joking with the others, the sound of Chuck Hille's radio transmission looping over and over in his mind. *2-Edward-59, I'm rolling Bolasky to the hospital.* They fucking left me there, he thought, staring at the gauze wrapped around Bolasky's arm. And for what? *That*?

HERMAN BROWN AND KEN MCDANIELS, BOTH SHOT AT THE INTERSECTION OF Limonite and Etiwanda, were treated and released, bullet fragments either extracted from their bodies or left right where they were. California Highway Patrol officer Bill Crowe had been kept longer while even more shrapnel and glass were taken out of his body. Remarkably, not even the wound from the bullet that had entered his arm and exited through his back was serious enough to keep him overnight and he too was released. A. J. Reynard, the youngest deputy on the Riverside force and the one who had inadvertently chased the yellow truck for a quarter mile down Bellegrave, remained in Riverside General Hospital. The first of two surgeries on his wounded elbow was scheduled for the next day.

D. J. McCARTY ALMOST DID NOT SEE THE PHOTOGRAPHER FROM THE *San Bernardino Sun* in time as he walked from the helicopter landing pad at Loma Linda University Medical Center. Chopper pilot Vic Brimmer gave D.J. the heads-up as they strode down the ramp together with Rolf Parkes just ahead of them. Uh, you might want to cover up that T-shirt. In the photo that ran in the papers the next day, McCarty is holding together both sides of the red windbreaker to hide the image of the Zig-Zag Man smoking a giant doobie emblazoned on the front of his T-shirt. The look on McCarty's face could be construed as a slight smirk.

The expression on the face of Rolf Parkes is decidedly different. It is the look of a man realizing how close he had just come to dying. The adrenaline that had kept him fearless in a pursuit under heavy fire was beginning to wear off. Parkes found himself overwhelmed with emotion. Under the bright fluorescent light of the emergency room, Rolf suddenly felt very far from home and utterly alone. He used a desk phone to call his wife. Susan was distraught. The department just called me and told me you had been shot in the head, she said. That's all they said, that you had been shot in the head. She began to cry.

To Parkes, Susan's voice was that of a widow having been notified of her husband's death. His death. Rolf began to sob, filled with an indescribable sadness for himself and for Jim Evans.

Susan insisted on driving to the hospital, but Rolf told her no. It was a long way and he would probably be leaving soon anyhow.

He hung up the phone and leaned against the wall but could not stop weeping. An instant later, he was screaming, his hands cupped over his right eye. There's something in my eye, he yelled. In an examination room, a doctor used drops of dye to study the eye under a black light. He carefully extracted a shard of glass two millimeters long from under the eyelid. It had been in there since the initial attack on Holmes Avenue, but only now was dislodged by his tears.

They put a patch on the eye and rolled Rolf into a room to wait for X-rays. San Bernardino sheriff's detective Carlos Acevedo came into the room and asked Parkes if he could interview him about the incident. Still on an adrenaline crash, Parkes could barely make it through the questioning, pausing frequently to choke back tears. Detective Acevedo concluded his report with a notation:

> I observed Deputy Parkes to be in an emotional state at this time in that
> he kept holding back and crying several times during the interview. The
> interview was concluded at this time.

D. J. McCarty looked at the chunk of flesh missing from his right elbow under the bright examination lights of the emergency room. This is probably going to hurt, the doctor said before commencing to dig around in the wound with the end of a long Q-tip. Every muscle in McCarty's body clenched down against the pain. He could feel something inside his left fist. Why don't you give me that? said an ER nurse. Bullets from Jim Evans's revolver dropped into the woman's hand. D.J. had no idea he had been clutching them since leaving the mountain.

The doctor told McCarty they were going to keep him overnight for observation. McCarty told them they were not. They argued with him. McCarty walked out. When he got back to his apartment somewhere near midnight, his roommate, Mike Lenihan, was sitting on the couch staring blankly at the television set. D.J. sat on the couch beside him. You okay, Mikey? he asked.

Sure, Lenihan said.

The image of Lenihan dragging the body of Jim Evans across the dirt on Baldy Notch Road returned to D.J. Shit, thought McCarty, Mikey was definitely not okay.

IT WAS 10:00 P.M. WHEN MARY EVANS FINISHED HER SHIFT AND PULLED THE big city bus into the lot at the Riverside Transit Agency where she had been a driver for the last few years. As she loaded her gear into a locker, a transit dispatcher called over to her.

Hey, there was a big shootout in Norco today, she said. Your husband doesn't work there, does he?

Mary looked at the woman. Not in Norco, but if there was a big shootout, he sure as hell would have been part of it. Did he call?

No, but your babysitter's been calling for you.

It's okay, Mary told herself. No reason to worry. She went to a phone in the office and dialed their babysitter Josie's house. J.B. Jr. was still there; Jim never showed to pick him up. Mary hung up and dialed the RSO. She was transferred to a sergeant. I heard there was a big shootout in Norco today, she asked the man in a firm voice. Can you tell me where my husband is?

There was a pause. I can't tell you anything over the phone, the sergeant answered.

I know he was involved, said Mary, and I want to know where he is.

We're sending a car over, the man said. That's all I can do.

A few minutes later, an unmarked car arrived at the municipal yard, a stone-faced man she did not know behind the wheel. When they got to the house on Oakley Avenue, neighbors were on the lawn and a fleet of RSO vehicles were lined up along the curb. Above the crowd towered one man. Mary immediately recognized six-and-a-half-foot-tall sheriff Ben Clark. So, this is how it happens, she thought to herself.

Mary marched straight up to Clark. Where's my husband? she demanded.

I think we should go inside, Clark said gravely.

It was getting near midnight and Mary was done with the bullshit. What time did he die? she asked.

Around four thirty, someone answered.

Are you telling me my husband died seven hours ago and you never even came down to get me? The bus depot is only two blocks down from your headquarters. Everyone in that department knows I work for the transit authority.

Mary turned her back on the sheriff and went into the house. It was filled with her friends and neighbors, all of them grief-stricken. Vince Kreter, a thirteen-year-old boy from across the street, was sobbing inconsolably. Jim had grown close to the young man after the death of Vince's father six months earlier. Mary's fifteen-year-old daughter, Michelle, sat trembling on the sofa, a neighbor trying to comfort her.

Mary sat down at the kitchen table, remembering how Jim had stopped by on his way out to his shift that very morning to check in on J.B. Jr. He had sat in that same chair holding the infant in his arms. "Jim, how come you never put that baby down?" she said to him, smiling. "Because I want him to know who I am," he had said. He looked up at her. "You know, Mary, some men never get to see their sons grow up."

"Excuse me, but there's something I have to do," Mary said, standing up from the table. She went to a back room, picked up the phone, and called Jim's parents in Texas. Jim's mother refused to believe her. "That can't be true. I was just out there with him. I was just there!" Mary heard the receiver being set on a kitchen table a thousand miles away, the mother's voice calling her husband to the phone. Mary thought of their house, all of Jim's awards and commendations proudly displayed on the walls. God, how they adored their oldest son. Jim's father refused to accept the news either. "I just can't . . ." His voice trailed away. For a moment, Mary could hear wailing in the background, and then the line went dead.

IT WAS 10:00 P.M. BY THE TIME ANDY DELGADO REACHED THE RSO. HE SAT alone in the pit outside the dispatch room waiting to be taken upstairs to be interviewed. Dave Madden came into the pit, stopped, and stared. Shit, Andy, I thought you were dead.

Rolf Parkes entered from the outside door. After having his head x-rayed and the glass fished out of his eye, he had been driven back to Riverside for one last departmental interview and to get his car for the drive home to Long Beach. Rolf had not seen anyone from his own department since being flown off the mountain and was eager to talk to someone. He sat on the bench next to Delgado. Evans is dead, Rolf told him. I know, said Andy. He sure came a long way just to get killed. Did we kill any of those guys up there? No, Rolf said. They all got away. A detective came into the pit and motioned Andy to follow him. Andy paused at the door and looked at Parkes. We just got our asses kicked, didn't we?

THIRTEEN MILES UP LYTLE CREEK CANYON AT A COMMAND CENTER SET UP AT Glen Ranch, preparations were being made to make sure Saturday, May 10, would be very different than the day before. Hundreds of heavily armed men were arriving with helicopters, dog teams, mounted search-and-rescue squads, and the most advanced equipment available to support them. The military offered up a helicopter gunship, night vision goggles, and a truck-load of arctic parkas to help with the massive manhunt that was to commence at first light. Just after midnight, the San Bernardino County Sheriff's Office put a call into the L.A. County Sheriff's Office, or LASO, with a request. In the predawn darkness with a cold rain falling, LASO SWAT personnel began arriving at Glen Ranch in buses. The L.A. Sheriff's Office had a fancy name for the specially trained two-man units they had been asked to send in, but most cops called them by their specialty: the Hunt & Kill teams.

Calvary Chapel ocean baptism, Corona Del Mar, circa 1973.
(Los Angeles Times)

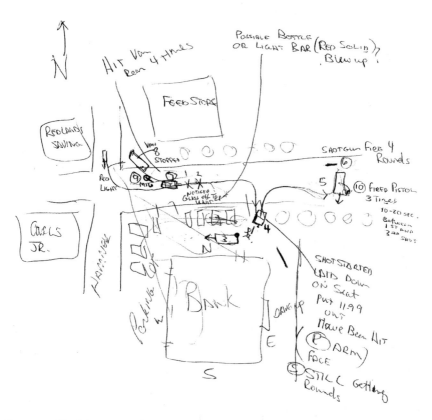

Diagram of firefight at Fourth & Hamner made by deputy Glyn Bolasky. Bolasky started at position marked "red light" and progressed through those marked 1–5. *(RSO)*

Riverside deputy Andy Delgado. *(Andy Delgado)*

Riverside deputy Glyn Bolasky. *(RPE)*

Deputy Chuck Hille holding Jim Evans Jr., with Mary Evans (LEFT). *(RSA/RPE)*

Hostage Gary Hakala. *(RPE)*

Mug shot of Manny Delgado from previous minor arrest. *(Orange County Sheriff)*

Aerial photo of Security Pacific Bank, looking East down Fourth St. Deputy Glyn Bolasky's vehicle is top left in roadway. *(RSO)*

Green van used in the robbery. *(RSO)*

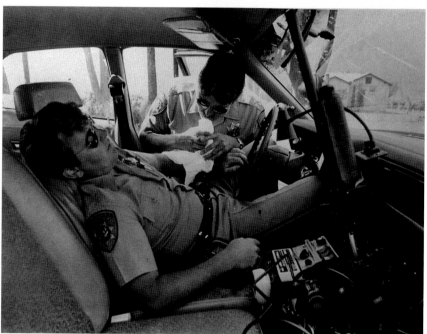

Bellegrave & Dodd: CHP officer Doug Earnest bandaging wounded patrolman Bill Crowe. *(RPE/Jim Edwards)*

Sketch showing position of shooters in yellow truck during the pursuit. *(RSO)*

Deputy James Evans. *(RSO)*

Deputy James McPheron (LEFT) and D. J. McCarty with ambush site model used in trial. *(RPE)*

Yellow truck abandoned at washout site. *(RSO)*

Washout, Baldy Notch Road. *(RSO)*

Bullet holes in the windshield of A. J. Reynard's 511 car. *(RSO)*

Rolf Parkes (LEFT) & D. J. McCarty (CENTER) airlifted to Loma Linda University Medical Center. *(San Bernardino Sun)*

George Smith under arrest. *(RPE)*

Christopher Harven (TOP
LEFT), Russell Harven
(LEFT), and a wounded
George Smith (TOP RIGHT)
in custody, Lytle Creek.
*(Top left and right: San
Bernardino Sun; left: RPE)*

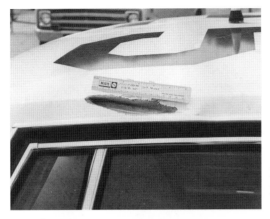

Damage to the roof of Andy Delgado's vehicle from a .308-caliber bullet. *(RSO)*

Thirty-two police vehicles were disabled or destroyed. Bolasky's vehicle at Fourth & Hamner (ABOVE), windshield of Jim Evans's unit (RIGHT). *(RSO)*

Russell Harven in courtroom. *(RPE)*

Christopher Harven during jailhouse interview. *(RPE)*

Smith with attorney Clayton Adams. *(RPE)*

Smith and defense investigator Jeanne Painter. *(San Bernardino Sun)*

11

SHOT THROUGH
THE HEART

May 10, 1980. San Bernardino National Forest, California.

GEORGE WAYNE SMITH WOKE WITH A START. HE OPENED HIS EYES AND blinked up at a sky just beginning to streak with purple light over the ridgeline to the east. He was confused and disoriented. How long had he been on this mountain? Had he slept through an entire day and into the next? He could not be sure of any of that, but there was one thing he did know: He was dying.

George sat up on the steep hillside and looked out over the blackness of Coldwater Canyon. A dusting of snow fell from his green military poncho. He remembered waking up in darkness, seeing the crystals of ice and snow sparkling as they fell around him and thinking perhaps his soul was being lifted up to meet his Lord in the sky. But then he lost consciousness and awoke to a hard, freezing rain. With the coming of daylight, it was a heavy, wet mist but still cold as hell, the temperatures hovering just above freezing. Even with the rain poncho, heavy boots, and gloves, he was soaked through, drifting in and out of a dream world of hypothermia.

He licked his lips. They were chapped and dry, his mouth parched. That had started while he was bleeding out in the back of the truck. It was the dehydration that goes along with hypovolemia. He reached down and felt the makeshift tourniquet tied around his thigh. The bleeding had mostly stopped, but the leg had a sickening numbness to it. Looking out over the canyon and contemplating his fate, George felt none of the comfort of a man destined for the Kingdom of Heaven; he felt like a man who had seriously fucked up. He leaned back and drifted into darkness.

"TRACKERS, REPORT TO YOUR COMMAND POSTS. TRACKERS, REPORT TO YOUR command posts," the temporary PA system blasted as the first slivers of light began to appear over Lytle Creek Canyon. The deputies, SWAT teams, and support personnel at the command post at Glen Ranch slowly emerged from wherever they had been seeking shelter throughout a night of frigid drizzles and downpours. The truckload of arctic parkas had helped somewhat, but it had been a miserable night.

Around midnight, a burst of gunfire was heard from somewhere in the mountains and rumor spread that the fugitives might be signaling to each other or perhaps had even killed one of their own. After that, it was just waiting for dawn to arrive and the expectation of an armed confrontation against four desperate men with nothing left to lose.

SWAT members made their way to a command vehicle, checked out M16 rifles, snapped in high-capacity magazines, and donned bulletproof vests. Others stood scarfing down plates of scrambled eggs cooked up by county jail inmates in a nearby chow trailer. Bloodhounds and German shepherds strained at their leads and circled their Fontana Police Department handlers, sniffing the ground around them. Mounted police teams gathered around a line of horse trailers. Trackers from the San Bernardino Mountain Rescue Team kicked at the dirt and waited to be teamed up with heavily armed escorts. After giving his men a final briefing, San Bernardino assistant sheriff Floyd Tidwell looked up from the terrain map laid out on the table. "Now go get those assholes and protect those trackers," he said.

At the head of one search team was sergeant Larry Richards of San Bernardino PD SWAT. Along with three of his men and three San Bernardino sheriff's deputies, Richards began his search at 8:00 a.m. at the site of the ambush on Baldy Notch Road. Richards's team would advance up the grade in the direction of a second tracker team equipped with cold-weather gear working its way down from the 7,800-foot summit of Baldy Notch.

At the washout itself, Richards's trackers picked up a trail of blood leading up the narrow fire road. If they had not already been on high alert, they were now. Not only were they at ground zero of the search, but there was a good chance that whoever had lost this much blood had not gone far. They fanned out and began creeping up the road while others swept the hillsides over the sights of their M16 rifles, looking for movement or muzzle flashes. After a few hundred yards, they came to the hairpin turn on the outside edge of the mountain leading to the backside of the ridge. It was the last place the fleeing suspects had been seen and therefore the first place they might be found. Richards and the others had been briefed on the terrain on the other side of the bend: a wide-open valley of steep hillsides dotted with pines and sloping into thick underbrush where they would be exposed on three sides. The suspects had explosives, shitloads of ammunition, and a strong preference for ambushing pursuers. Anyone engaging the suspects should be prepared for a ferocious firefight. And another thing, Richards was informed: The thick mist hanging in the canyon would prevent any early-morning helicopter support.

It was under these conditions that Richards and his team entered Coldwater Canyon. What they encountered was nothing like what they had been told to expect. Almost immediately, Richards heard a voice calling out from somewhere on the hillside. "Here!" it seemed to be saying. At first, the men thought it must be another law enforcement team. But then one of the trackers spotted something a few hundred yards down the embankment.

The men dropped low, spread out, and took positions. Within seconds, four high-powered scopes mounted atop M16 rifles were trained on a figure seated behind a thick manzanita bush waving his hands above the top of the brush line. The shouting continued. They waited, gun barrels steady.

Richards radioed command that they had made contact with a possible suspect, giving them his location. At Stockton Flats, personnel immediately deployed to positions at the top and bottom of the mountainside to reinforce

Richards's team. Once in place, Richards signaled to one of his SWAT officers, Jess Hernandez, to follow him down the hill. There was no need for Richards to remind his men of the standing order for dealing with an armed cop killer: If he makes one wrong move, shoot him dead.

It was slow going down the hill, traversing over loose shale and weaving between granite boulders and clusters of California chaparral. When they were close, Richards shouted for their suspect to raise his hands and keep them in the air. The suspect complied. When Richards and Hernandez got within a dozen feet, they ordered him to stretch out facedown on the hillside. "Please, I've been shot," the man said as his wrists were pulled behind his back and cuffed. "I've lost a lot of blood."

Hernandez searched the suspect, removed the Browning .45 from a shoulder holster. Richards popped the magazine out and then removed a live round from the chamber. When Hernandez rolled the suspect over, the cops got their first good look at one of the men responsible for the madness of the day before: round face grimacing in pain; dark eyes that seemed to be going in and out of focus; wild, curly black hair. He was shivering uncontrollably, wet blood staining his pants from crotch to knee. This dude is fucked-up, Richards thought. Richards radioed a "Code 4": situation stable, suspect neutralized, all law enforcement personnel okay. George Wayne Smith, the man who had vowed never to be taken alive, had just surrendered.

SAN BERNARDINO COUNTY SHERIFF'S HOMICIDE DETECTIVE ROSS DVORAK had just reached the command center at 9:00 a.m. when the call came in. A wounded suspect had been apprehended on a remote hillside in Coldwater Canyon and needed to be questioned before he died on them. Dvorak was told to report to chopper 40-King-1 for immediate transport to the area. A Vietnam combat veteran with eleven years on the force but only a year and a half in Homicide, Dvorak had a preference for Hawaiian shirts, a strong resemblance to actor Burt Reynolds, and a talent for creative interrogations that somehow still held up in court. After being choppered in to the base of the mountainside, it took Dvorak forty-five minutes through thick brush to reach the spot three hundred yards upslope where the suspect was being led down by two San Bernardino SWAT officers. The man was so weak he could be moved only forty to fifty feet at a time before needing to stop and rest, each time requesting that he be allowed to sleep. When he reached Smith, Dvorak switched on a tape recorder.

"George, I'm Dvorak from Sheriff's Homicide, you understand that?" he said. "What's your full name?"

"George Smith. Wayne Smith," George answered, panting heavily. "Ahh," he groaned. "Let me catch my breath."

"George, there's a possibility that you may die. Do you realize that?"

"Yeah," George answered.

"With that in mind," Dvorak said, "do you want to tell me anything about what happened?" Dvorak's strategy was to bait Smith into a dying declaration right there on the mountainside.

"Helicopter," George said, nodding down the hill at 40-King-1. "Then we'll talk."

"We're going to do what we can, George," Dvorak said doubtfully, "but the helicopter can't land here and we have quite a ways to walk before we can get you to where you're going to be picked up. Do you understand that?"

"Ahh, goodness," George groaned.

"What happened, George?" Dvorak asked.

"I took three in my leg at the bank."

"Did you get in a shootout with the cops at a bank in Norco? The Security Pacific Bank?"

"Yes," Smith acknowledged.

One of the officers took Smith's elbow, anxious to get his suspect moving down the hill again. "George keeps saying he's going to pass out on us," he told Dvorak.

"How many of you were there?" Dvorak went on.

"Chris, Billy, Manny, George, and Russ."

"Do you know their last names?"

"There's two Harvens, Chris and Russ. Two Delgados and me, Smith."

"Do you know that an officer has been killed?" Dvorak asked.

"What? I don't . . ." George stammered, breathing heavily.

"I'm telling you now an officer has been killed," Dvorak said, "and you will be taken into custody in San Bernardino County for the murder of one officer. Did you see them kill the officer?"

"No. I . . ."

"Did you fire at any officers in this canyon area?"

"I fired but it was just . . . There wasn't . . ." George's voice faded off. Whatever hope he might have been harboring about ever walking the earth as a free man again had just vanished. "Ahh, ahh," he grunted, partly in pain, but also out of sheer despair at the situation in which he now found himself. "No more questions," he said.

Dvorak shut down the tape recorder while Smith and the SWAT officers moved another forty feet down the hill. When George again requested time to catch his breath, Dvorak clicked on the record button and read Smith his Miranda rights. George did not acknowledge that he understood his rights when asked. Dvorak moved ahead with more questions anyhow. "How many other banks have you hit, George?"

"None. I'm not a criminal," George asserted weakly, edging down the hill, grimacing with each step. "This was just a desperate move for me."

"George, I find that hard to believe. You robbed the Security Pacific Bank in Norco, though, didn't you? You got in a shootout which killed a cop, didn't you?"

"I don't know if I did, no."

"You don't know that you didn't, though, do you?"

"No, I don't," George conceded.

"Somebody killed him," Dvorak said, "and you were shooting at him, right?"

George did not answer.

It was 10:45 a.m. by the time they reached 40-King-1 waiting at the bottom of Coldwater Canyon. In all, it had taken them more than two hours since his capture to bring George three hundred yards down the hillside. After a short ride in 40-King-1 to a larger landing area, Smith was hauled out and roughly carried to a larger Huey helicopter with medics on board to treat him. Dvorak climbed in with them. Someone warned him not to slip in all the blood. The Huey lifted off.

As the medics worked away, Dvorak tried to pin George down on the killing of Jim Evans. "That first car that showed up on scene, the officer got out, were you shooting at him?"

"Yes," George said.

"Did you hit him?"

"I just sprayed bullets, you know. Just a wild firefight."

"How about back at the bank?"

"Bullets everywhere," George responded weakly.

Dvorak asked him if they were firing automatics. "None," George answered. "They might have sounded like automatics 'cause all those guys was throwin' lead. But I didn't fire at the pin-down part," he added, contradicting his statement moments before that he had. "When the firefight started there, I just kept walking. I was in a kind of half a daze, getting ready to pass out. I was so bad hit I'd lost just boo-coo blood."

The recorder was turned off again as the chopper set down on the landing pad at San Bernardino County Medical Center, and Smith was transferred to a guarded room in the ER. Doctors and nurses worked on Smith, changing him into a gown, attaching EKG stickers to his body, starting IVs of saline and antibiotics. They sat George up in bed while detectives photographed him, his dark eyes looking directly into the camera. Investigators from other agencies entered the room. Dvorak turned the tape recorder on again.

"You planned the operation yourself?" asked agent Robert Gray of the Riverside office of the FBI, a heart-monitoring device beeping rhythmically in the background.

"Yes, I did," answered George, his voice soft and clear now. "It was mine. I told them what to do in the bank. I cased the bank. I made the bombs. I did all that."

Dvorak wanted to know about the others. "We're all really good friends," George explained. "And then we all ran into really bad luck all at once."

"Who got killed at the scene?" Dvorak asked.

"Billy, unfortunately."

"He was the driver of the van?"

"And one of my best friends, yes. And that officer that was ... Like I said, that wasn't supposed to happen."

"Huh?" said Dvorak.

"That officer wasn't supposed to happen. Billy wasn't supposed to happen. None of that was supposed to happen. I fucked up."

"How?" Dvorak asked.

"I should have made it a minute and thirty seconds instead of two minutes."

RUSSELL HARVEN AWOKE SOMETIME IN THE NIGHT TOO, BUT HE SAW SOMEthing different than crystals of ice falling. Curled beside a log for shelter and without a rain parka, Russ was soaked through and shivering in bursts that shook his entire body. He had dug a shallow trench under a fallen pine and piled dirt and rocks over himself for warmth, but it was no match for the bitter cold at seven thousand feet. That he might have just dug his own grave for the second time in twelve hours was an irony not entirely lost on Russ. He needed food immediately and another insulin injection within the next few hours. But insulin, along with everything else he needed, was in the trunk of his brother's Z/28 in the parking lot of a Little League field in Norco. When he dozed off, it was just his body giving out from sheer exhaustion. The sleep never lasted long. Every time he opened his eyes and looked down Coldwater Canyon, he could see the headlights of vehicles moving slowly up Lytle Creek Road, the beams of searchlights sweeping the brush far below. All those people are here for one reason, Russ thought: to hunt me down and kill me.

But this time when Russ awoke in the predawn darkness, he decided he'd had enough. Slowly making his way back up the hillside, he reached Baldy Notch Road and began walking down with the intention of surrendering or being shot to death trying.

Then something caught his eye far below where the hillside leveled out into the dry wash of Coldwater Canyon. There, a small orange glow danced in the darkness among a stand of pines. Russ crouched low at the edge of the road watching the flickering light of the campfire. It could be cops. It could be some oblivious camper.

When he eventually made it to the clearing, it did not surprise him to see his brother huddled near the flame. Slumped against a fallen tree trunk, Chris was breathing in shallow, quick breaths, each one a conscious effort. He adjusted his position, grimacing in pain. You got shot? Russ asked. Chris coughed and spit blood onto the dirt. Yeah.

Russ sat on the log and leaned in toward the fire. After a few minutes, the shivering subsided. He was dizzy and nauseated from the shotgun pellet striking his skull. His ears rang from all the guns going off around him, including the "Shorty" AR he had fired so many times.

Chris reached for a stick from a pile beside him and tossed it into the small fire. Russ saw his brother's lips move, but there was no sound. Russ asked, How bad you hit? Plenty bad, Chris said. They were silent for a while, staring into the fire. We're not getting out of this one, you know. Russ nodded. I know.

The fire went out from the rain and they could not get it going again. Chris stood up, coughed. Let's go. Russ picked up the pouch with the handguns and ammunition. Where are we going? he asked. Chris stood, trying to catch his breath. Anywhere, I'm cold.

Russ followed his brother, moving slowly down to the mouth of Coldwater Canyon where it opened up onto Lytle Creek Canyon. Chris grimaced with every misstep. They stopped frequently for him to lean against a tree or boulder to catch his breath. I'm gonna need to have this looked at real soon. Yeah, and I'm gonna need some food and another shot before I start freaking out. Chris squinted up into the low sunlight. Let's go.

They continued out to the wide Lytle Creek wash and headed down the canyon, keeping on the opposite side from the road. Russ was in the lead when he turned back to check on his brother. Chris had stopped and was looking across the wash to the road a few hundred feet away. Get on the ground, he told Russ.

JUST AFTER 8:00 A.M., SAN BERNARDINO ASSISTANT SHERIFF FLOYD TIDWELL rounded up captains Philip Schuyler and Charles Follett for a trip up to the SWAT command near Coldwater Canyon. The three hopped into a four-wheel-drive Jeep and began the five-mile trip up the dirt portion of Lytle Creek Road. Along the way, they picked up deputy Michael Smith of the SWAT force whose own vehicle had been unable to make the water crossing at the North Fork. About three and a half miles north of the command center, Deputy Smith spotted something on the far side of the wash. I got movement across the wash there, he shouted above the sound of the engine. Tidwell slammed on the brakes and all four men bailed out, guns drawn, and took cover behind the vehicle.

Across the boulder-strewn wash, two figures were walking along a knoll at the base of the mountainside. While not completely in the open, the two were nevertheless making no attempt to conceal themselves. One had his hands across his chest, the other had his tucked underneath a poncho. "Sheriff's officers, get your hands in the air, up where we can see them!" Tidwell called out to the suspects. One of the suspects stopped and looked in their direction. The one in front kept walking.

"Get down, get down now or we'll shoot you," one of the officers yelled.

One of the men raised his arms and lowered himself to ground, face-down. The other one then did the same.

The four lawmen advanced, taking turns covering each other. Two carried handguns pointed out in front of them; Tidwell carried a shotgun. Michael Smith carried a high-powered semiautomatic rifle with a scope he trained on the two suspects lying in the dirt. "You move or give us any problem and we'll shoot you," one of them said when they reached the two Harven brothers. "Let's shoot 'em right now," another one said.

Thirty minutes later, Floyd Tidwell rode into the command center at Glen Ranch like an Old West sheriff with the two most wanted men in the territory tied up in the back of his wagon. In this instance it was a Ford station wagon brought up to transport the outlaws down the canyon. Chris and Russell Harven found themselves circled by several dozen sheriff's deputies straining to get a look at the men who had gunned down one of their own.

In the photos that ran in the pages of the *Los Angeles Times* the next day, Chris Harven is in a hooded sweatshirt, still seated in the wagon with his legs in front of him, eyes averted down. He looks like a tough character, but one who knows he has been defeated. Russell is being led by his captors, hands cuffed behind his back, in boots, jeans, and ripped flannel shirt, the last shredded remains of a rain poncho hanging strangely from around his neck. Unlike his older brother, Russell is staring straight into the camera, scowling. With his scraggly beard and wet hair matted on his forehead, the Russell Harven staring back at readers looks like some sort of wild mountain man, a vicious outlaw entirely capable of gunning down a lawman in cold blood.

But the Russell Harven who was led into the command center was anything but a defiant outlaw. He was merely a frightened young man from the suburbs of Orange County who had gotten in way over his head. Once inside the ranch house, Russ spotted a fire blazing in the big stone fireplace. "Please let me stand by the fire. I won't move, I promise," he asked in a soft voice. Tidwell told him he could, and Russ stood there, teeth chattering, while more reporters moved in and deputies continued to enter the command center to gawk at the two cop killers. Russ watched as Chris was led out of the ranch house by two detectives to a waiting patrol car for transport to the San Bernardino County Sheriff's Homicide department for questioning. Chris didn't even look over as he was leaving.

"HOW MUCH DO YOU WEIGH?"

"With or without the lead?" Chris Harven said.

San Bernardino Homicide detective Larry Malmberg lit a cigarette and slid a Miranda waiver in front of him. Harven initialed each of the questions, signed the bottom, and slid it back. The chain-smoking Malmberg was a gruff veteran detective with a thick nose and bags under his eyes from frequent lack of sleep. Beside him in the interview room sat detective Roger Kuhns, who had driven down from the mountain with Harven. "You agree to talk to us about the charges?" Malmberg said.

"Whatever you want, start reeling 'em out," Chris said.

"Do you know what those charges are?"

"No," Chris shook his head.

"Bank robbery, numerous assaults on police officers, and a murder of a police officer. You understand those?"

Harven shifted in his seat. "I know what you mean. I just, you know, it's the first time I heard about a police officer being injured or killed. What was he killed with?"

"A firearm. He was shot."

"Where did it happen?"

"Lytle Creek area up above Stockton Campgrounds. You want to talk about it?"

"Yeah, whatever I can tell you."

"You can probably tell us a whole lot, man. Why don't you start from the beginning."

"You mean how the whole thing started?"

"There ain't no place like the beginning, right?"

"Well, I guess," Chris said. He thought about it. "Might say the whole thing started a couple years ago when my friend George split up with his wife. He went sort of a little nuts after that. He was living with me and my wife and that didn't work out, so my wife split. I had a job for seven years and they got rid of me so that's why I'm on unemployment. Manny, his wife's going to have a baby. He doesn't have any cash. Billy, he's got arthritis. He won't even be able to walk, or wouldn't have been able to walk, after he was twenty-five. He didn't have anything to lose. George lost his wife, his job, his family. My brother was against it but he went in just 'cause we're all friends. I didn't have to go in on it, but I had a lot of peer group pressure, I guess, so I went along with it. So we went down and hit the Security Pacific."

"So, all five of you got together and decided that you'd hit a bank. Is that it?" Malmberg asked.

"Well, not really." Chris shrugged. "I didn't decide to hit a bank. Russ didn't decide to hit a bank. Manny didn't decide to hit a bank. George decided to hit the bank. Believe it or not, before all this started out, I was a reputable citizen. The whole plan was stupid. Why we ever went through with it I'll never know."

"So George planned the whole operation?"

"Yeah."

"Well, it went pretty smoothly for no rehearsal. I mean, you guys went in there like a bunch of professionals from what I understand."

Chris shook his head. "I thought it was a botched job from the word *go*."

"What didn't you like about it?" Malmberg asked.

"Well, first of all, I don't like, you know, I don't believe in bank robbery. I don't believe in hurting people, I don't believe in killing people. If it wasn't for George, day after day. 'Are you going to be a yellow-belly or a coward?' I wouldn't never have gone in there. I know my brother wouldn't either. He was saying right up to the last minute, let's stop."

"But you did, so . . ."

"So we done it." Chris stared down at the table. "George's motto is, 'I'm not going to be taken prisoner.'" He shook his head, already informed of Smith's capture. "Right. Here he is down here now."

The interrogation went on for over an hour, with Harven confessing in detail to his own participation and that of the others. "What were you thinking about while all of this was going on?" Malmberg wanted to know when they were almost finished.

"Wishing I hadn't done the job. I can't deny anything about it, you know, the whole thing was stupid. I get what I deserve for being stupid. I mean you can sit there and go, your life's unhappy, you haven't got a job, nobody wants to give you a job, you haven't got a wife and family, all the bills are piling up and piling up . . . But that's no excuse and now I can't say why I did it."

"I'll tell you something, Chris," Malmberg said. "When you guys crossed over into our county, the information that we had is that you had a hostage. That's the only reason that you're alive right now."

"Well, probably you should have killed us because what we did was wrong." Chris paused. "So, what am I looking at?"

"You're looking at the death penalty," Malmberg said flatly.

"Oh," Chris said. "I guess I'm looking at the death penalty. When do I get to see an attorney?"

"When you ask for one."

"Anytime I want?"

"Anytime you want."

"You mean I can ask for an attorney right now?"

"Sure."

Chris nodded. "Maybe we better continue this on with an attorney since I'm going to get the death penalty, okay?"

"Sure enough," Malmberg said, snuffing out his cigarette and standing up from the table. "We'll terminate the interview at 11:10 hours."

"TODAY'S DATE IS 5/11/80, THE TIME IS 11:42 HOURS," SAN BERNARDINO DE-tective Hugh Gonthier said into the microphone on the table. "This will be an interview conducted at the sheriff's Homicide division. The persons present are sergeant Ron Durling, detective Hugh Gonthier of sheriff's Homicide. Interviewing a Russell Aaron Harven, date of birth 1/6/54."

Gonthier had already pegged Russell Harven for a "pleaser," ashamed of what he had done. He and Durling both agreed that all they would really need to do to get the guy to talk was to be nice to him, show him a little respect and kindness. "Russ, do you know what you've been arrested for?" Gonthier began.

Russ didn't know shit beyond that he was alone and in deep trouble. "Uh, yeah, I think so," he said, his soft, boyish voice a sharp contrast to his rough appearance.

"What did they say you were arrested for?"

"They didn't."

"You've been arrested for bank robbery and murder."

"Murder?"

"Murder."

There was a long pause. "I was thinking it over if I should talk or not," Russ said. "I'll . . . I'll talk, I guess."

"Before you got to the bank, how long did you plan to do that thing?" Gonthier asked.

"Uh, it wasn't too long. Chris said that everything was planned out pretty good and that George said everything was set and there wasn't gonna be any mistakes, but I figured, shit . . . you know, this is pretty risky business," he said, laughing nervously. "I didn't really want to go through with it. But I figured my brother's doing it, you know, so . . ."

Gonthier went through the sequence of events. Russ gave out information, but equivocated in his answers, pretending to forget simple, often meaningless, details. He seemed torn between coming clean and the urge to bullshit his way out of trouble.

"Okay, the cops show up; had you started to move the van?" Gonthier asked.

"I don't think so. Fired off a couple rounds and then, then we started to move."

"Who did you fire the rounds at initially?"

"Well, at the cops." Russ looked down, shaking his head. "Look, I know I shouldn't be spilling all this out, but shit . . ."

"Anytime you want to cease, we stop. You have the right," Gonthier said.

"Doesn't that make it basically harder on me or something like that?" Russ asked.

"Not necessarily. It's helpful to us, Russ, to find out what happened," Gonthier said, almost apologetically.

"Yeah, to help you get a good case to lock us all up." Russ stared at the floor, shaking his head. "Boy, are my parents gonna be surprised. They'll probably disown me. Course it doesn't matter, I guess; I'll be dead in a few months anyway." He looked up. "We didn't shoot any cops, did we?" he asked.

"One cop is dead," Gonthier informed him.

Russ leaned forward and let out a deep breath. "I feel I might be clamming up here in a minute."

"What do you mean?"

"I don't know if I want to do too much more talking. I'm getting fucking scared."

"You don't have to."

"Yeah, I know that," Russ said. "It's just that you guys, you know, being so nice to me and I feel like an asshole clamming up on you."

"Did you get hit at all from the exchange of gunfire?" Gonthier pressed on.

"One got me in the back of the head here," Russ said.

"Was anybody else hit?"

"Yeah, Billy got hit and Chris got it in the back and George got it in the leg. I think George's was pretty bad cause he was bleeding a lot in the back of that truck. He was expressing doubts as to his survivability. Billy, we left him in the van. I don't know what kind of condition he's in." Russ looked up. "How is he?"

"Billy's dead," Gonthier informed him.

Russ stared at the floor again.

"Who got the van again, Russ?"

"Billy and Manny and me." Russ thought about it. "Is that a charge against me?"

Gonthier nodded. "Kidnapping and grand theft."

"Well, I guess the dead cop and dead Billy, you're gonna put me in the chamber as it is, it doesn't matter anymore." He shook his head. "I'm slowly hanging myself here."

"Have you ever been involved in any type of offense like this before?" asked Gonthier.

"Uh-uh. Never robbed nobody, never had any weapons offenses, nothing. I'm not a violent person."

"Did your mom and dad have any idea this was going on?"

"No, they thought I was just going camping with Chris this weekend." He paused. "Wow, this is going to be a fucking shock to them."

"I've been asking you all the questions," Gonthier asked. "Are there any questions you'd like to ask us?"

"Well . . ." Russ said, thinking about it. "Not really. I know what's gonna happen." He gave a small laugh to emphasize the futility of it all. "This case is open-and-shut."

"Right now, as I've explained to you, we've got one officer dead, we've got officers wounded, Billy's dead, there's a stolen vehicle involved, there's a kidnapping involved, there's a bank robbery involved . . ."

"No doubt about it, we're dead," said Russ.

"Russ, let me ask you something. What were you thinking?" Gonthier said.

Russ shrugged. "I was thinking this is crazy but I didn't want to go to jail."

"Well, why were you shooting?" Gonthier asked, his tone almost one of a frustrated father wondering how the young man before him could have made such a terrible mistake.

"'Cause I didn't want to go to jail." Russ let out a breath. "Lot of good that did."

Gonthier gathered up his papers. "Do you have anything, Russell? Anything you want to say?"

Russ thought about it. "I got something to say. I'm just sorry I did this whole fucking thing, man. It doesn't carry no weight, but that's how I feel."

AFTER TURNING THE BEND ON BALDY NOTCH ROAD AHEAD OF THE OTHERS THE night before, Manny Delgado started to run. He just kept running and running up the road until he could run no more and then he went over the side. It grew dark, but he never stopped moving. Sliding, tumbling, crashing through manzanita and buckthorn that tore at his skin and clothing. If he got far enough away from the washout site, he could hide by day and move by night until he eventually made it out of there. After that, maybe melt away into Mexico with relatives or friends.

Manny also knew if he stopped moving, he would start thinking about Billy. No matter what happened, he would always have to live with that. But he sure as hell was not going to let them put him in a prison cell where he would have nothing else to do but think about it. He'd make it out of those mountains or take a bullet trying.

High up on the hillsides of Coldwater Canyon, he could see the lights of the men making their way up Lytle Creek. He pushed on, trying to make a last steep uphill climb to a rounded ridgeline that loomed a mile to the south. With each step up the sharp incline, the loose gravel and shale kicked out from under his feet, and he slid back, making scant progress. The effort was exhausting, like running up a sand dune. Finally, he traversed in switchbacks until he crested a domed ridgeline thick with chaparral as high as a man's head and penetrable only by crawling flat against the earth beneath the branches.

As daylight broke over Lytle Creek, Manny lay on his belly near the center of the thick stand of brush with a .38 in his hand, sucking rainwater out of his clothing and listening to the throaty baying of bloodhounds in the distance. By noon, the sun was cresting over the canyon, dissolving away the thick morning cloud cover. And then the helicopters came.

LASO DEPUTIES JOHN VIEW AND GLENN BARTHOLOMEW REACHED BALDY Notch Road above Coldwater Canyon and waited for the remainder of their element to get into position. Both View and Bartholomew were thirty-four years old with typical SWAT credentials: previous military service and five to ten years in law enforcement before joining the Special Enforcement Bureau. Together with deputy Steve Voors, View and Bartholomew made up one of two Hunt & Kill teams reporting to sergeant Tony Wilta. View was carrying a Remington 40-X high-powered rifle with scope and bipod. Bartholomew was armed with an Ithaca twelve-gauge shotgun and Voors an AR-15 firing .223 ammunition. It was the same configuration of weaponry with which George Smith had armed his own team of men the day before.

At 10:30 a.m., a sweep of Coldwater Canyon began with the main body of fifty men moving up from the base of the mountain in a southwesterly direction while the Hunt & Kill teams shadowed them from the high ground on Baldy Notch Road. At points throughout the mile-wide canyon, SWAT sharpshooters stood on craggy granite outcroppings, scoped rifles held at the ready as they scanned the landscape below for movement. View, Bartholomew, and Voors moved cautiously up the fire road, aware of just how exposed they were to anyone looking to take out another cop. An hour and a half into the sweep and one mile up Baldy Notch Road, they located fresh tracks. Whoever was wearing the boots with Vibram-type soles had been indecisive, walking back and forth at the edge of the road before going over the side.

The three men held their position and radioed for a tracking team. Fontana PD brought up a dog and handler under armed escort, but the overnight rain had washed away the scent, making the animal of little use. Several yards down the hill, the tracks seemed to double back on themselves and then head upslope. Sergeant Wilta broke up the team, taking Voors with him and swinging low on the hillside while View and Bartholomew followed the tracks along the high ground. It took an hour and a half to cover another mile while choppers crossed overhead fighting gusty winds, their spotters scanning the hillsides. As the two men ascended the side of the ridgeline, the tracks went into a dense stand of chaparral that covered the entire crest of the domed hilltop. Soon they were fighting through virtually impenetrable brush that reached above their heads. At times visibility was less than five feet and never more than fifteen. Bartholomew and View were less concerned about being ambushed than they were about accidentally stumbling across a desperate criminal armed with an AR-15.

At a break in the underbrush just below the crest of the ridge, Bartholomew and View paused and scanned the area in front of them. A San Bernardino Sheriff's helicopter rose up from behind the ridge with a roar of rotor blades and held a low hover fifteen feet above the ground, whipping the brush and kicking up a cloud of dirt. View noticed the spotter standing in the open door of the chopper looking straight down.

John Plasencia, who had been spotting on 40-King-1 with Ed Mabry during the pursuit through the canyon the day before, caught sight of a flash of blue among the green and brown brush. Pilot Terry Jagerson brought the chopper low, using the rotor blades to part the brush. They saw a man lying prone on the dirt wearing work boots, Levi's, and a blue sweatshirt beneath a dark green hunting vest with multiple pockets. The flash of color that had given away the man's position to Plasencia was the pair of bright blue dish-washing gloves used in the robbery that Manny had put on to keep his hands warm. Plasencia saw View and Bartholomew waving their arms to get his attention. The spotter made exaggerated pointing gestures toward the area just below the chopper. View gave Plasencia a thumbs-up and radioed the location over the LASO frequency. The two men checked their weapons one last time.

As they advanced in a low crawl, Jagerson kept the blades of the helicop-ter roaring directly over their suspect, blinding him in a cloud of swirling dirt and deafening him with the chopping of the rotors. "We'll hold here and cover him," Jagerson radioed. "We can split if the shit hits the fan."

View and Bartholomew crept slowly through brush so thick they could not even see the helicopter above them. They had crested the dome of the hill and were moving to the downslope side when Bartholomew saw a flash of blue twenty feet in front of them. The wind from the rotors jerked the bushes wildly side to side, exposing the subject in brief flashes. The two men lowered their weapons and advanced a few more feet to get a clearer aim with fewer branches obstructing their line of fire. When they attained their position, Delgado was only a dozen feet away, lying on his stomach, looking up at the helicopter with his right side exposed to the Hunt & Kill team. The two deputies settled into their firing positions with View sighting the .308 just under Delgado's armpit and Bartholomew leveling the Ithaca twelve-gauge at his torso. View gave his partner a silent nod.

"Freeze, Sheriff's Department, hold it right there," Bartholomew called out.

Manny whipped his head around and began to roll onto his left side. When he did, View and Bartholomew saw the steel of the handgun in his right hand and fired their weapons. Three rounds from the .308 and three loads of #4 buck slammed into the torso of Manny Delgado. Delgado pitched forward and lay motionless, one arm tucked beneath his body. The two men waited, weapons still trained on their suspect. "Get those hands out where we can see them," Bartholomew called out, but there was no response.

When further calls to Delgado produced no movement, View crept forward with his sidearm drawn while Bartholomew covered him with the shotgun. Reaching his suspect, View handcuffed Manny and rolled the lifeless body over. A .38 revolver lay beneath the body. View retrieved the gun and handed it to Bartholomew. View then squinted up at the helicopter still hovering low overhead and held out four fingers to them. Code 4: suspect neutralized, all law enforcement personnel okay.

Standing in the open door of 40-King-1, John Plasencia saw the signal and relayed it to Jagerson, who broadcast it over the San Bernardino radio frequency about the same time John View was radioing LASO personnel. A cheer went up at the command post and across the mountainsides of Lytle Creek Canyon. Hunt & Kill had done their job.

SUBJECT BODY IS COOL TO THE TOUCH, PATHOLOGIST DR. IRVING ROOT NOTED as he began to remove the clothing of Manny Delgado in the San Bernardino County morgue. As he pulled at the green hunting vest saturated in blood, several shotgun pellets fell out with a clatter onto the stainless steel table. Root scooped them up and handed them over to attendant Brian Hoak along with plastic and felt shotgun wadding that had been expended through the barrel of Bartholomew's Ithaca at such close range they penetrated Delgado's clothing. Root noted a tattoo on the upper right arm of his subject: the initials *M. D.* in script with the number *13* and a heart below that, all of it encircled in scrollwork.

Might be gang-related, sergeant Ron Durling speculated as he observed the autopsy.

Dr. Root addressed the right side of the subject's body peppered with buckshot. This could take a while. He began to count while examining each hole, starting with the lowest at midthigh. When he had examined the last of the punctures just north of the nipple line, Root called out the total. Sixty-two penetrating wounds from what appears to be #3 or #4 buckshot. Somebody whistled. Yeah, whoever was using that shotgun sure did a number on this one, Root said.

Next, Root studied a two-inch-diameter hole in the right shoulder, put there by John View and his .308. Root looked for an exit wound but found none. He studied the X-rays of the body posted on the light board. High-velocity projectile with fragments dispersed throughout the thoracic region, he said. He also noted a second two-inch hole in the right side of the subject. Same gun, same thing. Hoak scribbled the information on his notepad.

At last, Root addressed the hole in Manny Delgado's chest, just left of midline and below the inter-nipple line. Ten millimeters in diameter, abraded and inverted around the edges, he said, indicating an entry wound. Note greasy black gunpowder residue around wound. Straight-on contact wound. Root and Hoak logrolled their subject and checked his back. Root worked a probe through the wound on the chest all the way through to an exit wound under Manny's shoulder blade. Through and through, no projectile found. They rolled Manny back. Root checked the X-rays. Extensive fragmentation of the left cardiac ventricle with massive blood loss, he noted. The pathologist turned to the men from the San Bernardino Sheriff's Office. Who had the .38?

The guy on the table, Durling said.

Well, I hate to disappoint your friends over at LASO, Root said, but they didn't kill this guy. He killed himself.

Root removed his gloves and scribbled the last line of the report himself.

Cause of Death: Gunshot wound to the heart.

12

THE NORCO 3

May 18, 1980. Riverside, California.

JUST EIGHT DAYS AFTER THE NORCO BANK ROBBERY, AT 8:32 IN THE MORN-
ing, the earth began to shake beneath the Cascade Range sixty miles northeast of Portland, Oregon. Within seconds, there was an explosion with the
force of 1,500 Hiroshima atomic bombs, and an area of mountainside the
size of Manhattan gave way in the largest landslide in recorded history.
The mass of rock, dirt, and vegetation traveled fourteen miles at speeds of
150 miles per hour, burying everything in its way to a depth of 145 feet.
Through the gaping wound left in the earth, a fiery demon rose up from
the depths and broke through the surface, letting loose a dragon's breath of
glowing gas and rock superheated to almost 700 degrees that raced across
the landscape at 400 miles per hour. Almost instantly, every living thing
within eight miles—cattle, wolves, grizzly bears, salmon, human beings—
vaporized without a trace. Entire lakes evaporated. Four billion board feet
of timber was left lying flat, all of the scorched, felled tree trunks pointing north in an orderly fashion. Rushing down the mountain behind it all
came 46 billion gallons of meltwater sweeping up debris into a lethal slurry
that overflowed rivers, tore bridges from their moorings, and erased miles of
roadway in all directions.

But the monster was not done yet. Moments later, the earth shook again, and the mountain exploded a second time, sending a plume of 540 million tons of ash fifteen miles straight up into the sky, breaking through to the stratosphere within minutes. Inside the choking black cloud, lightning flashed while below the earth vomited rivers of molten rock. Within hours, ash began to bury Moscow, Idaho, and fell like tiny ghosts on Missoula, Montana. Three hundred miles away in Spokane, Washington, the streetlights went on as the midday sun turned to total darkness. Alone on a mountainside, trapped in the pitch black of a postapocalyptic wasteland, a man turned on his video camera to record what he was sure would be the final moments of his life. "Oh dear God," he gasped. "This is hell on earth."

Inside the Riverside County jail, one thousand miles south of Mount St. Helens, murmurs began among the inmates of a great catastrophe unlike anything the world had ever seen. A man stood looking through the bars of his cell, wondering if he would die there when California fell into the sea, as it surely would any day now. For Christopher Harven, the Jupiter Effect had come early. A few feet away, another man stared at a bare lightbulb, calculating how long it would take before Jesus lifted him up to meet his Lord in the sky. For George Wayne Smith, the Rapture was arriving right on schedule. Sitting on the edge of a metal bunk, a third young man eyed the other two with resentment and disgust. It's just a fucking volcano, thought Russell Harven.

While his brother and George were busy indulging in smug self-satisfaction over the fulfillment of their apocalyptic beliefs, Russ was focused on the real crisis facing them: the gas chamber at San Quentin. At a hearing four days earlier, the district attorney had formally requested the death penalty on a charge of first-degree murder with "special circumstances." The prosecutors had offered up a buffet of special circumstances from which to choose: evading arrest, killing a police officer on duty, lying in wait, homicide during the commission of a felony. Considering they had clearly committed all four of those acts, any one of which would send them to death row, Russ was fairly confident that's exactly where they were headed.

Through a family friend, Russ's parents were referred to an Orange

County defense attorney named Alan Olson. Olson agreed to have the court assign him to represent their youngest son despite having relatively little experience in serious criminal cases. Russ soon developed confidence in his thin, soft-spoken, and unassuming attorney, a former army captain in his early thirties with a wife and four children. Olson and Russ had something else in common, in addition to the effort to save Russ from the gas chamber: Both were diabetics, Olson having been diagnosed just two years before.

Olson had already begun pondering a "diabetes defense" for Harven, in which his client could not be held accountable due to being in a diabetic shock from lack of food at the time of the crime. Failing that, he would argue Harven should be spared the death penalty because his diabetic condition was, in fact, already a death sentence. To this end, Olson started referring to Russ's type of diabetes as "the terminal kind." Olson went so far as to opine to the press that his client might even die before standing trial.

Olson found his client to be cooperative and eager to please but mostly disinterested in his own defense. To Russ, the trial was nothing more than a charade with a foregone conclusion. He had fucked up and there was nothing he could do about it now. Olson summarized his client's feeling to reporters. "He was there, but it got completely out of hand. It was the worst mistake of his life." Olson added that his client "has expressed a lot of remorse." That was true, but Russell Harven's remorse was mostly for what he had done to his own life, not for what they did to Jim Evans. That fact that he might have been responsible for the murder of another human being was not something Russ wanted to contemplate. So he didn't.

If Russ was passive, regretful, and fatalistic in the face of his current situation, his older brother was none of those things. The last of the three to be released from the hospital, the slug from Jim Evans's .38 still lodged in his chest, Christopher Harven arrived at his initial court hearing appearing relaxed and confident, cracking jokes to his grim-faced captors as he was hustled into the building under heavy security. Guards with automatic rifles were placed around the courthouse and, once again, Riverside Police helicopter Baker-1 circled above him. Unshaven and unwashed since his capture, shackled at the ankles with his hands cuffed behind his back and secured to a leather strap, Chris nevertheless appeared defiant, his rugged good looks somehow enhanced by his outlaw status. When asked in the courthouse if he needed anything, Chris said, "Well, I have a lot of phone calls to make." He was told he would get only one.

Chris's court appearance was in sharp contrast to that of Russ and George Smith's the day before. Russ had stared in curiosity at waiting reporters and federal marshals, still looking every bit the ragged, bearded, scowling fugitive cop killer. Most there interpreted it as a hate-filled glare. Smith appeared utterly defeated, head bowed, eyes downcast, one foot wearing a green bathroom slipper and the other bare. Blood stained the cuffs of his orange prison jumpsuit where the ankle chains cut into his flesh with each forced step. Both looked distraught as the thirteen-page complaint against them was read aloud. At the conclusion, they were rushed out of the building and whisked off by heavily armed deputies in waiting vehicles.

Riverside attorney Jay Grossman had been assigned by the court to represent Chris Harven. An experienced and skillful criminal defense attorney, Grossman had recently gained some attention defending necrophiliac "Trash Bag Killer" Patrick Kearney in the slayings of an estimated forty-three young men and boys. But Chris had issues with the guy from the start. Unlike Russ, Chris had taken an interest in his own defense and soon became familiar with the lexicon of the law, speaking of "demurrers," "severances," and "Marsden hearings." In Harven's eyes, Grossman was dismissive of his suggestions, did not make enough trips to the jail to meet with him, and put too much focus on negotiating a plea rather than mounting a defense. Still, they pressed ahead for the time being.

RELEASED FROM THEIR RESPECTIVE HOSPITALS AND REUNITED IN THE SEG-regation unit of the Riverside County jail, the three Norco bank robbers soon reverted to their interpersonal hierarchy. At the bottom of the ladder was Russ, alternately screamed at or disregarded by the other two. George returned to the book of Revelation and the Rapture, God's ultimate jail-break. He was as convinced as ever in the Second Coming predictions of

Calvary pastor Chuck Smith as foretold in *The Late Great Planet Earth*. Just hang in there, he told his fellow inmates, Jesus is going to bust us out of here soon. With no other hope to hang on to, Chris and Russ did their best to believe.

Their stepfather, Walt Harven, was a pragmatic and practical man who knew his two boys were lost to him forever. By the time he slipped into a Riverside County jail visiting booth for the first time, he was resigned to their fate and saw no reason to reprimand them for what they had done. Speaking in a calm and matter-of-fact tone, Walt met with his youngest boy first. The conversation was disjointed and awkward, with Walt relaying mundane details of family members and activity around the Harven home. Russ responded with religious non sequiturs, desperately seeking to salvage some approval from the father he had disappointed for the last time.

"You're lucky to get Olson through his brother," Walt said at one point.

"Yeah, well, you know, Chris and me, we figure Jesus Christ has got to have some plans for us. There were a bunch of times when they could have killed us, but they didn't. We figure Jesus Christ is watching over us for something. They say when the Tribulations start, the righteous will come and set the prisoners free to fight the godless. And that's us."

"Very good," Walt said flatly, with all the enthusiasm of a man whose son had just told him he was going out to see a movie. There was a long, uneasy silence before Walt shifted back to small talk. "We got all kinds of mail from the relatives. The Purcells, Jim and Rose, both called . . ."

"How's Mom doing?" Russ asked.

Mae Harven was inconsolable and fell apart every time someone stopped by to offer their support or drop off a sympathy casserole. She could not bring herself to make a trip to the jail just yet, Walt told him, and had not gotten around to writing him because she was still so shaky she was unable to hold a pen. She had developed a stutter. "She's snapping out of it, slowly but surely," Walt said, with false optimism. "She'll come around."

"I'm really sorry that this happened," Russ told his father.

"Yeah, well, it happened."

"Well, I'm kinda sorry and I'm kinda glad because now I'm back to

Christ," Russ brightened. "Instead of going to hell, I'm on my way to heaven now."

"Yeah," Walt said doubtfully.

Russ asked if his father could get him a book by Carlos Castaneda and a copy of the Jerusalem Bible. They talked about cashing his tax return, his insulin dosages, and what they should do with his perpetually dead Volkswagen. Russ threw out a mishmash of quotes from Revelation, regurgitating George's old interpretations. The awkward pauses grew longer as the conversation continued.

CHRIS AND HIS STEPFATHER MAY HAVE BUTTED HEADS PLENTY OF TIMES through the years, but Chris knew if it were not for Walt, he and his brother would have had a pretty rough childhood. "How you doin', Dad?" Chris greeted him, and then immediately got down to business. "Well, I guess I ought to tell you what happened." He was desperate, he said, out of money, no job, wanted to die. So he went ahead with it. "I don't really know what got into me and Russ to get into this," he said. "It might be a small consolation to know that I, or I believe Russ, never shot anyone." The campaign to blame Manny for everything was already in full swing. "Once Billy got his brains blown out in that van, Manny went nuts." He said the only one firing at the washout site was Delgado. "Manny was just walking down the road, blasting away. So, both the Delgado brothers are dead," he added matter-of-factly.

"I didn't know them," Walt said. "Have I ever met them?"

"They're the two smaller Mexican guys that came over to visit Russ a couple of times before we got involved in this crap. They recruited him. I didn't recruit him; I didn't have the nerve." There was a pause. "So here we are."

"Yeah," Walt said sadly. "Yeah."

Chris filled the dead air with a recitation of biblical prophecy almost identical to Russ's minutes earlier. "I know that you have never really been one to be into God or Jesus or anything like that," Chris said. "But in this time of consolation, it would really do you a lot of good, Dad."

"You might be right," Walt answered, sounding unconvinced.

"Read Revelations, that's all this coming down now. You know that. You can see it. All the predictions are coming true."

Walt made a halfhearted attempt to engage on the subject of religion but soon gave up. He mentioned that there was a girl waiting to visit Chris and that he had offered to split his visiting time with her. So he and Chris would have only fifteen minutes together rather than thirty. But eight minutes in, both seemed to have run out of things to say.

"Anything you want to know?" Chris asked.

"No. Not really."

There was an excruciatingly long silence.

"Well, I guess I should talk to that girl, huh?" Chris said.

"That girl" would soon turn out to become Chris Harven's most loyal visitor. He had met Olivia Estrada just three months before the robbery and juggled her along with Nancy Bitetti right up until the end, each woman unaware that he was spending two to three nights a week with the other. Allowed only a half hour of visiting time a week, and his not-yet-ex-wife Lani also wanting to bring little Timmy to see him, Chris's juggling act was even more complicated now that he was behind bars. Estrada was eight years older than Chris, a born-again Christian with a ten-year-old daughter and a good job at technology giant Hewlett Packard. She was smitten with Chris from the start. One of their first times out together had been a trip to the gun store where Chris picked up the Smith & Wesson .45 Long Colt that, unbeknownst to Estrada, would be used in a gun battle with the cops. But hers was an affection seemingly undiminished by forty-odd felony counts, including first-degree murder. In their visit, Olivia seemed more than willing to continue the relationship, albeit now with a sheet of plexiglass between them.

"Everything got pressing," Chris tried to explain at the start. "I just went berserk. Things were going down in my life that I didn't like."

"I thought I was going to die when I found out," she said.

"What do you think now? Sorry you met me?"

"I won't ever be sorry of that. I'll just never understand why, that's all."

"I don't think I will ever understand why myself," he said. "I don't know where I went wrong. I strayed off God's path and here I am."

"I hope you are praying, Chris," she said.

"I am praying every night," he assured her. "I'm not alone. I have got my brother and God in this cell with me."

"When are you going to have surgery?" she asked, referring to the bullet still visibly lodged beneath the skin of his chest.

"They are not going to give me surgery. That bullet is going to stay there as long as I live." He told her that the slug "went into my back and around my rib cage and went around all my organs." He shook his head in wonder that it had not killed him. "Too many miracles have been happening to think that is it. I was just talking about Revelations before all of this came down. Something is going to happen down here. All the predictions, Israel and Egypt have all come true. Rioting in Miami. They beat a black man to death and let everyone go, the cops go, you know. Mount St. Helens erupted. All the predictions are coming true."

Time was up. A guard told Olivia she had to leave. "Take care," she said.

"Some miracle will happen," Chris said. "I know it will. And I will see you."

She looked at him through the plexiglass barrier. "Read the Bible, please."

"I have been. I have been," he assured her.

A few weeks later, Harven was scratching at what had become abscessed and inflamed tissue surrounding a visible lump under his left nipple. The skin suddenly opened up in an eruption of pus, and a .38-caliber slug of county-issued lead fell into Chris's hand.

WALTER SMITH HAD BEEN FOLLOWING THE STORY OF THE NORCO BANK ROB-bery on television for two days before he found out his own son had been hunted down and arrested for the crime. As he watched a reporter read off the names of the captured outlaws, Walter felt the blood drain from his face. It didn't make any sense. George was intelligent, the one everyone liked, the one the other children looked up to. George was the son who had taken it upon himself to attend church at an early age and never missed school. It was impossible that George would do something like this.

It took almost twenty phone calls and twenty-four hours before Walter was informed that George was at San Bernardino County Medical Center. Together with his younger son, Steve, Walter went to the hospital on Sunday afternoon and waited until he was allowed to see George. San Bernardino deputies stood in stony silence guarding the hospital room, hallways, and perimeter of the building. After being thoroughly patted down, Walter and Steve entered the room. What they saw shocked them. The son Walter had thought so highly of was pale and shackled to the rails of a hospital bed, naked except for a thin sheet covering his midsection. Walter held back tears and asked George how badly he was injured.

I'm all shot up, he told them. With his free hand, George pulled the sheet aside and showed them the bandaged wounds in the groin area and on his right thigh. There are no exit wounds. Those bullets will be in there forever. He did not mention that the "bullets" were actually only shotgun pellets. There were other injuries he was less clear about, suggesting they were additional gunshot wounds rather than simple lacerations from the brush in Lytle Creek Canyon. He told his father he was shot in the back by a police sniper and lost more than three thousand cubic centimeters of blood, about half his body's total volume. After his capture, he said he had been tortured on the hillside, told he would not be taken down or given medical attention until he confessed.

Did you do it? George's little brother asked him.

Yeah, George reluctantly conceded. He was there, but it wasn't his *fault*. The cops had overreacted and shot first. George had only tried to defend himself. He had been so badly wounded in front of the bank that all he could do was lie down in the truck and try not to die. I never even fired the gun, he told them.

Had Walter or Steve been allowed to read the medical chart in the room, they would have seen the following notation from Dr. Rudolph Holguin, who oversaw the evaluation of George Smith: "TM's showed bilateral perforations and dry blood in the ear canal secondary to concussion syndrome of the gun firing." In other words, George had fired the Heckler so many times that the concussion waves from .308 rounds going off next to his head had punched holes in the tympanic membranes of both ears.

Walter was locked in a cognitive dissonance between the George he thought he knew and the one who had just tried to rob a bank. Why would you do that, George? Walter wanted to know.

Because of what I have been telling you for years, George said. The end of the world is upon us. The signs are everywhere you look, the fulfillment of the prophecies is at hand. He didn't have a choice, he said. It was a matter of life and death. Without the money to buy that land and cabin in the mountains, how would he have been able to save them all from the catastrophes to come?

Walter knew all about George's plan for the remote mountain cabin in the hills. "Son," he had cautioned him earlier, "there is no such thing as a perfect utopia and that's what that would be." Not a churchgoer himself, Walter avoided arguing with George over his beliefs. But, then again, he never thought those beliefs would lead his son to this.

The detective told them they had to leave. Walter did not know what to say, so he placed a hand on George's arm. The guards did not try to stop him. It would be the last physical contact Walter Smith had with his boy for a very long time.

Like Chris, George had also been assigned an attorney to represent him. Unlike the calm and amiable Jay Grossman, the attorney the court handed George Smith was an absolute bulldog, both in looks and in temperament. Clayton Adams was a thirty-nine-year-old career criminal defense attorney with three years in the Riverside County Public Defender's Office. He had been astonished when he got the call on Sunday, May 11, saying he was assigned to represent the self-proclaimed leader of the most sensational crime the Inland Empire had seen since the Wineville chicken coop murders. Heavyset with a round face and cheeks well on their way to jowls, Adams was brusque and relentlessly confrontational in the courtroom. He had a reputation for being fiercely loyal to his clients with a willingness to scrap with prosecutors and witnesses over even the smallest details. But when it came to defending Smith, Adams began with something very big: the United States Constitution. Leaving the initial hearing in which prosecutors had asked for the death penalty, Adams had a short and direct statement for waiting reporters. "Death as a punishment for crime is nothing more than calculated, premeditated, administrative murder. I cannot and will not let it happen to George Smith."

Adams spent his childhood in Wisconsin before a stint in the navy brought him to the West Coast in the late 1950s. After an honorable discharge, he remained in California, earning a law degree from Lincoln University in Oakland. Despite sporting a faded tattoo outline of a spade on the back of his left hand and the accompanying nickname "Ace," Adams was no rebel or counterculture crusader. But it did not take long for him to reach the conclusion that the American justice system was unfairly stacked against the accused. "The prosecution is, in fact, the government and therefore advantaged with the skills and resources that only a wealthy government can provide." When it came to the reality of his role in the criminal justice system, Adams offered a mix of poetic pragmatism: "A criminal defense attorney is nothing more than a bracero toiling in the vineyards of justice. Sometimes the best you can do is try to keep the prosecution honest."

Their initial meeting on Sunday, May 11, at San Bernardino County Medical Center was brief. Adams laid out the general plan and what George could expect in the days following his release from the hospital. Adams would seek a severance to have George tried separately from the others. He would show a jury that George was wounded far too badly in front of the bank to have participated in any shooting after that, including the murder of deputy James Evans. And, as usual, Adams would contest every count, challenge every witness and piece of evidence from start to finish in hopes of chiseling off a charge here or there. Adams left the hospital impressed by his client's intelligence and willingness to accept advice. Unlike Walter Smith, Clayton Adams would never ask George why he had done it; such information was irrelevant to the case.

Clay Adams did one other thing that Sunday afternoon. After meeting with his new client, he made a call to the home of a defense investigator from the Riverside Public Defender's Office named Jeanne Painter. This was going to be a long and complicated case and the only other person on his team would be the investigator assigned to it. Adams wanted that investigator to be Painter. The thirty-three-year-old Painter was a highly regarded investigator with hundreds of felony cases under her belt. Like Adams, she was known as a fighter. Painter had also attracted attention among the tight-knit legal community in the Riverside criminal court for another reason: She was a very attractive young lady. In a profession still dominated by men, Painter had long bleach-blonde hair parted down the middle, high cheekbones, and a bright smile.

Like everyone else, Painter had been following the drama of the Norco robbery as it unfolded on Friday and into Saturday. The next day, the call came in from Clay Adams. "Guess which case you're about to get?" said Adams. "Oh, no," groaned Painter. The thrill of working such a high-profile case was tempered by the staggering amount of work she knew it would require. Well, she thought, at least I know what I'll be doing for the next year and a half.

HOURS AFTER GEORGE SMITH'S CAPTURE, HEAVILY ARMED RIVERSIDE COUNTY Sheriff detectives led by Riverside detective Joe Curfman surrounded the Mira Loma home, smashed windows, and crawled inside to find a radio still blaring rock station KMET. After sending in the sniffer dogs and bomb squad to check for booby traps, Curfman and the others emptied the premises of anything resembling evidence, including guns, ammo, bomb-making equipment, diagrams of the Security Pacific Bank, and a copy of *The Anarchist Cookbook*.

The site quickly became a local tourist attraction with carloads of gawkers rolling past day and night. Reporters stood on the roof of neighbor Denise Sparrow's house taking photos of the backyard fortress, including the now-legendary pit, the bottom of which could not be seen even from that lofty vantage point. Left unguarded, local youths graffitied the exterior walls, broke even more windows, and generally trashed the joint. Eventually, the property was sold and the measly proceeds sent to Chris's ex-wife, Lani.

The local press began referring to defendants as "The Norco 3" and sent reporters out looking for anyone who could provide information on the mysterious men responsible for the spectacular and bloody bank robbery. Mira Loma neighbors called them "weirdos" who rarely spoke to anyone and carried guns out to their mailbox. Of George, another said he was an unfriendly man, "nasty and foulmouthed," who beat up his German immigrant wife and threatened to kill her shortly before the two split up. George's former supervisor, Chuck Morad, said, "He was very violent. He hated authority with a passion." Morad characterized Smith as a "disgruntled troublemaker, a radical who would have been a real good general in a terrorist army." "They slept in the day and went out at night," said another neighbor, Anna Grimley.

Walter Harven told an *L.A. Times* reporter that his two sons might have planned and executed the robbery "under the ruse" of going on weekend backpacking trips. He referred to Russ as "an unemployed bricklayer" with a previous arrest for selling drugs and having once robbed a cash register at a shop where he worked at the mall. Walt told Russ it was all quoted out of context, which it was. A letter to the editor in the *Riverside Press-Enterprise* entitled "A Life for a Life" hailed efforts by a state senator to "get back to the death penalty," especially for the men who killed deputy Jim Evans.

The Norco 3 were so universally despised, authorities half expected vigilante townsfolk to storm the jail with burning torches. The only people who seemed to be on their side were a pair of armed bandits who robbed an apartment manager of $4,000 and then commanded their hostage to call television station KABC to demand the release of the Norco 3. Nobody, including the Norco 3, knew the outlaws or why they had made such a request.

Reporters also attempted to get information about the two dead men but were unable to find much about Billy Delgado beyond his physical ailments. What little they were able to dig up on Manny was positively glowing. Chuck Morad described Manny as "an ideal young man" and "a real nice guy whose mistake was getting in with George." Acquaintance LeRoy Lovato said Manny was "a hell of a nice guy. He was level-headed and to my knowledge had never been in trouble before."

On May 13, the *San Bernardino Sun* ran an article headlined "Did Norco Suspect Die by His Own Gun?" The article announced that the just-released autopsy report on Manny Delgado listed the cause of death as a self-inflicted gunshot wound through the heart. To the public, it was intriguing to consider the poetic notion of a fugitive bank robber so stricken with anguish and guilt over the death of his kid brother that he would put a bullet in his own broken heart. There was also a touch of Old West romance to be found in an outlaw who would rather die than be taken alive. The more likely possibility, that the weapon discharged when Delgado fell on it, was far less enticing to contemplate.

The autopsy report also generated a third theory, especially among some Riverside and San Bernardino deputies, that the Hunt & Kill boys had shot Manny with his own gun in revenge for the death of Jim Evans. In this narrative, after firing on Delgado, SWAT had approached their wounded suspect and, finding him still alive, pried the .38 out of his hands and shot him through the heart. It was not true. A closer reading of the article or coroner's report revealed that Manny's heart had stopped beating somewhere between the first and last shotgun blasts to strike him. In other words, only Manny himself could have pulled the trigger of the gun that killed him. But reality was no match for the sweet satisfaction of revenge, so the rumor persisted.

AS THE WEEKS WENT BY, ALAN OLSON BEGAN TO SEE AN ALTERNATIVE TO THE diabetes defense he had planned for Russell Harven. Russ might still be professing confusion over how he could have gotten himself involved in something like this, but his attorney believed he had the answer: The reason was Chris.

Olson had Russ evaluated by several psychiatric professionals. The first was a clinical psychologist named Kenneth Wright who administered to Harven a battery of standardized diagnostic tests including the Wechsler Adult Intelligence Scale. Wright's conclusion was that Russell Harven's intelligence was in the "superior" range and that "the potential is greater because his comprehension actually is much higher than the IQ score." However, additional findings based on the Rorschach inkblot and Thematic Apperception Test indicated that Russ had a severely reduced ability to fantasize and expand on thoughts and an almost total lack of introspection, rendering his functional intelligence below average. Wright said the tests showed that Russ would make "a great follower" who "does not have the wherewithal emotionally to lead people."

A second psychologist named George Chappell concluded that Russ was "a very passive, compliant person who sort of did what he was told" and had "very little insights or imagination or thoughts about his future or the consequences of what he may be doing." Chappell was plainspoken in his overall conclusion. "Basically, he was just a very passive guy who kind of went with the wind."

"The wind" in this case was most definitely his older brother, Chris. Dr. David Sheffner spent hours with Russ and interviewed family members and friends who knew both Harven brothers well. Long-time friend Bob Hennings said Russ "followed Chris blindly" and that Chris "exploited" Russ and "treated him badly." Russ had never been able to say no to Chris, said Hennings, providing multiple examples to Sheffner. Russ's ex-wife, Eileen, said Chris was "cruel" and abusive in general, but especially toward Russ.

Russ was a reluctant and unenthusiastic participant in the evaluation and, when asked directly, refused to blame Chris entirely for his involvement in the crime. But his comments about their relationship were revealing. "Chris always has to have his way and he'll do anything to get it," Russ said. Chris "has had his way all his life, pushing me all around. If I wouldn't have listened to him before, I wouldn't be where I am." Russ blamed himself as well, "because I was stupid enough to listen to him." When asked to describe his childhood, Russ said, "Happy, I guess. I had a good time except when my brother would start tormenting me." When they were younger and both living at home, Russ said, "I hated him." As an adult, "I guess I didn't like him too much." Russ characterized his brother's tactics at manipulation as alternately "screaming and yelling at me" and then being nice and speaking to him in a calm voice. "His reasonable act," Russ called it.

Sheffner termed Russ a "passive, dependent, rather non-functional individual" who most likely would never have participated in something like a bank robbery if it were not for the influence of his brother.

Alan Olson thought this could be Russell Harven's ticket out of the gas chamber, that he might even get a twenty-five to life from an especially sympathetic jury. All he needed was to get Russ's trial severed from his brother's. All three attorneys were filing for severance on behalf of their clients for various reasons, but Olson had the strongest case for getting a separate trial. Without Chris at the defense table next to him, psychiatric evaluations could be brought out more completely, specifically citing Chris as the reason Russ got involved in the crime at all. But with Chris as a co-defendant, anything that portrayed Chris as responsible for Russ's involvement would be considered prejudicial to Chris and therefore off-limits. Olson repeatedly made motions for severance, but the court was having none of it. The Norco 3 would be tried together.

JUST PRIOR TO THE PRELIMINARY HEARING, A SECOND COUNT OF FIRST-degree murder was added to the charges for the death of Billy Delgado. Under a doctrine known as the Felony Murder Rule, if anyone is killed during the commission of a crime, all participants in the crime are equally guilty, no matter who does the killing. To be found not guilty, the defense would have to show that either the cops or Billy himself had initiated the firefight in front of the bank. However, tests on the two guns in Billy's possession showed the teenager never fired a single round. That meant the defense would have to convince a jury it was deputy Glyn Bolasky who had fired the first shot.

Including this additional count of murder, the final list of charges against each of the Norco 3 stood at forty-six felony counts, including capital murder, kidnapping, arson, armed robbery, assault with a deadly weapon, and twenty-two counts of attempted murder of a police officer. With most of the preliminaries completed, the judge indicated the trial would likely start sometime in February 1981 and last six months.

It was Christopher Harven who caused the first significant delay in the timeline. On Friday, December 19, 1980, Harven's attorney rose to deliver arguments for a severance of Chris's trial from that of his little brother. But before Jay Grossman could begin, Chris stood and addressed the judge. "I must at this time respectfully request a Marsden hearing to hear a motion by myself for a substitution of counsel." Harven said he wanted Grossman jettisoned from his defense "due to the gross and shoddy nature of the negligent ineptitude in the preparation, or lack thereof, in this case." As evidence, Chris cited "the total disregard of my present counsel shown in his inactions on important motions I requested."

"You are asking then that the court appoint new counsel for you?" asked judge J. David Hennigan, just appointed to hear the trial.

"Yes, sir," answered Chris.

"This is the first time I heard of it," said Grossman, "but I formally move to withdraw."

At Harven's insistence, a Marsden hearing was held the following Monday so he could get his grievances against Grossman on the record. There, Chris asserted that Grossman had violated his constitutional rights. "I feel my present attorney has exchanged certain information with the district attorney."

The accusation sent the normally cool Grossman leaping from his chair. "That's absolutely preposterous," he yowled, and then gained his composure. "But I am not going to say anything further because of the attorney-client privilege."

By Wednesday, Chris Harven had his new attorney, a former Riverside deputy public defender name Michael Bancroft Lloyd. At thirty-one years old, Lloyd was only a few years older than his client. In fact, they had known each other as younger men. As a teenager growing up in the shadow of Disneyland, Chris frequently snuck into the park and rode the rides for free courtesy of a wider group of friends and acquaintances employed there. Lloyd was a friend of a friend who worked the Matterhorn ride and had frequently let Chris on without the required E ticket. When Chris entered the room to meet his new attorney for the first time, the two stared at each other for a moment. "You?" they said almost simultaneously.

Lloyd had a steady gaze, a baby face, and a hairline that had already retreated to the top of his head. He was a competent if unremarkable trial attorney who had graduated from Pepperdine University School of Law in Malibu just five years before and recently set up private practice on Main

Street near the Riverside courthouse. Lloyd did not mind the prospect of a lengthy, all-consuming trial. A high-profile case and a guaranteed $7,000 monthly income were not such bad things to have when establishing a new practice. Lloyd retained Bruce Cummins to handle the investigation duties.

After reviewing Chris's case, Lloyd decided he would need some mitigating circumstances to keep his client out of the gas chamber. What if, for example, his client's motivation for robbing a bank was not just pure greed, but an attempt to defend himself and his loved ones from a catastrophe of biblical proportions?

On Friday, March 27, 1981, Chris Harven sat down with *Riverside Press-Enterprise* reporter Chris Bowman for a rambling jailhouse interview. Seated beside Lloyd in the chapel of the Riverside County jail, clean-shaven with a neatly groomed mustache and sporting a shiny gold crucifix around his neck, Chris Harven first asserted his innocence and refused to talk about the incident itself. All he would say on the subject was, "I personally, and as to others involved in this case, did not murder Deputy Evans." But he was more than happy to talk about his belief in the coming Apocalypse and how it drove him to bank robbery.

"You can go into the Bible, into Revelations, and find out how it's going to end," he told Bowman. "It seems like the natural disasters talked about in the Bible are lining up. Earthquakes, floods, the drought in Africa, Mount St. Helens." When did he think the day of reckoning would come? Bowman wanted to know. "One might come to the conclusion that it could happen today. It could happen tomorrow." "Remember that comet we had?" Harven continued, referring to Kohoutek eight years earlier. "The Bible says that anytime a comet goes across, an empire falls. That one went right across North America. I think it's pretty well known that North America is an empire, regardless of the fact that Canada and Mexico consider themselves independent."

Leaning back in his chair with arms folded confidently across his chest, Harven told Bowman, "It starts in Revelations 17 . . . The whore of Babylon is going to be destroyed. I believe they are talking about the United States. What other country has, shall we say, led the world to moral decay? Before

Armageddon happens, the world will go through years of trials and tribulations. Many will die. At that time, Jesus Christ will return."

Harven then veered into his array of secular doomsday scenarios. "We're going to have a strange alignment of the planets in '82 or '83, which we haven't had since, I think, 1804. This, probably, definitely, will mean traumatic effects on the earth. It's called 'The Jupiter Effect' and it will affect tides, earthquakes, volcanoes. We're also into a very unusual sunspot." He went on, speaking in soft, measured tones. "We're getting into a dangerous nuclear confrontation with the Soviet Union, and I think that's what it's going to be that happens to us—a super Pearl Harbor."

Bowman asked about the pit he and Smith dug in the backyard. "Like you're sitting in your front room and a missile is on the way, film at eleven. We were going to go down there and sit it out rather than fry." "We always thought that it could happen any day," he added. "We had laid in months of stored food, lamps, oil, clothes, camping equipment, guns and ammunition for that day." Why so many guns? "To protect myself from marauders. You've got food. Nobody else has got food . . ."

In the article, which ran on the front page of the Sunday-edition County section, Harven stated he was "strong-willed" and confident about the outcome of the trial, despite the specter of death hanging over it. "Death does not frighten me," he said. "Why should it? You'd have to be faithless to be afraid of dying."

Chris Harven was not done with pretrial surprises. On June 8, 1981, just one week before the scheduled start of the trial, Chris and his most faithful visitor, Olivia Estrada, were married in what amounted to no more than a filing of paperwork at the county administrative building. The union went unnoticed by the press.

AS THE PROCESS OF GETTING THE CASE TO TRIAL LIMPED FORWARD, THE DE-fense attorneys continued their fight for a change of venue out of the Inland Empire. With all the press coverage, they contended, it would not possible to find an impartial jury there.

The judge agreed, moving the trial site from Riverside to San Diego County, to be held at the California superior court in the small town of Vista, seventy miles to the south. Prosecutors were not pleased. With a long trial ahead, this would mean regular two-hour commutes and long stretches in hotels away from family and office. Scheduling witnesses would be a nightmare, if they could get them to make the trip down there at all, which was exactly what the defense wanted. Their request for an additional six months to prepare for the trial was granted. When told by a reporter that the lead prosecutor had called the delay "excessive" and "not the right thing to do," Adams snapped, "I don't care what the D.A. thinks."

AFTER SIX MONTHS OF INCARCERATION AT THE RIVERSIDE COUNTY JAIL, THE Norco 3 finally had enough of the deputies running the place. On December 11, 1980, all three defendants filed separate affidavits to the superior court alleging harassment, bogus cell searches in the middle of the night, intentional sleep deprivation, and other offenses Chris Harven termed the equivalent of "torture." "The deputies congregate outside in the hall, talking loudly, ratcheting their handcuffs, shinning lights into our faces, and rattling the door until we are visibly awake." As a result, Chris said, he was so exhausted that he frequently fell asleep during court appearances.

Smith and Harven said the deputies were putting their lives at risk by keeping them in "the snitch tank" segregation cells and spreading rumors that they had either abandoned or ratted out Manny Delgado to the SWAT teams in Lytle Creek. They did this, Chris said, "to build up rumors against us so physical harm will result to us if we go to prison. If they couldn't kill us before, they want to make sure their rumors to the inmates will."

Chris offered that the only solution was to keep them out of any facility operated by the Riverside County Sheriff. "By the nature of the alleged crime, we are subject to harassment at every level. The deputies feel animosity to us above what they usually feel as a result and do anything to discomfort us. They get 'even' every day. It is ludicrous to expect them to act any other way." George Smith had a more succinct way of describing the untenable nature of the relationship. "You have handed them an ice cream cone—us—and told them not to lick it."

In truth, George, Chris, and Russ found the young jailers more annoying than threatening. It was the older deputies, the ones out working the streets, who were the most menacing. Those guys might not have had control over their day-to-day lives, but they spent a lot of time at the county jail hauling in prisoners and doing the substantial amount of paperwork that goes with any arrest. As a result, the Norco 3 were constantly coming face-to-face with men they had tried to kill. Many of them had taken bullets through their windshields; some still carried lead in their bodies. All of them had known Jim Evans.

When these deputies passed the segregation cells, they would often stop to stare at the three cop killers. Some told them flat out that they would kill them if they could. But mostly they just stared, their eyes saying it already. Among all the deputies, there was one who George Smith singled out by name in his declaration as particularly threatening, and who could sometimes be found lurking in the shadows outside their cell for no apparent reason. That deputy was Andy Delgado. "Deputy Delgado comes here by himself or with his friends," Smith wrote. "He does not work at the jail. He comes to look at the monkey. He tells his friends, Smith's the leader, a fact not in evidence. Delgado shot me, a fact not in evidence. But he comes here with death and malice in his heart, a fact in evidence."

13

BRICKS IN THE WALL

May 13, 1980. Riverside, California.

IT WAS A SUNNY DAY, LATE SUMMER, JUST MONTHS AFTER THEY HAD BEEN married. Jim Evans pulled the pickup off Van Buren Boulevard into the grounds of the Riverside National Cemetery. "What are we doing here, Jim?" Mary Evans asked her new husband. He smiled, the tan Stetson perched on his head. "Jim?" she asked again.

He drove in the main gate, winding through the beautifully manicured grounds of Lemay Boulevard, Eisenhower Circle, Normandy Drive. He stopped the truck and they got out. "This is where you're going to bury me," he told her, standing among the military grave markers. He squinted up into a bright blue sky at an aircraft roaring overhead on approach to March Air Reserve Base, just over the highway. "With those planes going over me."

TWO HELICOPTERS FLEW OVER RIVERSIDE NATIONAL CEMETERY. MARY EVans watched behind dark glasses as Baker-1 and a chopper from the DEA cut in low over Jim's flag-draped coffin in aerial salute and then arced high into the gloomy and overcast sky. In her arms, four-and-a-half-month-old Jim Jr. began to fuss from all the noise. Mary held him close.

She let her eyes settle over the crowd of mourners, hundreds of them and more still arriving even as the graveside service was underway. Around her now, almost one thousand law enforcement officers from fifty agencies throughout the state stood at attention in their dress uniforms. Nearby, fifty members of Jim's Fourth Battalion, 160th Infantry Regiment of the National Guard, were lined up, the edges of their hands touching their silver helmets in frozen salute.

Along with the baby, there were Mary's children from her previous marriage. Jim's parents, sister, and two brothers, all in from Texas, were still in stunned disbelief bordering on denial. Seated nearby were Julie Kay and Dallas, Jim's children from a previous marriage, along with his ex-wife.

Earlier, mourners had filled the six-hundred-seat pews of the Spanish-style St. Catherine's Church, stood along the side aisles and narthex, and spilled out onto the steps and lawn of the church. Along with all the cops and soldiers in their class A uniforms were friends, co-workers, and plain folk who had come in contact with deputy Jim Evans in one way or another through the years, teenagers in jeans and T-shirts, college students, office workers from the RSO, their babysitter Josie and her extended family. Municipal transit workers from Mary's department arrived, some of the bus drivers still in uniform with their ticket punchers dangling on chains about their waist.

A pew near the front was reserved for the wounded. Glyn Bolasky came, his arm in a sling. Herman Brown still walked with a noticeable limp. Ken McDaniels filed into the pew beside them, hairlike strands of copper shards still inhabiting his shoulder. Darrell Reed was brought in by ambulance and lay on a gurney in the center aisle, half of a round from a .308 still imbedded in his elevated left leg, an IV dripping antibiotics into his arm. Rolf Parkes stood beside him. A. J. Reynard had had surgery on his left elbow the night before and despite protests was not allowed to attend due to the possibility of infection. D. J. McCarty, his elbow wrapped in gauze, drove to the funeral with his roommate and partner Mike Lenihan. Both had witnessed Jim Evans die. They stayed with the other San Bernardino Sheriff's deputies and brass in the pews farther back.

Bill Crowe led the contingent of Riverside County Highway Patrol officers into the church, not just because of his role in Norco, but because of his close friendship with Evans. Crowe had expected to enter the church along with Doug Earnest, but at that moment his partner and surrogate big brother sat alone in a darkened bedroom staring into the carpet. The big patrolman had put on his dress uniform and polished up his wingtips, but when the time came to leave, he simply could not face it. It was not just the immeasurable sadness of losing Evans, whom Earnest had also known well. Earnest could not forgive himself for that moment when he thought he had led Crowe to his death at the intersection of Bellegrave and Dodd.

Dave Madden and Chuck Hille were among those who stood honor guard beside Jim's casket. Don Bender, the narcotics detective who had manned the CLEMARS radio up Lytle Creek, helped serve Communion. Seated beside Mary in the first pew was Bob Boytor, a friend and fellow deputy who had stood for Jim at their wedding in Las Vegas. Boytor was so stricken with grief that he could not bring himself to speak at the service. Evans's friend and first commanding officer at the RSO, lieutenant Bernard Bueche, gave the eulogy instead.

Evans lay in an open casket, dressed in his RSO uniform, his Stetson beside him and a photo of Jim Jr. placed in his folded hands. He still looked as handsome as ever, Mary thought, even with the piece of gauze covering the bullet hole in his right eye. At the close of the service, Mary kissed her husband's face, laid a single red rose in the coffin beside him, and was led from the church by Boytor as a recording of Pavarotti singing "Ave Maria" filled the cathedral.

The funeral cortege from St. Catherine's to the cemetery stretched for miles, led by 225 police motorcycles and cruisers, their light bars whirling, sirens off. Buses carrying 250 more Riverside deputies followed. As their limousine reached the intersection of Washington and Van Buren, Jim's father motioned silently to an open field where a dozen police and military helicopters had set down, the crews standing beside their craft saluting the passing hearse. Entering the cemetery grounds several minutes later, they heard the whining of aircraft engines high above and a dozen orange parachutes blossomed open against the gray sky, the paratroopers drifting just feet over the procession of vehicles to land over the fence on the grounds of March Air Reserve Base.

Two state troopers knelt before Mary to offer her the American and California state flags that had flown at half-staff over the capitol building in Sacramento a few days before. There was a sharp crack of gunfire as seven National Guardsmen raised M16 rifles with fixed bayonets toward the sky and fired the first of three salvos. Alone on a hillock overlooking the service, a trumpeter from the Los Angeles Police Department sounded taps. Mary watched the crowd breaking up as the ceremony ended. Well, she thought, things are about to get very lonely.

DEPUTY ANDY DELGADO STOOD AT THE BOOKING DESK FILLING OUT PAPER-work to process the prisoner standing handcuffed beside him. He glanced up at the two segregation cells located along the wall on the other side of the long, high counter. From that angle, Andy could see only a small slice of space behind the bars of the cells. He handed the paper and the prisoner over to the booking sergeant. Andy turned toward the elevator that would take him back down to his patrol car, but then paused and looked back at the two segregation cells. Inside one of them, a shadow moved across the wall and a tall man with black hair appeared and then receded again. Andy knew he should leave. There was nothing to find there, nothing to be learned from the men inside those cages. But the need to understand overcame him again.

Andy was not exactly sure what was drawing him to the segregation cages. He did not hate them. He was not there to taunt or tease or seek any kind of revenge. He had even considered leaving them a pack of Marlboros, the way a soldier offers a smoke to a prisoner of war. Not a peace offering, just a humanitarian gesture along with a subtle reminder of who the real losers had been that weekend. Mostly, Andy felt he needed to see who these people really were. What he had fought against in front of the bank was just a bunch of military ponchos and black ski masks—formless, faceless, and indistinguishable from each other. But inside those segregation cells were the human beings behind it all, real flesh and blood with blue and black eyes that stared back from their steel and concrete cave. Maybe if he could just get a good look at these guys, it would help him understand what the hell had happened to his life.

Andy approached the segregation cells and saw Chris Harven pacing the tiny room. Chris stopped and stared directly back at Delgado. When Andy did not move, Harven walked up to cell door and curled his fingers around the bars. One of the officers at the booking desk saw the two mad-dogging each other and gave Andy a little head nod to move on.

IT ALL MIGHT HAVE WORKED OUT IF ANDY HAD JUST TAKEN A FEW DAYS OFF after Norco, but he was back on the streets the next day. If you didn't take any lead, you didn't take any time. That was pretty much the rule. Besides, all Andy wanted to do was resume the life he had before the 211 tone dropped. Along with his promotion to detective had been the promise of a first assignment as an instructor at the Sheriff's Academy. Andy loved his training assignments in the Marine Corps, and it would give him a couple years away from street patrol, some time to lick his wounds before he was back fighting the bad guys.

If he had taken a few days off, he would have missed the flurry of second-guessing, exaggeration, and outright bullshit that started before Jim Evans's body had even been brought down off the mountain. Deputies who had never seen the yellow truck were suddenly telling tales of bullets cracking the sky above their patrol cars and near-death encounters. Others recklessly offered up opinions on what they would have done differently if it had been them at the bank, or at the intersection of Fourth and Hamner, or chasing armed suspects up a narrow mountain road. Why the fuck didn't Bolasky wait for backup? Why didn't CHP shut down I-15 or San Bernardino throw up a roadblock on Sierra? What the hell was Evans doing charging up a fire road completely outgunned? Why had Andy reported two hostages in the truck? I'd have iced those fuckers in Mira Loma if I'd known there were no hostages.

It wasn't true. No one had iced those fuckers in Mira Loma, San Bernardino, or anywhere else because no one had been in a position to take a shot from the time Andy fired his last slug at Fourth and Hamner to when Jim Evans emptied his .38 at the washout on Baldy Notch Road. "At that point, those guys were trying to kill anyone they saw," said one of the deputies in the pursuit. "If we'd had a shot, we would have taken it." Andy never acknowledged the second-guessing on the subject, but others knew some of it must have gotten back to him. "I'm sure he heard about it," said dispatcher Gary Keeter, who had no such criticism of Andy. "He had to know."

There were other developments that were far more concerning to Andy than all the big talk and second-guessing. On that first day back after the shootout, detective Joe Szeles was acting as shift supervisor and assigned Delgado to cover Rubidoux. "Hey, I'm the traffic car in Norco today," Andy told him. "The department doesn't want you guys in Norco for now," Szeles said. A few days later, there was another order from the department: They were no longer assigning Andy to the academy as a trainer. He was going straight into robbery detail, which meant right back on the streets. "The department wants you Norco guys close by, so we can keep an eye on you." Andy was bitterly disappointed, but he also saw a darker implication in the order. "So what are we now, damaged goods?"

WHETHER OR NOT THEY HAD "DAMAGED GOODS" ON THEIR HANDS WAS SOMEthing the RSO was only just beginning to understand in 1980. Along with no SWAT team, no helicopter, no bomb squad, no interagency communication system, and no high-powered weapons, the Riverside Sheriff's Department had no specific program for treating officers involved in traumatic events. If an officer felt he needed psychological counseling, the department's health insurance would cover it, but it had no set policy or contract with any trained psychiatric professionals. In this regard, the RSO was only slightly behind in a profession that had yet to address a condition known about for decades. Earlier that same year, the condition made its first appearance in the American Psychiatric Association's *Diagnostic and Statistical Manual of Mental Disorders* under a new name: posttraumatic stress disorder.

Whether referred to as "soldier's heart," "combat fatigue," "shell shock," or "combat stress reaction," PTSD was known as far back as ancient times. After a particularly brutal and prolonged campaign, Alexander the Great's men were said to have mutinied after suffering "battle fatigue." Greek historian Herodotus wrote of an Athenian spearman named Epizelus who, at the Battle of Marathon in 490 BCE, went blind after the soldier beside him was brutally killed, although the blinded soldier himself "was wounded in no part of his body." But it was not until the 1980 publication of the third edition of the *Diagnostic and Statistical Manual of Mental Disorders*, or *DSM*-III, that the psychiatric community clearly acknowledged causal events beyond just military combat.

Post Traumatic Stress Disorder (309.89)
Essential Feature. Characteristic symptoms following a psychological distressing event that is outside the range of usual human experience. The original stressor is usually experienced with intense fear, terror, and/or helplessness.

It was also noted that "The disorder is apparently more severe and longer lasting when the stressor is of human design," as had been the case with Norco. The symptoms had not changed much from the older editions of the *DSM*: anxiety, depression, feelings of detachment, isolation, recurrent dreams or recollections of the events. More acute symptoms included flashbacks, irritability, outbursts of anger, hypervigilance, and exaggerated startle response. The number and severity of the symptoms could vary from person to person, but many were already beginning to show up in the Norco deputies. Some recognized what was happening to them. Others, like Andy Delgado, did not.

IF THE RSO WAS BEHIND THE TIMES IN ADDRESSING PTSD IN ITS DEPUTIES, assistant sheriff Floyd Tidwell had made sure that the San Bernardino Sheriff's Office was not. Even before Norco, Tidwell realized involvement in shootings and exposure to violence was exacting a physical and emotional toll on personnel, resulting in increases in heart attacks, domestic violence, suicides, permanent disability, and early retirements. Tidwell's son had been involved in a shooting and he had seen close up the impact it had. He wrangled up $27,000 from the department budget to begin an evaluation and a counseling program. Psychiatrist Alice Pitman, an expert in the field of PTSD, was put on retainer. The department was now telling officers involved in violent situations that they were expected to participate in the program. "We've made it almost a mandatory thing," Tidwell said.

The need for compulsory participation was obvious. Without it, the deputies would not accept the help. "If you do, they're going to think you're crazy and you'll never get anywhere in this department," was the general feeling, according to deputy Jim McPheron. D. J. McCarty had a more succinct way of explaining the real reason most refused to even acknowledge they were having a problem to begin with. "Nobody wants to be seen as fucking weak." "Weak" if you had a problem, "crazy" the minute you stepped into a psychiatrist's office. Seek counseling in Riverside, RSO deputy Dave Madden said, and you were likely "to end up on the 'Rubber Gun Squad,'" the euphemism for a desk assignment given to cops deemed too psychologically unstable to carry a weapon.

Tidwell was having none of this macho bullshit. Having brought these horses to water, he was going to make damn sure they drank. The message for his deputies involved in gunfire on May 9, 1980, was simple: You're going. When psychiatrist Alice Pitman suggested a group session, Tidwell extended an invitation to all the agencies involved in the Norco incident. Most sent at least some of their men.

The session took place at the San Bernardino County Sheriff's Training Academy two weeks after Norco. The deputies, city cops, and CHP officers filed in and milled about talking with others and exchanging stories. Andy Delgado avoided the group and took a seat ahead of the others. Pitman told the participants they should say whatever they wanted about the experience, how it made them feel, and, if they felt comfortable enough, any issues they might be having in its aftermath.

As they went around the room, some of the men lowered their heads and spoke only briefly about their experience. For others, it just poured out. Rolf Parkes broke down in tears remembering how his wife had been informed that he had been "shot in the head" and was then unable to locate him for hours. D. J. McCarty was reserved in his comments. He was just sorry he could not have done more to save Evans. McCarty had something else he wanted to make very clear: "The only hero on the mountain that day was Jim Evans."

When it came to Andy's turn, he spoke in halting, measured tones. "I'm just sad that all this happened," he said, surprised at the tears suddenly welling up in his eyes. Pitman asked how he had been feeling since the incident. He paused for a long time, regaining his emotions and considering his words. "I'm sick of the shit," he said, unable to hold back his frustration, anger, and disillusionment with some of his fellow deputies. "I'm sick of being let down, people not backing me up when they should. I'm supposed to be able to depend on people in this department . . ." His voice trailed off. He might as well have been talking about all the people in his childhood who had let him down, just as he felt Bolasky and Hille had abandoned him in Norco. "I'm just sick of it all," he said, standing up from his chair. "I'm sick of the fraud." With that, he walked out of the session.

FOR GLYN BOLASKY, THE NIGHTMARES BEGAN JUST TWENTY-FOUR HOURS AFter the shooting. Lying beside his wife after all the local stations had gone to test patterns, he finally drifted off into a fitful sleep, his body awash in painkillers. In the dream, men were shooting at him, but he became paralyzed, unable to escape or fight back. He woke up with a start and then drifted off again. In the next dream blood was squirting in his face like a garden hose, the warm sensation of liquid so real it jolted him awake. It took even longer to get back to sleep this time, but once he did, it just started up again, the same goddamn dreams over and over. He thought that once he was off the painkillers, the nightmares would subside. They did not.

After Jim Evans's funeral, questions and doubts began to creep into Bolasky's consciousness. How was it possible that he was first on scene, had his car hit with more than forty rounds, and was wounded in five places, yet he survived while the deputy patrolling the farthest away from the robbery got killed? What if he had just stayed down and let the bank robbers drive off in the getaway van? Or what if he had been able to kill them all? Bolasky could not help thinking that if he had done either one, Jim Evans would still be alive.

Bolasky also had to come to terms with shooting a seventeen-year-old high school kid in the back of the head. No one was questioning Bolasky over the death of Billy Delgado except for Bolasky himself. Eventually Bolasky would come to a fragile understanding over the killing of Delgado, although he still found it too painful to say the boy's name. "That person didn't really die at my hand," he told *Press-Enterprise* reporter James Richardson. "I pointed the shotgun. Where the pellets went from there, I honestly believe God took it from there."

After two weeks off for his injuries, Bolasky returned to desk duty only to find himself overwhelmed being back in uniform. Just three days later, he walked into his supervisor's office and said it was too soon, he needed more time to straighten himself out. They gave him two more weeks and told him to see Alice Pitman. He went once. After the two weeks off, he still could not face it, so he used vacation time for an additional two weeks and went to Hawaii with his wife. There, he sat on the white sand in the shadow of palm trees waving in the tropical breeze, about as far away as a man could get from the dirt fields and traffic-choked intersections of Norco. It did no good. He continued to think about Evans and Billy Delgado and dream about warm blood squirting into his face. Bolasky also began to think about something else: How the hell could the department have let this happen to me?

GLYN BOLASKY WAS NOT THE ONLY RIVERSIDE DEPUTY QUESTIONING WHY the department had left them so ill prepared to take on a gang of heavily armed bank robbers intent on fighting to the death. What had started as grumbling escalated into widespread finger-pointing and accusations by rank-and-file deputies against their own department and sheriff Ben Clark.

In some ways, Ben Clark was an easy target for the fiasco of May 9. Although he began his career on the streets, Clark had risen to the top of the department through the administrative ranks. He was plainspoken and direct, his actions led by cold logic rather than momentary passions. Clark was widely acknowledged as the man responsible for the modernization of the Riverside County Sheriff's Department from a freewheeling organization severely short on procedures and training into a disciplined, well-organized law enforcement agency. Clark later brought his success to the state level and served as chairman of the California Commission on Peace Officer Standards and Training. By 1980, he was in his seventeenth year as the Riverside County sheriff, having been elected to the post four times. Much of Clark's appeal among voters was his budget efficiency and commitment to progressive policing and community relations.

It did not help Clark that just one county over was San Bernardino County sheriff Frank Bland, a rough-and-tumble, old-school cop's cop who had fought on Iwo Jima and came up through the ranks as a patrolman, detective, and then captain. It had been Bland who drove his personal department vehicle up Baldy Notch Road to bring down the body of Jim Evans. Bland had a fiercely loyal following among his deputies. Clark was not disliked by his deputies, but his biggest supporters were those among his own staff. "He was a man with absolute moral values, and he applied logic to all of his decisions," said Cois Byrd, who worked under Clark and would succeed him as sheriff.

Whatever equity Ben Clark had built up with his deputies over years of improved discipline and training seemed to evaporate in the days after Norco. What had been mostly insider squabbling became very public when the *Riverside Press-Enterprise* ran a four-part exposé titled "Staying Alive" on consecutive days the week of July 13, 1980. Ostensibly, the series was an exploration of lessons learned from the Norco incident and what could be done to address any deficiencies. But the opening lines of the front-page article in the Sunday edition clearly announced what it was really going to be about:

Riverside sheriff's deputies are angry. And they're scared. A fellow officer, James B. Evans, was shot to death during a robbery and chase that led into the San Gabriel Mountains. The deputies don't think their department is doing enough to prevent it from happening again.

Before the first installment of the series was over, the reading public was aware of just how pissed the deputies were at Ben Clark and the RSO. "Clark is dragging his feet on some changes and refuses to make others," Sheriffs' Association president Robert Russell was quoted in what was essentially a declaration of open revolt on behalf of the deputies. "He wants tempers to cool in hopes we will all forget the demands." The article added that "Police officials from other departments are also critical of Clark" and that they "agree with the deputies' contention that Clark's department lags seriously behind other police agencies in the areas of training and equipment."

Clark contested the accusations head-on. "Riverside's deputies are as well-trained and equipped as any police officers in the state." He did not run his administration by crisis, he said. "We will take our time and make the changes we honestly feel we need." While indicative of the sober and calculated management style that had made him popular in the past, he now sounded more like a man who did not see what the big deal was all about. What the deputies saw as evidence of a trend, Clark considered an anomaly not likely to be repeated. "In thirty years in law enforcement, I have never seen anything like the Norco incident."

It was not exactly what the public wanted to hear, especially after the paper took more than a dozen column inches to detail exactly how badly law enforcement had gotten their asses kicked that day. For a savvy politician who had won four major county elections in a row, the sheriff demonstrated a tin ear when it came to his remarks. When told the San Bernardino Sheriff's Office had concluded that the absence of CLEMARS was the reason Jim Evans drove straight into the ambush, Clark bristled. "No one will ever be able to convince me that if Evans's car radio had CLEMARS he would be alive today." As if to punctuate how alone Clark was in that belief, the *Press-Enterprise* ran a companion article titled "Evans' Unit Was Not Equipped for Crucial Warning," which contradicted Clark and included the heartbreaking final radio transmissions by Evans.

Not only did the series announce the rift within the Riverside Sheriff's Department, it revealed the animosity that existed between Clark and Riverside police chief Victor Jones, who ran his department from the building directly across the street: "Jones complains Clark is too often willing to fill gaps in his own force by relying on help from neighboring, smaller, better equipped police departments." After essentially calling the RSO a bunch of parasitic freeloaders, Jones went on to blame Clark for everything that went wrong that day. "I think had they [Riverside deputies] been afforded the best training and equipment available, the outcome would have been different." It was a particularly harsh indictment considering the "outcome" was the death of a deputy.

When the "Staying Alive" series turned its attention to guns, Clark conceded, "The bad guys simply had the better weapons." However, he dismissed the idea that high-powered rifles would have done his men any good.

The article went on to note that "some of Clark's deputies are unwilling to wait" for the department to move on the weapons issue and were now carrying semiautomatic rifles they had purchased on their own. "Most of the deputies are now carrying the guns the Sheriff said we can't have," an unidentified deputy said. "At shift change, there are a lot of AR-15s and Mini-14s going into the trunks and under the front seats of patrol cars." "I know that these weapons are against our policy, but I would much rather be tried by twelve jurors than carried by six friends," deputy Don Chennault wrote in the Sheriff's Association newsletter. The implication was clear: If the department won't protect us, we will protect ourselves.

The most startling revelation in the "Staying Alive" exposé was not how slow Clark and the RSO were to react, but the speed and degree to which the other agencies involved had moved to increase their own firepower. In the two months since the Norco bank robbery, the RPD had ordered a dozen high-powered rifles to go along with a dozen they already kept in the trunks of shift sergeants' cars. At the San Bernardino Sheriff's Department—which prior to Norco had possessed only the beat-up M16 used by D. J. McCarty— sheriff Frank Bland had "presented that county's Board of Supervisors with an extensive shopping list." Bland's wish list included three dozen automatic weapons as well as $5,500 to buy an M60 machine gun to mount on one of his choppers.

With his request for the M60, Bland had moved beyond the world of domestic law enforcement to that of military-grade weaponry, far surpassing anything found in the arsenal of any local police force. The M60, widely used in the Vietnam War, is a belt-fed machine gun capable of firing 750 rounds of .308 ammunition per minute. As over-the-top as Bland's request might have been, the contrast was not good for Ben Clark. While he was forming committees to study the issue, just over the border Frank Bland was making sure that the next asshole who shot at one of his choppers would get obliterated.

Compared to the impressive firepower his neighboring agencies had on order, the arsenal listed by Riverside chief deputy Sam Lowery in the "Staying Alive" article seemed almost quaint: several .30-.30 lever-action rifles, two bolt-action single-shot sniper rifles, and one AR-15, the whereabouts of which nobody was quite sure.

Shortly after publication of the article, Sheriff Clark strode into a scheduled budget meeting with the county supervisors and made a surprising announcement. "It is our intention to buy forty Mini-14 rifles so sergeant supervisors are equipped with the weapons." No one was more surprised than Robert Russell, the president of the Riverside Sheriffs' Association who had been so critical of Clark in the exposé. Russell, who also sat on the sheriff's weapons-review committee, said he was "amazed" by the sheriff's announcement. "Why was a committee set up to discuss this very same issue if the sheriff already knew what he was going to do?" Russell complained.

When asked about the change of heart, Clark refused further comment. Lowery deflected reporters' questions as well. "We are not going to talk about it anymore. All this is doing is stirring up trouble. We have enough of an emotional situation on our hands without adding to it."

Within months of the Norco bank robbery, Inland Empire law enforcement agencies, which had started the year with a handful of semiautomatic rifles, were now on their way to becoming some of the most heavily armed in the nation. The two sheriff's departments had gone from a pair of high-powered rifles between them to more than seventy-five and counting. Helicopters, which had been unarmed before Norco, now circled overhead with machine guns at the ready to rain dozens of rounds of ammunition down on hostile suspects. After firmly stating in the "Staying Alive" article that the RSO would have no use for a SWAT team, Clark announced he was forming eight of the heavily armed units to be placed throughout the county. An additional dozen Ruger Marksman rifles chambering .308 ammunition were ordered and put at the disposal of the teams.

Law enforcement officers throughout the Inland Empire knew they were experiencing a sea change in local police weaponry that was not likely to ever be reversed. After one hundred years of policing the Wild West with a six-shooter and a Winchester shotgun, sheriff's deputies suddenly had access to fifteen-round, high-capacity sidearms and rifles that could punch a hole the size of a fist through a man from half a mile away.

After the flurry of weapons acquisitions was announced, deputies Andy Delgado and Dave Madden were relaxing in front of the television set at Andy's house when the evening news showed video of German police guarding an event. On the screen, the federal Bundespolizei stood clad in body armor holding Heckler & Koch MP5 submachine guns across their chests. "See that," Andy said, nodding at the television. "That's the way it's going. That's how we'll all be armed soon."

DESPITE ORDERING THE NEW WEAPONS, HARD FEELINGS TOWARD SHERIFF Clark persisted among RSO deputies. They openly booed him at a Riverside Sheriffs' Association meeting. Much of the unhappiness was due to what they saw as a lack of recognition for their service that day. "We put our lives and souls and everything into this," deputy Rolf Parkes would be quoted in the *San Bernardino Sun* years later. "After the incident there was no support from the Riverside sheriff's office for any of us. We were not even thanked . . . They just forgot about us, put us aside."

Others felt the department was trying to brush the whole thing under the rug to avoid any further negative publicity related to the incident. When a local citizens group called the Law Enforcement Appreciation Committee held their annual event to honor Riverside officers from various agencies, the CHP recommended patrolmen Joe Haughey and Bill Crowe for their role in the Norco pursuit. The Riverside Sheriff's Office declined to nominate any of its deputies for their role in the Norco bank robbery.

All the discord between the deputies and their department came to a head on September 12, 1980, when the membership of the Riverside Sheriffs' Association returned a vote of "no confidence" in sheriff Ben Clark. "There is a great deal of emotion being exhibited in our department right now," Clark responded, "and a vote of this kind really is no help to me in administration."

AS FAR AS GLYN BOLASKY WAS CONCERNED, THE ONLY PERSON THE DEPART-ment had let down more than Jim Evans was Glyn Bolasky, and he was not being quiet about it. Andy Delgado might have had his differences with the Norco deputies after the incident, but Bolasky's complaining did not sit well with him. From the time Andy first saw him in the hospital hours after the shootout, he was convinced Bolasky's injuries were not nearly severe enough to warrant his leaving the scene while the shootout was still in progress. "Sure, Bolasky did a few good things there; he stood up and shot at those guys," Andy said. "But after he was wounded, he was worthless. And he took another guy with him," he added, meaning Chuck Hille.

Andy was also disgusted with his fellow deputies for being so openly contemptuous of their own sheriff and department. The Darrell Creed code of ethics demanded a level of respect for one's department and the institution of law enforcement itself. Andy's faith in all of those might have been eroded, but he remained faithful to the principle.

By mid-July, Bolasky was back full-time but still restricted to dispatch duty due to injury. The assignment had effectively kept Delgado and Bolasky from crossing paths. But one afternoon while pulling file numbers near the dispatch center, Andy spotted Bolasky talking to a few other deputies in the hallway. According to Andy, he heard Bolasky complaining bitterly about the department and then saw him lift his badge up and pretend to spit on it.

What the fuck's wrong with you? Delgado said, approaching Bolasky. We just finished burying a guy and you're disrespecting the same badge he wore? The two exchanged words. Andy's anger spiked, and he lunged at Bolasky. In an instant, the two were pushing and threatening to throw punches until the other deputies jumped in and separated them.

By the end of the day, news of the confrontation between Bolasky and Delgado had spread. The impact among the ranks of the RSO deputies was profound: Not only was Norco tearing apart the relationship between the deputies and their department, but now they were turning on each other.

JUST ONE MONTH PRIOR TO THE NORCO BANK ROBBERY, AN ALBUM BY ROCK group Pink Floyd finished an astonishing fifteen-week run at the top of the Billboard album chart on its way to becoming the best-selling album of 1980. *The Wall* was a semi-autobiographical chronicle of a rock star's downward slide into isolation and alienation, with each traumatic event a metaphorical "brick" pushing him closer to self-destruction.

For Andy Delgado, Norco had become just another brick in the wall he had built up around himself since childhood. After speaking out at the group counseling session and the fight with Bolasky, Andy felt like a marked man. Now it seemed people were gunning for him, trying to bait him into getting into more trouble.

Within weeks of the fight with Bolasky, Andy had a run-in with another deputy, this time in public. Angered over a comment made behind his back, Andy radioed the man for a 1087 meet-up at the Carl's Jr. parking lot directly across the street from the Security Pacific Bank. Once there, he dressed down the junior deputy. Soon the two were out of their patrol cars screaming accusations and poking fingers in each other's chests in the middle of a crowded lot. A citizen reported the confrontation and the two men were called in by their superior to explain themselves. In the end, only Andy received a reprimand for having instigated the incident.

The flare-ups, confrontations, and shouting matches continued. By the first anniversary of Norco, Andy was carrying two handguns while out in the field—one in a shoulder holster, one in his boot. He did not try to disguise the reason for this. "If I can't count on people in this department to back me up," Delgado let it be known, "then I'll do it myself." He was also spending more time drinking with his buddies, had dropped out of college, and had a failing marriage. "I was not a very pleasant guy," he would later admit.

After yet another confrontation, Andy arrived at the RSO one morning to find a letter on his desk from workman's comp informing him that a claim had been filed on his behalf. The notice instructed him to see a psychiatrist for evaluation. If Andy wasn't going to get help himself, the department was going to do it for him. Andy stormed into the captain's office and set his service revolver and badge on the man's desk. "If this is what you fuckers want," he yelled, shaking the letter at the captain, "then here you go."

The captain, a man Andy did not dislike, tossed his pen on the desk. "Goddamn it, Andy," he bellowed, pushing the hardware back at Delgado. "Put that fuckin' shit back on right now, get back to work, and go see that doctor." The department was not ready to give up on one of their best detectives yet.

AFTER THE FIGHT WITH DELGADO, IT DID NOT TAKE LONG FOR THE RELATION-ship between Bolasky and the RSO to sour even further. Bolasky's criticism of the department continued and the brass was not happy about it. At the end of July, acting station commander lieutenant Walter Kelly called Bolasky in on a day off to discuss the deputy's dissatisfaction with the department. The two men argued, and Kelly kicked Bolasky out of the office.

It was the last straw for Bolasky, who immediately walked across the street to the headquarters of the Riverside Police Department and asked for a job, just as he had been threatening to do for weeks. To Bolasky's immense surprise, he was led into the office of chief Victor Jones. Bolasky was direct: Can I come over here? he asked. Jones, eager to steal the hero of Norco away from his rival Ben Clark, said he could. Bolasky then walked back across the street and resigned from the Riverside County Sheriff's Department.

Three weeks later, Glyn Bolasky was a member of the Riverside PD.

He felt relieved to be making a fresh start, hopeful that the change in environment would help put Norco behind him. Like any incoming officer, he was assigned a six-month field-training program under the supervision of veteran officer Dennis Doty. Doty immediately spotted problems. Bolasky was jittery, his behavior erratic. He was having issues driving a police vehicle. Most of all, he seemed preoccupied with the Norco shootout, bringing it up constantly. "I like the guy," Doty confided in fellow officer Mike Watts, "but he just can't get over Norco."

Bolasky knew he was struggling. Even the most routine traffic stops were stressful. On November 5, two months into the training program, Bolasky was involved in a high-speed pursuit in the La Sierra area that ended in the arrest of armed robbers at gunpoint. "From that moment on, I didn't care about law enforcement as much," Bolasky said. "Why am I doing this?" he began to ask himself.

The change in enthusiasm was obvious to all involved. Supervisors, including Doty, wrote unfavorable reviews of Bolasky's performance. It was about that time that fine strands of copper shrapnel began showing up in Bolasky's eyes, a testament to the insidious nature of a full metal jacket .223 and its ability to damage the human body on levels both catastrophic and minute. Although the effect on his eyesight was minimal, it spooked the shit out of him, making matters worse. Higher up the administrative chain, a fear was developing that if Bolasky could not get over Norco, he might end up filing a claim against the RPD for lifetime retirement benefits.

On January 12, 1981, Victor Jones and the Riverside Police Department cut their losses and fired Bolasky, labeling him a "vicarious liability." When asked by reporter James Richardson why his department had not done more to help Bolasky, "Jones said he doesn't have the budget for psychologists or psychiatrists, so he retires officers when they have mental fatigue." The comment demonstrated that there was at least one law enforcement agency in the Inland Empire even further behind the RSO in its attitude toward PTSD.

Glyn Bolasky probably would have preferred a different headline to Richardson's article that appeared in the *Riverside Press-Enterprise* on April 12, 1981. "The Day a Man's Life Took a Sharp Turn—Norco Shootout Survivor Now a Washed-up Ex-Officer at 24" was an interview piece chronicling Bolasky's fall from Norco hero to unemployment in less than a year. Accompanying the story was a photo of a thoughtful young man, arms folded, his eyes shifted off camera. In the interview, Bolasky was introspective rather than bitter, conceding that he had declined further counseling offered by the Riverside Sheriff's Office upon his initial return. "I just didn't understand maybe the whole scope of things," he said. The article ended on a melancholy note. "I'm the hot potato nobody wants," Bolasky said. "I wouldn't be here if I hadn't been shot in Norco that day."

ON NOVEMBER 24, 1980, A DEADLY CONFLAGRATION ERUPTED JUST OFF THE Cajon Pass at a scenic overlook known as Panorama Point, just over the ridgeline from Lytle Creek Canyon. Aided by one-hundred-degree heat and dry Santa Ana winds gusting to ninety miles an hour, the flames raced down the canyons toward San Bernardino, burning at a rate of five thousand acres per hour. Firefighters never stood a chance.

By the time the Panorama Fire was contained on December 1, it had consumed 310 homes in Waterman Canyon and the city of San Bernardino. One of those destroyed belonged to deputy Jim McPheron. Mac lost everything but his family. Among the charred wedding photos and melted Little League trophies was a framed piece of windshield with a bullet hole through it. The section was one of two cut from McPheron's patrol unit, framed and presented to Mac and D. J. McCarty by their fellow deputies.

It was a devastating end to a devastating year for the big, amiable deputy. After watching Evans shot in front of him, McPheron knew he had finally seen enough. Within a week, McPheron embraced the department program and sought counseling.

One June 22, 1980, *Riverside Press-Enterprise* reporter Ilene Aleshire featured McPheron in an article titled "The Stresses of Crime" that focused on the emotional toll exacted by a career in law enforcement. He called the shooting in Lytle Creek the last straw. "I told the captain, 'I've got a problem and I really don't know how to deal with it. I have a lot of in-built tension, I don't know how to release it. I'm arguing with my wife, yelling at my kid.'" McPheron was taken off patrol duty and reassigned to the Civil Processes division, serving property-seizure notices in lawsuits. After Norco and the Panorama fire, McPheron was happy to get off the streets for a while.

D. J. McCarty had lost none of his swagger as he and deputy Mike Lenihan walked into their mandatory counseling session with psychiatrist Alice Pitman; if anything, it might have increased. McCarty didn't need any fucking psychiatrist, and he all but let Alice Pitman know it. The two had gone from Jim Evans's funeral straight to Pitman's office and spoke with her together. How were they doing? Fine. Just part of the job. Did they need to take some time off? Time off for what? Either of you want additional counseling? Fuck no! McCarty was courteous but dismissive, almost smirking at the suggestion. Lenihan, as usual, was a man of few words who tended to follow D.J.'s lead. Neither was good at expressing their feelings even if they had wanted to, and neither one wanted to.

Young, Irish cops. It was a bad combination for any psychiatrist to try to crack, even one as experienced and capable as Pitman. As she ushered them to the door at the end of the session, Pitman offered up a warning: "Your machismo is going to put you right back on the street," she said. "And you'll be just fine. For a while, anyhow. But a year from now you'll be back scratching down my door." They gave Pitman a shrug and a little salute good-bye and went on their way, Lenihan back to his darkness, D.J. back to drinking and fucking and pretending nothing was wrong.

CALIFORNIA HIGHWAY PATROL OFFICER BILL CROWE WAS ON ROUTINE SHIFT when he pulled off the freeway to buy a soda at a local gas station. It had been about a year since Crowe was shot up at the corner of Bellegrave and Dodd. The image of Russell Harven, hair and beard whipping in wind, looking over the barrel of an AR-15 had never left him.

Crowe pulled in behind a Volkswagen Beetle and walked toward the market while the VW idled, waiting for the next open fuel pump. As he approached the small car, the last person he expected to see behind the wheel was the man who had almost killed him in Mira Loma. With his adrenaline spiking and every defense mechanism firing off at once, Crowe drew his gun, leveled it through the window of the VW, and told the man with the long brown hair and scraggly beard not to move. When the frightened man whipped his head around, Crowe realized he had made a huge mistake. Lowering the gun and muttering an apology, Crowe went back to his patrol unit and drove away.

With his heart still pounding and sweaty palms gripping the steering wheel, Crowe drove directly to the CHP station and told his superiors what had happened. Of all the agencies involved in Norco, the Riverside CHP had done the least to address the issue of PTSD with its officers. The department realized their mistake and ordered Crowe and Doug Earnest to seek help. For Crowe, talking with other cops involved in shootings helped and he began to move on. But Doug Earnest would never fully get over what happened at the intersection of Bellegrave and Dodd. Even decades later, the big patrolman could barely speak of it without being brought to tears.

FOR MARY EVANS, IT HAD BEEN A PARTICULARLY CRUEL YEAR SINCE THE KILL-ing of her husband. *Press-Enterprise* reporter Sandy Pavicic interviewed Mary for a one-year anniversary article titled "Slain Deputy's Widow Tells of a Long Year's Nightmares, Memories." Pavicic noted that among all the plaques, certificates, awards, and mementos in the widow's living room honoring Jim Evans's military and law enforcement careers, there was not a single photograph of the man Mary called the love of her life. "I took them all down and put them away," she said. It was just too painful to see him every day. As for the honors, "I don't pay any attention to them," she said. "If I did I'd probably take them down."

Among the collection was a proclamation by the board of supervisors, recognition by the American Legion, and the California Military Cross awarded to him by his National Guard unit after posthumously promoting him to captain. Awards from other city, county, government, and citizens' groups hung on the walls. A rocking horse bought by deputies and presented to J.B. Jr. by Chuck Hille sat in the hall, while a real horse given to the boy by a prominent local attorney stood chewing hay in a nearby corral. Absent was any recognition from the Riverside County Sheriff's Department.

When it came to the fate of the three men who had murdered her husband, Mary expressed a lack of faith in a California judicial system that was widely viewed to be populated with liberal judges unwilling to enforce the recently reinstated death penalty. "People come up and say, 'I bet you really hope those guys get the death penalty.' I don't count on them getting the death penalty. I hope they get it, but I don't count on it. They've already taken a part of my life."

With the trial scheduled to begin in just four weeks, Mary Evans thought she would soon have her answer. But neither Mary nor anyone else could have foreseen that what appeared to be an open-and-shut case was about to become one of the longest and most expensive trials in American history. And by far one of its strangest.

14

CONTEMPT

June 15, 1981. Vista, California.

AT ELEVEN THIRTY IN THE EVENING OF MARCH 16, 1977, FOUR YOUNG MEN ranging in age from sixteen to eighteen knocked on the door of a prominent Riverside criminal defense attorney named David Hennigan. Alone in the house were Hennigan's fifty-two-year-old wife and nineteen-year-old daughter. When Mary Hennigan opened the door, the four teens announced that their car had broken down and asked to use her phone to call for assistance. Immediately sensing danger, Mary refused and shut the door.

David Hennigan had the misfortune of arriving home at the same time. One of the teens stepped from behind a bush and aimed a shotgun at the attorney. Hennigan was marched to the door and forced to open it. Once inside, the fifty-five-year-old attorney tried to persuade the four youths to take what they wanted and get out, arguing that he was a defense attorney who often defended young men just like them. The argument abruptly ended when the kid with the shotgun fired a blast into the ceiling. David Hennigan was tied up and forced into a closet where he listened helplessly as his wife and daughter were sexually assaulted.

Momentarily left alone by her attackers, Mary Hennigan bolted from the house, ran to a neighbor's, and called police. The four intruders fled but just blocks from the scene encountered units from Riverside Police Department. As they forced their way around a unit blocking their escape, the suspects fired the shotgun at the patrol car. The officers returned fire, riddling the suspect vehicle with fifteen bullets, hitting eighteen-year-old Marvin Green in the head and sending the car crashing into a stone wall. Green and the others were quickly captured.

Eventually, the case wound its way through the court system and all were found guilty of crimes ranging from rape and kidnapping to armed robbery and attempted murder. But in the weeks following their sentencing, a rumor began to spread through the Riverside legal and law enforcement community: During the penalty phase, Hennigan had made a plea to the court for leniency on behalf of the four teens who had attacked his wife and daughter. Although never substantiated, the rumor persisted. After all, anyone who had worked with Hennigan knew such a thing was not entirely impossible. When asked about the event, an attorney who worked at the law firm of Hennigan, Butterwick & Clepper responded, "Yeah, I can see him doing something like that." A second agreed that it would be consistent with his personality to want to show compassion for young men who had taken a criminal turn.

J. David Hennigan, Dave to friends and colleagues, had spent time in the public defender's office before joining up with two fellow attorneys to launch a private civil and criminal defense practice. Hennigan was a jovial, outgoing Irishman from St. Louis who served in the Pacific Theater in World War II, earned a law degree from George Washington University, and was respected among the Riverside legal community. He had a solid understanding of the law but was not above occasional courtroom histrionics. Once, while defending a client charged with drunk driving, Hennigan drank a can of beer during his closing argument just to show that it did not impair his abilities.

Hennigan, like defense attorney Clayton Adams, felt that the justice system was unfairly stacked against defendants, especially the poor. He believed deeply in the right of the accused to an adequate defense and fair trial. He felt that in most criminal acts, there were mitigating circumstances beyond the control of the actor, usually due to injustices inflicted upon them during childhood. His Roman Catholic faith informed him that all acts could be forgiven, all lives were redeemable, and that the death penalty was immoral. However, he was also faithful to his professional oath to uphold and obey the law, even if that included capital punishment.

A little more than a year after the home-invasion incident, Hennigan received a call from Anthony Kline, the judicial appointment secretary for governor Jerry Brown. Kline offered Hennigan a position on the California State Superior Court. Hennigan had never put himself forward for a spot on the bench, but after thoughtful consideration, he accepted. When the Norco case came to trial two years later, the Honorable J. David Hennigan was "next in the barrel" in the case assignment rotation.

The district attorney's office was not thrilled that a former criminal defense attorney with relatively little judicial experience would be presiding over the trial. The case of the Norco 3 was only the second capital murder trial in Riverside County since the reinstatement of the death penalty in California and promised to be a bitterly contested, lengthy, and high-profile case. In the opinion of many within the office, there were plenty of seasoned ballbusters on the Riverside bench better suited for this type of free-for-all.

Even less thrilled were the deputies at the RSO, who were familiar with Hennigan's stance on the death penalty and the rumors surrounding the 1977 home-invasion trial. "A guy who asks the court to go easy on the punks who attacked his own wife and kid," Andy Delgado said about Hennigan's appointment. "And that's who they assign to the trial of a bunch of fucking cop killers."

THE DISCONTENT ON THE PART OF THE DEPUTIES WAS NOT ENTIRELY DIrected at Hennigan. The attitude of law enforcement in general toward the California criminal justice system in 1980 was one of disillusionment and disgust. The system, and particularly the liberal-minded California Supreme Court led by chief justice Rose Bird, was seen by many as easy on criminals, hostile toward law enforcement, and vehemently anti–death penalty. Of the sixty-four capital cases reviewed by the Bird court, sixty-one death sentences were overturned. Bird herself voted to overturn in all sixty-four. If there is one thing judges and prosecutors have in common, it is a hatred of being overturned. Both knew the trial would be an exercise in tiptoeing through a field of legal land mines laid by the defense and intended to blow up during the appeal process.

The man in charge of dodging land mines for the prosecution just happened to have been trained as a mine warfare technician in the navy during the Vietnam War. Deputy district attorney Jay Hanks had been put on the Norco case immediately and was busy collecting evidence even before the last of the suspects had been brought off the mountain. The plan was for Hanks to cover the case until another prosecutor was freed up to take it over. However, district attorney Byron Morton quickly realized that the scope of investigation and a capital murder trial would require one of his best prosecutors and assigned Hanks the job. Hanks was a sharp and effective trial attorney but had not litigated a case in more than two years. Instead he had been working in an administrative capacity under Morton and was clearly being groomed for a bigger role in the department.

Hanks relocated from the Midwest to California when his father, a trial judge in Illinois, retired to Riverside. His older brother Hardin "Bud" Hanks was a deputy with the RSO and had been a friend of Jim Evans. After his stint in the navy, the younger Hanks earned his undergraduate degree from UC Riverside and put himself through Pepperdine University School of Law in Malibu while working as a sixth-grade schoolteacher. Hanks was admitted to the California Bar in 1974 and joined the district attorney's office shortly thereafter. In his midthirties when assigned the Norco 3 case, Hanks had a wife and two small children and drove around in a beat-up sports car he called "the Crime Fighter." While the heavy workload had caused Hanks to sock on some extra weight around the middle, he was still active and could hold his own in pickup basketball games with courthouse colleagues. A hard-charging prosecutor, he was nevertheless known for his good humor and quick wit inside the courtroom and out. When he learned that Christopher Harven had dubbed him "the Bad Year Blimp," Hanks embraced the nickname and started using it himself.

Hanks needed an additional attorney to help with the enormous amount of evidence and number of witnesses involved in prosecuting three defendants, each with forty-six felony counts against them. He chose Kevin Ruddy, a native Southern Californian who had earned his undergraduate and law degrees from the University of San Diego and joined the DA's office in 1977. Ruddy was a six-foot-two, thirty-year-old ex-basketball player with a calm disposition and methodical approach to trial preparation that made him well suited for organizing and presenting large amounts of evidence. It was decided that Ruddy would handle the thirty-six counts committed in Riverside County including kidnapping, the bank robbery, multiple counts of attempted murder of a police officer, and the killing of Billy Delgado under the Felony Murder Rule. Hanks would prosecute all the crimes committed in San Bernardino, including the one charge that could send the Norco 3 to the gas chamber at San Quentin: first-degree murder with special circumstances in the death of deputy James B. Evans.

Hanks obtained the final member of his team when, days before the start of the trial, the DA's office hired Joe Curfman away from the RSO to act as lead investigator for the prosecution. Curfman had been in charge of the Norco investigation for the Riverside Sheriff's Office from the beginning.

By June 1981, Riverside County had secured housing arrangements in Vista, a sleepy community just seven miles inland from Oceanside, for the four county employees working on the trial full-time. A three-bedroom house in a suburban neighborhood was rented at $1,200 a month to accommodate Hanks, Ruddy, and Curfman. In practice the house served as a crash pad for the rotating cast of attorneys, investigators, and 128 witnesses for the prosecution who would come and go as needed. The fourth county employee, defense investigator Jeanne Painter, was put up at the Vista Way Inn motel at a rate of $375 a month. The private-practice defense teams headed by Michael Lloyd and Alan Olson settled into monthly motel rentals with maid service and convenience kitchens paid for out of their own pockets and billed back to the county.

Just days before the start of the trial, Clayton Adams abruptly resigned from the public defender's office. George Smith immediately filed a motion to force the county to retain Adams as a private-practice defender, citing his Sixth Amendment right to a speedy trial. Facing the possibility of a long delay or mistrial if they assigned Smith a new attorney, the court had no choice but to give in and retain Adams for more money than he would have made working for the defender's office. Having successfully executed the well-orchestrated bump in salary, Adams rented himself a room at the Vista Way Inn motel directly below Jeanne Painter, both courtesy of a housing allowance from the County of Riverside.

IF ANYONE HAD THOUGHT THE TRIAL OF THE NORCO 3 WAS GOING TO PROCEED smoothly or rapidly, they were quickly disabused of that notion on the opening day, June 15, 1981.

Instigated by Chris and George in hopes of forcing a severance, Russell Harven announced he no longer wanted Alan Olson as his attorney. "Mr. Olson hasn't had any murder trials," Russ stammered uncertainly, "and some of the motions I have wanted filed, he never did." It was far from the confident and aggressive performance his older brother had displayed when firing his own attorney, Jay Grossman, six months earlier.

Hennigan was having none of it. "I don't know if any of the other attorneys have had this experience, either," he responded, referring to a capital murder trial. "None of the judges in Riverside County have heard such a case." Sensing Russell's heart was not in the request to begin with, Hennigan softened to an almost fatherly tone. "Mr. Olson has been with you from the beginning. He has been very competent. I'll deny the motion for now."

Outside the courthouse, Alan Olson told reporters the whole thing was nothing more than "pre-trial jitters" on the part of his client.

Things got more complicated when Hennigan granted a defense motion for a closed jury selection process, excluding both the media and public. While the Riverside and San Diego papers appealed the judge's decision, the *Press-Enterprise* ordered reporter Bob LaBarre to continue to seat himself in the courtroom gallery at the beginning of every session throughout the day. For weeks, LaBarre dutifully entered the courtroom and took his seat, only to be formally, but good-naturedly, expelled from the courtroom. LaBarre would then rise and shuffle out to the hallway like a dejected sad sack until the ritual was to be repeated all over again the next time. The charade was mercifully terminated when the California Supreme Court upheld Hennigan's right to conduct jury selection behind closed doors.

The defense's second major motion was to object to the long-established practice in capital murder cases of automatically excluding prospective jurors who express extreme views regarding the death penalty. Hennigan granted the request along with what he thought was a compromise: "Anti-death" and "auto-death" jurors could sit for the guilt phase of the trial and be replaced with open-opinion alternates for the penalty phase. Jay Hanks was irate, voicing his displeasure in the court and to the press. Alan Olson took a swipe at Hanks, telling a reporter, "It will mean we will have a fairer jury. That's why Hanks is so upset. A fair jury is detrimental to the prosecutor's case."

The defense teams were not nearly through with their attempts to shove a stick in the spokes of justice, filing another barrage of motions to delay the start of the trial. "Jury selection in the trial of three men accused of killing a Riverside deputy sheriff would have begun today but for three obstacles: the defense lawyers," wrote reporter Pauline Repard in the *Vista Press.* "Collectively, the three challenged practically every aspect of the justice system."

Michael Lloyd objected to San Diego's method of drawing names for jury duty using only voter registration rolls and filed a motion for a change of venue to San Bernardino County. Hennigan resolved that issue with a simple question to the defendants themselves: "Do you *really* want to be tried by San Bernardino County jurors?" After a ten-minute recess, Hennigan had his answer: Fuck no, they didn't want to get tried in Cow County. Alan Olson found an administrative error on the part of the prosecution that automatically triggered another one-week delay to July 7. Clayton Adams demanded the trial be moved to a larger courtroom to accommodate three defendants along with their legal teams, saying the small courtroom "will effectively destroy the defense." Adams's attempt to rearrange the furniture himself resulted in a screaming match with Lloyd before a veteran bailiff stepped in to stop Adams. "What the hell do you think you're doing?" the man barked. Another wrench was thrown into the trial process when eight hundred San Diego County sheriff's deputies went on strike over wages requiring all 289 Vista inmates to be bused to jails in neighboring counties. In a discussion between the Norco 3's attorneys and Hennigan over how the defendants should be transported a total of 140 miles back and forth from Riverside to the Vista courthouse each day, the judge cracked, "Maybe we should let them find their own transportation; they seemed successful at getting a pickup truck."

On July 7, 1981, the voir dire process officially got under way with Hennigan announcing a confounding series of never-before-seen jury selection procedures in which jurors would be prescreened individually rather than in groups. Befuddled attorneys on both sides spent more than an hour trying to clarify the new procedure, which would add two ponderous steps and countless hours to the process. With Hennigan making changes and adjustments on the fly to satisfy numerous objections, the whole thing became so convoluted that a flummoxed Clayton Adams finally threw up his hands in frustration. "I'm lost. I just don't get it." When Jay Hanks pointed out they would have to read the entire forty-two-page complaint against the defendants to each juror individually, Hennigan was annoyed. "If you insist that be done, get your tonsils oiled. Because if you insist, you'll do it."

Once the process got started, things moved so slowly that before the first day was over, Hanks was imploring the judge to scrap the new plan and go back to screening jurors in groups. Hennigan stuck to his guns. Instead of the intended twenty minutes, questioning of the first prospective juror took seven and a half hours over three days, ending with marine corporal David Wright dismissed from jury duty. Seventeen other scheduled juror appointments had to be canceled in the meantime. "Did you ever feel like you were swimming in a pool of molasses in thirty-degree temperature?" Hennigan confessed to reporter Bob LaBarre. "That's how it's been."

When Hennigan tried to speed things up by imposing a time limit to voir dire, the increasingly petulant Michael Lloyd ceased questioning prospective jurors altogether. "The whole jury-picking process is a farce," he told a local paper. "I will not take the responsibility for this," a disgusted Clayton

Adams growled to a reporter. "I told the judge three months ago that it was [an] error."

The drawn-out jury selection process was especially hard on the physical and mental health of the defense teams. They were living out of hotel rooms away from their families and carrying enormous workloads, all in the name of a cause that was thankless, unpopular, and borderline hopeless. Michael Lloyd became so ill at one point the trial was delayed for a week. On Tuesday, July 21, Alan Olson approached the bench to inform Hennigan that he was having heart palpitations and numbness of the lips. Hennigan called a recess, and Olson was taken to a nearby VA hospital where doctors informed him he was having a heart attack. "The trial is taking its toll on him," his brother and investigator, Roger Olson, told reporters. Olson remained hospitalized until cleared to return to the courtroom the following week, where jury selection resumed after a nine-day delay.

NO ONE WAS FRAYING FROM THE STRESS AS MUCH AS CLAYTON ADAMS. HE had become increasingly exasperated with the runaway selection process and what he perceived to be the prosecution's intentionally slow response to discovery orders to produce evidence and documents. Already significantly overweight, Adams was sleeping in a motel bed and hauling around heavy boxes of law books, which soon caused an existing upper back condition to flare up. The pain became chronic, radiating up his neck and into his arms and causing debilitating muscle spasms that made the long days standing and sitting in court almost unbearable.

It all boiled over in the courtroom on November 19, 1981. When Adams ran long on questioning a prospective juror, Hennigan stepped in to limit him to one final question. While the woman was answering, Adams cut her off to clarify a sentence. The judge was annoyed. "Let her finish her answer," he said.

"Well, Your Honor, you interrupt me more than I interrupt you," Adams fired back in a display of open disrespect not normally tolerated by judges.

With the day's session already running over, Hennigan put an end to it. "I am going to call a halt, Mr. Adams, to questioning, and I'm going to declare that Mrs. Morris is not disqualified as an automatic-death-penalty person."

Adams was livid. "Your Honor, I object for the record to the Court's constant interrupting and changing Counsel's questions and leading the jurors," he said. "And, in fact, I insist that this procedure be changed, or I intend to take some drastic steps, Your Honor."

"You may take what steps you wish," Hennigan cut him off. "I have ruled." He rose from his seat. "We're in recess until tomorrow morning at nine o'clock."

Adams didn't move. "I will request a brief interview with the Court in chambers."

"Tomorrow at nine o'clock you may have so," Hennigan said firmly.

"I will not be here tomorrow morning at nine o'clock, unless I have that interview tonight."

Hennigan paused, blindsided by Adams's blatant defiance. "If you wish to see me, you will see me tomorrow morning at nine o'clock," he said.

"I will advise the Court that I will not be here."

"If you are not, Mr. Adams, you will be in contempt of court."

"Thank you very much, Your Honor," Adams said. With that, he turned his back on the judge, packed up his briefcase, and left.

When court reconvened the following morning, Hennigan took his seat on the bench and scanned the participants arrayed before him. "The record may show it is now 9:40. Counsel are present, except Mr. Adams is not present. Mr. Bailiff, have you seen Mr. Adams in the hall or anyplace else?"

"No, Your Honor, I haven't."

"Ms. Painter," Hennigan asked investigator Jeanne Painter, sitting alone at the defense table with George Smith, "do you know the present location of Mr. Adams?"

"No, I don't," she said.

"Was he in the city?"

"No." Painter shook her head.

"It appears to the Court in the absence of some good cause that a direct contempt of this court has probably occurred." Hennigan turned to Michael Lloyd. "Mr. Lloyd, you have spoken on the phone to Mr. Adams this morning?"

Lloyd stood. "Yes, I have, Your Honor. Just moments ago."

"Can you relay any message to the Court as to why Mr. Adams is not present, or an excuse for not being present?"

"I don't know of an excuse in the legal sense," Lloyd began. "I know of the reason for his not being here." Hennigan asked to hear it. "Basically, Mr. Adams felt that there were major differences between the court and himself as to the voir dire process." Lloyd went on to explain that Adams's "condition" for returning was a meeting with the judge in the absence of the other attorneys. Lloyd quoted Adams directly: "Well, if I can't come in and talk to the court on the record and ex parte in chambers, then I am not going to come in."

Jay Hanks could take the display of gross insolence no longer. "I would state so the court might know precisely," he sputtered, "I find that this laying down of conditions to return to this court is reprehensible. It is beyond comprehension, frankly, from my perspective. I believe that it is contemptuous in the extreme, and that such conduct should not be tolerated by the court."

Hennigan told Lloyd to inform Adams that he had two hours to get his ass into the courtroom or a warrant would be issued for his arrest.

Lloyd did indeed pass the information on in a call to Adams immediately upon recess, after which the AWOL attorney was back in the courtroom and standing before the judge at 1:35 p.m. that afternoon.

"Mr. Adams, it appeared to the court this morning that you were in contempt of this court by failing to appear at a time that was set."

"I simply wanted to request the court to reconsider and permit voir dire uninterrupted," Adams argued defiantly. "And I am prepared to say at this time that if the court is not inclined in its discretion and generosity to reconsider and grant what I view as a very simple request . . . then I am still at this time prepared to risk contempt in order to reserve those rights for my client."

"If the request is that the court not participate in voir dire," Hennigan cut him off sharply, "the request is denied." Hennigan then ordered Adams to appear for a contempt hearing before a different judge.

"I am prepared to face the consequences," Adams announced melodramatically.

When Adams appeared for his trial on the contempt charge one week later, it was before the Honorable Charles W. Froehlich Jr., a judge with little tolerance for frivolous arguments in his courtroom.

"I believe at this time it would be appropriate to, in addition to a denial of the contempt, enter a plea of basically temporary insanity," Adams's attorney Adrian Roth said, "and request for an appointment [with] doctors to examine Mr. Adams as to whether at the time of the alleged contempt Mr. Adams had a sufficient mental disability."

"Counsel, that's a spurious motion," Froehlich scoffed. "Motion denied."

Unable to secure a delay, Roth declined to mount any defense at all. Froehlich moved straight into his verdict. "It's clear to the court that he had the ability to appear, had no excuse or reason for failing to appear," he said of Adams. "There is no excuse for that kind of conduct unbecoming an officer of the court. Mr. Adams must be found in contempt of court and he must be punished."

In pronouncing the sentence, Froehlich did not mince words about how he felt about Mr. Adams and his behavior. "I should say that it's difficult to conceive of any action by an attorney that is more contemptuous of the court's processes than this one. The court will sentence him to five days in jail and a fine of $500."

The judge agreed to Roth's request that any jail time should be postponed until the completion of the Norco trial. With that, Froehlich gaveled the case closed. It had taken all of twenty minutes for the judge to try the case and sentence the defendant when Adams and Roth had expected to draw it out for months. When Michael Lloyd heard about Froehlich's squashing of Adams's attempts to mount a defense, he was livid and dashed off a letter to the *Press-Enterprise* for publication in the December 10 Reader's Open Forum section.

Slathered in melodrama, hyperbole, and self-righteousness, Lloyd railed against "a closed mind by a particular judge" who had deprived Adams of his constitutional right to defend himself. "I cannot think of any action by the government more contemptuous than denying due process of the law; denying the constitutional right to defend oneself when accused." Lloyd went on to refer to the judge as a "governmental employee who abuses the legal system." Within days of the letter's publication, Froehlich slapped Lloyd with a contempt charge of his own and fined him $500.

Prosecutor Jay Hanks had been so irked by Lloyd's editorial that he jumped into the fray himself. His own letter to the editor titled "Not Used to the Pace" appeared in the *Press-Enterprise* nine days after Lloyd's. Dripping in sarcasm, Hanks ridiculed Lloyd. "His tirade about the San Diego Judiciary was unfounded, unfortunate, unnecessary, and worst of all, silly." Hanks contrasted Froehlich's "deliberate speed" with the "sedentary" pace of Hennigan's Norco trial. "Undoubtedly Mr. Lloyd would have preferred that the San Diego Court adopt a pace similar to that reflected in the Norco bank robbery trial. The fact that the San Diego Court would not do that speaks volumes about many things." Anyone intimate with the Norco trial to date knew that by "many things," Hanks actually meant "one thing": J. David Hennigan.

As the voir dire processes mercifully limped over the finish line, everyone involved was showing signs of battle fatigue. All three defense attorneys had broken down physically at some point—Adams's spinal pain had put him flat on his back for a week in October—and two stood convicted of contempt. It was not until December 15, fully six months after the trial start date, that twelve jurors and eight alternates were seated in what was the longest jury selection process in California history.

WITH THE DEFENSE NOW FULLY AND PUBLICLY AT WAR WITH THE PROSECU-tion and judge, another front opened up with an entirely different warring party. To say that the Norco 3 and the San Diego deputies running the Vista jail had gotten their relationship off on the wrong foot would be an understatement. That the deputies would be unhappy with a bunch of cop killers from Riverside crashing their facility was entirely predictable. However, George Smith and Chris Harven had already established up in Riverside that they were not the type to take any mistreatment lying down. With the help of their attorneys, the inmates fought back with a steady stream of complaints, petitions, and demands. Through most of the jury selection process, the feuding between the two sides had been conducted outside the courtroom of Judge Hennigan and included mostly petty incidents. However, that was about to change in an altogether unexpected way.

On November 30, 1981, Clayton Adams had a representative for the Vista jail hauled in front of Hennigan to protest a disciplinary action that had been taken by the jail against George Smith. The reason this particular matter deserved the attention of Hennigan, Adams contended, was that his client had been denied due process and was now being held alone in "deadlock" isolation for the infraction, thus inhibiting his ability to participate in his own defense. Although Hennigan would punt the matter back to Smith and the jail to resolve, the official "Inmate Status Report" documenting the November 26 incident was introduced into the hearing. According to the deputy filing the report, the following events occurred:

> On the above date at approx. 0145 Hrs., I was making a security check of North Wing Housing ... As I got to the area of rooms 6, 7 & 8, I smelled the odor of burning marijuana ... Both Deputy Clark and myself then started checking the area of rooms 6, 7, & 8 for the smell, we both found that the smell was the strongest in front of room #7 ... I then opened the door to room #7 and observed Smith flushing a crumpled pack of "Salem" cigarettes down the toilet. As Clark and I entered the room, we were both met with an excessive odor of burning marijuana. Smith then moved from the toilet to the bunk. I then asked Smith if he would explain to me what was going on, and Smith stated "No!"

The report went on to note that although no marijuana was found in the cell or on Smith, the inmate was "sluggish" to the deputy's commands, his eyes were "red and bloodshot," and that he walked with a "staggering gait." In other words, in the opinion of the deputies, George Smith was baked. The report concluded that "Smith should be rolled-up" to a different module for further discipline and subjected to periodic strip searches.

Although an accusation of drug use within the jail facility was not as heinous or unusual an infraction as one might think, there was a larger issue of concern to the jailers: Someone was smuggling drugs into the Vista county jail for George Smith. The deputies had a pretty good idea who it was. Although no accusation was made in court that day, a clue as to who the deputies suspected was contained in a seemingly innocuous handwritten note at the end of the formal incident report:

Reference:

The previous evening of this incident (11-25-81), inmate Smith had a two-hour visit with J. Painter, an investigator with his attorney.

15

THE INVESTIGATOR

November 26, 1981. Vista, California.

JEANNE LANE WAS VERY MUCH A SOUTHERN CALIFORNIA CHILD OF THE 1960S.
Born in 1948, she came of age at the dawn of everything that the decade came
to represent, both good and bad. In addition to a love of the Rolling Stones,
she had an affinity for underdogs and outsiders, a healthy distrust of authority, and an understanding that not everyone in America was treated equally.
Jeanne was no radical or extremist, but like many girls of the era, she did not
feel encumbered by the limitations placed on women of previous generations.
Lane was a Riverside girl, born and raised. Although the Inland Empire often
tended toward provincial, blue-collar, and close-minded, it was still Southern
California, and it was still the 1960s. For a whip-smart, free-spirited young
woman determined to make her own way in the world, there were few better
places to be.

Lane was politically aware from a young age, but mostly spent her high
school years hanging out with friends, going to rock concerts and escaping
the choking heat and smog of Riverside for the beaches of Orange County
whenever they could find someone to give them a ride. She was well liked but
hung mostly with her own group.

Staking her claim to what was then every Californian's birthright to excellent higher education at an astonishingly low cost, Lane entered the University of California, Riverside, in 1966, straight out of high school. After the fleeting optimism of 1967's Summer of Love culture, the political and social skies quickly darkened into the age of assassinations, race riots, and Charles Manson. According to the dictates of the era, Jeanne became a more serious person. She majored in political science but found many of the electives recently introduced into the curriculum to be a frivolous waste of time. With graduation a semester away and still unsure of what she wanted to do, Lane took an internship with the Riverside Office of the Public Defender.

From the start, Jeanne was hooked on the high stakes of criminal law. Even though the internship required only eight hours a week, Lane was at the defender's office every hour she was not in classes. At school, she found herself slogging through required courses such as "Mexican Folk Medicine." But down at the defender's office, things could not be more serious. She quickly found herself working side by side with hardened criminal defense attorneys representing the likes of accused murderers, rapists, and armed robbers. The contrast was dizzying for a young college girl from the middle-class suburbs of Riverside County.

With her bachelor's degree completed, Lane continued her work with the defender's office. Already familiar with the job, she charged straight into her duties, first with misdemeanor cases and then felonies. She was known as a fearless investigator, not afraid to pick up a phone or knock on the doors of witnesses, even if they didn't want to talk. If stonewalled by police or prosecutors on discovery requests, she was more than willing to pester them to comply. Along the way, she got married and became Jeanne Painter and soon had a baby son.

Jeanne Painter was clear-eyed when it came to her clients, the majority of whom were guilty as charged, often of crimes of an unforgivable nature. However, some were not and others often had excessive or additional bogus charges tacked on. It was obvious to Painter that, once caught up in the machinery of the American judicial system, they didn't stand a chance, especially the ones without the means to hire a private attorney. In that regard, she could have sympathy *for* her clients without sympathizing *with* them.

She was no lover of "bad boys," but grew fond of a few clients after working with them for long stretches of time, slugging it out in the trenches on their behalf.

When Clayton Adams joined the defender's office in 1977, the two were frequently paired on cases, chiseling away on often-hopeless causes in search of the best deal possible for their client. She admired his pragmatic and determined approach to defense. The work appealed to Painter's moral sensibilities on many of the same levels it did to Adams's. "I don't think either one of us ever could have prosecuted anyone," she said.

After marrying young, Painter was divorced in 1974 and once again single at the age of twenty-five. Carrying herself with confidence, Painter turned plenty of heads and drew the occasional unwanted comment from the men around her. But Jeanne always kept it professional, dating only outside her profession. When she remarried in 1978, to a young man named John Ditsch, few in the defender's office had any idea. She continued to use the name Painter and never spoke of the man her colleagues would never meet.

AFTER A DOZEN YEARS WORKING THE RIVERSIDE CRIMINAL JUSTICE SYSTEM, Painter had become a fixture around the county jail. She rarely had any trouble with those overseeing the captivity of her clients. But in Vista, Painter was on foreign soil, dealing with San Diego deputies who extended their dislike of cop killers to include those who defended them. Whereas visitor searches at the Riverside County jail had become quick, perfunctory affairs for Painter, they were far more thorough and time-consuming in Vista. She cooled her heels for long stretches in interview rooms waiting for her client and encountered jailers who called "time's up" on her with a cold finality.

It did not take long before Painter decided to make a stand against the jailers. Leaving the facility after a visit with Smith, Painter asked the deputy on duty to return a cassette tape player, which she had left with the guards upon entering. Sure, the deputy said, handing her back the recorder. As she headed for the door, Painter noticed that the tape in the recorder was missing. She turned back. "Where's the tape that was in here?" she asked the man.

The deputy gave her a smirk and a shrug. "There wasn't any tape in it when we got it," he said.

Painter took a few steps toward the man and fixed him with a determined stare. "Give me back my goddamn tape," she said.

The smirk dissolved from the man's face. "Let me check," he said. He opened a drawer, took out the tape, and handed it to Painter. She left without another word, but she had drawn her line in the sand. Things did not get much better for her after that, but at least they did not get any worse. For now.

THE TROUBLE BETWEEN GEORGE SMITH AND THE JAILERS HAD STARTED IM-
mediately. Within a week of his arrival at the Vista jail in late May 1981, Smith had penned a handwritten statement to the court complaining about his treatment. "Since I have been in this jail I have been shackled in all cases but exercise. No other inmate at this facility is treated this way to my personal knowledge except the Harven Brothers." Smith also complained, "I've been told that even when my family visits I'll be shackled like an animal." He also protested the jailers were interfering with his visits to the facility church. "I'm rather dismayed at this treatment and request that it stop."

With the statement in hand, Clayton Adams dragged the head of the Vista jail, captain Robert DeSteunder, into court to answer accusations of inhumane treatment of his client. The other defense attorneys quickly joined in on the complaint. Adams knew his leverage point with DeSteunder: Any actions that unreasonably interfere with the ability of a defendant to participate in the preparation of his own defense could result in a mistrial. The last thing a jailer wanted to be responsible for was causing a mistrial. Adams focused the complaint on the excessive shackling, especially the jail policy that the defendants have only their writing hands unchained during visits with their attorneys and investigators. Adams also cited the jail's refusal to provide Smith with a four-foot-high metal filing cabinet for his legal papers, a request DeSteunder dryly characterized as "unreasonable."

When Adams challenged DeSteunder to characterize his deputies' attitudes toward their prisoners, the captain was remarkably frank. "Why are we bothering with a trial?" was the general feeling among the troops, DeSteunder reported. "It's obvious that these are the people who did it. They were chased from the bank robbery to the point of arrest. Why are we wasting the taxpayers' money to go ahead with this charade?" DeSteunder went on to add that Smith was only making things worse by repeatedly addressing the deputies as "boy."

"Inhumane Treatment of Suspects Charged" ran the headline in the *Vista Press* the next day. Irked by the press coverage and strongly urged by Judge Hennigan to avoid any conduct that might result in a mistrial, the jail relented on most of the issues except for the filing cabinet.

Adams then turned his wrath on the San Diego deputies who guarded the courthouse, asking Hennigan to dismiss every last courtroom bailiff for misconduct. While Hennigan rejected the request, he did give stern orders regarding recent conduct. They were to "avoid any overt expression of opinion with facial expression," and ordered to stop talking to reporters about the defense attorneys. In other words, cease all the smirking and eye rolling in court and quit talking shit about the defense attorneys to reporters in the hallway. And whichever bailiff wrote "Cop Killers" on the court assignment sheet instead of the defendants' names had better knock that crap off right now, too.

Michael Lloyd caused the jail a major headache with his successful demand that DeSteunder double the existing visiting hours for Chris Harven, and by extension all other prisoners, to meet the state guideline of two thirty-minute visiting periods a week.

Chris Harven got an opportunity to put his contempt for the Vista deputies on full display in a dispute involving the confiscation of a notebook after he was accused of passing a note to a fellow inmate without permission. In front of Judge Hennigan, Deputy Rosall stated that Harven had "coerced" an inexperienced trustee to pass the note for him. "May I speak now?" Chris asked impatiently once Rosall was done. "There is not coercion. That's a lie. The problem is that this man has had an attitude problem toward us." Chris got his notebook back.

Not to be left out, Alan Olson made his own demand on behalf of his client after jailers put an end to the backgammon games Russ Harven frequently played with investigator Roger Olson. They warned Olson that he and his brother would get their visitation rights cut down if they brought in any more board games. Olson immediately took his protest to Judge Hennigan.

"I think I have a right to play Go Fish, Old Maids, or Monopoly with my client."

Olson then took his backgammon crusade to reporters standing in the hallway outside, explaining that playing the game was "a relaxant" for his client that allowed him to more effectively participate in trial strategy. "They just don't want him to have any fun," he added, without any apparent irony.

Two days later, DeSteunder relayed Hennigan's ruling to jail personnel in a departmental correspondence dated February 16, 1982. "As a result of court action today, the following is in effect: Inmate Russell Harven will be allowed to play backgammon and cribbage with his attorney's investigator in the interview room." The memo also contained a second instruction from DeSteunder to his staff that had far more serious implications: "Investigator Jeanne Painter has been ordered to leave medication of any kind in her car or elsewhere when entering the jail."

AFTER SUFFERING SO MANY HUMILIATING DEFEATS IN THE COURTROOM, THE jailers saw the November 26, 1981, marijuana bust of George Smith as the first clear chance for them to strike back. But it was by no means their last. On January 10, 1982, one week into witness testimony, the deputies at the Vista jail caught George getting high in his cell again, under essentially the same circumstances as the first.

The report of the incident noted "there is a possibility Smith may be smuggling narcotics into the jail via his contact visits." The report made no specific mention of Painter, but it didn't have to; the only "contact visits" George Smith was allowed were with his attorney and investigator.

A January 30, 1982, incident report titled "Search of Investigator Painter" noted that "While going through her purse I found a prescription bottle containing tablets of Donnatal." It went on to say that the jailers had checked the *Physician's Desk Reference* and "It was found that one of the ingredients contained in Donnatal is phenobarbital." The jailers held on to the bottle and returned it to Painter when she left but only after she had been given a stern warning. "Miss Painter was again advised not to bring any personal or unnecessary items into the jail."

On February 11, Painter was written up again. "Investigator Painter entered VDF on 02-11-82 (Thur.) at approximately 1917 hours for a visit with Smith," the incident report read. "During a search of her purse I found a prescription bottle about half full of tablets of Donnatal." Painter was warned again. Just two days later, George Smith was caught smoking marijuana in his cell for the third time. The fact that Smith's marijuana incidents all corresponded with visits from his investigator convinced the Vista jailers that Painter was the one smuggling it in.

Painter vehemently denied any wrongdoing and complained to Adams that the jailers were harassing her, impeding her ability to adequately prepare for Smith's defense. Within a week, Adams had filed a lawsuit against John Duffy, the sheriff of San Diego County. Adams subpoenaed the jail for a slew of records including "Reports relating to jail visitations to petitioner by Counsel herein or Counsel's investigator, Jeanne Painter; particularly reports relating to allegations, suggestions, or suspicions of contraband smuggling into the jail facilities by Counsel herein or Counsel's investigator, Jeanne Painter." What he received in response to the request included one document Painter would have preferred not to be entered into the court record.

The incident report dated November 27, 1981, one day after George Smith's first marijuana bust, stated that when Painter arrived for a visit with Smith, a female deputy was summoned for a routine search. After finding nothing on Painter's person, the guard wrote:

I also conducted a security search of her briefcase during which I observed several packages of pictures. Looking through these pictures I found approximately twelve pictures of Miss Painter nude in various positions. Painter stated, "they are for my husband."

At that point, the guard returned the photos and "advised Miss Painter not to show the photos to her client and that unnecessary personal effects should not be brought into the jail."

Riverside public defender Malcolm MacMillan dispatched his chief investigator, Theron Bursell, to Vista to look into the allegations. Painter fiercely denied that the jailers had ever found such photos and that the accusation was a complete fabrication by vindictive San Diego deputies. According to Painter, the only photographs she had ever taken into the jail were of her and her son being baptized in Long Beach Harbor. No action was taken against Painter. "There wasn't anything [Bursell] could come up with that would justify me doing anything about it," MacMillan said.

Whether the photos had been of an ocean baptism, herself "nude in various positions," or both, it said a lot about how far Jeanne Painter had fallen under the spell of George Wayne Smith and the degree of manipulation of which he was capable.

BY THE TIME THE TRIAL WAS MOVED OUT OF RIVERSIDE, JEANNE PAINTER HAD already spent dozens of hours in small, windowless interview rooms with George Smith. That was just the life of an investigator working on a complicated case involving massive amounts of evidence. But once things got moved to Vista, Painter's world became upended. In Riverside, Painter was surrounded by personal and professional support systems. No matter how grim and hopeless her caseload might be, no matter how many witnesses might have slammed doors in her face, no matter how grueling the workload, Painter was in an office filled with people who were on her side and with whom she could vent her frustration, get answers to her problems, and share in some gallows humor. Even the "other side," the prosecutors and Riverside deputies running the jail and courthouse, could usually be counted on for a hello or an occasional joke. And at the end of the day, she could go home to her own apartment and the unconditional love of her son or out for a drink with friends or drop in for dinner with her parents who lived nearby.

In Vista, all that went away. Painter was in hostile territory. The deputies guarding the jail and courthouse were unrelentingly rude and aggressive. Things had grown so ugly between the defense and prosecution that the best she could hope for with the usually amiable Hanks, Ruddy, and Curfman was cold civility. She knew Michael Lloyd and, to a lesser extent, Alan Olson, but they were drowning in their own workloads; their allegiance was to their own clients, not hers. She was fond of Clayton Adams, where she could still get some sympathy and advice, but Adams was fighting physical pain and too buried under the stress of his own situation to be of much help and support to Painter outside the context of the trial itself. An eighteen-year-old staff member from the Public Defender's office named Debbie Rose was assigned to assist Painter and both was helpful with the workload and provided some additional companionship, but the two were almost a generation apart. For the most part, Vista was an emotionally lonely existence for Painter.

Her attempts to contact prosecution witnesses were met with a level of anger and rejection she had not experienced on any case before. It was entirely understandable that people who had been kidnapped, shot at, had guns stuck in their faces, cars rammed in intersections, bullets fired through their windshields, or been ordered to get down on the fucking floor might be reluctant to speak with an investigator defending the man they believed responsible. But instead of a "sorry, but I really don't want to talk to you," Painter was now getting a lot of "I don't have to talk to you, so fuck you, lady"–type hang-ups. The bank employees were under orders from Security Pacific not to speak to her, and the dozens of cops who were listed as either victims or witnesses . . . well, that was never going to happen either. With a success rate hovering just above zero, Painter spent many long moments staring at her motel room phone wondering why she should even try.

Getting her hands on evidence or discovery documents from the DA and law enforcement was just as frustrating. With no email, internet, or cell phones in existence, getting access to these often required waiting for envelopes to arrive in the mail or crisscrossing the traffic-choked Inland Empire to pick up boxes and documents from the front desks of crime labs, sheriff's offices, or the DA. Too often, they were not there as promised. So she had to go back. And back.

Living out of the motel room was wearing her out. Fourteen-hour workdays and trips in her VW Bug back and forth between Riverside and Vista were fraying her nerves. She missed her home, her co-workers, her family, her friends. She missed her kid. It all came to a head one day as she was making the short drive from the motel to the jail to meet with George Smith.

She had been feeling anxious that morning. Sitting at a stoplight, a nameless terror suddenly swept through Painter. She could hardly breathe, felt utterly paralyzed, was sure something terrible was about to happen. Somehow she managed to negotiate the VW into a convenience store parking lot and buy a Coke. Trembling, she continued on to the jail. Once locked inside the cramped interview room waiting for Smith, Jeanne fell apart. The place felt as tight as a coffin being lowered into the ground. She leapt from the chair and began to pound on the door, screaming, "Let me out! Let me out!" When they opened the door, she pushed past the guard and ran from the jail. Nobody asked her if she was okay. Nobody cared.

Back at the motel, an alarmed Clayton Adams tried to calm her, gave her a Valium, and urged her to see a doctor. She did. They gave her a prescription for a sedative, phenobarbital, mostly to help her sleep. None of it helped very much. The attacks continued, her baseline anxiety level inching up by the day. She escaped to Riverside whenever she could, but once back in Vista, it started all over again. The trips to the courthouse became exercises in pure terror. There were no friendly faces or people she could talk to about what she was going through. Except one.

Soon jailhouse visits with her client were more than just another stop in her busy day. The time with Smith became a refuge from the emotional storm raging within her and the animosity directed at her from without. He calmed her, purred helpful advice, and listened patiently, all the while staring back with his soulful brown eyes. He quoted scripture, prayed with her, and told her to seek comfort in the Lord Jesus Christ. She did, and along with her son, participated in a mass ocean baptism in Long Beach Harbor just as George had done with Calvary Chapel at Pirate's Cove almost a decade before.

George helped her with the mundane tasks of investigation work. Instead of sitting alone on her motel bed putting together evidence books, she gathered up the enormous stacks of police reports, pretrial transcripts, witness statements, and interview notes and brought them to the jail. They spent hours together organizing the mass of documents into three-ring notebooks. As long as they looked busy, the guards let her stay, but only because they had to. In the courtroom, they sat side by side, George often helping her locate specific documents on the fly as needed by Adams.

By all accounts, George Smith could be genuinely caring, generous, and sincere in his desire to help others. But there was the other side of George that too often surfaced. It was a willingness to put those around him at great risk for little gain. In the case of the Harven brothers, they lost their freedom. For the Delgado brothers, it had cost them their lives. With Jeanne Painter, it was her career and reputation. When it came to the Harven and Delgado brothers, George Smith had already done as much damage as he could possibly do. But with Jeanne Painter, there was a lot more still to come.

16

ON BEHALF OF
THE PEOPLE

January 4, 1982. Vista, California.

ON MONDAY, JANUARY 4, 1982, ALMOST TWENTY MONTHS AFTER GEORGE
Smith had charged into the Security Pacific Bank screaming, "Everyone hit
the fucking floor," deputy district attorney Kevin Ruddy rose to his feet to
tell a jury why the three men before them deserved to be put to death. Ruddy
was careful not to overload the jury with details of the chaos of that day. In
his soft-spoken, often monotone voice, he opened by introducing the jury to
the accused.

"We have a bank robbery. But how does a bank robbery begin? It has to
begin with people. Ladies and gentlemen, it began with five people." George,
Chris, and Russ watched him warily. "Those three people sitting at the table
who are on trial for these crimes," he said, standing near the well-groomed
young men in their suits and ties. "Their appearance is somewhat different
today than it was on May 9, 1980. You will notice a photograph over by the
witness stand." He motioned to a display with three enlarged color photographs, three feet high by two feet wide, of each of the defendants taken
within hours of their capture. The contrast was profound. Chris Harven,
dirty and still in his wet sweatshirt and oversize blue gloves, stared emo-
tionlessly at the camera. Russell Harven was filthy in a ripped shirt and torn

jeans, with stringy hair, shoulders hunched and arms held out from his mea-
ger frame like some sort of Appalachian swamp monster. George Smith was
shown being propped up to a seated position in a hospital bed by an emergency room doctor, EKG leads stuck to his skin, an IV line running into his
left arm. His hair stuck out wildly, and on his round face was the expression
of a man who knows all hope is gone.

"These five people who got together to rob a bank were all friends,"
Ruddy said. "They included the two sets of brothers and the brains of the
operation, George Smith."

Although Ruddy let the events of the day provide most of the drama, he
was not above a flair for the theatrical when it came to the physical evidence
brought in to punctuate his case. Spread on a table was the murderous arsenal
of firearms and homemade bombs. Ruddy held up the carbon-black Heckler
.308. "George Smith armed himself with this, a .30-caliber military assault
rifle." He lifted the riot gun recovered from Baldy Notch Road. "Manny Delgado armed himself with this, a folding stock, twelve-gauge shotgun." Some
jurors visibly winced at the sight of the vicious-looking weapon. He showed
off Billy Delgado's unfired AR-15 and the "Shorty" AR-15 used by Russell
Harven. Absent from the table was Chris Harven's Heckler, used by Manny
during the pursuit and ambush. It had never been found.

Ruddy then lifted a case of ammunition boxes. "Obviously with lots of
rifles and pistols, they need ammunition," he said. "Hundreds upon hundreds upon hundreds of rounds of ammunition." With that, Ruddy turned
the box over, spilling dozens of empty bullet boxes onto the table.

Ruddy then focused on the ambush in Lytle Creek that killed Jim Evans, the one charge that could send the Norco 3 to the gas chamber. Ruddy
showed a photo of Evans's unit with the bullet holes through the windshield.
"James Evans was able to extricate himself from that vehicle," Ruddy said,
picking up Evans's .357 revolver from the table. "And James Evans took out a
rather small, pitiful weapon . . . and he began to fight back with this, fight for
his life. James Evans was accustomed to fighting for his life. James Evans had
been a Green Beret in Vietnam." After noting that Evans was able to wound
Chris Harven, Ruddy dropped the only real surprise of the day. "He ran to

the back of his car and crouched down, unloaded his gun, loaded it again, and stood up to fight again. And a bullet fired by Russell Harven entered James Evans at his eye and exploded in his brain and James Evans was dead."

At the defense table, Russ had been absently twisting and stretching a rubber band around his fingers, as he had come to do almost constantly while in the courtroom. He looked up at the mention of his name. It was the first time the prosecution had formally named their triggerman. Suddenly, Russ felt like the only dead man in the room. "Russell Harven will tell you that he was carrying this gun," Ruddy said, lifting the "Shorty" AR with one hand, "this gun which killed James Evans."

Ruddy concluded his opening holding the "Shorty" in one hand and Jim Evans's .357 in the other. "Ladies and gentlemen, nothing can describe events better than physical evidence . . . what Jim Evans had." He paused, holding the small revolver out for the jury to see. He then held out the wicked-looking "Shorty" AR. "And what these people had."

After Ruddy completed his opening, all three defense attorneys opted to defer the presentation of their opening remarks until the prosecution completed its case. It was clear from the start that the battle for the lives of the Norco 3 was to be waged on two fronts: who fired first in front of the bank, the cops or the robbers, and who shot the bullet that killed Jim Evans. Alan Olson summed up the defense's position on both outside the courtroom after Ruddy's opening. "All their ballistics shows is that the suspects and the cops were firing. Our ballistics prove it was the cops."

THE OPENING WITNESSES FOR THE PROSECUTION WERE FAMILY MEMBERS OF the accused and the dead. Ruddy's only purpose was to establish that the three defendants and the dead Delgado brothers had all been friends and that Smith and Chris Harven owned lots and lots of guns. The ex-wives of George and Chris had both remarried since the robbery. Hanne Smith was now Hannelore Palmer, and Lani Harven had become Galena Thomas. Both appeared for the prosecution, but only because they had no choice. The defense used the opportunity to sneak in testimony from both that, in their opinion, their ex-husbands were nonviolent people. Ruddy challenged that contention on the redirect of Lani. "Mrs. Thomas, as to your opinion of George Smith being nonviolent, would it change your opinion of him if you found out that he had planned and carried out a bank robbery?"

"I would object, Your Honor," Clayton Adams called out. "May we approach the bench on this? I think we need to get some ground rules straightened out on how counsel is to approach character testimony. He does not seem to have a grasp on it at all."

The testimony of Manny Delgado's wife, Juanita Delgado, and father, Manuel Sr., were sobering affairs, reminding everyone in the courtroom that Norco had taken its toll on more than just the police officers involved. Again, Adams used the cross-examination to lay some foundation to his claim that the police had been the aggressors and acted with excessive force. "Mrs. Delgado, I realize this is probably a little difficult for you," Adams began. "But as far as Manny's death goes, do you know how he died?"

"He was shot by a SWAT team," Juanita answered softly.

"Do you know how many times he was shot or how many wounds were in his body?"

"Not exactly."

"It was over sixty, wasn't it?"

Alan Olson tried to establish what would be another recurring theme for the defense: blame Manny whenever possible. It was in all three defendants' interest to paint a picture of Delgado as being completely out of control after witnessing the death of his little brother in front of the bank. When Manuel Sr. took the stand, Olson asked if his two sons had been close. Manny Sr. said they had. "What effect do you believe the witnessing of one of the death of the other would have had on the one who remained alive?" Olson asked.

"I think it would drive him nuts," the father of the two dead boys said.

TWO WEEKS INTO THE TRIAL, THE FIRST IMPORTANT WITNESS TOOK THE stand. Hostage Gary Hakala's testimony was critical to the prosecution if they were to nail down a kidnapping conviction. Other than the two murder charges, the kidnapping count was the most serious. Hakala's testimony should have been relatively straightforward but ran into trouble on cross-examination. Hakala was already on the lookout for deceptions when Alan Olson rose to begin questioning. They first clashed over Hakala's testimony that he had been repeatedly hit over the head with the butt of a handgun by Manny Delgado. Holding a copy of Hakala's testimony from the preliminary hearing, Olson questioned him about why he had never mentioned being hit on the head when asked about it before.

"I interpreted that as asking me the most important things as to what happened to me when the first man first entered the van," explained Hakala, already getting irritated.

"You didn't think it was important, then, that you had been hit on the head?"

"A lot worse things happened to me that day than being hit on the head with a gun," Gary answered sharply.

Olson paused. "Mr. Hakala, if you would like to stop and take a break at any time during this cross-examination, please say so."

"Keep going," Hakala said, glaring at Olson.

Olson and Hakala would have other flare-ups, but they were just a sideshow to what was the most important part of the questioning for the defense: Who exactly kidnapped Gary in the parking lot of the Brea Mall? Olson asked Hakala if the prosecution had ever shown him a photo of Manny Delgado. Hakala said yes. "Do you know what that photograph depicted?" Olson asked.

"It was a dead man," Gary answered, referring to the autopsy photo he had been shown.

"Who did you tell Mr. Hanks it was?"

"I told him it was the first man that had entered my van," Hakala said, positively identifying Manny as the ringleader and his main tormentor that day.

Olson motioned to the three defendants in the courtroom. "Do you recall testifying to the effect that you had seen photographs of all of these men from Mr. Hanks before the preliminary hearing?"

"I have seen photographs of these men."

"And did you tell Mr. Hanks at that time, when he showed you those photographs, that these were not the men?"

"These men that are in the courtroom today are not the men that initially picked me up," Hakala confirmed with 100 percent conviction.

"None of them?"

"That's correct."

"Showing you People's 19, do you recognize this man?" Olson said, holding up the arrest photo of a scruffy, rain-soaked Russell Harven.

"Yes."

"Is he one of the ones who grabbed your van?"

"No."

"Are you sure of that?"

"Yes."

Russell Harven had admitted on tape that he and the Delgado brothers carried out the kidnapping and carjacking, but now Ruddy could only look on as the prosecution's only witness to the act definitively ruled out Harven.

When asked what one of the missing two men looked like, Gary said, "I remember him being young and of Mexican American descent." However, when shown an autopsy photo of Billy Delgado following the incident, Gary had said, no way, definitely not the same guy.

Olson then held up photos of the two getaway cars. "Can you say with certainty that neither this car which appears to be a blue Z/28 nor this car which appears to be a blue Matador were there?"

"Yes."

"You have no doubt about that?"

"No."

Olson then got right to the matter, referring in part to a rather harmless interview Hakala had given to the trashy tabloid the *National Enquirer* in exchange for $500, money Hakala said barely covered the replacement of the shattered windshield of his van. "Do you recall in any of your interviews, either to the *National Enquirer*, the police, the FBI, or anyone else, ever telling anyone that you still feared for your life because you thought or were sure that one man got away?"

"I can tell you that right now."

"You can tell me what right now?"

"That I believe that there is still a man out there."

With that, Hakala had handed the defense what no prosecutor ever wants introduced into a trial: the missing-man theory. Kevin Ruddy chose not to question Hakala on redirect about his emphatic assertion that there was a sixth man involved in the crime.

Hakala's insistence on sticking to his story said a lot about who he was and all he had gone through as a child. He had not survived being orphaned at an early age and then raised as an outsider on the high plains of Wyoming by being tentative or unsure of himself. Gary Hakala was tough and more than a little stubborn. He knew what he had seen that day, goddamnit, and it wasn't Billy Delgado and it wasn't Russell Harven. As far as Gary was concerned, there must have been others involved, and that was that. Gary was simply telling the truth as best he knew it.

During the testimony of bank witnesses a few days before, the defense brought out a curious, but seemingly unimportant, detail that was now starting to make a lot more sense. Several witnesses stated they had heard the bandits call out the name "Jerry" multiple times during the robbery. Customer James Kirkland said he heard one of them shout, "Jerry, let's go, let's go." Others heard "Jerry, get the money," or "Hurry up, Jerry." Gary Hakala offered that he had heard the names "Arthur" and "Tony" used inside the van.

Ruddy was not overly concerned; it wouldn't be the first time criminals used fake names during a holdup. But with the missing-man theory now in play, it was clear where the defense had been headed in bringing out all the mentions of "Jerry." It would be another few months before the issue became central to one of the strangest twists in a trial that was already becoming stranger by the day.

RUDDY AND JAY HANKS DECIDED TO TELL THE STORY OF MAY 9, 1980, THROUGH witnesses called in order of the events as they unfurled. Bank customers and others told of having rifles stuck in their faces by masked men, teller drawers emptied at the end of a shotgun, being paraded into the vault and dumping all the cash into a bag, and a man who walked the floor calling out "time" before the bandits fled to a waiting van. The only traction the defense was able to get out of several of the early witnesses was to sow some doubt as to which side had started the firefight outside the bank. Several, like customer James Kirkland, stated they thought the robbers had already climbed inside the van when the shooting started. One said she had seen Bolasky standing behind his unit firing while still in the parking lot.

However, others backed the prosecution's version of events by testifying to hearing the gunshots that blew out Bolasky's light bar moments after turning left onto Fourth Street. The parking lot directly outside the bank entrance also happened to be littered with spent shotgun casings and rifle shells matching only the suspects' weapons, while cartridges from Bolasky's two guns had been found only beside his vehicle in the middle of Fourth Street.

Still, the defense had no other choice than to hammer away on the issue with every witness, just as Alan Olson said they would. "There's a big question in my mind who fired first," Olson told reporters. "I'm going to dispute every bullet fired."

Within minutes of Gary Hakala stepping down from the witness stand, Glyn Bolasky took his seat on it. Again, Ruddy guided his witness through the events of the day. Again, the three defense attorneys attempted to discredit the testimony. The defense contended that Bolasky entered the bank parking lot, got out of his car, and opened fire on the van before the suspects fired a shot. Unable to shake Bolasky's version of events except for inconsequential inconsistencies, they turned to attacks on his character.

Clayton Adams tried to portray him as a psychiatrically unstable cop with an itchy trigger finger. "Now you no longer work for the Sheriff's Department, right?"

"That's right."

"In fact, you quit the Sheriff's Department?"

"I resigned."

"And after you left the Sheriff's Department, did you take another job?"

"I did."

"With who?"

"Riverside city as a police officer."

"And were you terminated from that job?"

"I was," admitted Bolasky. Bolasky explained that after observing him out on the streets, RPD felt he had become a "vicarious liability" due to what happened to him in Norco and terminated him to avoid financial responsibility.

"Any mention of erratic behavior?" Adams wanted to know.

Bolasky said there was nothing in the termination papers to that effect. When pressed later by Michael Lloyd on specifics related to his termination from the RPD, Bolasky said they "only told me that the Norco bank robbery might have had some scarring on me."

"And did they enlighten you on what scarring effect it might have had on you?" Lloyd asked.

"Very briefly. Just said that the Norco shooting, or after getting shot five times, or five different areas, and killing a subject, may have caused [me] to no longer enroll in police work anymore."

On redirect, Ruddy asked Bolasky if the termination had anything to do with his performance during the probationary period. "They said job performance regarding anything that had been done wrong, they said, no," Bolasky answered. "Everything was going well in that area."

Adams attacked that characterization on re-cross. "You indicated that you did not meet or make your probation?"

"Correct."

"But there were other reasons, isn't that true, that were told to you, either behind closed doors or in some other fashion?"

"There were other reasons I was told, yes."

"One of the reasons stated was your erratic behavior?"

"Yes. There was an evaluation report."

"And in that evaluation report, did it mention erratic behavior on your part?"

"It may have regarding driving," Bolasky conceded.

"Did it also mention an inability on your part to deal with blacks or other minorities?"

"I don't know if it said that in that fashion," answered Bolasky. "It mentioned an item that I may have had—if I recall correctly—a conflict regarding a black juvenile."

Adams did not have any evidence to pursue the line of questioning further, a direct result of having had his request for access to police disciplinary reports and psychiatric files on all the police officers rejected almost two years before.

With his testimony finished, Glyn Bolasky had satisfied all duties and responsibilities related to his career in law enforcement and left the profession, never to return. All that his heroic actions in front of the Security Pacific Bank had gotten him were nightmares, an accusation that he had abandoned a fellow officer, and the destruction of his career. He had received no recognition by the Riverside County Sheriff's Department in the two years since the gun battle that almost killed him, only a final gratuitous insult from Alan Olson. "From his testimony, you would think he was a hero," Olson told reporters afterward. "But nobody is calling him a hero. Why is that? Maybe he was trigger-happy at the time."

Chuck Hille's testimony essentially corroborated Bolasky's. He recounted what he had found when he first reached Bolasky. "Deputy Bolasky looked like he was going into shock. He was pale and white. As he spoke he made little sense. He said numerous times he had been hit. The blood was squirting out."

On January 25, detective Andy Delgado entered the courtroom wearing a dark suit and striped tie, with his hair grown out over his ears, a full beard, and large-frame eyeglasses. It was a sharp contrast to the clean-shaven, short-haired deputy who had repeatedly emptied his shotgun into a group of bank robbers while under heavy fire. Although well groomed, Andy looked as though he might have been working undercover to infiltrate a Mexican drug cartel. In truth, he had not been doing much of anything related to police work for weeks. After years of swimming upstream against what he saw as racism and incompetence among some of his fellow officers, Andy knew he needed a break. He was wrung out from scratching and clawing to stick up for himself ever since he was a small child. When the psychiatrist he had been ordered to see recommended that Delgado take some time off, Andy took him up on it. He stayed away from the department, took and taught classes, stopped shaving, and let his hair grow out. It was in this state of career purgatory that Andy Delgado took the stand.

After the accusation that Andy was stalking their cell and the stare-down with Chris Harven through the bars at the Riverside County jail months before, the defendants had a rather low opinion of the deputy they tried to kill on Hamner Avenue. "He was the one we all thought was your typical psycho cop," Harven said. But after nine hours on the stand, most of it on cross-examination, the defense was unable to make any of those sentiments stick. Despite his fiery personality, Andy was as cool a customer in court as he had been on the streets. The thrust of the defense position was that Andy had been firing wildly from so far away that it was one of his shotgun pellets that had wounded Glyn Bolasky. Alan Olson even went so far as to imply that it was Andy who shot fifteen-year-old Jody Ann Tygart in the back as she was crossing Hamner during the driving lesson with her father.

On February 4, 1982—one week after testifying in the Norco trial—Andy was back in the offices of the RSO in a meeting with sheriff Ben Clark and deputy chief Cois Byrd. Standing before the two top-ranking members of the department, Delgado knew what was coming. You've done a good job for us, Andy, Byrd said, but you have to go. Byrd and the others were sorry to lose one of their best detectives and a man they liked personally and admired professionally. But those around Andy could see things he was not entirely able to see himself. He was spiraling, and being at the RSO was making it worse. They wanted him to take a voluntary medical retirement for posttraumatic stress disorder.

Andy resisted. He was too much of a fighter, and this felt too much like giving up. You can't force me to retire, he protested. But Andy could see the writing on the wall. When he left the office, he filled out the forms making it official. Detective Andy Delgado had been medically discharged by the County of Riverside for posttraumatic stress disorder. Cois Byrd made sure all the paperwork went through smoothly so that Andy received all his retirement and pension benefits.

It had taken twenty months, but now two of the three deputies who had shot it out with the escaping bank robbers at the intersection of Fourth and Hamner were out of the only career they had ever wanted. For Andy, the source of his disillusionment and unhappiness might have been building for years, but like Bolasky, it was impossible to ignore the moment everything seemed to change. "Before, it was like I could do no wrong," Delgado told a psychiatrist. "But ever since Norco, it seems like I can't do anything right."

WITH THE BATTLE BETWEEN DEFENSE AND PROSECUTION OVER WHO FIRED the first shot in front of the bank over for now, the prosecution methodically walked the jury through the pursuit into Wineville, Mira Loma, onto Interstate 15, and up Lytle Creek. One by one, civilians and cops told the harrowing details of their encounters with the armed men firing from the yellow truck. Along the way, the defense continued to badger the prosecution witnesses.

The law enforcement officers, mostly experienced veterans on the witness stand, generally kept their answers short and their tempers in check on cross-examination. It was the civilian witnesses who were most likely to punch back when the defense attorneys went on the attack.

As predicted, Clayton Adams was as crafty as he was combative. James Kirkland was barely eighteen when Chris Harven aimed the Heckler in his face. Adams did his best to make Kirkland out to be a confused teenager who could not tell the difference between movies and real life.

"Now, James, you watch a lot of war movies and a lot of TV, don't you?"

"I watch TV, yeah."

"You watch a lot of war movies?"

"Not a whole lot."

"You like them?"

"I see them every now and then."

"See movies about bank robberies and stuff like that?"

"Sir, everybody has, haven't they?"

Adams abandoned the line of questioning when it became obvious that Kirkland was not some kid he could push around. In fact, before it was over, Kirkland seemed as though he might be the only adult in the room.

Janice Henker (Janice Cannon at the time of the bank robbery) was driving up Hamner Avenue when she passed the yellow truck while the men in the back fired at deputy Darrell Reed's vehicle and then turned and fired upon her. Like most victims of a violent crime, Henker did not anticipate being victimized all over again in the courtroom.

Adams quickly went after Henker for having met briefly with the prosecution in the hallway prior to testifying. "Did they show you a police report or anything to help you for your testimony?" Adams asked.

"I have had nightmares for years," Henker shot back. "I didn't need any preparation."

It was a mistake that opened a can of worms Adams was happy to spill out for the jury to see. "And it is your dreams that you are testifying about today, isn't it?"

"No. My dreams were created by the problem that brought us here today," Henker snapped, growing agitated.

"You have been having a lot of emotional turmoil because of this event and the dreams you have been having, isn't that right?"

"On occasion."

"And yet, it was you that went and contacted the sheriff? They didn't contact you, did they?"

"That's right. It was me that got fired at," Henker replied. She looked over to the defense tables. "I would be glad to tell you how I became a witness in this case," she added, as if to say the only reason I'm here is because of those fuckers right there.

From there, things boiled over between the two, with Henker's voice rising with each answer in a rapid-fire exchange.

"Excuse me, Your Honor," Ruddy finally intervened. "This is really degenerating."

Hennigan agreed and tried to calm Henker. "Just answer the question and don't get mad at Mr. Adams."

"I love it when she gets mad at me, Your Honor," Adams said, baiting the woman. "You are more than welcome to get mad at me, Mrs. Henker."

Alan Olson, who most everyone other than Russell Harven had been convinced was in way over his head, had finally found his footing. Olson seemed anxious to prove himself early on. Like a pipsqueak on his first day at a new school deciding to walk up and punch the first kid he saw, Olson picked a rather unlikely target to attack.

Kimberly Scott got off work at the Westminster Mall the afternoon of May 8, only to find the rear license plate had been stolen off her car. The plate later showed up on the bumper of Manny Delgado's Matador parked at the Little League lot on Hamner. Her testimony was simple and brief: I walked into the parking lot and my license plate was gone. But Olson chose to harangue and bicker with the woman. "Did you report this incident?"

"Immediately. Both the police and the Motor Vehicles." Olson asked for an exact time. "I drove home first, I think," she answered, trying to think back. "I don't recall. That was a very long time ago."

"So, you wish to change the 'immediately' then?" Olson challenged her, as though the woman were intentionally lying about such a trivial matter.

Scott was taken aback by the reproach. "Pardon? No. I don't recall. I stated that."

"Well, a moment ago you stated that you called the Motor Vehicles Department and the police immediately."

"I told you. I think it was after I got home," Scott said.

"Okay," Olson said doubtfully.

"Okay?" Scott parroted sarcastically.

Mikel Linville, who had his yellow pickup truck stolen at gunpoint by Chis Harven, got into it with Olson over whether anyone had ever really aimed a gun at him that day. "So, he wasn't taking any careful aim at anything then?" Olson asserted as much as asked.

"Do you want to hear what I have to think about that?" Linville said. "I think he was pointing it directly at me."

"But you really don't know where he was pointing it, since there were so many vehicles?"

"That's what you might say."

"It's an assumption on your part, is it not?"

"It's an assumption on your part," Linville fired back.

The long-haired Linville then had the added indignity of Olson randomly asking him, "Had you been using any drugs that day, Mr. Linville?"

"No, I had not," a surprised Linville answered.

The only witness to be treated gently by both sides was Sheila Deno, the bank customer who had entered the lobby in the middle of the robbery and frozen when an inattentive Russell Harven pointed the "Shorty" AR in her face. The naturally nervous Deno had practically begged Ruddy not to make her testify and entered the courtroom in the third trimester of pregnancy with a note from her doctor stating that the stress of testifying could cause her to miscarry. Hennigan attempted to calm the trembling young lady while at the same time cautioning the attorneys not to step over the line. "Mrs. Deno, I assure you nobody is going to jump on you today," Hennigan said in a fatherly voice. "I'm sure that counsel, for their own sake, are not going to do anything which will upset you." Deno's testimony was brief and uneventful and she left the building just as pregnant as when she had walked in.

The issue of dreams surfaced again when deputy Rudy Romo took the stand later in the trial. Romo was speeding down Bellegrave alongside Bill Crowe and A. J. Reynard when he ducked just before a bullet blew the headrest off his seat. Romo was asked by Ruddy to described what George Smith looked like when he saw him firing from the truck on May 9. "In my own words? Scumbag." He was pressed on why he could give no details before but could now make a positive ID in the courtroom. "I kept flashing back to the face in the dreams I was having," Romo said. Hennigan ruled that the identification of Smith and Harven based on dreams was inadmissible. "I don't have to be a psychiatrist to know this," Hennigan remarked. "The trauma of how close he came to death, plus seeing the photos in the newspaper, there's no question it all feeds into our dreams." The story was picked up by the AP wire and blasted across the country.

Prosecution witness testimony had its colorful and dramatic moments. Rolf Parkes told of being trapped against the corral fencing while the truck methodically drifted into his lane and a .223 round creased his scalp at close range. Dave "Mad Dog" Madden told of bullets zipping over his head and sparred with Adams in his usual irreverent deadpan delivery. Adams referred to Madden as a "creature." Madden just smiled; it was not a nickname the Klingon-speaking deputy necessarily objected to. When asked if he could identify the gunman who shot him, CHP officer Bill Crowe raised his arm and pointed directly at Russell Harven. "Seated there." Detective John Burden held up George Smith's samurai sword found inside the van. Riverside PD bomb squad sergeant Bill Miller used an unloaded shotgun and dowel-mounted beer can bomb to demonstrate how it would be used as a grenade launcher. Both images ran in the *Riverside Press-Enterprise* as the paper chronicled the events of the trial on an almost-daily basis.

On March 18, 1982, a silver-haired, elderly gentleman in a three-piece suit entered the courtroom and took a seat in the spectator gallery. "I want to see the defendants and get a general feel for the proceedings," the father of James Evans told James Richardson of the *Press-Enterprise*. "My principal purpose is because of Jim," said Bernard Evans. "It's a little hard for me to explain. It's just something I feel I should do." As they took their seats at the defense tables, Evans laid eyes on George Smith and the Harven brothers for the very first time. "I sort of caught my breath. There's the guys responsible for my son's death." Evans attended for several days and stayed at the prosecution's house in the Vista suburbs as a guest of Jay Hanks. Jim Evans's mother, Martha, stayed home in Texas. "She doesn't feel like she can go through that," Bernard Evans said.

AS THE WITNESSES TESTIFYING ABOUT CRIMES COMMITTED IN SAN BER-nardino began to take the stand, Jay Hanks took over the helm from Kevin Ruddy. The dislike the defense had for Ruddy was nothing compared to what they reserved for Hanks. As head of the prosecution team, he was the one they held responsible for what they saw as witness coaching, feet-dragging on disclosure requests, and other actions they openly referred to as misconduct. "Until The People want to be gentlemanly about this," Adams threatened at one point, "I will withhold everything I have from them, just as they are withholding it from me." After one such attack, Hanks exploded. "I resent this continued attack by Mr. Adams without any justification. He continues to make bald nonfactual accusations accusing the prosecution of not complying with discovery." "Let's stop calling names back and forth," a beleaguered Hennigan urged.

In another instance, Hanks objected to Adams continuing a line of questioning despite sustained objections against it. "I am asking the Court to admonish counsel to leave the area," a frustrated Hanks demanded. "I would love to leave town," Adams commented dryly. "I would desire the Court to ask him to leave town too," Hanks responded. None of it was said in jest and nobody in the courtroom laughed. Things had gotten too raw between them.

At times, the animosity veered into the realm of the absurd. One of the rubber bands Russell Harven compulsively stretched between his fingers accidentally got loose and shot Hanks in the rear end. In what the press dubbed the "Pencil Fencing Incident," Olson and Hanks threw pencils at each other during a particularly combative argument in front of the jury. The spectacle was so unseemly that Michael Lloyd objected. "I realize the people's emotions are rather high key in a case of this nature, but I would request the Court prohibit both counsel from throwing pencils in court." Alan Olson jumped in. "I would join Mr. Lloyd in the request that the district attorney not mimic in his childlike manner things he thinks funny about this case." "I will admonish all counsel, don't throw pencils," Hennigan scolded.

LATER IN THE TRIAL, AN INCIDENT OCCURRED THAT RAISED EYEBROWS INSIDE the courtroom and out. Clayton Adams was in the process of cross-examination when he noticed something strange. "No offense intended to the court," Adams protested at the next recess, "but I did want the record to reflect that while I was cross-examining the witness Charles Vasquez this morning that the Court was, from the bench, photographing jurors." Asked about the incident by a reporter afterward, Hennigan said, "We've been together a long time. I like having a memento of them." The AP wire story about the incident was headlined: "Judge in Robbery-Murder Trial Photographs Jury for Souvenir." A quote from Jay Hanks summed up the sentiments of anyone who had been following the proceedings from the start: "For this trial, it's not weird."

With all the drama, colorful testimony, and unseemly squabbling, word was out that there were some very strange happenings going on at the Vista courthouse. Soon veteran court watchers and just plain folk were lining up in the hallway outside the courtroom of Justice Hennigan to snatch up seats in the gallery for the best show in town. Ahead of them lay the most dramatic and contentious fight of the entire trial, over the single question most likely to determine whether the three defendants before them would live or die: Who really killed deputy James Evans?

17

FRIENDLY FIRE

April 12, 1982. Vista, California.

D. J. McCARTY SAT ON A BENCH IN THE HALLWAY OF THE SUPERIOR COURT IN Vista, hoping to God no one would notice him. The place was a zoo, spectators packing the seats inside the courtroom and spilling out into the hallway hoping someone might leave so they could take their place. The newspapers called them "court watchers," but to McCarty they were nothing more than complete strangers. For D.J., the prospect of being questioned in front of a room full of strangers was nothing short of horrifying. Despite his gregarious nature and self-confidence, D.J. had no experience speaking in front of crowds and had only been on the witness stand once in his life, and then only for five minutes. And now he was supposed to sit there and talk about . . . this?

"Which direction did Deputy Evans turn when he was hit?"

"Toward me."

"Could you see he was wounded?"

"Yes."

"What did you see that indicated he was wounded?"

"Massive hole in his head."

D.J. adjusted his tie, shifted in his seat, and took deep breaths to calm himself. His heart was beating so hard he could see the lapels on his suit coat moving up and down. The waiting was killing him. Not just the thirty minutes sitting outside the courtroom, but the five days since Jim McPheron had ended his testimony. McCarty had been scheduled to take the stand right after Mac, but Jay Hanks decided to slot in another witness, a sergeant from the California Highway Patrol, before him on short notice. Once it became clear that the sergeant's incident reports and testimony included things he could not have witnessed, it turned into a feeding frenzy that ran all the way through the end of the week. McCarty had spent it driving back and forth the two hours each way between Vista and San Bernardino, his anxiety level rising. By Friday, he had caught the flu and spent the weekend sweating and puking. And then the call came in from Joe Curfman: You're going on Monday, for sure. So here he was, feeling like shit and still waiting while the CHP guy finished getting his ass shoved through the cross-examination meat grinder.

McCarty noticed several people outside the courtroom stealing looks at him. Of course they knew who he was. He was the reason they were here, the main attraction of the entire trial. He looked like a cop, too, midtwenties, six foot two, broad shouldered, with his dark suit, trimmed mustache, and hair parted on the side and swept low across his forehead. One of the court watchers, almost all of them nosy old retirees, nodded in his direction and whispered something to the old crone beside her. D.J. could feel himself rising off the bench, ready to bolt from the courthouse. He took another deep breath and settled down. "You just sit up there looking like the all-American boy and you'll be fine," Curfman had told him.

Joe Curfman had been a lifesaver for McCarty. Curfman was the real deal, with hundreds of felony investigations under his belt. "Handsome little fucker and funny as shit," D.J. described him. The veteran calmed McCarty with his cool confidence and easy smile and gave him good, simple advice: Keep your answers short, stick to your story, and don't let them get you mad. Once you lose your shit, those defense attorneys will pounce.

A guy in a suit walked up and introduced himself. A reporter. Would D.J. talk to him when his testimony was over? I doubt it, D.J. smiled weakly.

Talking to the press was the last thing McCarty needed. Even reading the papers had been a mistake. Now that the trial had turned to the killing of Evans, it always seemed to make note of what McCarty was being accused of by the defense, as though it deserved serious credence: "Defense attorney Clayton Adams has said he will attempt to show that it was McCarty who killed Evans, and not the suspects."

Once that stuff began to show up in his hometown paper, the whispers and speculation started. "That guy had no business being up on that mountain with a gun he didn't even know how to use," one loudmouth veteran deputy announced in the locker room. Others just shrugged. D.J. knew it was the same thing that went on in police departments everywhere: cops popping off without thinking, never considering the consequences. He tried, but it was impossible to ignore it. McCarty knew what had gone down on Baldy Notch Road that day, but the truth didn't matter. The only thing that mattered was what the jury decided. What if they came back with forty-five "guilty" verdicts and one "not guilty" or some reduced charge in the death of Evans? It would follow him forever. The fucking thing would . . . *define* him.

The courtroom door opened and Curfman came out. Just a few more minutes, he said. D.J. swallowed hard and nodded. Curfman studied him. It's gonna be fine. Yeah, said D.J.

If I had it to do all over again, D.J. thought, would I really go charging up that mountain with a gun I had never used before? If I had known I would experience the terror I felt up there or see the things I saw, would I have made the same decision? What if I had known I would end up being accused of killing a fellow cop, or sit on a witness stand in front of a room full of strangers while some asshole defense attorney tried to make me out to be some glory-seeking cowboy? I was young, too eager for the fight, too many goddamn John Wayne movies. But I never wanted any of this.

"No one had assigned you this job? What I mean is, as far as the assignment of Deputy McCarty to be the one to carry the AR-15 up, that was still all volunteer, wasn't it?"

"Yes."

"In fact, you were off duty?"

"Yes."

"You could have just checked out?"

"I was off shift."

"In fact, you were on your way home, getting ready to go home?"

"Yes."

"And you decided to stick around for the action?"

"I don't believe so."

"In any case, you beat whoever was available to the AR?"

"I wouldn't call it beat. I didn't consider it a race, Counselor. Somebody had to bring the weapon out."

In his incident reports and preliminary trial testimony, McCarty had been consistent on the key points. He never loaded the gun on the way up the canyon because he was too busy working the radios and too worried that McPheron might drive the Ford Fairlane into Lytle Creek. At the ambush site, he was still in the passenger seat when Evans was shot.

Only after that had two rounds come through the windshield of the Fairlane, one hitting McCarty in the elbow and causing him to dive out the driver's-side door. After fumbling to load the weapon, he had, by his own admission, raised the gun over the top of the door and closed his eyes, "spraying" gunfire across the width of the road. The M16 was capable of firing in fully automatic mode, but McCarty never thought to switch the setting and had fired in semiautomatic mode instead.

All the defense had to do was tweak a few details to turn the whole story around. Of course McCarty loaded the gun on the way up and switched it to automatic mode. Who goes to a gunfight with an unloaded gun? When the shooting started, McCarty threw open his passenger door, jumped out with his fully loaded gun, closed his eyes, and began spraying automatic gunfire all over the place, unable to control a weapon he had never fired before. When Jim Evans heard gunshots coming from behind him, he whipped his head around to look and a bullet from D. J. McCarty's gun struck him in the right eye, killing him. Friendly fire, happens all the goddamn time.

McCarty was just too ashamed to admit what really happened, they said, and was hiding behind the "thin blue line" of fellow cops lying to protect him, all of it aided and abetted by a prosecutor willing to do anything to send three men to the gas chamber.

D.J. eyed the thick binder sitting on the bench next to him stuffed with incident reports, a transcript of his pretrial testimony, and some other documents he could refer to while on the stand. He had gone over his preliminary testimony a week before, using a yellow highlighter to mark places that might give him some trouble. Any time you take the stand, you're the one who's on trial, he had been warned. D.J. thumbed through a few pages of the pretrial transcript. He closed it again and set it on the bench. Just a bunch of minor bullshit, nothing he needed to worry about. But what about the other guys? What had Lenihan and McPheron said on the stand before him? D.J. wondered but knew better than to ask. Sharing prior witness testimony with another witness was not allowed. "You can't control what anyone else says," was all Jay Hanks would say on the subject.

DEPUTY MIKE LENIHAN WAS TWENTY-FOUR YEARS OLD WHEN HE TOOK THE stand for the prosecution on April 1, 1982, almost two weeks before McCarty. D.J.'s friend and former roommate was thin and soft-spoken, with an intensity about him that belied an underlying shyness. Lenihan had been in the patrol unit immediately behind McPheron and McCarty when the pursuit reached the washout high up Baldy Notch Road. On direct questioning by Hanks, Lenihan recounted how he had slammed on the brakes, jumped out of his car, and saw Evans get killed before McCarty fired a shot. However, in recalling the flurry of activity, which unfolded in a matter of fifteen to twenty seconds of total chaos while he was under heavy fire, Lenihan's memory flip-flopped the order of the two events. Clayton Adams was quick to point out the inconsistency on cross-examination.

"After you observed the brake lights going on, what was the next thing that you observed, the very next thing?"

"The next thing I observed was shots going through his back window."

"When was the first time you observed Deputy Evans in the washout area?"

"I was behind the driver's door, I noticed—he was later identified as Deputy Evans—behind his unit."

"This was already after the bullets going through the window of McPheron/McCarty's unit?"

"Yes."

"Okay. And Deputy Evans was still alive then?"

"Yes."

Lenihan's account contradicted McCarty's version that Evans was shot before the rounds came through the windshield of the Fairlane. Lenihan also unwittingly substantiated an important element of the defense's friendly fire argument.

"Could you estimate how many rounds he fired . . ." Adams asked regarding the first volley of fire by McCarty.

"It was a burst of gunfire. It was an automatic weapon he was firing."

"So he cranked off a burst of automatic fire, too much rounds for you to count, essentially?"

"Yes."

This was important to Adams because it supported the defense's assertion that McCarty had been "spraying" bullets around in fully automatic mode, which makes it notoriously difficult to control a weapon, especially for someone untrained on the M16.

DEPUTY JIM MCPHERON TOOK THE STAND TO TESTIFY FOR HANKS ON APRIL 2. McPheron's direct testimony supported McCarty's version of events almost perfectly. A little too perfectly in the opinion of Alan Olson, who went after McPheron for inconsistencies with his earlier testimony at the pretrial hearing.

"Now, it's your testimony that you are certain that the weapon was not loaded before you got to Lytle Creek, the AR?" Olson asked. McPheron confirmed he was certain it was not. "Okay. Court and Counsel," Olson announced, holding a copy of McPheron's preliminary trial testimony aloft and calling out the page number. "Page 1056, line 14 . . . through 22."

> Question: Did you observe the AR-15 to have a clip in it at that time?
> Answer: I don't recall, sir.
> Question: Is your answer to that you don't recall whether there was a clip
> in there or not or that you don't remember observing the rifle?
> Answer: I knew he was holding the rifle. However, I do not recall whether
> there was a clip in the rifle at that time.

McPheron stuck to his current testimony. "The clips were not inserted into the weapon during the time we were driving up there, sir."

McPheron recalled in detail watching McCarty attempting to load the magazine into the M16 while crouched down behind the door and seeing it repeatedly fall out before D.J. finally got it to catch.

Olson thumbed through the copy of McPheron's pretrial testimony again and read.

> Question: Did you ever observe McCarty loading that AR-15 or loading
> a clip into it?
> Answer: I don't remember, sir.
> Question: And you had McCarty in your view, did you not?
> Answer: Yes.
> Question: And you saw him fire the weapon, is that correct?
> Answer: Yes, sir.
> Question: However, you did not see him load it before. Is that correct?
> Answer: I don't recall seeing him load the weapon, no sir.

Olson then retrieved the report written by detective Peggy Williams concerning her incident interview with McPheron the night of the shootout. "Did you tell Detective Peggy Williams that you believed that McCarty and the deceased Riverside deputy had gotten hit simultaneously; however, Mc-Carty was able to continue firing?" he asked.

McPheron stared down at his copy of the report. As written by Williams, it suggested McCarty was already firing when Evans was shot and then was able to *continue* shooting afterward.

"Yes, that's what is down there. Whether it was put to her that way, I'm not sure."

"She made that part up?" Olson sneered.

Both Olson and Adams spent an extended amount of time grilling McPheron on his psychological state, referring to the two prominent newspaper articles in which McPheron had discussed the emotional impact of Norco and the stress of police work in general. Clayton Adams was particularly nasty in his questioning. "Incidentally, have you resolved your psychological problems that you were receiving counseling for?"

At one point, McPheron recited a list of heartbreaking and gruesome things he had experienced in his career and the toll they had taken. Afterward, Adams questioned his sincerity by noting the mementoes and newspaper clippings McPheron had a habit of collecting. Referring to the piece of windshield with the bullet hole that McPheron had framed, Adams used his last re-cross to take a parting shot at the big deputy.

"Deputy McPheron, as I understand it, you would like to be able to forget all about these incidents in your past so that perhaps your stress-related problems might go away."

"It would be nice," McPheron agreed.

"By the way, where did you keep that windshield in your home, that memento?"

JAY HANKS NEVER BELIEVED D. J. McCARTY SHOT JIM EVANS. HE CALLED THE accusation "foolishness" on the part of the defense. He was less certain about whether it had been Russell Harven or Manny Delgado. There had been three men firing .223-caliber weapons on Baldy Notch Road and only two were still alive. There had been three ARs involved in the gunfight, but only two were ever found. Chris Harven's HK93 used by Manny Delgado still lay hidden somewhere in Coldwater Canyon, its location a secret Manny had taken to his grave. But for Hanks, the decision of whom to blame for the murder of Deputy Evans was a simple one. Manny Delgado had already received his death sentence. The only person sitting in the courtroom who had been firing a .223 that day was Russell Harven. That is, until D. J. McCarty walked in to take the stand.

"THE PEOPLE CALL DANIEL McCARTY."

Moments after McCarty was sworn in, the jury was removed from the courtroom so that Judge Hennigan could hear a motion by the defense to forbid McCarty from specifically identifying Russell Harven in court. Sitting quietly on the stand listening to the arguments, D.J. got his first glimpse of the existing acrimony between the defense and prosecution. When Hanks attempted to enter into evidence an artist rendering of the ambush, Olson and Lloyd objected to stick figures representing their clients being included in the sketch. Adams, on the other hand, demanded that one representing George Smith be left in. Hennigan granted the requests of all three defense attorneys.

"I'm objecting, Your Honor," Hanks said, exasperated at Hennigan's decision.

"I know you are," said Hennigan.

"My objection is no good, Your Honor?"

"That's correct."

"If I get this right—if I understand this correctly—that drawing can't come in if I offer it because the defense objects, but part of it can come in if the defense wants it even though I object?"

"Yes," Hennigan said.

"Well, that seems fair to me," Hanks said sarcastically.

When Hennigan suggested they could use scissors and cut the offending figures out of the exhibit, Hanks was beside himself. "It's my exhibit," he protested. "You're going to cut up my exhibit, Your Honor?"

"I would agree with Mr. Hanks, that he is correct, the exhibit should remain intact," Clayton Adams said. He suggested a photograph of the exhibit be chopped up instead. "I would think that he would be thanking me for that," Adams added when Hanks continued to argue with Hennigan.

"Don't hold your breath," Hanks snapped.

"Well, it's unusual to have found for a fleeting instance Mr. Hanks and Mr. Adams on the same side," noted Hennigan before ordering the photograph of the exhibit to be cut up.

"I'll do it," Adams said, raising the scissors to begin cutting.

"Give me that," Hanks growled, grabbing hold of the scissors. The two men engaged in a brief tug of war before Hanks successfully jerked them out of Adams's hand.

"I beg your pardon," Adams yowled. "Pardon me. May the record reflect Counsel has yanked it out of my hands and is apparently now attempting to cut the photograph?"

You gotta be kidding me, McCarty thought.

After an hour of debate, Olson was able to successfully prohibit the identification of Russell Harven in the courtroom. But within moments of beginning his testimony in front of the jury, Hanks did ask McCarty to identify someone else. "As you look around the courtroom, do you see anybody in the courtroom that you recognize to be the person that was standing in the roadway when Evans fell?"

"Yes, I do," said McCarty.

"Please point him out."

McCarty raised a finger and aimed it at the defense table. "The man in the blue suit, with the red tie, with his hand on his face."

"Wearing glasses?"

"Yes, sir."

"May the record reflect the witness has identified the defendant, George Wayne Smith?"

"It may," said the judge.

Hanks kept the questioning of McCarty lean, not wishing to put too much out there for the defense to try to use against him. Although his anxiety had somewhat subsided now that the questioning had begun, McCarty still spoke in a soft voice recounting the killing of Evans, getting wounded himself, diving out the door, and then driving off the suspects with the M16. The jury listened intently, the spectator gallery silent.

Hanks had McCarty step down from the witness stand and approach what was referred to as People's exhibit 245, or as Hanks called it, "The Mountain." The Mountain was a scale model of the washout site on Baldy Notch Road that Hanks had commissioned from the graphics department of the Los Angeles County Sheriff's Office at a cost of $1,000. Using topographical maps and personally inspecting the location, a designer named Michael McClure used chicken wire, a compound plaster called Sculptamold, gravel, and handmade landscape elements to create a remarkably accurate six-and-a-half-foot-long, two-foot-wide representation of the scene. The Mountain took up constant residency in the courtroom for several weeks. The defense refused to use it and Alan Olson had taken to referring to the monster as "Mount St. Harvens" while outside the presence of the jury.

D.J. painstakingly placed a miniature truck, police vehicles, and plastic figures in their various positions during the ambush. Having been permitted to identify him in the courtroom, Hanks and McCarty freely referred to one of the figures as George Wayne Smith. However, because the identification of Russell Harven had been denied, McCarty had been instructed to not refer to any figure or person he might have observed as Russell Harven. But during questioning by Michael Lloyd, McCarty slipped up.

"And your attention was focused on him?" Lloyd asked, referring to the figures McCarty had seen standing by the truck during the ambush.

"It was the whole shot, the blurs, the movement," McCarty answered. "That's why it was focused, like I say, on Harven."

Hennigan jumped in immediately, before the attorneys even had time to object. "The jury is instructed to disregard the identification or statement of name there."

Olson had been reading over papers at the defense table when McCarty identified his client. His head shot up. "Excuse me, Your Honor? May I have that last answer read back? I wasn't paying attention."

Hennigan refused to have the answer reread, not wanting to reemphasize the gaffe again in front of the jurors.

"I am forced to move for a mistrial at this point," Olson said at a sidebar on the subject.

"I am going to deny it," Hennigan responded.

"I think the witness, Your Honor, should be admonished in the presence of the jury and that the People should also be admonished in the presence of the jury," Clayton Adams jumped in. "This to me is clearly unconscionable. There is no question about it. You can tell him not to blurt things out that he has been instructed not to."

Hennigan rejected the idea of a public scolding of McCarty and Hanks before the jury. Hanks was instructed to whisper to McCarty not to do it again, but it was unnecessary; D.J. had been sitting there listening to the discussion the whole time.

Direct questioning of McCarty took less than a day, with Clayton Adams taking the first cross-examination of the witness, as usual. Adams sparred with D.J. over testimony that he did not know how to load the M16 even though he had fired AR-style rifles before.

"So you had, in fact, fired an automatic weapon of the .223-caliber in the past; that is, before May 9, 1980?" Adams asked.

"Semiautomatic, yes," D.J. corrected.

"All right. The only difference being where one was automatic and the other one had the semiautomatic/automatic mode; is that correct?"

"Yes."

"Other features about the weapon being identical?"

"No."

"No?"

"No."

"Okay. What were the differences between the weapons then; that is, the weapon you had on May 9, 1980, and the one that you had fired in the past?"

"This weapon here is an assault rifle. It is a military-type rifle. The other weapons that I had fired are basically like a hunting rifle."

"With magazines that feed in and load them?"

"Yes."

"In much the same fashion as the one that you had on May 9, 1980?"

"None whatsoever."

"None whatsoever?"

"None."

"It didn't concern either one of you that neither one of you in that vehicle knew how to use that weapon?" Adams asked.

"Oh, it concerned me."

"Not enough to stop, though?"

"No."

When it was his turn, Alan Olson challenged McCarty's claim that he never loaded the gun en route.

"Now, at that point did you realize or were you prepared to be the one to fire that weapon when necessary?"

"Yes."

"In fact, that was your singular mission, to get to the front and use it, wasn't it?"

"Yes."

"Did you think of loading it on the way up?"

"I thought about it."

"And you thought it wasn't a good idea or what?"

"I thought it was a better idea to watch McPheron at the time."

"You thought it would be a better idea to watch McPheron and arrive with an empty weapon?"

"At the time that I was driving up the hill with Deputy McPheron, I really wasn't worried about anything except winding up in the ditch."

"At what point did you become worried or concerned about McPheron's driving?"

"When I got in the car with him."

"You thought it would be a better idea to arrive with the weapon and just instantly load it when you got there?"

"Yes. I was planning on getting the weapon operating when I needed it, when I got to the point."

The cross-examination finally came to the actual firefight itself. The defense began laying the foundation that McCarty accidentally shot Evans while standing just outside the passenger door. That would have put McCarty in a position of firing in the direction of Evans crouched less than a dozen feet in front of him. At the heart of their argument were five empty .223 shell casings found in the dirt outside the passenger door of McPheron's unit, a bullet hole in the passenger door that could only have been made if the door was open, and the incredulity that McCarty would remain in the passenger seat doing nothing for ten to fifteen seconds while Evans was shot down in front of him.

The presence of the shell casings outside the door was neutralized by testimony that the ejection pattern of the M16 was to jettison spent casings out the right side of the weapon a distance of three to four feet. If McCarty fired the weapon from the V of the open driver's side door as he contended, it would have sent ejected shells skipping over the hood of the vehicle and onto the dirt on the passenger side.

But Alan Olson challenged McCarty's story that after being wounded he had kicked open his own door before diving out the driver's-side, accounting for the bullet hole in bottom of the open passenger door.

"Now, as I understand it, you kicked your passenger door open as a diversion; is that correct?"

"Yes."

"Okay. As I understand your testimony, you pulled up, Evans gets out, goes from [position] E-1 to E-2. Meanwhile, you are simply sitting there for ten or fifteen seconds observing things in disbelief, as though you were in a movie?"

"Yes."

"At that point, after Evans is hit, rounds come through, you, yourself, are hit and you duck or dive to the left, putting your right arm up—was it your right arm?"

"Yes."

"And, I take it, your head was towards the driver's side at that point?"

"I was moving in that direction, yes."

"And you kicked the door open?"

"Yes."

"Kicked it with your foot and grabbed it with your hand?"

"Uh-huh."

"So somehow you stretched and reached the door handle?" Olson said, in obvious disbelief.

"Yes."

THROUGHOUT THE FIRST TWO DAYS OF TESTIMONY, HANKS AND THE DEFENSE attorneys continued to battle each other, sometimes in open court. When Alan Olson began to get far afield in his initial cross, Hanks simply called out, "Objection. Ridiculous."

"Sustained," Hennigan agreed, without even waiting for Hanks to elaborate.

Referring to the San Bernardino deputies as "banditos," Olson later suggested that Jim McPheron might also have been firing a second AR-15 converted to fully automatic by a Fontana sergeant whose hobby was firearms. "This is crazy," Hanks objected.

"If it's really crazy, you ought to appreciate it," Olson said.

"Just for clarification," Hanks asked Hennigan. "The Court is going to permit questioning of this officer who's not qualified as an arms smith in the AR-15, to testify about another sergeant who is an arms smith, if I'm understanding this correctly?"

"I don't think you understand anything," Clayton Adams interjected.

"Oh, go get lost, Clay," Hanks shot back.

The defendants were not shy about displaying their disbelief at some of McCarty's responses. Chris Harven was the most demonstrative in his disgust, folding his arms behind his head, leaning back in his chair, and shaking his head whenever he found one of McCarty's remarks to be especially preposterous. George Smith, sitting beside investigator Jeanne Painter, mostly stared flatly at McCarty. Russell Harven fiddled with his rubber bands, a slight smirk on his lips, his attitude toward D.J.'s testimony the same as it was toward the whole trial in general: a complete joke.

For his part, McCarty had worked up a particular dislike of Clayton Adams. Following a recess on the third day of testimony, Michael Lloyd spotted something rather unusual he felt he should bring to the attention of Hennigan and the other attorneys. "I don't know if there is a problem or not," he said, after convening the defense and prosecution teams at the bench. "But as we were coming in the court and Deputy McCarty was going to the stand, apparently there was a note in his binder that dropped out. No one saw the note drop out, but my investigator, Mr. Cummins, did see one of the jurors pick up the note and hand it back to Deputy McCarty."

"Without reading it, apparently?" Hennigan asked.

"I don't know if he read it or not. I went up to Deputy McCarty just before we started and asked to see the note, and the note is rather derogatory towards one of the defense attorneys."

"Why don't you tell us what the note said?" asked Hanks.

"I am not exactly sure of the wording," said Lloyd, "but it was something to the effect, 'Do you think you are going to have a job after this, Mr. Adams?'"

"I would be more than happy to tell them, I don't have a job at all," Adams said, more bemused than anything. "I am glad it was brought to the attention of all concerned, but I don't want to make a big thing out of it."

McCarty maintained a sly innocence about the note when asked about it later.

ON HIS FINAL RE-CROSS, ALAN OLSON BECAME OVERT IN HIS ACCUSATIONS against McCarty, even attempting to bait him with thinly veiled accusations of cowardice.

"Does the window appear to be up or down?" Olson said, referring to a photograph of the passenger side of McPheron's unit.

"It appears to be down."

"When you were carrying the weapon, did you have it pointed out the window?"

"No."

"Towards the window?"

"Possibly."

"And you, instead of sticking it out and firing, just sat there and observed Evans die? You did nothing for ten or fifteen seconds; is that correct?"

"Yes, sir," McCarty said.

"Any fire from behind Evans?" Olson asked, later.

"Not while he was alive," McCarty said.

"Did you ever go out the passenger door?"

"No."

"Did you ever give a different version of what happened up there to, say, Detective Jordan?"

"Not that I recall."

McCarty and Hanks knew that the report written up by RSO detective Mike Jordan was going to be problematic. McCarty had encountered Jordan as he was walking down the Baldy Notch Road to be helicoptered out to the hospital. Jordan asked McCarty the name of the deputy who had been killed and became upset when D.J. confirmed it was Evans. McCarty turned Evans's revolver over to Jordan. As the two walked down the hill in the direction of the makeshift landing site, they had an informal conversation.

On his cross-examination turn, Clayton Adams attempted to impeach D.J.'s version of events using testimony made by Jordan during the preliminary hearing regarding their conversation. "Do you remember telling Detective Jordan that Deputy Evans abandoned his vehicle and came back to his unit on the right-hand side, and you stated that as you were firing, Deputy Evans fired one shot at which time Deputy Evans was struck?"

"No," McCarty answered.

Calling an extremely reluctant and irritated Mike Jordan to the stand as a witness for the defense, Jordan's pretrial testimony was read into the record.

> Question: Did McCarty tell you what he was firing, what weapon he was firing when Evans was hit?
> Answer: No.
> Question: Did he say where he was when he was firing and Evans was hit?

Answer: I believe he said he was behind him or alongside him. I can't
remember.

Question: McCarty said he was behind or alongside of Evans firing when
Evans was hit; is that correct?

Answer: That's what I recall, yes.

D.J. was at a loss to explain Jordan's testimony other than that the man
had been distraught at the time upon learning his friend Evans was dead.
On the stand, there was not a lot McCarty could do other than deny that he
had ever said those things to the detective while walking down Baldy Notch
Road in the cold and darkness of May 9, 1980.

"Do you remember telling him any of that?" Alan Olson asked.

"I don't remember telling him any of it," McCarty answered flatly.

As McCarty's three days of grueling testimony wound down, Alan Olson saved his best shot for the very end. Olson went after McCarty over
an apparent contradiction in the condition of the rear window of Evans's
vehicle. McCarty testified in the preliminary that Evans's rear window had
been completely blown out of its frame, not a shred of glass left. Evidence
photographs clearly showed the window to be shattered, with multiple bullet
holes through it, but most of the glass remaining. It was not an especially
important discrepancy, but Olson was mostly using it as a set-up for his
grand finale.

"Officer McCarty, are you positive that you did not personally kill James
Evans?"

"Yes, I'm positive."

"As positive as you were about the window?"

D. J. McCarty stepped down from the witness stand just after 3:00 p.m.
on the afternoon of April 14, 1982, relieved to be done with the ordeal of
testifying but far from certain what the jury might decide after hearing it.
On his way out, George Smith glared, and Russell Harven smirked. Chris
Harven leaned forward and flashed D.J. the middle finger while shielding
the gesture from the sight of the jury with the other hand. D.J. left the courtroom, walked past a waiting reporter without comment, climbed into the

root beer–colored piece-of-shit Impala the department had been loaning him for the trips to Vista, and drove home to San Bernardino.

D. J. McCARTY WOULD NEVER SEE THE NUMBING AMOUNT OF BALLISTICS TES-
timony presented by both sides that followed his own. He would not be there when a nuclear chemist named Dr. Vincent P. Guinn testified for the prosecution that after bombarding sample bullets with radioactivity and then measuring for trace elements, he was certain the fatal round came from the boxes of ammunition used by Russell Harven and Manny Delgado. Or when the defense countered with Lawrence Kovar, who ran the same "neutron activation" tests and agreed with Guinn that it had to be the PS-79 manufactured bullets, but then revealed that dozens of PS-79s had been found at the Fontana substation mixed in with the rest of the ammo for the M16.

He would not be around when Michael White, a criminalist with the department of justice, discredited a claim by the defense that McCarty might have hit Evans while firing through his own windshield from the inside by proving the bullet holes in McPheron's windshield had come from the outside. Or when the blood splatter experts for the defense contradicted his story by saying the spots around where Evans fell indicated the bullet must have been fired from McCarty's position behind him.

He would not hear criminalist Ronald Ralston declare that the lead taken from the brain of Jim Evans was too mangled to trace back to any one weapon. Or Donald Dunn, a ballistics expert for the defense, who asserted that there was indeed enough left of the slug to conclude that it could not possibly have come from either Russell Harven's "Shorty" AR or McCarty's M16, the only two guns available to test.

D.J. would miss the spectacle of Clayton Adams's bitter accusations against Hanks and the San Bernardino Sheriff's Office for conspiring to withhold, steal, and destroy evidence that would have linked the bullet to McCarty. Or Jeanne Painter taking the stand to describe how she had tried for months to get Hanks to comply with an order to produce the only remaining round from McCarty's M16, only to finally be given a useless slug of lead that had been destroyed when pried out of its casing for testing by the prosecution.

And McCarty never knew that justice J. David Hennigan had made the highly unusual request to the jury that it make a "special finding" to determine who had been the killer on Baldy Notch Road that afternoon. Or that a bailiff had handed out a slip of paper to the jury foreman that read

SPECIAL FINDING:
We find that the bullet which killed James Evans was fired (by)
(mark one only)
George Smith _____
Russell Harven _____
Christopher Harven _____
Manuel Delgado _____
A Police Officer _____
We cannot say beyond a reasonable doubt who fired the bullet _____

And D. J. McCarty would be nowhere near Vista, California, when the ballot was handed back to Hennigan with a single checkmark indicating the jury's finding. The only people in the courtroom whose opinion mattered had decided that the killer was the only person with nobody in the courtroom to defend him: Manny Delgado.

18

SCANDAL

April 28, 1982. Vista, California.

ON THE EVENING OF APRIL 28, 1982, TWO WEEKS AFTER D. J. McCARTY HAD completed his testimony in the trial of the Norco 3, a booking clerk at the Vista Detention Facility assigned to the visiting-area observation booth saw something happening in one of the interview rooms. Nancy Garcia watched carefully. Then she left the booth and hurried to notify her supervisor, deputy Larry Van Dusen. Van Dusen entered the observation booth and took a close look. Moments later, there was a sharp knock on the door of the interview room, startling the man and woman inside. The door flew open and Van Dusen announced that the interview between the prisoner and the member of his legal team was now terminated. What for? the woman wanted to know. Van Dusen ordered her to pack up her documents, escorted her to the reception area, and ejected the woman from the jail.

Van Dusen's report to the commander of the Vista jail, Captain Robert DeSteunder, would say that Garcia had notified him that "suspicious activity of a sexual nature appeared to be occurring in interview room C." When he went to see for himself, Van Dusen reported that he observed investigator Jeanne Painter "grasping Inmate George W. Smith in the area of his crotch ..." When the press got ahold of the story the following day, they were less obtuse about what Van Dusen had allegedly seen. "Jail officials ejected Painter from jail last Wednesday night and banned her from interviewing Smith in person after a jailer allegedly observed her masturbating Smith ..." The same article in the *Vista Press* went on to quote attorney Clayton Adams as saying, "We deny everything."

On April 29, with the prosecution calling in its final ballistics experts and wrapping up its case against the Norco 3, all court proceedings came to a screeching halt.

"The record may show defendants and counsel are present. There is no member of the jury present. I intended to take up, Mr. Adams, the matter you mentioned to me this morning," Judge Hennigan said at the opening of the session. "I would suggest that this would be better discussed in the closed court without members of the public present."

"I agree, Your Honor," said a visibly distressed Clayton Adams.

"Very well," said Hennigan. "The Court will order the courtroom cleared. Captain DeSteunder may remain, but other members of the public are asked to leave. Mr. Bailiff, you will put a 'Closed Court' sign out."

"I have read the report that the Court gave me this morning, the incident report," Adams began. "The point I wanted to make is that I am not prepared to address any of these charges in the report other than to deny them entirely. Beyond that, I would just indicate to the Court that because of what happened last night, i.e., that my investigator was apparently ejected from the jail premises last night during the course of her meeting with my client, I am not prepared to go forward today. It does not appear that I will be prepared to go forward for the remainder of the case in that this final insult is such that my investigator simply will not be going forward on this case any longer. So I am without an investigator. I personally will not tolerate this kind of conduct," Adams continued, growing more upset. "I will no longer have any dealings whatsoever with the jail until such time as I have to turn myself in to become their prisoner," he added, referring to the five-day sentence for contempt looming in his future.

"Had you personally had any problems or limitations in your visits with your client, Mr. Adams?" Hennigan wanted to know.

"I have avoided such visits for this very reason: I don't want to become a subject of false reports, false charges, false innuendos, as my investigator has. So I have studiously avoided that. You can check the records," Adams added. "I haven't even had a visit in the jail probably for over a month."

"Usually the person who visits the jail and talks to the client is the attorney rather than the investigator," the judge said, surprised that Painter had been the one conducting all the jailhouse meetings. "This is not a usual case. I am not implying any criticism of having the visits through the investigator," he added. "But there is no reason you could not see your client in jail, as far as any communication that is necessary."

"Well, that is your opinion, Your Honor," Adams protested. "I am not going to subject myself to this kind of abuse. I am just not going to do it. I don't think I am required to do so. I know of no ethical or moral requirement or canon that requires me to do so, and I refuse to do so."

"Do I understand that Ms. Painter has withdrawn herself from this case completely?" Hennigan asked.

"I can't make any representations at this time, Your Honor. As far as I am concerned, no human being should have to put up with the kind of abuse that she has suffered up to this point. She is not here today. She was not able to accomplish her task last night. I am not prepared to go forward today."

Hennigan kept calm and methodical as Adams grew more upset, trying to keep the situation from turning into an absolute disaster. For Adams to lose his only investigator—especially one playing as critical a role as Painter—two years into a death penalty case could easily trigger a mistrial, or at the very least leave it wide open for reversal on appeal. Hennigan was doing everything he could to keep Painter attached to the case in a way that would not compromise Smith's right to an adequate defense.

"Is there any reason she could not continue her function as an investigator in serving subpoenas on witnesses, talking to witnesses, arranging evidence, and assisting you in that respect?" Hennigan asked.

"No. I am telling you, Judge, the woman is a nervous wreck. She has given all she can give and taken all she can take. When she called me last night, she was in tears. And like I said, she was an emotional/mental basket case. The jail has succeeded in doing what they wanted to do."

"Is she still assigned to this case by the Public Defender's Office?"

"I haven't the vaguest idea, Your Honor."

"Very well," Hennigan sighed. "I would appreciate it if you would find out from her as quickly as possible if there is any reason she could not continue her functions in this case other than visiting the client at the jail."

"Whatever the Court wants to do, Your Honor, except my feeling is that that will not be acceptable. She is the one who has been the investigator on this case for almost two years now. She is the only one who knows where everything is, who has her finger on the pulse of the case."

"Is there any other problem she is having other than her problems in connection with visiting your client in jail?"

"Yes, of course," Adams said. "She has health problems. She has other problems that I don't care to go into detail."

After deciding to recess the case for the remaining two days of the week to get the mess sorted out, Hennigan proposed he and Adams call public defender Malcolm MacMillan to find out whether he intended to leave Painter on the case or assign a new investigator to replace her.

"It should be evident to the Court and everyone concerned that a replacement for Ms. Painter wouldn't solve the problem," Adams said, growing more distraught. "Whoever replaces her would have to redo everything."

"That would seem unlikely," Hennigan responded. "I presume that whatever she has done, as far as getting witnesses and making investigations, has been recorded in some way so that counsel must present it and is aware of it. I would be very much surprised if she was doing an investigation and keeping it all in her head without any memorandum or notes or reports to the attorney."

"No, Your Honor. It's all verbal and most of the time she doesn't even tell me. I tell her to do things. She does them. I haven't the vaguest idea how she accomplishes them and I don't care." Hennigan asked again about her performing other functions. "She does when I ask her," Adams replied.

"Well, then, you can ask her and certainly she can do that without having to go to the jail today, tomorrow, or Saturday or Sunday," Hennigan said.

With that, all the frustration, crushing workload, physical pain, months of sleeping in a motel room, and fights with the jail and prosecutors seemed to overwhelm Adams, unhinging him. "Your Honor, as far as I'm concerned, personally I am no longer going to continue in the fashion that I have. I will be present in court and I will be available from the hours of 8:00 to 5:00 for each day that the court is in session. I no longer intend to work evenings. I no longer intend to work on days that the court is not in session, nor do I intend to work weekends."

"The Court will not be in session today and tomorrow, primarily, Mr. Adams, so that you may work."

"Well, in this particular instance, today and tomorrow, yes, Your Honor, because I have agreed to it. But, after those days, Your Honor, it's 8:00 to 5:00 and if it doesn't get done, it doesn't get done."

"That, as I say, Mr. Adams, is a matter between an attorney and his conscience, his client, and sometimes the state bar. I cannot order you to put in time." Hennigan attempted to calm the distressed attorney before him. "You have done a good job on the case. I think you have worked very hard on it. And, as I say, I'm not in a position in which I can order you how to budget your time or try your case."

"Well, I'm trying to be honest with the court, Your Honor. It's my feeling that no one, attorney or otherwise, has to take this kind of abuse. And I no longer intend to do it. I have been doing it for two years, and I'm not going to continue."

"Well, I thought we had said that the abuse you have been talking about has been primarily in the relationship with the jail."

"I think there has been a lot more than that. I don't think it's appropriate to go into the record on it at this time. But I have personally endured a lot of abuse that I have never experienced before until I became involved in this case."

"All right," sighed Hennigan. Figuring he had done all the fixing he could for the moment, the judge ended the session and left with Adams to make the call to the public defender Malcolm MacMillan. MacMillan did not answer or return their calls.

UPON HER EXPULSION FROM THE JAIL, JEANNE PAINTER FLED VISTA FOR THE sanctuary of her Riverside home. Already plagued by anxiety attacks for months and now anticipating humiliation and unemployment, Painter felt her world crashing down around her. That night, she called Adams in tears and explained what had happened, adamantly maintaining her innocence, as she would unwaveringly throughout the ordeal. Whatever that booking clerk and deputy thought they saw never happened, she said. With cameras excluded from the interview rooms to preserve attorney-client confidentiality, there would be no conclusive evidence to support either side. According to Painter, the incident was nothing more than the latest attack by a bunch of jailers who had it in for her from the start. For Adams, who would stand by Painter throughout, it was another chapter in the jail's attempt to sabotage the defense of an inmate they had grown to loathe even more than when he first arrived.

It did not take long for the public humiliation of Jeanne Painter to commence. Despite the closed-court proceedings and Hennigan sealing the incident reports, multiple newspapers blasted the accusations against Painter across the pages of their Friday, April 30, editions. To Adams's dismay, the articles included details from the incident report, quotes taken directly from the April 29 trial transcripts, and comments by public defender Malcolm MacMillan and Vista jail commander DeSteunder. "She can interview him on the telephone, but we are not going to allow her to meet with him," DeSteunder was quoted as saying.

Adams marched into the courtroom on the morning of Monday, May 3, convinced he knew who had tipped off the press. "Good morning, Your Honor," said Adams, decidedly calmer than he had been the week before. "I think at the outset I would like to say that over the recess time that we have had here, I have had a little chance to reevaluate my position. And I realize now that no matter what happens that I cannot restrict myself to working from 8:00 to 5:00 and not working extra hours and so forth."

"However," Adams added, "at this point I feel that it's appropriate and necessary for me to move for a mistrial in this case as it relates to my client. There has been widespread publications relating to this particular issue in the press. A good deal of press in the Riverside area. And I have in front of me now, and I would submit to the court, a copy of the *San Diego Union*, which is the local newspaper. On the front page of the County section there is a full spread, including a photograph which depicts my client, myself, and Miss Painter."

Adams moved on to fingering the culprit he suspected was behind it all. "Further, it's my representation, based on information and belief gathered from my sources within and without the Prosecutor's Office in Riverside County and from my sources within the staff of the *Press-Enterprise*, that these articles were generated as a direct result of Mr. Hanks providing copies of the incident report. And how he got that report in the first place I'll never know, which was ordered sealed by the court. And the reporters that—or at least one reporter, who had access to that report, used it as a basis for the subsequent publications. I would suggest to the Court that Mr. Hanks is in contempt. I would ask the Court to cite him for contempt at this time. And I would urge the Court to grant the mistrial based on the publicity here."

Hennigan turned to the deputy district attorney. "Mr. Hanks, there is an accusation against you. What is your response?"

"It's untrue," Hanks said. "I provided no copies of the report to anyone, nor did I show the copies of the report to any members of the media. However," Hanks confessed, "I did discuss the contents of the report with members of the media."

"Did you receive a copy of the report from Captain DeSteunder?"

"I did. I received, I believe, a copy from—I believe it was from Captain DeSteunder. I did receive a copy of the report from the Sheriff's Department."

"I see," a very unpleased Hennigan said.

For Clayton Adams, it was unambiguous evidence that the prosecution was engaged in ongoing and improper collusion with the jail and law enforcement agencies to undermine the defense. "I don't understand why the prosecution or how the prosecution even had a copy of that report. This is not a matter of public record, as far as I know. Police reports are not a matter of public record," he said sharply. "I would indicate to Mr. Hanks and to the Court that my position is that that report was taken back to the Riverside office, copies were actually run off and posted around the office. Now whether Mr. Hanks cares to deny that it was he who disseminated that report, that's fine. But the point is, a copy or copies reached the hands of the press and it was as a direct result of Mr. Hanks's activity. And I would urge the Court—"

"Mr. Adams has a habit of making bald-faced accusations without substantiation," Hanks cut in. "No copy of that report, of my report, was ever made. My report remained in my hands at all times. Although I did discuss the contents of the report with a number of different individuals, I never had the report duplicated. To my knowledge, there was no report ever posted in the District Attorney's Office. And I'm simply unaware of any further of these allegations. I discussed the contents with both members of the District Attorney's Office and also with members of the media who called me on the phone."

The admission that he had revealed the contents of a sealed report to the press was unsettling. The implication that Hanks might be reveling in the misery of Painter and stoking the gossip mill now in full swing was at the very least unseemly. But Jay Hanks was certainly not the only source of information. True or not, the story of a beautiful thirty-three-year-old investigator jacking off a cop killer inside a jail interview room was simply too juicy to keep secret for the multitude of jailers, deputies, and courthouse staff who knew the details.

"This report does not really relate in any way to the guilt or innocence of the defendants," an exasperated Hennigan said. "And the motion for a mistrial is denied."

"And the request for a citation of contempt as to the prosecution, Your Honor?" Adams asked.

"That is also denied as of this time."

Hennigan then called in the jury. "I would like to ask you: While I have told you not to read articles relative to the [case], did any of you actually see this article? If so, would you raise your right hand?" With possible jury bias from the story at the heart of Adams's request for a mistrial, Hennigan had been hoping no hands would rise. No such luck. "Very well," he sighed. "Let's see, Mr. Moreno, Mrs. Bourguignon, Mr. Perk, and Mrs. Galanter."

Hot on the tail of a salacious jailhouse sex scandal, the papers quickly dug up more dirt on Painter from sources within the Riverside legal and law enforcement communities. Along the way, someone got their hands on the November 27, 1981, Vista jail incident report accusing Painter of bringing in photographs of herself nude "in various positions" and including the investigator's explanation that they were "for my husband." Wondering who this husband might be, a reporter managed to confirm what Painter's colleagues at the Riverside Office of the Public Defender suspected or already knew. Placed near the bottom of the April 30, 1982, article in the *Vista Press* announcing the scandal was a single paragraph containing a bombshell.

> Painter has been involved in several of the Public Defender's major cases in recent years. In 1978 she married one of her clients, John Ditsch, after he was convicted of second-degree murder. He has been serving time in state prison since then.

Two days later, on May 5, Adams again moved for a mistrial upon learning that Painter had been placed on leave by the public defender's office. "Not only has she been relieved of her duties with respect to this case, but with respect to all of her duties in the Public Defender's Office."

Again, Hennigan rejected the motion. "I am going to deny the mistrial at this time, at least until we see what the situation is next Monday."

Adams said he doubted anything would get done by Monday. "To me, this is a deliberate sort of a thing anyway. Somebody wanted this to happen, and it happened."

Before ending the discussion, Hennigan made a decision he hoped would guarantee Painter would remain on the Smith defense team, one way or another. The judge acknowledged that he did not have the authority to tell the public defender what to do concerning an employment issue, but he would refuse to enforce any ban defender Malcolm MacMillan might place on Painter regarding her ongoing participation in the case. Hennigan told Adams to instruct Painter to be in attendance when Adams returned to court the following Monday, May 10.

After speaking with Painter, Adams was in full expectation that he would once again have his lead investigator on his team and at his side. He then left for a long-planned three-day legal seminar in Georgia. But when he returned, he was surprised to encounter yet another obstacle in his battle to get his investigator back. The source of the problem was one of the last people he would have expected.

AFTER ONCE AGAIN DISPATCHING HIS DEPARTMENT'S LEAD INVESTIGATOR, Theron Bursell, to look into the allegations against Painter, public defender Malcolm MacMillan made his decision. On May 6, 1982, MacMillan sent a letter addressed to Jeanne Painter-Ditsch notifying her of "our intent to terminate you from your position as Senior Defender Investigator with the Office of the Public Defender for the County of Riverside." The letter went on to give an effective termination date of the following Thursday, May 13.

In addition to citing the Vista jail allegations against Painter, MacMillan added a second reason. "As a result of your acts on April 28, an article appeared in the *Press Enterprise* on April 30, 1982. As a result of this article and the comments and observations made by persons having to deal with this office, the effectiveness of the female investigators employed by this office has been reduced. The morale of these employees has been adversely affected." In other words, MacMillan was saying, not only have you humiliated yourself, you've humiliated every other woman in this office. It was a vicious accusation to make against a woman who had always valued and returned the support of her female colleagues.

In response to the termination notice, Jeanne Painter retained counsel to defend herself against the allegations and fight to get her job back. Her choice of attorney was a curious one.

"THIS IS THE FIRST TIME I HAVE SEEN THE LETTER ADDRESSED TO MS. PAINTER," Judge Hennigan said, reading over the termination notice. It was Monday, May 10, Clayton Adams's first day back in court after the Georgia trip. "Ms. Painter apparently is still employed by the Public Defender, until at least this Thursday," commented the judge, scanning the room for the presence of Painter, whom he expected to be back at the defense table.

Adams too was surprised to find Painter missing. "When I left on Wednesday," he said, "it was my understanding that she would be here prepared to go forward this morning. As the Court can see, she is not here and the Smith defense is once again without an investigator." Adams then addressed a situation that had been even more surprising to him. "The subsequent information that I learned is this: that during my absence, somehow Mr. Lloyd became involved in the case and apparently is representing Ms. Painter in her difficulties with the county. And he has advised her not to be here. So I have got co-counsel who is advising my investigator not to be present in the courtroom."

To find Michael Lloyd, his closest ally and friend in the trial, suddenly standing in the way of getting his investigator back was intolerable. Lloyd knew how important Painter's help was to Adams and that her absence, even for a week, would be severely damaging to a case Adams had put his heart, soul, and sanity into for two years. Not to mention the stress and added workload it would heap onto a man who was already near his breaking point. Lloyd might have seen the two roles as completely independent of each other, but Adams did not.

"And the retainer as to Mr. Lloyd happened while I was gone," Adams went on. "And I'm not sure what the status is here, but at this point, Ms. Painter is following Mr. Lloyd's advice as to whether to appear in court or not, is the way I understand it. Now, doesn't that on its face create some kind of a conflict, where the co-counsel's attorney is telling my investigator what to do?" Once again, Adams was becoming increasingly distraught. "I would ask the Court, Your Honor, how can I and my client be assured of what the situation is when she reports to Mr. Lloyd as opposed to me? We're not independent any longer. Our defense has been splintered. In fact, it's been destroyed in my view."

Adams argued for a motion for a brief suspension of the trial until it could all be sorted out. Rather than being obstinate or combative as he had in the past, Adams practically begged Hennigan. "We're floundering here, Your Honor. And it's not the fault of the defendant. It's not the fault of defense counsel. I'm just asking for what I believe is reasonable." Adams ended with a final, desperate plea. "I'm a voice in the wilderness at this point. And all I'm asking for is just a brief couple of days."

"I'm going to deny the motion to suspend the case temporarily," Hennigan announced, to the dismay of Adams. The judge then addressed Michael Lloyd regarding the conflict of interest. "Whether Ms. Painter follows the instructions of the attorney whom she has been appointed and hired to assist, or that of Mr. Lloyd, is up to her. I do suggest to Mr. Lloyd that there is a possibility of a conflict of interest in a situation like this. And I suggest that to Ms. Painter too."

"I frankly don't see the conflict," Lloyd said. "I have informed Ms. Painter of the possibility of a conflict, and we have taken great pains to make sure that this does not arise."

Adams took exception to Lloyd's statement. "I would suggest to the Court that the conflict is just very evident. I told Ms. Painter to be here this morning. He told her not to be here. She is not here. So Mr. Lloyd's remarks are just not well-founded."

With everyone having presented their arguments, Hennigan acted decisively. "Insofar as any orders by Mr. MacMillan that she not do any further work on this case, I will and do overrule Mr. MacMillan on that on the basis that regardless of her employment, she is now and has been for some time assigned to this court to assist an officer of this court."

"Your Honor, I would seek a couple minutes to at least make a phone call and I would advise her to come back into court," Lloyd requested.

"Would ten minutes be sufficient, Mr. Lloyd?"

Twenty minutes later, Clayton Adams's investigator was back in the courtroom seated beside him at the defense table, albeit with the attorney now positioned between Painter and Smith for the duration of the trial, as ordered by the Court.

On May 13, 1982, three days after returning to the courtroom, Jeanne Painter was officially terminated for misconduct by the Office of the Public Defender and began her career as a private investigator on retainer to Clayton Adams. One day later, the prosecution rested its case against George Wayne Smith, Christopher Harven, and Russell Harven after four and a half months and 120 witnesses.

After her dismissal from the defender's office, it would have been much easier for Jeanne Painter to simply walk away from the case and avoid all the waiting reporters, knowing looks, snickers, and whispers she would be subjected to around the Vista courthouse. But she had always been tough, independent, and gutsy. She also had a kid and needed the steady money. There might have been another reason Jeanne Painter was willing to endure the daily humiliations to remain on the defense team. That reason was George Wayne Smith.

TWO WEEKS LATER, JEANNE PAINTER TOOK THE STAND AS A WITNESS FOR Clayton Adams, although purely in her capacity as an investigator on the case. However, when it became clear that Adams's primary purpose was to have Painter state that, in her opinion, Jay Hanks and the prosecution had intentionally withheld evidence, Hennigan called the attorneys to the bench for a sidebar. The judge got right to the heart of the matter.

"Now, one other thing I see coming up that I wish to make certain that we do not get into, in view of the fact that her background and closeness to the case has been established, Mr. Hanks, do you intend to go into any question of the matters that came up two weeks ago?"

"To be quite frank with the Court, I hadn't decided if I at this point intended to impeach her by her—how shall I say—closeness to the defendant."

"Well," Hennigan said. "I think I am going to forbid anything which would amount to impeachment on claims that have not been proved as scurrilous matters, and so on. On the other hand, a proper method of impeachment is bias. And a legitimate relationship with a client—let me state it since we are out of the presence of the jury, because I have heard rumors." Hennigan paused, uncertain if he should even bring it up. "Does she have any marital plans with Mr. Smith?"

19

WHO THE FUCK IS JERRY COHEN?

May 17, 1982. Vista, California.

ON THE EVENING OF MAY 17, 1982, ALL THREE DEFENDANTS, THEIR ATTOR-
neys, and investigators in the trial of the Norco 3 met for what was assumed
to be a perfunctory final review and coordination of the individual defense
cases to begin the following morning. Judge Hennigan had granted the request by the defense to meet at the courthouse in what would be the first
and only time all nine would be together outside the courtroom. Before the
meeting, Jeanne Painter had an idea to lift the spirits of the three defendants.
After dining out with Clayton Adams, Painter ordered three steaks to go.
Telling the courthouse guards the containers were just leftovers, the investigator brought them into the meeting room to the delight of George, Chris,
and Russ. After five months of prosecution witnesses, they would at last have
a chance to go on the offensive. But the warm glow of unity and cooperation
was to last no longer than the steaks, never to be experienced again.

After consulting among themselves for more than seventeen months, the
last thing Clayton Adams and Alan Olson expected were any surprises. But
when Michael Lloyd finished outlining his strategy for the defense of Christopher Harven, the others in the room exchanged looks of stunned disbelief.

Clayton Adams took a deep breath and folded his hands on the table. If you really want to go ahead with this, that is your right. As long as it doesn't interfere with the defense of our clients.

Lloyd then broke the news that he had every expectation of putting Chris on the stand to testify.

That was a problem, said Adams. A big problem. Of particular concern to Adams and Olson were comments made by Chris Harven during the interrogation by detective Larry Malmberg the day of his capture. By testifying, Chris would be subject to cross-examination by Jay Hanks in which the prosecution could bring in statements implicating George and Russ that Hennigan had previously ruled inadmissible. All three attorneys had fought exhaustively to keep these statements out, but now Lloyd was going to ruin all of that just because he wanted to roll the dice on some wacky defense doomed to certain failure.

The February ruling by Hennigan had been a partial victory for both sides. In their respective interrogations, all three defendants had not only confessed in detail to their own guilt, but explicitly implicated their co-defendants. Hennigan had ruled the prosecution could introduce the contents of the interrogations, with one important limitation: Due to the hearsay and Aranda-Bruton rules, only statements made by a defendant about himself or his own actions would be allowed. But if Chris took the stand and contradicted his statements to Malmberg, Hanks would be allowed to impeach his testimony by reading the verbatim excerpts from the parts of the confession that had been previously excluded by Hennigan. Whatever his intention, Chris would be effectively testifying against the others.

The meeting quickly grew contentious as Olson and Adams made it clear they did not appreciate being bushwhacked by Michael Lloyd at the eleventh hour. From the start, Clayton Adams had been the de facto leader of the defense team both by virtue of his greater experience in felony cases and by force of personality. He had usually been first to cross-examine prosecution witnesses, defending not only the interests of George Smith, but also matters common to all three defendants. Olson and Lloyd swooped in afterward mostly to address any remaining issues peculiar to their own clients. As such, it had long been agreed that Adams would go first with the Smith defense, launching the initial and most complete attack on the prosecution's case. But what Lloyd told them that night changed everything. Adams would now have to completely adjust his opening statement and witness list to defend his client not only against Jay Hanks, but also Christopher Harven. Adams's position was simple: You want to spring this shit on us at the last minute, then you go first. Olson concurred. Michael Lloyd did not.

IN THE DARKNESS, THE THREE DEFENDANTS RODE IN THE INMATE VAN BACK to the Vista jail. You were captured in the mountains with that cop's bullet in your back, asshole, George growled in a low voice, seated one row behind Chris. How are you going to explain that?

Don't worry about it, Chris said, staring out the window. I'm not going to say a fucking word about you or Russ up there.

You won't have to; Hanks will say it for you, George said. We were never going to turn on each other, remember?

We were never going to get taken alive either, remember?

George sat back in his seat. I wonder what they're going to think about it back in the tank.

Chris turned to look at George, his face visible in the alternating light as they passed beneath the street lamps. Don't even think about putting a snitch jacket on me, he warned.

They were silent for a while.

What the fuck, Chris? Russ said in the darkness. All you've ever done is what's best for Chris.

Yeah, well . . . Chris stared out at a world of fast-food restaurants, gas stations, and car dealerships, one where he was now considered too dangerous to exist. A car came to a stop at the light beside them. Chris stared down at the young woman behind the wheel. No more of that either. Throughout the prosecution's case, Chris had a growing feeling that George, Russ, and their attorneys were taking an every-man-for-himself approach, frequently disregarding previously agreed-upon tactics. Maybe now it was time to look out for himself too. You know something, he thought. Fuck you guys.

"I TOLD MR. LLOYD I'M NOT GOING FIRST," CLAYTON ADAMS TOLD JUDGE HENNIGAN on the morning of May 18, 1982. "That's it. That's the rule. I'm not going first."

"Mr. Adams, I'll remind you, you don't necessarily make the rules in this case," Hennigan said. The judge had entered the courtroom that morning expecting Adams to begin his opening argument only to find he had yet another situation on his hands.

"For the identical reason stated by Mr. Adams, I have the same problem," Alan Olson told the judge with equal finality.

"All right. Do you agree, Mr. Lloyd, that in view of your position on this, that it would be logically better for you to open the defense case?"

"No," replied Lloyd.

"I gather everybody wants to go last. That cannot be," sighed the beleaguered judge.

The three attorneys declared that whoever went first would need at least another week to prepare for opening and witnesses in light of Lloyd's revelation. Hennigan reluctantly agreed to the continuation and then ordered the bailiff to dismiss the increasingly frustrated jury for another entire week. "As far as who goes first, in view of the attitude of all three defendants, I think the only way I could handle that is to draw lots or something and decide who will go first."

This made nobody happy. "If I should lose in the lottery, I will lose big," Alan Olson complained. "It is as simple as that."

"I would oppose any kind of chance or gambling, whatever you want to call it, in a case of this nature," Adams added.

Hennigan could find no other alternative. "All right, gentlemen," he said. "I will do what I suggested. I'm going to get three slips. And I have written One, Two, and Three on them." They each picked a slip. "All right. Who got what?"

Olson held up his slip with the number 2 written on it. "I got Three," said Lloyd. Clay Adams crumpled up the slip of paper in his hand, disgusted with the whole situation. "I defer to Mr. Lloyd," he said dryly.

"Mr. Adams, you will commence your case with your opening statement on Monday at nine o'clock and will be prepared to have your witnesses follow on that."

CLAYTON ADAMS FELT AS THOUGH HE HAD ACHIEVED THE MOST IMPORTANT part of his defense efforts on the part of George Smith during cross-examination of the prosecution witnesses. Through his own witnesses, he set his sights on having Smith's mountainside confession to detective Ross Dvorak thrown out. "We intend to produce evidence that the taped interrogation of George Smith was not only conducted under the most cruel kind of circumstances, but that there is definite evidence of tampering, tampering to the extent that certain deletions have been made."

There was no question the breaks in the tape by Dvorak were unusual and at seemingly random intervals. An acoustic expert named George Papcun testified that after analyzing the tapes there was clear evidence of tampering, which Adams contended were deletions by police of all the time George had said he no longer wanted to speak with Dvorak and had requested an attorney. Additionally, Adams called in doctors and produced medical reports showing that Smith had lost so much blood that he was not competent to waive his Miranda rights.

With his military background and desperate need to prove the fatal bullet did not come from Russell Harven's gun, Alan Olson had become the ballistics and criminology expert of the group. After all his haranguing of prosecution witnesses, it was the testimony of one of his own that allowed the least experienced of the defense attorneys to score what might have been the single greatest success among them. It was Olson's ballistics expert Donald Dunn, with his comparison of lands and grooves in bullets to specific gun barrels, who convincingly ruled out Russ Harven as the killer. Never mind that Dunn all but destroyed the friendly fire defense in the process by also ruling out D. J. McCarty's weapon. For Olson, it was far more important to keep the fatal bullet out of his client's gun than it was to put it into McCarty's.

After fifteen witnesses, Olson rested his case. It had taken Adams and

Olson a total of three full weeks to present their cases. As they left the court-room on Friday, June 4, there was nothing left for them to do but wait and see what surprises Michael Lloyd had up his sleeve.

ON THE FOLLOWING MONDAY, LLOYD DROPPED THE SAME BOMBSHELL ON THE jury that he had on the other two defense teams a few weeks before. "What I will prove to you is that Christopher Harven didn't have any guns that day in any of those crimes. He did not have any guns with him, and he did not participate in the crimes as they are alleged. What we'll show to you in our defense is that the idea for the robbery, the conception of the robbery came from Billy and Manny Delgado. They enlisted the help of one of their friends by the name of Jerry. His last name is Cohen, *C-O-H-E-N*."

The jurors stared back at Lloyd with knitted brows and looks of general confusion. There were hushed whispers among the spectators. Six months into this damn trial and suddenly . . . this? Who the fuck is Jerry Cohen?

As the jury looked on in bewilderment, Lloyd outlined how poor judg-ment, bad luck, and exploitation at the hands of a mercurial figure named Jerry Cohen had led his client to be charged with forty-six felony counts he did not commit. According to Lloyd, Chris had backed out of the heist at the last second and was not even there for the robbery of the bank or the shootout at the intersection of Fourth and Hamner. Yes, Chris had driven the stolen truck all the way up to the washout and then fled into the mountains, but only after being picked up while walking on Hamner north of the bank and forced to by Manny Delgado and Cohen.

Perhaps the most fascinating character in the trial of the Norco 3 was a man who did not even exist. As presented, Jerry Cohen was a composite of George Smith in attitude and Chris Harven in actions. It was Jerry Cohen who had planned and led the robbery, who was the dominant personality of the group, the one who pressured the others to follow through with the scheme when they had wanted to back out. That guy inside the bank vault, outside the bank shooting a Heckler .223 at Glyn Bolasky, stealing a truck at gunpoint, sticking a .45-caliber revolver out the driver's window to fire bullets into the patrol units of Rolf Parkes and Herman Brown? Yeah, that was Jerry Cohen, too. Jerry Cohen had also been the third guy along with Manny and Billy who kidnapped Gary Hakala and stole the van. So where was Jerry Cohen now? Well, just like Gary Hakala said four months ago: "I can tell you that right now that I believe that there is still a man out there."

Through cross-examination of prosecution witnesses, Lloyd had already established no less than five witnesses having heard the robbers call out the name "Jerry" inside the bank. Glyn Bolasky testified to seeing a man in a khaki poncho much like those worn by the bank robbers running north on Hamner less than a minute before the 211 tone went out. And then there had been Gary Hakala's definitive statements that none of the three defendants in the courtroom had been involved in stealing his van and that neither of the getaway cars parked at the Little League field at Detroit and Hamner had been the car in the parking lot at the Brea Mall. Over the next two weeks, Lloyd called an additional fifteen witnesses who either saw people they thought were suspects fleeing in various places along the pursuit route or testified to seeing five suspects in the yellow truck at points along the pursuit.

NEAR THE END OF HIS WITNESS LIST, LLOYD CALLED JUANITA DELGADO BACK to the stand a second time. Still just barely over twenty years old, Delgado was somber and uncomfortable as she briefly testified that, no, she did not remember meeting, or her husband Manny ever mentioning, anyone named Chris Harven. Excused from the stand, Juanita Delgado lingered for a moment, her eyes searching the three men responsible for leaving her a widow and her children fatherless.

"Could I ask a question?" she said softly. "Where is Chris? Who is Chris?"

"The gentleman who is seated right next to me is Chris," Michael Lloyd said.

"Oh, okay," she said, studying Harven. "I just wanted to know."

WITH ALL THEIR WITNESSES CALLED, LLOYD AND HARVEN WERE NOW FACED with the task of weaving a tale which would somehow stitch together all the threads of corroborating details about Jerry Cohen while also explaining away a vast amount of glaringly contradictory evidence, most of it coming from Chris himself.

"Please state your name for the record."

"Christopher Gregory Harven."

Chris Harven took his seat on the witness stand dressed in the dark suit, white shirt, and blue tie he had worn most days of the trial. He was clean-shaven except for a neatly trimmed mustache, hair cut stylishly short and parted down the middle.

"Do you know of a person by the name of Jerry Cohen?" Michael Lloyd began, after walking his client through a brief set of autobiographical questions.

"Yes, I do," Chris answered, speaking softly in his deep, baritone voice.

"When did you first meet him?"

"I must have met him in late February or early March of 1980."

"Who introduced him to you?"

"Manny."

Chris said Cohen was not a friend, just some dude who would come by occasionally when Manny and Billy were at the Mira Loma house.

"Could you give us a description of what Jerry Cohen looks like?"

"Roughly, five foot ten, a hundred and sixty-five to a hundred and seventy pounds. Brown hair, much redder than mine, sort of what you would call the Prince Valiant style. Parted in the middle, a mustache and a goatee that I believe ran along the edge down to here."

"And the complexion of skin, was it about the same complexion, or was Jerry darker or lighter?"

"Jerry always had a good tan."

Chris described Cohen as a Caucasian who often affected Chicano ways.

"What kind of car did Jerry Cohen drive?"

"A 1963 blue lowrider. Very metallic blue in color. Lowered. It was a nice car."

"Did you know the make of the car?"

"Chevrolet."

Not coincidentally, that was precisely the vehicle Gary Hakala had described seeing in the Brea Mall, right down to the color, make, style, and year.

Originally, Harven had just thought of Jerry Cohen as odd, but soon developed a dimmer view of the man. "He had radical ideas that didn't correspond with the views with the rest of us, especially myself. He had a tendency to think that guns were power. He had a tendency to think that, you know, that there was different ways of making a buck. You know, he just had all sorts of ideas that were not consistent with my train of thought."

Chris tried to explain his motivation for becoming involved in the robbery plan to begin with, elevating it to a higher calling than simple greed.

"Was there any particular interest that you had in common?"

"Yes. All of us were interested in survivalism."

"What purpose did you have as to being a survivalist?"

"Well, I feared there would be, and I still do, that there is going to be tremendous social upheaval around the world, wars, famines, droughts, economic collapse, so on and so forth. And I feel that I want to be among the ones that survive when it's complete and ran its course."

Harven explained that his failure to back out earlier than the morning of the robbery was also noble in nature. "Other people were recruited into this operation that were dependent on me. There was the old 'am I going to let everybody down?' thing, so I just, you know, went along." He said he had tried his best to talk the others out of going through with the heist. "I had told them this is completely out of our department; that one thing was going to lead to another; that this whole thing is rotten; it is not going to work. And that, you know, I tried to persuade them all to give it up." Failing at this, Harven felt he owed it to the others to keep his word and participate. "I couldn't let the people down that were in on this." On the day of the robbery, Chris said he brought all his guns and ammo along as planned because he promised he would.

Upon meeting up with Manny, Billy, and Jerry Cohen in the parking lot of the Little League field later that day, Harven professed shock at discovering there had been a kidnapping. "'What's this?' I go, 'This is just what I said, one thing is going to lead to another. I mean, this wasn't agreed upon; that guy wasn't agreed upon.' I go, 'It's gotten completely out of hand.'" Again,

Chris argued not to go forward. "And then I turned to them and I said, 'But it's not too late. We can just leave this guy and leave this van and we'll get in our cars and forget it.'"

Chris had convinced everyone to give up on the job except Jerry Cohen. "Jerry would go, 'You're just screwing up the operation. Every time we get together you always screw up the operation. You're always talking this way or that way.' And why don't I just shut up."

Harven said he finally gave up. "It got to the point where I wasn't making my point, nobody was going along with me and I told them that, 'Hey, I'm getting out,' you know, and they're telling me, 'Go ahead and get out, we want you to get out.'"

From there, Chris said he was unceremoniously booted out of the van at the Kmart parking lot, but not before Jerry Cohen forced him to leave his guns behind. "I had it moved over by the door, and at the point where I got out, Jerry put his foot on it and said, 'Hey, we are short of rifles anyway; you are screwing up the operation all the way around. You got your skin; you got what you want, just get out of here.'"

"Okay. Did he say anything else to you at that time?" Lloyd asked, leading Chris to an explanation for a critical flaw in their sixth-man defense: Why had Harven never mentioned Jerry Cohen before now—not to detective Larry Malmberg, not to investigators, not even at the preliminary hearing?

"He said if I ever open my mouth about his involvement, that he knew where my girlfriend lived; he knew where my son lived; he knew where my mom lives, and he knew where to find me." In other words, Christopher Harven was not only willing to rob a bank to save his loved ones from the coming Apocalypse, he was also willing to go to the gas chamber to save them from Jerry Cohen.

Unarmed and left behind, Chris wandered around Kmart for a while and then set off on a three-mile hike straight up Hamner Avenue to get to his Z/28 at the Little League field. On the way, he passed directly in front of the Security Pacific Bank. All was quiet. "Just a normal Friday," Harven said. "I was thinking they didn't go through with it." Moments later, Harven said he heard gunfire erupting from the area of the bank just 250 feet to the south. "I thought, 'God. Here it is. Something went wrong. Something happened.'"

Harven promptly hoofed it north on Hamner until, minutes later, a yellow truck he had never seen before pulled up to the curb beside him. The passenger door swung open and Manny Delgado stepped out holding Chris's HK93. "I heard my name. I looked over to the side and Manny had the door open, and Jerry was waving to me. They said that everything went haywire. You know, 'Get in, we will give you a ride. We shook the cops.'" Chris decided to accept the ride to his car in the interest of getting the hell away from the bank. "What were you thinking at the time you got in the truck?" Lloyd asked. "I was very, very, very confused and very, very scared."

Then began the wild ride through Wineville and Mira Loma with Jerry Cohen behind the wheel, Manny sitting out the window shooting at anything that moved, and Chris Harven sandwiched helplessly between the two.

"I believe, just after Sixth Street, that I heard some fire coming from Manny. And I turned over and looked at him, and looked in the direction his body was pointing, and saw a police unit over on the opposite side of the street."

"What did you do at that time?"

"Grabbed him and hauled him back inside. I was asking, what the heck he was doing? He said, 'Hey, they killed my brother. You know, we're all going to get killed. They are going to'—You know, he started rambling on and on in that sort of demeanor."

"Was he angry to you?"

"I think he was angry at the world in general. Me in particular."

"What was he angry at you about?"

"He said later on in this thing, he said that if I wouldn't have got out when I did, his brother would still be alive."

It was during the attempt to carjack Robert LeMay's van at the Can Do Market that the elusive Jerry Cohen finally bailed out of the truck and vanished into broad daylight, never to be seen again. Asked why he did not take the opportunity to do the same, Chris said, "Well, there was police in the area, and I didn't particularly want to hang around for questioning, so I drove and left."

From that point on, blame-Manny-for-everything became Harven's primary defense. Chris said that all the times he slowed the truck on Interstate 15 and in Lytle Creek was not to ambush police, but an effort to extract himself from the situation. "What the hell are you doing?" Manny said to him a one point. "I'm pulling the truck over before somebody gets killed. I'm getting out here." Manny responded with a threat: "Well, if somebody gets killed, it's going to be you, if you chicken out on us again."

Testifying to his actions at the ambush site, Harven did not have all that much to lie about, considering he had not been accused of engaging in the firefight that killed Jim Evans. "You know, I opened the door. I said, 'This is it. This is where I get out. I can't go no further. I'm leaving.'" Chris said that after taking the bullet in the back, his first thought was that it must have been Manny who shot him. "He felt I was responsible for the death of his brother. I wasn't helping them with anything at the end."

With the explanation for his actions on May 9, 1980, complete, Chris tried to explain why he had confessed to things he had not done in the interrogation by detective Larry Malmberg. He told them he feared his whole family would be killed if he didn't "ride the beef" for Jerry Cohen. "I just substituted my name for Jerry's" to avoid ratting out Cohen, he said.

FROM THE MOMENT CHRIS HARVEN TOOK THE STAND TO MOUNT HIS SIXTH-man defense, the scene at the Vista County Courthouse devolved into a circus. Veteran court watchers knew to be observant of courtroom etiquette, but now their ranks were swollen with a rabble of amateur gawkers. "The Court will notice that the courtroom is, spectator-wise, filled. In fact, it is over capacity. I think there are people we can't even get in," Clayton Adams said to Hennigan at the first break in Harven's testimony. Always finicky when it came to courtroom distractions, Adams complained about one man in particular "who is commenting on the questions being propounded to the witness, Christopher Harven, the expected answers, and then giving his opinion as to the credibility of the witness, and guffawing, and things of that nature." Hennigan admonished the spectators not to comment inside the courtroom or outside in the presence of the jurors.

Clayton Adams received a sharp reprimand from Hennigan when he requested ten minutes to run back to his hotel to retrieve the transcript of Chris Harven's interrogation, which he had not anticipated needing that day. "I find it hard to believe that a competent lawyer would not be prepared to believe that Mr. Lloyd would be asking his client about the statement made," Hennigan scolded.

Adams, taken aback and feeling undeserving of such harsh words, shot back at the judge. "Let me make it clear on the record, I guess I am incompetent then. For the record, I am incompetent. I did not anticipate this. My client does have incompetent counsel. I request ten minutes to go home." An irritated Hennigan granted the request and Adams hustled off to retrieve the document.

Michael Lloyd's direct questioning of Christopher Harven had taken a day and a half. During the break prior to the start of cross-examination, one of the yahoos from the spectator gallery approached Michael Lloyd in the corridor. "I was believing this Jerry Cohen business for a few days," he said. "But last night I started thinking a nice Jewish boy would never get himself in something like this." Lloyd was unfazed. "Well, he could be Irish, you know," he told the man.

On cross-examination, it did not take Jay Hanks long to get into reading the unabridged transcript of Harven's interview with Detective Malmberg.

During direct, Lloyd had asked Chris to explain how he was able to provide so much detail to Malmberg about activity that went on in places he now claimed he had never been. Two reasons, Chris said. Russell Harven had filled him in on a lot of the details while sitting around the fire in Coldwater Canyon. Everything else, Chris said he filled in based on the roles each were supposed to play inside the bank according to the plan.

Hanks read from the transcript, each time asking Chris if the statement was something he had observed firsthand, had been told by Russell, or was speculating on based on the plan.

"Do you recall being asked: 'You went to the cage or the vault?' And your answer: 'To the vault.' Was that based on something you had been told or on speculation?"

"That was based on my understanding of where Jerry went."

"Do you recall being asked: 'Who goes where armed with what and who does what?' Do you remember saying: 'Well, hum, Russ went to the other door'?"

"Yes."

"Was that based on your personal observation or something you were told or speculating about?"

"It was something I was both told and also per the plan before."

With the questions and answers right in front of him in black and white and also on the tape recording of the interrogation Hanks would later play for the jury, all Chris could do was confirm his statements and sit there looking like the biggest fucking liar in the world while Jay Hanks shredded his Jerry Cohen story line by line, paragraph by paragraph.

Hanks used the interrogation transcript to implicate George Smith as the mastermind behind the crime, the role Chris had tried to assign to Jerry Cohen during direct testimony.

George was the one who ran the whole show, told us what we were going to do, what bank we were going . . . See, that's George's bank, right? Cased it out, you know, when he was in there doing his bank work, you know.

George said he wasn't going to be taken prisoner, you know. He armed up and told us all to do it, too.

When George decided we were going to go in there, he said he was going to go heavily armed; he said he liked to have some grenades, you know; he said that in the service they made grenades with Coke cans and all that, so him being my roommate, George and I manufactured them together. I helped him.

Hanks was also able to get Chris to implicate George further through direct questioning:

"Mr. Harven, did you ever tell the police that it was the result of your constantly being pressured by George Smith day after day that resulted in your doing it?"

"Yes, I did."

"Did you ever say, 'I had a lot of peer pressure, I guess, so I went along with it. So we went down and hit Security Pacific'?"

"Yes, I said that."

The worst damage to his co-defendants came from several statements Hanks managed to elicit from Chris directly during questioning over the whereabouts and actions of Russ and George during the pursuit and shootout with Evans.

"You have told us that Manny and Jerry and you were in the cab. Where were Russell and George?"

"Russ was in the back attending to George."

"George was lying down in the back?"

"He was in a severe state of shock. He was bleeding to death."

"Was Russell lying down also?"

"No. He was leaning over George."

"Did you ever see him with a weapon?"

"When I was driving, occasionally I would be looking in my mirror or looking back through the glass, and I saw that he had one in his hand."

"Did you hear the gunfire coming from the back of the truck?"

"Yes."

It got worse for George and Russ when Hanks used the transcript to grill Chris over the details of what happened in the firefight that killed Jim Evans.

"Do you recall being asked: 'So you didn't fire at that point?' Your response: 'No. I was just bookin' it up the road.' Question: 'So Manny, Russ, and George were firing then?' Your response: 'Well, I know … they probably all fired. Like I said, I can't say that I personally saw them all. I know that we fired. Not we meaning me, but I know …' Did you make that statement to the police?"

"Yes."

"Who is the 'all'?"

"Members of the group other than me."

To the legally untrained, even the veteran court watchers in the spectator gallery, what Chris Harven had just done to the cases of his co-defendants might have gone unnoticed amid the spectacle of his own self-immolation. But every legal professional in the room and the defendants understood completely. From the start, the defense attorneys recognized their primary objective was to keep their clients out of the gas chamber. Key to that, in this trial and certainly on future appeal, was to have their respective client's confession ruled inadmissible. All three could make a reasonably strong case on grounds of duress and diminished capacity: George from blood loss, Chris from having been shot in the back, and Russ for having gone almost twenty-four hours without food or insulin. But Chris had effectively become the prosecution's star witness. Even if Russ and George's confessions were tossed out, Chris's testimony and confession transcript would still help prove their participation in virtually every crime they were charged with, especially the killing of Evans. In short, it was possible that Chris Harven might have just cost his brother and best friend their lives.

The significance of Harven's testimony had certainly not escaped reporter Bob LaBarre. "Defendant Implicates Brother, 'Best Buddy'" ran the headline to LaBarre's story in the *Press-Enterprise* the next morning. LaBarre wrote that Chris had "placed his brother, Russell A. Harven, 28, and friend George W. Smith, 29, at the San Gabriel Mountain scene where Sheriff's Deputy James B. Evans was killed more than two years ago. Moreover, he placed his brother and Smith in the back of a stolen pickup from which he had heard firing during a chase into the mountains."

In an antechamber just off the courtroom, George Smith confronted Chris and Lloyd, demanding that Harven end his testimony immediately before Jay Hanks inflicted any further damage when resuming cross-examination the next day. They refused. Jeanne Painter told George it was too late anyhow. For Chris to plead the fifth now would make it even worse.

Outside the courthouse, Clayton Adams was livid as he spoke to reporters. "There's no question he is trying to dump responsibility on others. He doesn't care if it's Jerry Cohen, his brother, or his best buddy. He's a coward."

When asked how Russell reacted to his older brother placing him at the murder scene with a gun in his hand, Alan Olson replied, "Not very well."

Michael Lloyd countered by claiming it was really Russell and George who were screwing over Chris by continuing to keep Jerry Cohen's participation a secret. "I don't think there's much love lost between them after his brother let him sit for two years without coming forward. Same is true of his best buddy."

DAY TWO ENDED WITH YET ANOTHER SURPRISE. BEFORE LEAVING THE COURT-room, Clayton Adams had something to tell Judge Hennigan. "I would also bring to the Court's attention that it is my understanding, or at least the information that I have at this time, that my investigator has been cleared of any wrongdoing with regard to the jail—the false jail report that I brought to the Court's attention some weeks ago. It has been determined that that report was, in fact, false and unfounded. She is being reinstated in her position at the Public Defender's Office. For that reason, I would request that the Court permit me now to rearrange my seating arrangement here back to the original positions because there is no longer any reason for it and never was to begin with."

"I see no reason why not," Hennigan said. "Let's hope there are no further problems or accusations."

Acting as Painter's attorney, Lloyd told reporters that the position of the table in the interview room in relation to the observation booth proved the jailers' allegations to be unfounded. "It's not that the charges can't be substantiated. They are false." Painter told reporters that she had been constantly harassed during her visits with Smith, including being intentionally tripped and, in one incident, thrown up against a wall. "People don't realize the things that have happened to me in there."

"There's no doubt in my mind about what I saw," deputy Larry Van Dusen commented in the article. "I knew what they were doing." Commander Robert DeSteunder announced that his ban on face-to-face visits between Smith and Painter would continue. If they wanted to meet, the two could do so over a telephone with a sheet of plexiglass between them.

WHEN COURT RECONVENED THE NEXT DAY, ALAN OLSON HAD SOMETHING HE wanted to address with Judge Hennigan prior to admitting the jury to the courtroom. "I would object to proceeding today in light of the condition of Mr. Christopher Harven and the obvious implications to the negative for my client," Olson told the judge.

"The record should reflect what counsel is speaking of," Jay Hanks said.

"I'm talking about the condition of Christopher Harven, who has an obviously damaged face," Olson said.

"In order to make it clear," Hanks added, "it appears that the defendant, Christopher Harven, has suffered an injury to his face. It appears that the left side of his face is slightly swollen and also red and there are abrasions on the left side of his face across his forehead."

"Your Honor," Olson continued, "because of the obvious implications that may befall my client quite unfairly, I would ask for some kind of an admonition to the jury that my client had nothing to do with these injuries, which are quite obvious. They are all over his face."

"I think the best way would be to have Mr. Lloyd take that up in questioning. Mr. Harven can indicate at that time that no co-defendant had anything to do with it."

"I'm not going to indicate that, Your Honor," Lloyd responded. "I have no evidence that no co-defendant had anything to do with it."

"Do you have any evidence that they did?"

"No. I have no claim whatsoever."

"Well, if you don't ask him, I will," said Hennigan. "Mr. Christopher Harven, to the best of your knowledge, did the co-defendants have anything to do at all with the marks which appear on your face?"

"None whatsoever, Your Honor," Chris answered.

What actually happened to Chris Harven's face would remain a matter of intense speculation. What was not under dispute was that within three and a half hours after returning to the jail, somebody beat the shit out of Christopher Harven. The consensus among court watchers was that George Smith had done it. Others thought Chris had asked another inmate to rough him up to support his Jerry Cohen defense. Harven would later say it was done by other inmates when George put the snitch jacket on him after Harven refused to discontinue his testimony. But, under questioning on re-direct, it was clear who Michael Lloyd wanted the jury to believe was behind it.

"Chris, how did you get those marks on your face?" Lloyd asked.

"These marks?"

"Yeah."

"Not keeping quiet."

Jay Hanks was immediately out of his seat objecting and requesting a sidebar at the bench.

"What is the relevance of the present marks that he has?" Hennigan asked Lloyd out of earshot of the jury.

"His answer will be that they are in retaliation for testimony he has had here at trial involving Jerry Cohen."

"This is outrageous," Hanks said. "Surely counsel doesn't think that that is admissible, that this man is going to testify that somebody else attacked him because he identified this person who is supposed to exist named Jerry Cohen?"

Despite Hanks's protests, Hennigan ruled that he would allow the questioning.

"How did you get the marks on your face?" Lloyd resumed.

"I was beaten."

"And do you know the reason why you were beaten?"

"Yes. They told me to shut up."

"Well who were they?"

"Inmates."

"The inmates, did they say anything in reference to your being hit?"

"Yes. They told me to shut up and I had better stay off the stand."

For the remainder of the guilt phase of the trial, Chris was housed in the jail infirmary and a protective cell, away from other inmates, including George Smith.

HAVING READ THE ENTIRE INTERROGATION TRANSCRIPT INTO THE RECORD, Hanks spent the remainder of his cross-examination mocking the plausibility of Harven's story. Hanks ridiculed the notion that as the van carrying his brother and best friend sped off to commit a crime Chris felt was doomed to certain failure, Chris's first thought was to go into Kmart to beat the heat.

Hanks used Harven's account to portray him as callous and self-serving.

"Now when, after hearing the gunfire and seeing this strange truck appear, you got into that truck not knowing where your best friend and your brother were at, is that correct?"

"I didn't know at the time that my brother and George were in there; that wasn't really a thought on my mind."

"You were approximately 259 yards away from the area where possibly your best friend and your brother had been engaged in a gunfight during a bank robbery, correct? Did it occur to you to go back those 259 yards to the intersection of Fourth Street to check and see whether or not your brother was wounded or killed at the intersection?"

"I wasn't going to go anywhere near the intersection."

"Did it occur to you to go back to that intersection to see whether or not your closest and dearest friend, George Smith, was wounded or killed at that intersection?"

"Not at all."

Hanks questioned Chris about his and George's motivation for arming up so heavily for the robbery attempt. "The catastrophe that this country is going to go through in two or three years, that was going to result in the collapse of social order; isn't that correct?"

"Yes."

"You and George believed it was imminently necessary that you two get out of Southern California, didn't you? Did you believe that your survivability would be increased if you could get to a mountainous area someplace in Utah or Colorado?"

"Yes, I did."

"Mr. Harven, you felt that if you had to stay in Southern California another two or three years with the impending social collapse, that you wouldn't survive, didn't you?"

"That thought had crossed my mind."

"Isn't it true, Mr. Harven, that your opinion was you were all young men and you weren't afraid to die? Isn't it true that you took these thousands of rounds of ammunition and these bombs, gas masks, all these weapons, because you were convinced that you would die anyway if you had to stay in Southern California?"

"That's incorrect."

"Mr. Harven, didn't you believe, and weren't you convinced, that it was necessary for you to succeed or die in this attempt?"

"No."

IN ALL, CHRIS WAS ON THE STAND FOR FOUR DAYS, THREE OF WHICH WERE under cross-examination by Hanks, Olson, and Adams. At the conclusion of the testimony, Jay Hanks commented derisively to the press that the whole Jerry Cohen story could be summed up by the two-letter identifier the court had assigned to one of the last pieces of evidence submitted in the case: "Chris Harven's—BS."

On June 30, 1982, the prosecution and defense rested their cases after six solid months and more than two hundred witnesses and nine hundred exhibits. Despite the two sides' frequent displays of personal dislike for each other throughout the trial, most of it had been out of presence of the jury, restrained by the rules of courtroom decorum, and cut short by the authority of Hennigan. But with the following day's closing arguments, the rules would be loosened and the gloves allowed to come off. In statements intended to address the guilt or innocence of the defendants, both the prosecution and defense attorneys would instead direct their harshest accusations at each other in a display of vitriol rarely seen inside a courtroom.

20

STOCKHOLM SYNDROME

July 1, 1982. Vista, California.

THE JURORS AND SPECTATORS WHO ENTERED THE COURTROOM OF THE SAN Diego Superior Court were greeted with quite a spectacle. Ceremoniously laid out across the courtroom floor was the entire arsenal of weapons used by the Norco bank robbers on May 9, 1980. All the long guns and handguns, ammunition, defused grenades, launchers, bomb-making equipment, knives, gas masks, canteens, walkie-talkies, a machete, and what had come to be their symbol of excess: George's samurai sword. The collection took up so much space that its creator, Jay Hanks, had to step over the items as he roamed the courtroom floor delivering the first of two closing statements.

Hanks began with the first comprehensive narrative of motive for the crime the jury had heard.

"These two men being religious, believing themselves capable of making interpretations of biblical prophecy, and being survivalists. The combination of these two things resulted in those forty-five crimes. They had interpreted biblical prophecy and decided that the world that we know, our civilization, was going to suffer a tremendous upheaval. That upheaval was going to occur by, at the outside, 1985.

"There would be . . . that kind of complete social breakdown, a situation where people would be desperate for food, shelter, where individuals would be set upon one another because of their need for food and their need for clothing.

"This, however, was not the end of their planning. You see, to live in Southern California during the breakdown was almost certain disaster. If you lived here these roving hordes of individuals who were seeking to take away from you your means of existence, and without any civil authorities to stop them, you would be at their whim.

"The best place to survive would be on a mountaintop in a sparsely pop-ulated area, go to Utah, Colorado, Wyoming, buy yourself a little place out away from everyone, sufficiently barricaded so you could defend it."

Hanks then connected the beliefs with the crime.

"They arrived at the conclusion that it was all or nothing at all. They were going to get the money, and they were going to acquire the means to leave Southern California and find themselves their safe haven to protect themselves from this cataclysm, or they were going to die trying."

Hanks could have easily argued that all the mishmash of religiosity and doomsday scenarios was nothing but a smokescreen to cover up a far less no-ble motivation. But instead, he appeared to attribute their decision to com-mit the crime in the manner they did to honestly held religious beliefs. "This type of cataclysmic behavior was coming about," he told the jury, "and these men believed it. This was a heartfelt belief." It was a characterization the de-fense would be happy to embrace when the time came.

Hanks then turned his focus to the exhibition of weaponry on the floor. "As a result of this, they acquired the materials, their survivalist materials, and they acquired a vast array of them," he said. "They equipped themselves admirably for killing human beings."

He stepped cautiously through the display and picked up the most inex-plicable item of all. "Why would he take a samurai sword which was chromed and a decorative device and sharpen the edge of it, ruining the chrome dec-orative value but making it a lethal weapon? Why? As a last resort, George Smith was going to pull out his samurai sword, if necessary, and continue fighting. Do you remember George's motto, 'We'll not be taken prisoner'?

"You'll notice that I have got here the pictures of the five men who perpetrated these crimes," Hanks went on, indicating easels supporting the three-foot-high photos of George, Chris, and Russ taken soon after capture. Along with them now were similarly sized photos of a mugshot of Manny Delgado from his minor arrest in Orange County and an autopsy photo of Billy Delgado. Before each photo were the weapons with which each had been armed.

"Russell Harven, the weapon he had," Hanks said, standing before the photo of Russ. He moved to the second photo. "George Smith, his weapons. Christopher Harven, his weapons. Manuel Delgado and his weapons. With one exception. Christopher Harven's rifle was never recovered. Belisario Delgado and his weapons." Hanks held up Jim Evans's .38 revolver. "Those four men armed with all of this against James Evans."

Hanks did not miss an opportunity to take a jab at Chris Harven while he was over there. "Okay. Now, over here, ladies and gentlemen, is the picture of Jerry Cohen," he said, framing his hands over an empty space beside the final photo. "And these are his weapons," he added, indicating the empty floor in front of the nonexistent photo. "Chris Harven is a liar."

"Make no mistake, ladies and gentlemen, they were prepared for a war," Hanks said, wrapping up his initial statement. "And they were engaging in one. It was a one-sided war. It was a war that they had prepared for and no one else. It was a war on their terms. They initiated the place. They selected the arms. But it was a war nonetheless. For that and because of that, I ask you to do what the law and justice demands."

IN HIS CLOSING ARGUMENT, CLAYTON ADAMS REITERATED HIS DEFENSE THAT George Smith was "legally unconscious" after being shot in front of the bank and could not have participated in any of the crimes from that point on, the empty .308 shell casings littering the entire pursuit route notwithstanding. With many of the normal courtroom constraints gone, Adams had saved his energy for an all-out attack on the prosecution and "their agents, the police."

Adams said he and Smith had not contested the offenses for which he was guilty. "The Smith defense has always worked to expose the truth and the whole truth as to any given issue in this case." However, he said, "the prosecution's case is based primarily on fabrication, falsehood, and collusion." Adams accused Hanks of intentionally defying discovery orders, adding that even the jailhouse accusations against Jeanne Painter were part of the strategy to hobble his defense. Adams said the misconduct went far beyond foot-dragging and bad faith "even to the extent of actual theft of evidence by a prosecutor," in this case a bullet from D. J. McCarty's gun. "This was a very important piece of evidence, the only surviving bullet that Deputy McCarty had in his weapon up on Lytle Creek on May 9, 1980. I had found it. Mr. Hanks went over and stole it, took it apart, just totally destroyed any hope that I might have had for accomplishing that which I had hoped to do," Adams said, his blood boiling. "Now, I don't know about you folks, but I expect a heck of a lot more integrity from a person who claims to be a prosecutor and a representative of the People of the State of California.

"Simply put, in my opinion," Adams concluded his attack on Hanks, "I think we have demonstrated that the prosecution will stop at nothing to get a conviction in this case, including lying, cheating, and stealing."

Adams also had harsh words for the cops, especially those involved in the firefight that killed Evans, and for one officer in particular. "We have amply and routinely exposed bias, favoritism, motives, and willingness to actually testify falsely by prosecution witnesses in this case. I suggest that Officer McCarty's testimony is so demonstrably false, it should be disregarded. I suggest to you that every officer's testimony up there is false and should be disregarded."

Adams let it be known that his contempt was not limited to the other side, striking back at Chris Harven's claim that George had pressured him into participating. "When you take a witness like Christopher Harven who is up there doing everything he could to relieve himself of liability, I think it's an exhibition of his own belief that he can manipulate people and get them to believe what he wants them to believe, get them to do what he wants them to do. I suggest to you that if anybody planned this particular robbery, it was Christopher Harven.

"For those reasons and the other reasons that I have stated," Adams concluded, "I think that in all fairness, and in order for you to do that which is right in this case, that you should convict only of those charges that are undisputed, admitted by the defendant, and acquit him of all other charges."

ROBBED OF HIS ABILITY TO PIN RUSSELL HARVEN'S INVOLVEMENT IN THE crime on his older brother, Alan Olson's summation was a combination of the diabetes defense and a portrayal of his client as the bungling doofus, so hapless he could not possibly have committed the crimes for which he was charged. "He did an incompetent job," Olson said of Russ's responsibility to guard the door inside the bank. "All he had to do was see to it that no one left or came in. A simple job. But people came up to the door, came in, and left. He, in fact, had his back to the door." As he often did in the courtroom, Russ nodded off during his attorney's attempt to save his life.

Olson characterized the police as "a brotherhood of Barney Fifes," comparing them to the famously inept deputy from the popular television comedy series *The Andy Griffith Show*. He referred to the RSO investigator as "the rotund Officer Burden," and gun store owners as "merchants of violence." He accused Glyn Bolasky of starting all of the shooting at the bank and blamed the death of Evans on "grossly unprofessional" conduct by the officers in the Lytle Creek pursuit. "These country policemen did not have the necessary training. Police did all the killing. The defendants did all the fleeing."

Olson characterized the prosecution's case as one of quantity over quality. "I would refer to Mr. Hanks's witnesses as similar to snowflakes: As many as you can count, no two exactly the same." Olson closed by lamenting that he would now have to stand by helplessly and watch Hanks lie his ass off with no opportunity at rebuttal. "Now, I will sit down and begin to sizzle. God help you all in your deliberations."

MICHAEL LLOYD CLOSED HIS DEFENSE OF CHRISTOPHER HARVEN WITH A RE-telling of the Jerry Cohen story despite Jay Hanks's dismemberment of the tale. Lloyd attempted to give the story a coherent flow, but the contradictions were still glaring.

"Jerry Cohen, a person who now, even as I speak, secrets himself away, a person sits here on trial for Jerry Cohen's crimes." Lloyd noted his own attempts to find the elusive Cohen. "I would like nothing better than to bring in Jerry Cohen, but it didn't happen."

Lloyd continued to contend that the jailhouse beating Harven took during his testimony was proof that Chris's fear of retaliation by Cohen was very real. "I'm sure the district attorney is going to come up and say that is a hoax. You look at me and you look at Christopher Harven, and you remember when he had that beaten and bloody face and you tell me it is a hoax. That is real. It is here. It's not a hoax."

Having earlier blamed Manny and Cohen for instigating and planning the robbery, Lloyd now pointed the finger at George Smith. "We have lots of evidence in here that George was the brains of the operation. George planned this. George Smith is kind of a leader. The others were sort of followers."

Chris's objective was not self-preservation, Lloyd said, but a selfless attempt to protect his loved ones. "The motto of a survivalist is to protect your family, not yourself." His belief that catastrophic events would soon befall mankind was not the product of a delusional mind, but an entirely reasonable one. "There are millions of people out there that believe the same way he does." He implored the jury to absolve Harven of responsibility for becoming involved in the robbery at all because of the immense financial and personal pressures he was under at the time. "I want you to feel what he felt and decide if you would have done the same thing."

"Christopher Harven backslid from God," Lloyd went on. "When the chips were down, he kept firm and he left, and he told the others not to do it. I don't know if you want to call it conscience or God is telling you to do something, but when you know it is wrong sometimes you have to stand firm even under all pressure."

Lloyd concluded his closing argument. "I want you to be sure of your decision, because Christopher Harven, as he sits in that chair, does not deserve to be there. He deserves the same thing you are going to do and that I am going to do after this case is over with. We are going to go home to our families. That is where he deserves to be."

JAY HANKS WAS SPITTING MAD AS HE ROSE TO DELIVER HIS REBUTTAL OF THE defense attorneys' statements. It wasn't just the accusations made against him by Adams, Olson's disrespect toward the officers, or the ridiculousness of Lloyd's Jerry Cohen defense. It was the months and months of pointless delays, and what he and Ruddy felt was a consistent display of insolence, impertinence, and contemptuous and childish behavior on the part of all three.

Lloyd was petulant and unprofessional, and his investigator had lied on the stand about searching for Cohen. Adams had alienated just about everyone in the courtroom at some point while Jeanne Painter was jacking off George Smith in an interview room. Olson was bush-league and needlessly mean-spirited toward witnesses, and his investigator, brother Roger Olson, was just plain lazy. Hanks and Ruddy would give them credit for one thing: If the defense's only goal had been to make a complete mess of the trial, they had certainly done that.

"They are all lying," Hanks mocked what he saw as the defense's outlandish conspiracy theory. "Riverside Sheriff's Department, liars. Riverside Police Department, liars. San Bernardino Sheriff's officers, liars. San Bernardino Police Department, liars. California Highway Patrol, liars. They all got together at some sort of meeting and conspired and made this all up? You know, if you were to believe this, this makes Watergate pale by comparison. Nobody has ever bothered from the defense to tell you why. Amazing. These cops are all liars, and why? What are they lying for? What are they going to get out of it? Nothing. Nothing. Absolutely nothing. It's stupid. It's silly."

Standing feet from the defense table, Hanks raised a finger at Alan Olson. "Russell Harven's attorney argues to you that, 'Look at it. They couldn't wait to get to the front of the line,'" he said, referring to Olson's characterization that police officers had been reckless glory seekers. "These men in the back, Russell and George, firing away. And what happens when these [police] men come into court and tell you what happened? He calls them 'Keystone Cops, country policemen, Barney Fife tactics.' It's amazing. They come in here to be insulted and vilified because they put their life on the line. It's incredible."

He moved over to the Smith defense table and leveled a finger at Adams. "He calls them creatures, liars, perjurers. It's intolerable."

Hanks still had ammunition left over for Michael Lloyd. "When we cut through the whole thing, get done with all the crap that we have heard for months, we get right down to the bottom line. Jerry Cohen never did exist. It is ridiculous. We spend all of this time to be insulted by that sort of thing?"

As for their accusations of misconduct against him: "I have realized from the beginning of this that somehow the defense saw a clever tactic out of this case was to attack the prosecution, that somehow it would make it appear less heinous as to what they did if they tried to impute some sort of evil or vile deed to the prosecutor. You may recall that Russell Harven's attorney asked you to 'Gee whiz, don't let the DA get up there and give all these evil connotations to what Russell said.' Evil connotations? Can you believe that? How am I going to give that a good connotation? What am I going to say about that that's good?"

One by one, the prosecutor attacked and ridiculed the defendants' cases.

"George Smith's defense doesn't exist. He was unconscious. He was bleeding so badly that, shucks, he can hardly lift the gun up when he fired at D. J. McCarty. Poor George. Why, George was wounded so severely there at the bank that he was unconscious thereafter. The only thing that there is that deals with unconsciousness in this case might be a description of his attorney's state of mind during the presentation of the evidence."

Adams tried to defend himself. "I would object to that as a denunciation of the defense, the defense counsel, and the defendant."

It only made Hanks even angrier. "Poor, unconscious George. In his confession, he admits trying to shoot the helicopter. Poor unconscious George.

"What about Russell?" Hanks went on. "What about the diabetic Russell? Well, let's see. He was standing in the back of the truck shooting at everybody he could. He stood up and he shot Bill Crowe a few times. He was leaning over firing in all directions. This insulin reaction is violent stuff, folks, and it makes you go out and rob banks and shoot and kill people.

"The real reason we're here is because that man died," Hanks said, pointing to a large photo of Jim Evans. "He died up here on this road. Who killed him? Russell Harven. Russell Harven shot and killed him as he was fighting for his life. So unnecessary. So totally unnecessary."

Hanks had saved his last attack for the defendant for whom he had the most contempt. "I'm going to take the circumstance now and address myself to the phantom Jerry Cohen, the individual that suddenly and mysteriously appeared. The defense, as to Christopher Harven, is that he wasn't there, that somebody else named Jerry Cohen was there instead of him. If you buy that, I have some property in the Everglades I'm sure you will be interested in.

"Christopher Harven is a liar," Hanks said, his voice rising. "And I sometimes think that he would probably lie when the truth would do him just as much good. The most important thing in his life was his family, right? That's the most important thing in his life. That is the reason he was so tormented when they left him. It is not surprising his wife left him. He had two other women on the string. But it is the most important thing in his life.

"Finally, his wife leaves him and takes the child, and he is so distraught over it, he moves in with another woman. And while he is living with the other woman, he is carrying on an affair with the third one. He is a liar. He lies to serve his own purposes. He lies about everything. He even lied when he talked to Malmberg. Whenever he thinks it is to his advantage, he will lie. He doesn't care if it is under oath or not, he will get up there and lie."

Hanks moved over to the photo of Evans. "Now the same four men are cornered. What do they do? They line up behind the truck. They walk down that road, and they kill Jim Evans. Evans shot Christopher Harven, managed to get him." Hanks paused and shook his head. "Damn shame he didn't kill him."

Hanks was particularly galled at what he saw as Harven's complete lack of remorse, citing Chris's joke about the bullet still in his body, within minutes of being told of the death of an officer. "You can even hear at the start of the case about how flip he is about the whole thing. He [Malmberg] was getting the vital statistics out of Christopher Harven:

'How much do you weigh, Chris?'

'You mean with or without the lead?'"

In closing, Hanks stood directly in front of the jury box. "Ladies and gentlemen, the reason we're here is because those three men are responsible for the death of James Evans. They killed him. They each had a finger on that trigger. They all pulled the round that went through his head. Each one of those men killed him. I don't ask you to convict them because of what you may consider some obnoxious or unprofessional or offensive conduct that may have gone on during the trial. I ask you to convict them because they are guilty."

WITH THE CONCLUSION OF HANKS'S STATEMENT ON THE AFTERNOON OF July 8, 1982, both sides had finally rested their cases in the guilt phase of the trial of the Norco 3. Hennigan announced he was dropping one incidental charge due to insufficient evidence, reducing the total number of felony counts to forty-five. After four and a half hours of jury instructions from the judge, the jurors were transported directly from the courthouse to a motel in nearby Oceanside where they would be sequestered until reaching a final verdict. Armed United States marshals were posted at the hotel for their protection as well as to see that there were no violations of the sequestration. Although the yearlong trial had strained them to the limit and they were anxious to get the ordeal over, foreman Paul Dillinger guided them through a methodical, thorough, and thoughtful deliberation that lasted for fifteen days.

Just after 7:00 p.m. on the evening of Friday, July 23, Dillinger sent word to the court that they had reached a verdict on all 135 counts. Hennigan had ordered defense and prosecution teams to remain close enough to reach the courthouse within thirty minutes, but now the judge was nowhere to be found. Ruddy and Hanks rushed to the apartment complex in which the judge was living and were met there by a marshal from the court. After jumping a security gate and pounding on the apartment door, the marshal had just decided to kick in the door in case there was a medical emergency when Hennigan walked up. He had been out for an evening stroll and lost track of time in idle conversation with a stranger about flowers. With the judge located, they jumped into cars and raced toward the courthouse. In the Vista jail, guards brought the three defendants their suits. They were quickly loaded into a transport van, their mood a mix of anxiety, fatalism, and vague hopefulness.

By 7:45 p.m., all the players were assembled in the courtroom, along with a packed spectator galley that included friends and relatives of the defendants, all having been screened through metal detectors before entering. Seven armed marshals positioned themselves throughout corridors and inside the courtroom.

"Mr. Dillinger, you are the foreman. Do I understand that you have reached verdicts on all the matters?"

"Yes, we have."

"Will you hand them to the bailiff and we'll ask the bailiff to give them to the Court." For five agonizing minutes, an expressionless David Hennigan leafed through the thick pile of papers while the courtroom looked on in dead silence. When he was done, he turned to clerk Geni Hays. "I'll hand you the verdict sheets and ask you to read them. I'll hand you first separately those relating to count 46 and ask you to read those first," Hennigan said, deciding to begin with the most serious charge of all: murder in the first degree of deputy Jim Evans.

"In the Superior Court of the State of California, in and for the county of San Diego, case number CRN 6940, The People of the State of California, Plaintiff, versus George Wayne Smith, Christopher Gregory Harven, and Russell Aaron Harven, Defendants.

"Verdict: We, the jury in the above entitled action, find the defendant George Wayne Smith guilty of violation of section 187 of the penal code, the murder of James Bernard Evans, and fix the degree as murder in the first degree."

In the gallery, Walter Smith, who had attended every day of his son's trial believing in his heart that George had never killed anyone, looked on without expression as the jury was individually polled as to their verdict.

The clerk continued. "We, the jury in the above entitled action, find the defendant Christopher Gregory Harven guilty of violation of section 187 of the penal code, the murder of James Bernard Evans, and fix the degree as murder in the first degree."

To no one's surprise, the Jerry Cohen defense had failed.

"We, the jury in the above entitled action, find the defendant Russell Aaron Harven guilty of violation of section 187 of the penal code, the murder of James Bernard Evans, and fix the degree as murder in the first degree."

The courtroom remained silent and the defendants and their attorneys expressionless as the clerk read the verdicts on all 135 counts. Like the trial itself, the process seemed to go on forever. When she was done, the defendants each stood guilty of all forty-five charges against them. The jury also found that the murder of Evans had been committed under "special circumstances" that qualified the convicted men for the death penalty.

Outside the courtroom, Jay Hanks gave his investigator Joe Curfman a hug. "I was confident the jury would see through the farce and sham that constituted the defense in this case," he said. Clayton Adams said the guilty verdicts on all charges were "a total shock" and that the jury "went for the throat." Michael Lloyd also professed shock but refused to label the Jerry Cohen defense a complete flop. "They had a doubt in their minds," he said. "But they didn't know if they understood what the law says about reasonable doubt." Alan Olson said he was "surprised and disappointed" by the prosecution's clean sweep. However, he did see one small victory in the special finding that Manny Delgado had fired the bullet that killed Evans. "They didn't buy my arguments," he said, "but they didn't buy Hanks's either."

When contacted by a reporter, D. J. McCarty said he was "dancing" at news of the verdict. "I feel relieved," he said of the jury's special finding that the bullet that killed Evans had not come from his gun. But he was not surprised. "Hey, I was up there. I saw what was happening." Mary Evans told a reporter, "Since the jury has been out I've had a lot of sleepless nights. I'm glad. I could jump up and down. Maybe I shouldn't feel this glad, but I feel glad." "It's been a long ordeal," Walter Smith said, looking noticeably drained but loyal to his boy to the end. "There is one thing I know, and my son knows: He did not kill anyone."

AFTER QUELLING A THREATENED WALKOUT BY EXHAUSTED JURORS OVER A $2.50 per day cut in compensation by the county, Judge Hennigan commenced with the penalty phase on July 27, 1982. "Mr. Olson, you may make an opening statement and then call your first witness."

Alan Olson called a procession of family, friends, neighbors, and even Russell's fourth-grade teacher who described him as a shy and sensitive child who had struggled to come to terms with his diabetic condition. Olson continued to call the disease a death sentence, and that handing him an additional one would be cruel and pointless. The condition "had robbed him of at least one third of his life span. The general consensus among doctors is that Russell has ten to fifteen years to live, and he's going to die a very distressing death."

The psychiatric professionals who had evaluated Russ soon after the crime portrayed him as a follower, easily talked into anything and unable to foresee the consequences of his actions. While still not able to specifically accuse his older brother of having pressured Russ into participating in the robbery, Olson was able to indirectly, but clearly, get the point across that Chris had dominated and tormented Russ all their lives. From there, the jury was left to connect the dots.

The most puzzling of the penalty cases was the one that was never presented. Chris Harven simply gave up. He instructed Lloyd that no witnesses be called on his behalf. There was no point trying to convince those people of anything. They can kill me if they want.

Lloyd convinced Chris that he should at least present a closing defense argument. Lloyd went all-in on the Jerry Cohen defense to the jury, saying that Harven should be sentenced to life "so I can find Jerry Cohen and prove to you that you were wrong." To punctuate just how wrong they felt the jury was, the two refused to stand at any time during the penalty phase when jurors entered the courtroom. Lloyd explained to reporter James Richardson that he and Harven had "no respect for the jury. I asked them to follow the law and they didn't do that. They let their passions get away from them and they ignored solid evidence to the contrary." It was a perplexing antagonization of a panel who held Harven's life in their hands.

Lloyd concluded his comments by saying the penalty phase was meaningless anyhow because his client, like his younger brother, had already received a death penalty. Except in this case, the sentence had been self-imposed by an act of courage. "When Chris got up and testified against Jerry Cohen, he's bound to die in prison."

Clayton Adams brought to the stand an array of immediate family, in-laws, ex-girlfriends, and childhood friends to vouch for George Smith's history of honesty, trustworthiness, and devotion to God. Rosie's brother Ralph Miranda recounted their Calvary Chapel ocean baptism together at Corona Del Mar in 1973. He said how much Rosie leaving him had hurt George. Michael Fantino talked about writing praise songs with George, hoping one of the bands on Calvary's Maranatha record label would record one.

Hannelore Smith (now Palmer) said George was compassionate, gentle, a loving father, generous to a fault. When asked if her daughter was in the courtroom, a relative in the spectator gallery lifted up five-year-old Monica for the jury to see. But Hanne had also found many of his beliefs strange. "Did you ever feel toward the end of your marriage he was starting to get weird?" Hanks asked on cross-examination. "Like I say, I did not agree with his wanting to go to the mountains. It seemed weird at the time."

A grave and defeated-looking Walter Smith fought back tears as he tried to explain to the jury that George had been an accomplished, loving, and loyal son who had done nothing but try to help others his entire life. He described how two failed marriages had left him devastated and preoccupied with the End Times prophecies of the book of Revelation. "Why did he become involved?" Clayton Adams asked him. "That's a question I have asked myself a thousand times. The only logical answer I can come up with is George was trying to achieve his utopian goal, to get a place out of state in the mountains, take his mother and dad, family and friends."

Others told how George had brought them to know the Lord as their Savior in an honest attempt to save their souls. "He talked about the Lord with me every chance we got," his brother-in-law Michael Halbach said. George had urged Halbach to help him find a mine shaft somewhere where they could grow food and protect themselves from roaming hordes of marauders. His sister Patricia sobbed on the stand speaking of how her loyal and dependable brother's religious beliefs intensified in ways that affected even his appearance. "He told me he wanted to grow his hair long because Samson got his strength from his hair." George urged her to bring her family to ride out the nuclear apocalypse in the pit at the Mira Loma house. "We could even bring our animals."

With all the witnesses now called, a man the jury thought they'd never hear from rose to argue why they should not put him to death. Prior to the start of their penalty case, Adams requested that George Smith be named co-counsel, allowing him to question his own witnesses and participate in closing arguments. The motion was granted by Hennigan over the objections of Jay Hanks. Even after months of trial and the hours of family and friends trying to tell them who George Smith really was, the man behind everything remained a puzzle to all.

It may have been in his best interest for George to present himself as a complicated man driven by a mix of sincerely held religious beliefs and a complex psychological makeup beyond his ability to control. For most of his life, he had somehow been able to channel extreme intelligence and a personality pathology that included elements of grandiosity, self-righteousness, and self-importance into admirable achievements and acts of compassion toward those around him. He had been responsible and self-sufficient from an early age, dutifully served his country and the God of his understanding, been a good provider for his family and a law-abiding contributor to society. But when put under the pressure of downturns in his life, the deeply ingrained personality traits that had served him so well suddenly conspired to propel him into a crime of horrendous consequences.

But in the end, it was not Smith's inclination nor within his ability to untangle psychological complexities he could not recognize within himself. When the time came for George to tell the people who sat in judgment of him who he really was, all George Smith could do was try to convince them of his beliefs and how they justified his actions.

"Good morning. I ask your indulgence in this. I'm not learned as counsel who knows how to present something like this, but I'll do the best I can. First and foremost, George Smith did not kill anyone; did not attempt to kill anybody; did not want to kill anybody."

His status as co-counsel dictated that George refer to himself only in the third person, lending an additional tone of arrogance to his presentation.

"Mr. Hanks does me a great honor by saying he [George Smith] is a prophet, that he was inspired by God. God has no purpose in this. There is no justification for this. George Smith was wrong. Jesus Christ doesn't condone this action, that's why George Smith has been whipped severely, but found pardoned under Christ.

"George Smith is no man's leader. He treated every man as an equal and exalted himself to no one. He says George Smith values his life above others, but you have heard testimony time and time again, George Smith's main concern was of others rather than of himself. You have heard evidence about George Smith's childhood. It was an average childhood. Nothing different. George Smith worked with the school newspaper, played in sports, and sang in the choir. Those are not the acts or the personality of someone who is a monster. George Smith is not a monster."

Smith went on to tell how his experience in the military taught him to recognize just how close mankind had brought itself to the brink of destruction. "George Smith has extensive military knowledge because of his MOS [Military Occupational Specialty], and the stuff he was taught was all classified. So he knows the reality of nuclear warfare, and people do not know how close we actually are to it. Yes, that made him religious, for he felt and was certain that weapons of war are only made for one purpose, and that is to be used. The hole in the backyard was not for, as Mr. Hanks asks you to believe, the last-ditch stand to fight police, or whatever; it was simply a bomb shelter."

George opened a version of the King James Bible. "I wish at this time to read a section out of Revelations 20, Your Honor, since Revelations was brought up continually in this matter."

He read the passage he felt clarified his actual beliefs. "Then I saw an angel come down from Heaven with the key of the abyss in his hand . . ."

He closed the book and veered into the realm of esoteric theological debate. "You heard testimony relating that George Smith thought that he would be left behind. What I have just read to you now is different. It doesn't say that. George Smith has read the Bible cover to cover. He has read many, many, many books on many, many, many different people's opinion as to the Bible. Mr. Hanks would have you believe that I was some kind of mad prophet, but then Hal Lindsey and Chuck Smith and Carruthers and all the others would be mad prophets, according to him. I understand Margaret MacDonald's theory of the Rapture, which you will not find anywhere in the Bible."

He said his confession on the mountainside was nothing less than the admirable act of a dying man. "When you look at George Smith's character and you know his personality, the evidence shows that when faced with death, knowing he is going to die, wanting to die at that point, that he would take the blame for everything under the sun. And that is what George Smith did."

Smith called D. J. McCarty "a paradox" of contradictory statements and accused SWAT members of murdering Manny Delgado. "Sure as we're all here today, you in your hearts know that they murdered him and the justification is that because we're criminals supposedly. But them sticking that shotgun in his side and pulling the trigger, does not justify, nonetheless, but it's still murder."

It was Smith's contention that if he had really wanted to kill anyone, he could have. "George Smith has been around guns most of his life; he is what you call a crack shot. When it came time to go to heaven, he was not going to go to it with the blood of Americans on his hands. When it came to the quick, he would rather shoot the car than the man and that is consistent with George Smith's religious convictions. He's not a murderer. He's not a killer. The United States' enemies are George Smith's enemies. The Christian enemy is George Smith's enemy. Communism and dictatorships are George Smith's enemies, not the American people."

"Why I went?" Smith began, with the first and only explanation of his actions the jury would hear from the defense during the entire trial. "It is a complex thing. It's nothing I am proud of. I am sorry I went, and I am sorry all this happened. I guess the closest theory to it would be when my father testified that George Smith was looking for a utopia. Errors in his ways are there. He knows he was wrong. Do not take my lack of fear as a contempt of this Court or these body of people. I accept what I cannot change. I cannot change your verdict. I have no ill will for any person here. I have no ill will for the Court. I have no ill will for Mr. Hanks."

Smith headed into his conclusion with a statement that would bring the blood of many in the courtroom to a boil. "I just have to keep my faith and know that wherever Christ leads me, I shall follow. Manuel Delgado and Belisario Delgado, I believe, died under the grace of Christ and they are waiting for George Smith in heaven now. I hoped and prayed that Jim Evans died a Christian.

"All I wish to say, I guess, in final and in closing here, is that George Smith, his Lord and Savior is Jesus Christ. I have to confess that amongst men to show you that I am for real. And I wish you all wings of an angel, and when you run, not to grow tired, and when you walk, not to grow faint."

When his testimony was over, George had brought the jury no closer to understanding a man whom they might soon order to be put to death. He remained a puzzle of great contradictions. On one hand, selfless, kind, and generous. But in deciding to rob a bank and arm himself to kill others if needed, he displayed a self-righteous superiority that put his needs and beliefs above all others, even if it meant the death of total strangers. George might never have set out to kill anyone on May 9, 1980, but when the time came, he did, or at the very least, tried his hardest to.

EVEN WITH THE END OF THEIR ORDEAL IN SIGHT, THE JURORS REMAINED frayed and edgy. After nine days of deliberation, foreman Paul Dillinger sent Hennigan a 550-word note that it was turning into a complete mess and that they were not even close to agreeing on sentences. The problem, Dillinger said, was that several of the jurors had made up their minds on a verdict before deliberations had begun and were making the others feel they were being "railroaded" into coming to a quick decision. "The majority of the jury feels that we haven't really even begun the process of a fair deliberation. We have not yet discussed most of the elements of the instructions." Some of the jurors refused to even discuss the case with the others. Dillinger felt "that an exhortation by the court to 'unmake up' their minds will not change anything." For the calm and methodical Dillinger, it was clear he was getting to the end of his rope too.

Hennigan called the jurors into the courtroom on August 13 to address the problem. He told the jurors they had a duty to discuss the evidence with the others. "Stubbornness is not a good attribute of a juror," he said, before sending them back to the motel to try again. Late the following day, the jury threw in the towel. They were hopelessly deadlocked, Dillinger told Hennigan, eight for life, four for death. Hennigan thanked the jury for its service. They were free to go. "It was a very difficult, trying experience," juror Vicki Regan said. "Something I want to forget for a while." "I got a few bars to hit," John Sowell said, clearing out his possessions from the Oceanside motel.

Press-Enterprise reporter James Richardson, who had sat through so much of the trial, had a theory about why the jury could never come back with a death verdict. "Stockholm syndrome," he said, referring to the bond that can sometimes develop between captives and captors after going through a long ordeal together. "After spending so much time in that room together, there was no way they were going to sentence those guys to death."

A MONTH LATER, THE THREE CONVICTED MEN SAT LISTENING AS THEIR life-without-parole sentences were pronounced. Christopher Harven chatted with attorney Michael Lloyd while judge J. David Hennigan pronounced his fate.

Russell Harven sat alone on a bench behind Alan Olson, staring expressionlessly into space. When Olson objected to sending the defendants back to Riverside jail, calling it a "dungeon" and a "hell hole," all the acrimony that had been built up between Olson and Hanks finally erupted. "Could we do without the pejoratives?" Hanks snapped. Olson leapt to his feet, angrily threw off his suit coat, and screamed at Hanks. "Could you do without your coat outside?" Two bailiffs jumped up and stepped between the two as Olson continued to shout at Hanks while the prosecutor stood grinning at his enraged adversary.

In a separate hearing on September 25, 1982, George Wayne Smith remained convinced to the end that he had been unjustly convicted and unfairly sentenced. "This is a one-hour indiscretion that could lead to a life of torment. I don't think society demands that much of an example." The probationary report prepared to help guide the judge in his sentencing said that Smith had shown no remorse. However, George Smith had regrets. "If I could turn back the clock. If I could lay down my life and the other three could come back, I would do it. It's something I have to live with for the rest of my life."

On November 15, 1982, the sentences were finally affirmed, two years, six months, and six days after five men attempted to rob the Security Pacific Bank in Norco, California. When it was done, Jay Hanks stepped out a courtroom door into an alley, raised his hand above his head, and shouted, "It's all over!" In a house in Irving, Texas, a phone rang with the news and, once again, a mother sobbed. "It never goes away," said Martha Evans.

MARY EVANS RODE THE HORSE HARD THROUGH THE RIVER BOTTOM, AMONG the willows and cottonwoods, the hooves thundering on the sandy wash beneath her. She slowed the big animal to a walk and they went along like that, breathing deeply from the exertion. They came to the small stream at the center of the channel and paused, Mary listening to the water flowing over the rocks. The news had finally come in from Vista. A hung jury. So, this is the way it ends for the three of them: life. Not the way it ended for Jim.

She rode the horse out of the wash and up a long trail to the top of a dry and dusty hilltop and looked out at the wide sweep of the Inland Empire spread out below her. The animal kicked at the dirt and nosed the blanket of dead grass that covered the hillsides in all directions. A setting sun filtered through the brown smog. From that spot, Mary could see where everything had happened, but only on a clear day, of which there were few. Fifteen miles west was Norco and the intersection of Fourth and Hamner where events were put into play that led to the death of her husband. Twenty miles to the north, the mouth of Lytle Creek Canyon opened at the base of the towering San Gabriel Mountains where he died. Eleven miles due south was Riverside National Cemetery where his body now lay. That she could see, even through the layer of smog. A hot wind blew back her hair. *You were the love of my life.*

She leaned forward and patted the horse's neck. Desperado, given to J.B. Jr. by a local attorney within weeks of his father's death. The boy was two and a half now. She thought of Jim seated at the kitchen table the morning before he went off to die, cradling the baby in his arms. *Jim, why don't you ever put that baby down? Because I want him to know who I am.* She had kept all the photos, the medals and awards and the news clippings to be brought out at a later time. One day he will, she thought. She turned the horse and headed back down the trail.

EPILOGUE

ON SEPTEMBER 9, 1982, JUST DAYS BEFORE HIS SCHEDULED SENTENCING, George Wayne Smith submitted a one-page handwritten note to justice J. David Hennigan requesting a hearing for a "motion for new counsel" to have Clayton Adams removed from his case. "As the Court has noticed, he fought with Court, all counsel, court clerks, court security, and client and investigator. He stated to this Court he has had fits of insanity, and I put that mildly." He went on to say Adams and Alan Olson "both lied to me" about presenting witnesses that he requested. "His batting average is 0–45," he wrote, referring to the guilty verdicts. He said that the jury indicated Adams "was the biggest trouble as to my case." The note was signed, "Christ be with you and your family. Your brother, George Wayne Smith."

Meeting in chambers with Hennigan and Adams two days later, George Smith was irate at what he felt was grossly inadequate representation that had landed him in jail for life. He called Adams a liar, mentally ill, incompetent, negligent, ill prepared, and neglectful of him as a client.

Adams defended himself and his strategy, but it was obvious he felt betrayed by the man whose life he had fought so hard to save. "I'm trying to be professional about this, but I simply cannot help it because I know I broke my heart over this case. I can't believe this has actually happened. All I can do is sit here and tell the Court my heart is no longer in this case. I just can't do it."

Clayton Adams went on to a long career in criminal defense as "a bracero toiling in the fields of justice." Decades later, he showed no bitterness over the case. He summed up his defense strategy in a single sentence: "I was trying to save George's life." He referred to Alan Olson and Michael Lloyd as "professionally and personally competent." He had nothing but admiration for Jeanne Painter, calling her "investigative knowledge and experience, excellent," and her support in the courtroom "like clockwork." He remained convinced that Painter had been set up by the Vista jail and had done nothing wrong. He still believed Jay Hanks committed "prosecutorial misconduct by interfering with defense expert witnesses and intentionally disregarding standard discovery orders." Of their animosity in the courtroom, Adams said, "Any suggestion of aggressiveness or confrontational behavior is considered a two-way street."

Despite his client's post-trial attack, he still referred to George as "intelligent, attentive, and courteous" and their relationship on the case "open and cordial." "If you see George," he said almost four decades afterward, "tell him I said hello." As for his performance in the trial, Adams said, "Some folks said the defense won the case, others were not so generous. You decide." Adams died in Modesto, California, in 2016.

ON APRIL 16, 1983, GEORGE WAYNE SMITH AND JEANNE PAINTER WERE MAR-ried through a filing of paperwork with the County of Sacramento, near where Smith was being held at Folsom State Prison.

The anxiety attacks and emotional strain that had afflicted Painter for most of the trial continued afterward. In September 1982, Painter filed for disability and workers' compensation with the county, saying the stress of the trial and allegations of sexual misconduct had rendered her unable to continue at the Office of the Public Defender. "At this point she is 100 percent disabled because the doctor won't let her work," said her attorney, Michael Lloyd. Days later, Painter also filed a $4 million lawsuit for libel and slander against Riverside and San Diego Counties over the jailhouse accusations.

It took Jeanne Painter only a few years to file for divorce from Smith. Several years after that, George displayed one final act of disregard for a woman who had been loyal to him beyond any reasonable expectation. Included in his 1989 trial appeal was an argument against Clayton Adams for "Failure to control his defense investigator, Jeanne Painter." "Appellant Smith argues that his investigator Jeanne Painter was allegedly observed by a deputy performing oral sex with appellant Smith inside an anteroom to the court during a recess." In the response to the appeal, deputy attorney general Holly Wilkens noted that an investigation "cannot locate any reference in the record" of the court or anywhere else to support the allegation.

If there was anyone who had been misunderstood and unfairly treated in the trial of the Norco 3, it was Jeanne Painter. It is true that Painter was successful in a high-pressure world of extremely high stakes. But what had been forgotten along the way was that she was still a young woman buffeted about by uncertainty, anxiety, and the pressures of trial work. Painter was never delusional about the crimes committed by George Smith, but she was a passionate and compassionate person. After years alongside Smith in a battle to save his life against a system she felt was unfairly stacked against him, Painter had found it difficult to simply walk away from someone for whom she had fought so hard. It did not help that this particular someone was the intelligent, charismatic, and often manipulative George Wayne Smith.

Eventually Jeanne Painter's anxiety began to subside and her life slowly returned to normal. After leaving the defender's office, she started an independent private investigation firm in the Riverside area. Shortly after divorcing George Smith, Painter married a local attorney with whom she raised children. They were married for more than thirty years. Jeanne Painter Callaway died in 2018. Her obituary invited donations in Jeanne's name to Death Penalty Focus, a nonprofit dedicated to the abolishment of the death penalty.

AFTER RECEIVING $150,000 FOR TWELVE MONTHS' WORK, THE NORCO TRIAL had left Michael Lloyd's newly opened Riverside law firm nearly bankrupt. Lloyd remained in criminal law until 1999. Alan Olson returned to his practice in Orange County and gained some attention for his defense of James O'Driscoll, convicted of stabbing a teenager to death inside the Disneyland theme park in 1981.

AT THE CONCLUSION OF THE NORCO TRIAL, PROSECUTOR JAY HANKS WAS named assistant district attorney, the number two in the department, responsible for running day-to-day operations. In 1988 he was elected justice to the Riverside Municipal Court and two years later to the California State Superior Court for the County of Riverside, where he served for another twenty-five years. Hanks lives in Riverside.

Kevin Ruddy went on to become one of the most prolific prosecutors of major crimes during his time with the Office of the Riverside District Attorney. Ruddy brought to jury verdict thirty-five murder cases, including some of the most notorious in county history. He was named chief deputy DA in 1999 and supervised the Major Crimes department for ten years. Ruddy retired in 2009 and remains in Southern California.

In 1984, Joe Curfman was named the district attorney's chief investigator, where he served for twenty years overseeing the bureau that grew to 125 members across Riverside County during his term.

By the conclusion of the trial, both the defense and prosecution had positive and negative things to say about justice J. David Hennigan's handling of the trial of the Norco 3. "That's usually a sign that a judge has done his job," a colleague of Hennigan's said. Most had an unfavorable opinion of the jury selection process; however, one of his rulings during that stage had likely avoided a mistrial months later. Hennigan continued to serve on the superior court for many years and passed away in 1997.

DAMAGE AND MONTHS OF POLICE CONFISCATION OF HIS VAN COST GARY Hakala his canning business within a year of being taken hostage in the parking lot of the Brea Mall. Gary returned to his first love as an educator, teaching mathematics at the high school and junior college level and coaching wrestling, volleyball, and track. He was named Teacher of the Year for the city of Beaumont in 2007. A grandfather of eighteen, Hakala lives in Riverside County where he is a real estate investor, NRA pistol instructor, and kayaking teacher.

ANDY DELGADO WOULD NEVER FULLY FORGIVE GLYN BOLASKY AND CHUCK Hille for leaving him alone under fire in front of the bank that day. "I had a three-minute gun battle with the robbers. I wasn't happy being left there to die," he told the *Press-Enterprise* thirty years after the event. The way Andy remembered it, he had been in the middle of gunfire when he heard Chuck Hille's transmission that he was rolling Bolasky to the hospital. The recording of the radio traffic reveals that Hille's transmission, made moments after turning off Fourth Street, had come two minutes and eleven seconds after Delgado reported the yellow truck had left the scene. However, there is also no question that Bolasky and Hille had ceased engagement in the firefight prior to that, effectively leaving Andy alone from the moment he arrived on scene.

But details and data do little to get to the heart of what happened during those four minutes of madness in front of the Security Pacific Bank. All three deputies acted heroically, all felt fear, all did what they thought at the time was right. "When I got shot, I wasn't a cop anymore," Bolasky would later say. "I was a human being trying not to die. I went into a self-defense mode. It was a caveman mentality with only one thing in mind—survival."

For Chuck Hille, reconciliation comes only in understanding what the others were experiencing in the moment. "I'm sorry Andy still feels that way," Hille said years later. "We never made a decision to leave him alone, but in the end, we probably did."

After leaving law enforcement, Glyn Bolasky joined the United States Air Force, rising to the rank of lieutenant colonel as an electronic warfare officer. He frequently speaks to law enforcement and other groups, applying the lessons of Norco to the modern world of terrorism.

Chuck Hille left the sheriff's office several years after Norco, tried his hand at acting, and ran a carpet store. In the aftermath of the terrorist attacks of September 11, 2001, he began to hear more about posttraumatic stress disorder and realized he had been suffering some of the symptoms himself since his experience in Norco. He decided then he wanted to use that experience to help others and obtained an advanced degree in psychiatry. Dr. Charles A. Hille has a successful therapy practice in Riverside County, much of it counseling sufferers of posttraumatic stress disorder.

Andy Delgado enjoyed great professional and personal success after leaving the RSO. He re-enrolled in college and earned a master's in business administration from the University of Redlands. He joined the San Diego Probation Department and rose to the rank-equivalent of lieutenant and was the architect of a landmark youth offender program. After retiring, he taught U.S. history at a local high school for ten years along with criminal law and administrative justice at the junior college level.

At age forty-five, Andy Delgado finally found the family he had been denied early in his life when the children of his biological father, Leonard Monti, embraced him as one of their own. He had been in touch with Monti, the restaurateur from Phoenix, and the other children off and on since high school. After the death of the family patriarch, Andy reunited with the extended family in 1998. They soon began encouraging him to "officially" become one of the Monti family. "What's this Delgado name? You're not a Delgado." In 2001, Andy Delgado filed the paperwork and became Andrew Monti, finally shedding the last name he never should have had in the first place.

Dave "Mad Dog" Madden was named detective in 1988 and worked in an array of investigation assignments including auto theft, robbery/homicide, major narcotics unit, and criminal intelligence. He served as a sniper in the RSO SWAT unit. He retired in 2009 and currently works in plainclothes executive protection.

In 1985, A. J. Reynard transferred to the Inglewood Police Department in South-Central Los Angeles. During an undercover drug buy, Reynard was shot three times, including once in the back of the head. Regaining consciousness, Reynard and his partner shot and killed the attacker. Tired of being shot at and weary of the bureaucracy and politics of law enforcement, Reynard retired in 1995, went to culinary school, and worked in the kitchen at the prestigious Miramar Resort. After several years, he switched to a career in education, teaching law and criminal investigations for almost twenty years at Yucaipa High School in San Bernardino County. He lives in Big Bear Lake, California.

A week after the Norco bank robbery, Rolf Parkes made his scheduled move to the Irvine Police Department in Orange County, where he worked as a detective on arson investigations and spent seventeen years on the SWAT unit. At the request of his new department, Rolf was instrumental in creating a police training video about the incident that is still used by law enforcement agencies throughout the country today.

RSO deputies Ken McDaniels, Herman Brown, and Darrell Reed, all wounded in the pursuit, recovered from their injuries and went on to long, successful careers in law enforcement. After an equally successful career, Fred Chisholm retired to Arizona. Gary Keeter, the patrol deputy who had found himself behind the dispatch mic that day only because of an injured knee, went on to become one of the top police dispatch instructors in the country. The actions of the dispatch team of Keeter, Gladys Wiza, and Sharon Markum during the Norco pursuit is credited with having prevented an even greater loss of life.

Twenty years after the Norco bank robbery, the Riverside Sheriff's Department finally officially honored the deputies involved. In a 2000 commemoration ceremony organized by the Sheriffs' Association, Glyn Bolasky, Chuck Hille, Andy Delgado, and Rolf Parkes received the Medal of Courage for "acts of heroism performed at great risk to life and limb." Although long overdue, the recognition did much to repair the damaged relationship between the deputies and the department and, in some cases, lingering resentments toward each other. "Some didn't want to come, they asked why bring this all up again," said Laura Bakewell, who coordinated the event. "Some of the deputies arrived angry, but by the end of it, they left crying and hugging each other."

ON A ROUTINE TRAFFIC STOP ON MARCH 14, 1987, CHP OFFICER DOUG EAR-nest had his gun taken away by a disturbed marine. Kidnapped and forced to drive on a chase with law enforcement over three counties, Earnest finally convinced the man to throw away the gun and apprehended the suspect himself. That he had been involved in two harrowing incidents in his career says much about how perilous the life of a law enforcement officer in the Inland Empire could be. In each instance, Earnest acted with supreme brav-ery, although the two events left him shaken. After serving with distinction for more than twenty years with California Highway Patrol, Earnest finally retired. He passed away in 2016.

Patrolman Bill Crowe went on to become the first drug K9 officer for the California Highway Patrol, roaming the highways of Riverside County with his partner Ebbo. Crowe transferred to the Northern California city of Redding and served on the Special Investigations Unit. One day he received a call from Riverside CHP. "You want your dog back?" Ebbo proved as faith-ful a pet as he had been a partner, helping Crowe and his wife raise their son, born one week after the return of the dog. Crowe retired in 2002. Bill Crowe and Doug Earnest remained lifelong friends.

DESPITE A MULTITUDE OF HEARTBREAKING EXPERIENCES THROUGHOUT HIS law enforcement career and the loss of his home in the Panorama fire, deputy James McPheron maintained his optimism and gentle ways. He served out his career with the San Bernardino Sheriff's Department and continues to live in the area. One of his prize possessions remains the scrapbook and me-mentos of his life as a peace officer.

Deputy Mike Lenihan rose to the rank of lieutenant at the San Ber-nardino Sheriff's Office, most of it in the Homicide division. He retired after thirty-five years of service and passed away in 2018.

Not long after having tracked the yellow truck up Lytle Creek canyon in San Bernardino Sheriff's helicopter 40-King-2, pilot Ed Mabry and spotter John Plasencia were on routine patrol over the county when Mabry suddenly turned the craft around and returned to the Rialto airfield. Mabry departed the chopper without explanation and disappeared into the control building. When a confused Plasencia asked an officer inside what was going on, the man said simply, "He's done." Plasencia believes Mabry's abrupt departure from piloting was a direct result of the remorse he felt over their inability to warn Jim Evans in time of the impending ambush on Baldy Notch Road.

WHEN D. J. McCARTY WALKED OUT OF THE COURTHOUSE ON APRIL 13, 1982, he was done with Norco, but Norco was not done with him. At a SWAT training facility several years later, he found himself sitting in a classroom when one of the instructors slipped a VHS tape into a video player. What flickered to life on a large monitor in the darkened room was the training film Rolf Parkes had made about Norco for the Irvine Police Department. McCarty watched as the face of a wild-haired George Wayne Smith stared out at him from the monitor. "A known and admitted anarchist . . ." a professional narrator informed the viewers. As the film continued, images that McCarty had fought hard to forget began to flash through his mind.

When his name was mentioned in the film, several heads turned to look at him. A fellow officer leaned over and whispered, "You were in that thing?"

Just over thirty minutes into the tape, D.J. heard the voice of Jim Evans for the first time in his life. McCarty listened to the smooth West Texas drawl as the pursuit headed up Interstate 15 and into Lytle Creek. *We are a quarter mile from the ranger station on Sierra Road in the National Forest and they are firing like crazy.* As the chase went onto the dirt road, Evans's voice began to grow tighter, asking more frequently about possible ambushes. McCarty's mind leapt back to those moments riding in the passenger seat next to McPheron trying to get to the front, the M16 held between his knees. Why the hell didn't he move over and let us pass? *Okay, we're hit!* the voice on the tape screamed. D.J.'s heart leapt, and his memories took over from there: Evans jumping from the car as his rear window explodes; backing up in combat stance, emptying his .38; ducking down to reload. Don't come up the same place you went down, Evans. Don't come up in the same place.

McCarty knew it was time to get some help. He soon found himself in the office of a therapist named Nancy Bohl-Penrod. "If you could be doing anything in your life right now," Bohl-Penrod said in their first session, "what would it be?" D.J. thought about it. "Two things. First, I'd be a Civil War soldier on horseback with a rifle riding my way back home west." What's the second thing? "Commander of my own starship." It was the start of the road back.

D. J. McCarty was awarded the Medal of Valor by the San Bernardino Sheriff's Department for his actions on Baldy Notch Road. His career with the San Bernardino Sheriff's Office spanned thirty-three years. In addition to SWAT, he served in the career criminal division and the Undercover Narcotics Bureau, rose to detective, and retired as a sergeant in 2010. He lives in Arizona with his wife and works in the field of executive protection.

MARY EVANS IS A RETIRED REALTOR LIVING IN SAN JUAN CAPISTRANO. SHE has seven grandchildren and two great grandchildren. James B. Evans Jr. lives in the area with his two young children. Decades after his death, James Evans was posthumously awarded the Riverside County Sheriff's Department's highest honor, the Medal of Valor.

AT 11:00 A.M. ON DECEMBER 2, 2015, TWO ISLAMIC EXTREMISTS ARMED with AR-15 semiautomatic rifles, thousands of rounds of .223 ammunition, and homemade pipe bombs burst into the Inland Regional Center in San Bernardino, California, and opened fire on an employee meeting inside. Within minutes, fourteen were dead and twenty-two seriously injured. The suspects fled the scene, immediately sparking the largest manhunt in the Inland Empire since the search for the Norco bank robbers thirty-five years before.

But this time, law enforcement agencies came equipped with more than just a single beat-up M16. Hundreds of officers from seven different agencies—including Norco participants, San Bernardino County Sheriff's Department, CHP, and Rialto and Fontana city police departments—swarmed the region armed with semiautomatic weapons, such as the Ruger Mini-14 .223 rifle and the Glock G22 pistol. Police traversed the streets of San Bernardino in BearCat armored personnel carriers while the skies above swarmed with police choppers now equipped as "gun platforms."

Trapping the fleeing SUV in a suburban neighborhood four hours later, the two suspects were killed in just over five minutes with a hail of 440 rounds of police gunfire. Afterward, one of the dead suspects was dragged from the SUV using the mechanical arm of a Rook armored critical incident vehicle, while remote control robots from the bomb squad searched vehicles and houses nearby. Had the incident occurred in any major metro area in the country, the response would have been the same.

In the immediate aftermath, local police officials cited the lesson learned from Norco as the genesis of the Inland Empire law enforcement's ability to rapidly deploy with such overwhelming force to neutralize superior firepower. In a 2017 article for *Vice* by Daniel Oberhaus entitled "How a 1980 Bank Robbery Sparked the Militarization of America's Police," a quote from Rolf Parkes pinpointed the evolution to a specific moment and the actions of a single deputy: D. J. McCarty.

> When backup for the responding officers finally arrived, bringing a single AR-15 in tow, the robbers fled into the woods. . . . "When the suspects hear[d] that rifle, they realize[d] their firepower [was] now being matched," recalled responding officer Rolf Parkes. "There would have been a lot more dead cops on that road if not for that weapon."

IN A MEDIA STORAGE ROOM AT THE RIVERSIDE COUNTY BEN CLARK TRAINING Center, the possessions of George Smith sit frozen in time. Unopened mail, Mastercard bills, mortgage papers, half a pack of Benson & Hedges menthol cigarettes, a film canister of marijuana and a one-hitter pipe inside a baggie, and a savings account deposit book from the Security Pacific National Bank in Norco. On a piece of lined notebook paper is a list of cities with phone numbers and addresses for parks and maintenance departments he had been contacting for a job: Anaheim, Brea, Fullerton, Norco . . . Beside most is scrawled the word *no*. Inside an envelope is an uncashed federal tax return check along with a handwritten note. "Hi George. We are doing fine. We went to Catalina, Knott's Berry Farm, and Farmer's Market. Monica is doing fine but it is hard on her also. I will call you after my parents leave. See you soon. Hanne & Monica."

Almost forty years behind bars has given George Smith a perspective that had eluded him in the years immediately following his crime. "I do have empathy," he would write in 2018. "I am ashamed, embarrassed, and deeply sorry for all that happened on May 9, 1980. It was a tragedy for everyone, especially to the Evans and Delgado families. I wish I could do or say something that would mean something comforting. A great deal of introspection also showed me I need to apologize not only to the Evans family and Delgado family, but to all who were injured and had anything adverse happen to them." He added that "I had rationalized my actions contrary to my faith" and that he had been "hypocritical and wrong on so many levels."

George Smith has been a model prisoner active in counseling fellow inmates in their quest for spiritual belief. He is currently housed at the Richard J. Donovan Correctional Facility in San Diego County. The prison is also home to Robert F. Kennedy assassin Sirhan Sirhan, Manson Family killer Tex Watson, Beverly Hills parent-murderers Lyle and Erik Menendez, and serial rapist Anand Jon. The facility maintains five interfaith chapels.

A MAN WALKS INTO THE ROOM WITH A SLY, ALMOST MISCHIEVOUS SMILE ON his face. He is in his midsixties with a potbelly, the long beard and hair much as it was thirty-five years earlier, only now snow white. The eyes are the same too, squinty with a bit of a sparkle. If he auditioned for Santa Claus at the local mall, he'd probably get the job. But he can't. This is the Inmate Visiting

Center of Unit A at the California State Prison in Lancaster, high on the desert plain east of Los Angeles. Russell Harven has been here a long time, and he is never getting out.

"I appreciate you meeting with me," the visitor says to the man he has known only through letters. "Yeah, we'll see about that," Harven says doubtfully, taking a seat across the circular table. "My brother is giving me a lot of shit for this." Russ is talking about his older brother, Chris, currently held up north in a Vacaville prison. The two had been cellmates for most of the last fifteen years, and he expects to be transferred up to Vacaville soon where they will be again. Russ sees it as a blessing and a curse. On one hand, at least it's someone he knows. On the other hand, it's Chris. The dynamic has not changed all that much in thirty-five years.

The visitor center is full of men in denim shirts and pants, almost all black or Hispanic. They sit chatting with their mothers, holding children, or walking with their wives hand in hand around the caged-in outdoor area. To look at them, most don't seem like such bad guys at all. But there are others who pimp-roll into the room, badass and menacing. If they think about an old white inmate like Russell Harven at all, it is probably dismissively. But there is not one of them in the room who has a conviction record approaching anything like his.

Harven seems to respond to all the visitor's questions as best he can, even if the answers are simple and uncomplicated. "I've spent most of my life trying not to think about what happened that day." In his letters and as he speaks, the superior intelligence range in which he tested just after Norco is obvious. He refers to himself as having been "indolent" and "fatalistic" in the years leading up to Norco. He does not lay any blame on his brother, says it never occurred to him that it would end up in a gunfight. If it had, he never would have done it. When asked if he thinks one of them killed Jim Evans, he looks away. "God, I hope not."

Like his brother, Russell is still angry about the trial. No question the cops lied, covered up, destroyed evidence. The prosecution couldn't prove who shot the bullet, so they should have gotten twenty-five years to life under the Felony Murder Rule instead. "I am somewhat bitter about getting that sentence," he says. "I used to be a happy-go-lucky, devil-may-care type. Now I am a bitter old man waiting for my toe tag."

After two hours, the visitor runs out of questions, so they spend the last hour shooting the shit about seventies rock music and L.A. radio stations they used to listen to, the lousy Mexican ragweed, the smoggy days, sneaking into Disneyland—all the stuff teenagers growing up in Orange County did back then. For a while, they are just two guys sitting around talking about the old neighborhood. They try to figure out if they might have gone to some of the same concerts. Cal Jam II at the Ontario Motor Speedway, the Stones at Anaheim Stadium, Queen, Aerosmith. "What about the AC/DC *Back in Black* tour at the Orange Pavilion in San Bernardino?" the visitor asks. Harven's mood changes. He shakes his head. Of course he wasn't there. It was September 1980. By then, Russell Harven had already thrown his life away.

The guard calls out visitor hours are over and Harven stands. Before shaking hands and thanking him again, the visitor cannot help but ask what is both the best and stupidest question one can ask someone who has done something unimaginable: "Why did you do it?"

"Simple," Harven says without hesitation. "Because I thought we'd get away with it."

NOTE ON SOURCES

THIS BOOK IS THE RESULT OF FOUR YEARS OF RESEARCH. THE METHODOLOGY was simple: Track down every document, contact every surviving person involved, and follow any thread wherever it led me. Research sources included forty thousand pages of trial transcripts, dozens of boxes of physical evidence and trial exhibits, unedited recordings of police radio traffic and suspect interrogations, and thousands of pages of police investigation reports, photographs, witness interviews, and other documents from five law enforcement agencies. While it sometimes took years to locate or secure approvals, all the agencies involved ultimately allowed me access to everything remaining in their archives, most of which had never before been released.

There are many ways I could have chosen to write the story of Norco, but my intention from the start has been to tell a true story truthfully and transparently. Everything presented, whether in dialogue or narrative, is as factual as I could determine based on a wide range of sources.

Mistakes, contradictions, and inconsistencies in witness accounts and evidence are not uncommon in criminal cases, especially one of this magnitude. Most concerned incidental details. In those few instances where I was unable to resolve through referencing multiple sources, I either decided which was more likely or attributed to their source within the narrative. When concerning more important information, incidents or conflicts and disagreements between people, each point of view or version of events is represented or clearly noted in the narrative. Significant challenges to evidence and witness accounts and testimony by defense attorneys are an important part of the story and contained directly within the accounts of the trial.

Of course, data and hard facts do not tell the whole story. I also spent hundreds of hours interviewing those involved on all sides and facets of the story. Most were conducted face-to-face in diners, private homes, cop bars, prison visiting rooms, and a multitude of other locations. In the case of the major players, there were multiple conversations totaling dozens of hours with each and countless smaller follow-ups to clarify details and facts. Additional information on the people involved came from family, friends, and acquaintances through interviews and testimony transcripts from the penalty phase of the trial.

For many, it would have been easier and far less painful not to revisit the events of Norco. But after years of just wanting to forget, most now felt it was more important that the story be told. I am grateful to all for their courage and candor. Most who spoke or corresponded with me are listed in the acknowledgments, but some wished not to be recognized. Very few individuals declined to be interviewed or participate in the making of this book.

Anything in quotation marks is taken verbatim from publications, documents, recordings, transcripts, or dialogue reported directly to me in interviews. Dialogue based on the recollections of those involved appears without quotation marks. Radio communications are verbatim and expressed in italics. Some of the above was condensed and edited for flow and context, but never to alter meaning. In rare cases when one or more participants were no longer alive, I relied on secondhand accounts, but from as many sources and in as limited a way as possible.

Any errors contained herein are unintentional, but entirely mine.

REGARDING THE USE OF FIREARMS AND AMMUNITION TERMINOLOGY IN THIS book, much care, research, and consulting of experts was undertaken to accurately represent the weapons used in the Norco event. However, I made the decision in a few cases to use terminology consistent with common usage and used overwhelmingly by those involved, even if technically inaccurate. It should be clear to the reader in all cases what is being expressed.

The following are terms used interchangeably along with their correct definition:

- A *bullet* is the projectile fired from a gun. A *round* includes the bullet, shell casing, and gunpowder unit loaded into the gun. Here, as it was then, the term *round* may at times be used to indicate what is actually a *bullet* (e.g. "I just took a round in the shoulder"), but never the other way around.

- A *magazine* is a container that holds multiple rounds under spring pressure for auto-feeding into the chamber of a firearm. A *clip* connects multiple rounds together into a single unit. As *Guns & Ammo* magazine explains it: Clips feed magazines. Magazines feed guns. Both *banana clip* and *jungle clip* are misnomers refering to what are really variations of high-capacity magazines. Everything used in Norco was a *magazine* but almost always refered to as a *clip* by those involved.

- The term *assault rifle* has become a particularly politically charged term in recent years. No politics are intended by its use in this book. The traditional definition was limited to rifles capable of firing in fully automatic mode. However, some sources, including *Merriam-Webster's Collegiate Dictionary*, have recently broadened the definition to include any rifle capable of firing in at least semiautomatic mode. Each were used in the Norco shootout. I have chosen to refer to both types as *assault rifles* to be consistent with the terminology used by law enforcement officers and investigators at the time. However, the capability of each specific weapon used is clearly differentiated in the text, and at no time do I refer to "semiautomatic" gunfire or weapons as "automatic."

ACKNOWLEDGMENTS

I WOULD LIKE TO THANK THE FOLLOWING PEOPLE AND ORGANIZATIONS FOR
their help and cooperation in the making of this book:

A. J. Reynard, Andrew Delgado Monti, Bill Eldrich, Capt. C. Brandon
Ford, Capt. Leland Boldt, Clayton Adams, Cynthia Lumley, D. J. McCarty,
Dan Smetanka, Danielle Simson, Darrell Reed, Dave Madden, David Tem-
pleton, Dawn Stott, Debbie Rose, Dennis Johnson, Doug Earnest, Dr.
Charles Hille, Frank Girardot, Fred Chisholm, Fred Grutzmacher, Gary
Hakala, Gary Keeter, Gerard Brooker, Herman Brown, Holly Wilkens, How-
ard Leslie, James and Olivia Houlahan, James Kirkland, James McPheron,
James Richardson, Jeff Ourvan, Jennifer Lyons, Jerry Baker, John and Judy
Houlahan, John Burden, John Plasencia, John View, Joseph Wambaugh, Ju-
lie Gilbert, Justice Jay Hanks, Kari Tesselaar, Kenneth McDaniels, Kevin
Ruddy, Kurt Franklin, Larry Malmberg, Lt. Jacqueline Horton, Mary Ev-
ans, Melvin Bukiet, Mike Lenihan, Mike Watts, Mikel Linville, Nancy
Bohl-Penrod, Paul Dillinger, Pete Kurylowicz, Phillip Gay, Robert Hellman,
Robert Noe, Rolf Parkes, Rosie Miranda Johnson, Ross Dvorak, Sgt. Will
Edwards, Shawn Kelley, Sheila Marten, Sheriff Cois Byrd, Shirlee Pigeon,

Stacey Sanner, Steve Cunnison, Steve Harmon, Tom Mellana, William Crowe, William Edwards.

California Office of the Attorney General, Los Angeles County Sheriff's Department, Riverside County Sheriff's Department, Riverside Sheriffs' Association, West Redding Fire Department, Mark Twain Library, Ben Clark Training Center, San Bernardino County Sheriff's Department, the FBI, California Highway Patrol.

Thank you also to all who preferred not to be acknowledged here.

© Olivia J. Houlahan

PETER HOULAHAN is a freelance writer contributing to a wide range of publications. In his career as an emergency medical technician, he has written a number of articles related to his profession. He holds an MFA from Sarah Lawrence College. A native of Southern California, Houlahan now lives in Fairfield County, Connecticut. Find out more at peterhoulahan.com.